Acknowledgments p.62 Board of Trinity College, Dublin; p.82 Hamlyn Group Picture Library; p.108 right Alte Pinakothek, Munich; p.184 Tate Gallery, London; p.201 National Portrait Gallery, London; p.222 Tate Gallery, London; p.258–9 bottom Kodak; p.295 Glaxo Laboratories Ltd.; p.332 left Prensa Latina Servicia Fotografica; p.332 right National Film Archive; p.341 Hamlyn Group Picture Library; p343 National Aeronautics and Space Administration, Washington DC.

Contributors Kenneth Allen
Janice Anderson John Bailie Neil Curtis
Peter Eldin Neil Grant Lynne Sabel
Philip Steele

Illustrations for this book are taken from the following books published by the Hamlyn Publishing Group Limited: All Sorts of Aircraft Answer Book of Astronomy Answer Book of History Famous Military Battles Famous Sea Battles Kings and Queens of World History Rulers of Britain They made History The Hamlyn Children's Encyclopedia The Hamlyn Children's History of the World The Hamlyn Junior Science Encyclopedia The Hamlyn Younger Children's Encyclopedia

First published 1977
5th impression 1981
Published by The Hamlyn Publishing Group Limited
London · New York · Sydney · Toronto
Astronaut House, Feltham, Middlesex, England
© Copyright The Hamlyn Publishing Group Limited 1977

ISBN 0 600 38743 7
Printed and bound in Spain by Graficromo, S.A.–Córdoba

1,000
Great Events

Edited by
Lynne Sabel and Philip Steele

Hamlyn

London · New York · Sydney · Toronto

Introduction

This book describes one thousand of the greatest events that have occurred in the history of civilization. Some of them are great advances in the history of man – great medical or scientific discoveries for example. Others are disasters caused by man's inhumanity to man – such as the Thirty Years' War, or the dropping of the atom bomb – not 'great' but unfortunately important historical events.

Many of the events in this book are cultural milestones, famous books or paintings. And many events may not seem important to you at all: popular music or social customs may not seem to be as significant as revolutions and wars, but they are nevertheless useful pointers.

This book covers the last seven thousand years of the world's history. This seems like a long time, but it is quite brief compared with the four million years or so that man has walked the earth. Yet man himself is a real newcomer on the earth, although he has had more impact on his surroundings than any other creature.

The origins of the earth

It is estimated that our planet was born as much as *4,500 million* years ago. It has often been stated in the past that the world began as a hot, fiery ball. This is no longer thought to be true. A modern idea suggests that the earth and its satellite, the moon, were formed by the cold accumulation and compaction of gas and dust particles in space. As the earth compacted, enough heat was generated to start certain materials breaking down. These materials, known as radioactive elements, released even more heat. The earth now seems to be cooling down again but at the centre of the planet today the temperature is still estimated to be as much as 2,700°C. You can get some idea of just how hot this is by remembering that water boils at a mere 100°C.

Life begins on earth

It is all too easy to take for granted the variety of living creatures, including ourselves, that the earth supports. We should remember, however, that so far as is known at present, earth is the only planet in the solar system to support such a complicated living web of animals and plants and that it took a very long time for the first primitive life to develop.

In fact, it was about 1,300 million years after the birth of the earth before the first, tiny, simple, algae-like plants evolved. Before this time, there existed complicated chemical substances and it was not until these were able to reproduce themselves that they could be considered as living things. Traces of these first living forms can be found fossilized in rocks 3,200 million years old in southern Africa.

It was not until 600 million years ago, at the beginning of a period in the earth's long history that we call the Cambrian, that there seems to have been a sudden upsurge in the variety and numbers of animals and plants, although life was still mainly represented by two groups of sea animals – trilobites and brachiopods. Trilobites are now extinct but they were related to insects and spiders. Brachiopods are similar in appearance to cockles, although they are not related, and there are still members of this group alive today.

There were no vertebrates (animals with backbones) alive at this time. It took yet another 100 million years before the first fishes appeared in Ordovician times, and a further 100 million years before they became well established in the Devonian period. It was at this time too that the land began to be colonized by the first primitive pond plants, which could in turn support animals similar to our modern spiders, centipedes and snails.

From water to land

There were two types of Devonian bony fishes, characterized by having either *ray fins* or *lobe fins*. Those with lobe fins, the lung fishes, were able to support their body weight on land and breathe air, so that they were able to withstand periods when the lakes dried out during the desert conditions of the Devonian. These became the amphibians. There are amphibians alive today, such as frogs. Amphibians have never been common and they are perhaps more important as the first stage of a line of evolution which ends in the world's most advanced creature – man.

The age of the dinosaurs

You will have realized that the last 600 million years are divided into periods which are characterized by the appearance of certain life forms; we have already looked at the first few. From the amphibians, reptiles evolved in Carboniferous times some 300 million years; in the next period, Permian, they became very important.

Then, between 230 and 180 million years ago a group of creatures evolved to dominate the Earth, the dinosaurs, including some of the most formidable flesh-eating creatures the world has ever known, such as the terrible *Tyrannosaurus rex*.

Evolutionary changes in time led to the development of the warm-blooded birds from reptiles with the appearance of *Archaeopteryx* in late Jurassic times, about 150 million years ago, although the first mammals had already evolved by then. Mammals did not begin to occupy the important place they now hold, however, until the extinction of the dinosaurs made room for them.

The origins of man

The early mammals evolved to more advanced forms. Most remarkable of all the mammals were the primates. One branch of primates, the ancestors of modern apes such as the chimpanzee, took to the trees. The other, living in open country, took to the ground and evolved the characteristics of man – they walked upright, could use their hand with precision, and they developed their brains.

The earliest member of the family of man, *Ramapithecus*, lived some fourteen million years ago, but not until five to two million years ago did a more human-like primate appear – *Australopithecus*.

Homo erectus, who lived in China and Java about one to half a million years ago, mastered the use of fire: man had emerged as a unique creature. Gradually man's tools and weapons became more sophisticated, as his brain became superior. Neanderthal man, a direct ancestor of modern man, lived in Europe about 70,000 to 40,000 years ago. The first modern man, known as Cro-Magnon man, made his appearance in Europe some 35,000 years ago.

Early cave paintings tell us a great deal about primitive man.

The birth of civilization

From about 1 million to 10,000 years ago, large parts of the earth were periodically covered with ice. When these Ice Ages were finally over, and the Northern Hemisphere became warmer, man began to settle down and live as a farmer. The agricultural societies that grew up in the fertile valleys of the Middle East formed the basis of modern civilization: it is with the culture of Sumer and the Nile delta about 5000 BC that we shall commence our look at the events that have shaped man's history.

The Sumerians worked hard farming their land and building villages.

c. 5000 BC
Sumer, cradle of civilization

Civilization was born more than seven thousand years ago between the rivers Tigris and Euphrates. Here, within a broad and fertile valley was the settlement of Sumer. The area on which it was built was later given the name of Mesopotamia, 'the land between the two rivers' (now Iraq). The name in time applied to the whole length of the valley in which other early civilizations were also destined to settle.

The Sumerians built huts, clustered together to form villages, domesticated animals to give milk and meat and skins for clothing, and grew wheat, barley and other crops. They still hunted, but now, for the first time, they no longer relied on hunting to keep alive. So they were able to live in one place without being forced to a nomadic life, like all others before them.

The Sumerians invented the first written language: a form of abbreviated picture language called cuneiform (or wedge-shaped), written with reed pens on soft clay which was later baked. The invention of the wheel is also attributed to the Sumerians who must have been a most industrious and inventive people.

c. 5000 BC
Settlement of the Nile Valley

Egypt is the 'gift of the Nile' wrote Herodotus, an ancient Greek historian, for without this river the country would not have come into being. Then, as now, the plains on either side of the Nile were flooded each year and the black, fertile soil that was left was ideal for crops that quickly ripened beneath the blazing sun.

The first to settle in the Nile Valley were primitive people who, in time, learned how to build huts, grow crops and domesticate cattle. Their settlements stretched along the Nile's banks for some 1,200 kilometres, yet were rarely found more than fifty kilometres from the water's edge. The rest of the country was then, as now, a desert of sand and stone.

From the earliest times, the land was divided into two parts – Lower Egypt (the Delta area) and Upper Egypt (between the Delta and the Cataracts). About 3200 BC these were united and ruled by Pharaohs, to become a golden civilization that lasted for thousands of years until the death of Cleopatra in 30 BC, when Egypt became a Roman province.

The Egyptians were a nation of artists. They made jars of clay, decorating them with beautiful, brightly coloured designs; they created fine sculpture from stone but, above all, they knew how to *build*. It is from the massive remains of their temples and their tombs, the walls of which are still decorated with scenes of their everyday life, that we are able to know how they lived, worshipped and died.

From the annual rising of the waters of the Nile evolved the first 'calendar' of 365 days, which consisted of twelve months of thirty days with five holidays over.

c. 5000 BC
Australo-Melanesoid settlement of Malaya

Whilst civilization as we know it was being born in the Nile Valley and the Middle East, the rest of the world was

peopled by more primitive tribes. It was around 5000 BC that the people of Australia, Polynesia and New Guinea, of the Australo-Melanesoid racial type, moved westwards into Malaysia, where small groups of this origin are still to be found.

c. 3500 BC
The discovery of bronze

Weapons and implements of bronze have been found in Egyptian tombs of 2500 BC, but it is known that this metal was used by primitive man at least a thousand years before that. The discovery of this metal marked a great step forward in human progress.

Bronze is an alloy, the result of two or more metals being fused together and then allowed to cool. It is composed of copper and tin and although the proportions may vary slightly, the usual is nine parts of copper to one of tin.

For centuries early man used copper, extracting the pure metal by 'smelting' lumps of the copper ore on the hot stones they used for cooking. In many places, copper ore and tin stone occur in the same veins and it is believed that, through carelessness rather than skill, the early smelters, quite by chance, hit upon the harder and better metal created by the alloy.

The first bronze objects were cast in open moulds. The shape of the object was laboriously chipped from the surface of a flat stone, the heated metal was poured into it then covered with a clay cap to prevent too early cooling.

c. 3000-2000 BC
The rise of Minoan civilization

During the period of pre-history, an early sea people began to settle along the borders of the Aegean Sea, spreading southward into Macedonia. Their principal settlement was on the island of Crete.

At first they lived in caves but soon found out how to build, first huts and then rectangular buildings with flat roofs and with doorways that always faced east so that the inhabitants woke up to the first rays of the sun. These were the early Cretans, and they were fine craftsmen, for remains of their pottery, sculpture, metalwork and jewellery prove them to be far superior to other nations of the time. This was mainly due to the fact that, for centuries, they were secure from invasion thanks to a powerful fleet, and their artists and artisans were left free to develop all the arts and amenities of life.

Their king was called Minos – as the kings of Egypt were always called Pharaoh – and in time the people of the island became known as Minoans. The supremacy of their sea power dates from 2000 BC when they began to open up the trade route from Crete to the Middle East (see c.1700BC The Building of Knossos).

c. 2870 BC
The settlement of Troy

For centuries, Homer's *Iliad* (written, it is believed, about 850 BC) was believed to be merely an imaginative poem, but nothing more. Even the city of Troy, and its ten-year long siege by the Greeks, was thought to be a legendary place and happening.

One man who believed the story im-

An archaeologist working on the site of ancient Troy.

plicitly, however, was a German, Heinrich Schliemann (1822–90), who spent the latter part of his life and much of his considerable fortune, in seeking the site of Homer's Troy. He began his work at Hissarlik, at the southern end of the Dardanelles, where an old mound looked very promising. Almost immediately he found pottery, weapons and other articles and then went on to uncover temples and palaces.

Altogether he found *nine* cities, one on top of the next, the earliest, at the bottom of course, dating from about 2870 BC and marking the site of the first neolithic settlers.

c. 2700-2600 BC
The building of the pyramids

Standing like great sentinels in the desert, the three great pyramids of Gizeh seem to have resisted time itself. Largest of them is the Great Pyramid, built to house the mummy of the Pharaoh Khufu, better known by the Greek spelling of his name – Cheops. It is the only one of the original seven wonders of the world that still exists.

It was built of limestone and granite, more than two million blocks of stone being used, some of which weigh fifteen tonnes.

Each side of its base is 230 metres long, its height 138 metres. It is said that one hundred thousand slaves toiled for twenty years to build this mighty monument to a dead king, but they only worked for three months at a time, the annual three-month period when the Nile flooded its banks.

The granite was brought from Aswan, being floated about 900 kilometres downriver to a specially built wharf at Gizeh. It was then dragged up giant causeways, to be fitted into place. The other two pyramids, those of Chephren and Mycerinus, like Khufu, kings of the 4th Dynasty, whilst not so large, were built in a similar fashion.

c. 2500 BC
The building of Mohenjo-daro

As with the Sumerian nation which developed between the Tigris and the Euphrates, and Egypt which originated in the Nile valley, the third oldest civilization also developed beside a river. This was the great state which grew up in the Indus river basin. Its capital, built about 2500 BC, was the amazing Indian city of Mohenjo-daro, constructed almost entirely of bricks made from sun-dried mud and clay, held together by mortar.

For its time it was far in advance of any other city. It was built to a plan obviously drawn up at its foundation, for the streets, laid out in rectangular blocks, were similar to those of a modern American city. It covered an area of some ten square kilometres and housed up to 50,000 people, a vast number for those days.

A bearded god from Mohenjo-daro.

Indeed, the more one examines Mohenjo-daro, the more modern it appears; a sophisticated drainage and sewerage system existed beneath the streets and in many houses, revealing a high standard of private and public sanitation.

The inhabitants lived a full and active life and, judging by the number of amusing clay figures and toys that have been found, a happy one, too.

c. 2500-2000 BC
The first Andean civilization

The earliest people to settle in South America were nomadic hunters and fishermen who had moved slowly southwards from North America. They spread into various areas, but the highest civilization of South America was in Bolivia and Peru, especially in the high Andes, where the newcomers settled in small villages, grew maize, squash and manioc, and domesticated llamas.

c. 2350 BC
The first astronomical observatories

The ancient peoples – the Babylonians, Egyptians and Chinese, all believed that the heavenly bodies influenced the lives of men. The Babylonians, particularly, thought that the position of the stars represented messages from the gods and their priests spent much of their lives studying the firmament with great care. They divided the heavens into regions and the various groups of stars into constellations, naming them after gods or objects. These were later renamed by

The Babylonians used their knowledge of mathematics and geometry in their study of the stars.

the ancient Greeks, to give us the twelve signs of the Zodiac.

In time they became very familiar with everything that was visible in the night sky, predicting what was to happen in the future. From this science came astrology, and the priest-diviners, after carefully observing the stars, would perform religious rites to ward off evil influences. To enable them to do this work, observatories were built upon the flat roofs of their temples.

c. 2400-2183 BC
Sargon founds Akkad

When the palaces and temples of Sumer rose from the flat but fertile Euphrates-Tigris valley, it was inevitable that many of her neighbours looked with envy at the riches of the country. Over the years, in consequence, border raids became commonplace.

To the west of Sumer lived several tribes of Semitic nomads and about the middle of the third millennium BC, these fierce tribes united under a great leader, Sargon. His first achievement was to crush the Sumerians. He then went on to conquer all the lands 'from the rising to the setting of the sun', thus creating the first empire in history. His people were known as Akkadians, a name they took from the district of Akkad (or Agade) in the northern part of the Plain of Shinar, which in time was to include the cities of Babylon, Kish, Sippar and others.

c. 2400 BC
The Aryan migrations

It is believed that in the Neolithic age, northern Europe had one original language from which most of the modern European languages have derived, and that between Central Europe and Western Asia were tribes which used only one. For convenience they have been named the Aryan peoples and their language,

A Chinese nobleman is escorted home while farmers work his fields.

the Ayran tongue. These tribes originally came from the region of the Danube and South Russia and slowly spread southwards to warmer climes.

Originally, most of the countries of Europe had been peopled by a race which had spread from the Mediterranean known as the Iberians. They were dark and rather short and were soon pushed back by the advancing waves of the tall and fair Aryans who moved through central and southern Europe and thence into India leaving many settlements in their wake.

c. 2205-1122 BC
Emergence of Chinese civilization

Civilization came to China when a number of Stone Age villages were built along the banks of the Hwang Ho. Little is known about these primitive people.

The first great dynasty in China is known as the Hsai dynasty and was created by the legendary Emperor Yü in the twenty-third century BC. Like the Pharaohs of ancient Egypt, he and the monarchs that followed were considered divine, and were given the title, 'Sons of Heaven'.

11

The Hsai dynasty gave way to that of the Shang which was led by their Bronze Age King T'ang, usually regarded as the first emperor of all China, who raised an army to overthrow the last of the Hsai kings, a tyrant. T'ang's dynasty began the Middle Kingdom era which lasted from about 1500 BC for some five hundred years. During this period, the country organized government, the arts and trade flourished, and the country was at peace.

During the Shang dynasty, bronze utensils were made which are considered to be amongst the finest the world has ever seen. Writing, based on pictures, also appeared in China at this time. Silk made from the world's first domesticated silkworms was to give China the monopoly of growth and manufacture it was to hold for thousands of years. Lacquer was also discovered during this rewarding period. The Chinese used it for the preservation and decoration of articles of wood and leather, whilst their carving of jade, a technique known as early as 2000 BC, was the envy of the world.

The last Shang emperor, sated with orgiastic revelry, burned himself in his palace (c. 1122 BC) and the new rulers of China became men of the house of Chou.

c. 2200 BC
Indonesian settlement of the Malay Peninsula

The many islands of Indonesia were originally colonized by primitive peoples who came from the mainland of southeast Asia. In time, some of them decided to move on, and paddling their double-hulled canoes, they reached Malaya to become the ancestors of the Orang Malayu, the dominant race peopling the Malayan peninsula today.

c. 2100 BC
The building of Ur

At that point where the Tigris came closest to the Euphrates, a city was built called Ur, which became the capital of the Sumerians. Although the original people of Ur had been farmers, a new generation of builders, artists, priests and scribes arose who brought true civilization to the city.

The Sumerians used the cuneiform system of writing and were skilled mathematicians. They counted in tens and, curiously, also in sixties; a fact which has resulted in a circle having 360 degrees, the hour sixty minutes and the minute sixty seconds.

A magnificent ziggurat (literally translated as 'mountain top') was discovered at Ur. This building had 'stepped' sides, like a series or blocks placed one upon the other and joined by stairs. Originally the temple of the moon-god, Su'en, it measured more than 200 metres at the base.

The headdress of a Sumerian queen and the sculpture of a ram in a thicket, both discovered at Ur.

The power of the Hittites grew as they developed the art of refining iron ore.

c. 2000-1200 BC
The first use of iron

What is now called the Iron Age began at the time of the Hittites, a fierce nation of Aryans who had conquered the Anatolian peninsula. United under their king, Labarnas, the Hittites began to extend their frontiers in all directions – to the Aegean Sea in the west, and eastwards and southwards to the plains of Syria, south of the Taurus Mountains.

They proved invincible because, before any other nation, they had discovered the art of refining iron ore. They first heated the ore until it became a paste-like mass, then as it cooled, they hammered it into the desired shape, whether weapon or implement. Their method was crude and the iron far from pure, but it was infinitely superior to bronze which was far 'softer' and had a tendency to bend.

The power of the Hittites grew, but was disturbed by internal troubles until King Telepinus (c. 1525–1500 BC) made the succession to the crown hereditary and founded what was, in fact, the true Hittite empire. The Hittites defeated a strong Egyptian army under their hero King Rameses II (reigned 1292–1225 BC) in 1286 BC, and although their own em-

pire was to disappear some fifty years later, in the Syrian provinces their culture persisted for another five hundred years.

c. 2000 BC
The rise of Babylon

For centuries the fertile valley between the Tigris and the Euphrates had been under the control of the Sumerians. They finally grew weak with time, however, and were defeated by invading Semites who founded a nation of city-states. These city-states were constantly at war with each other until a king ascended the throne of a hitherto unimportant city called Babylon.

This new king, Hammurabi, was determined to bring the land back to the peace it had originally enjoyed under the Sumerians. He raised a standing army – the world's first – and proceeded to attack and destroy the other rival cities one by one. In time he had made himself master of the whole of Mesopotamia and of Assyria, an area which, taking its name from his own city, was then known as Babylonia.

With peace restored, Hammurabi began to build new temples, strengthen city walls and construct vast irrigation works. It is as a law-giver that he is most remembered, however, and for centuries other nations used the Law Code he developed. Also, copies of many of his letters (written on tablets of baked clay) have been found in the ruins of vast libraries that he had built.

c. 2000 BC
The Bronze Age reaches Europe

Round about 2000 BC Britain and her near European neighbours were subjected to an invasion that was to change their whole way of life. It came from the strange tribes known to anthropologists as the 'Beaker' folk, early metal-smiths who knew how to produce weapons and implements in copper – and the metal drinking vessels after which they have been named. As they moved, so they took the secret of this new craft with them. By 1800 BC they had spread across Europe and with their superior weapons easily overcame the primitive peoples of the Stone Age whom they met. They then began to intermarry with those they had conquered and a new form of civilization came to Europe.

By about 2000 BC Bronze Age people had reached Europe, bringing with them their bronze tools and weapons.

Almost all southern Britain was taken over by them and the unique monuments that they erected such as Stonehenge, Silbury and Maiden Castle, date from this time. The most imposing is Stonehenge, described as 'northern Europe's first architecture', which stands today as a unique monument to the industrious builders of some four thousand years ago. Its most remarkable feature concerns the transport involved in getting the great stones to their final resting place. As the wheel had not then come to Britain, rollers, sledges – and a great deal of manpower – must have been used.

c. 2000 BC
The Jomons settle Japan

The first truly civilized people of Japan were the Jomons, originally a group of hunters who invaded the country and settled in the hinterland. Later Jomons, coming from China and Korea, settled in

the lowland areas where they developed into a nation of farmers. They were also skilled potters, many fine examples of their work having been found.

c. 1900 BC
Abraham leaves Ur

Mentioned in the Bible as Ur of the Chaldees (*Genesis 11, v. 31*), this city had been the home of the great Hebrew leader Abraham before he and his family left the city on the long journey to Canaan.

Patient excavation of Ur, begun in 1923, revealed that it had been a city of large, two-storied villas, many with up to fourteen rooms, including lavatories, with the walls plastered and white-washed.

Such discoveries made many people change their minds about Abraham's boyhood – there was no rough living in tents for *him*, at least, not until he was an adult and wandering in the desert.

The Hyksos armed with bows of horn and leather, invaded Egypt in horse-drawn chariots.

Abraham and his followers eventually settled in Hebron, a part of Lower Canaan, mixing with earlier Semitic settlers from Mesopotamia. Abraham became regarded as the first Patriarch, the father of the Jewish people.

c. 1750-1560 BC
The Hyksos invade Egypt

After nearly one and a half thousand years, Egypt was facing a grave threat to its existence. The power of the Pharaohs had diminished and the whole country was in a state of chaos. The Nubians, the Thebans and the Libyans had all attempted to invade but, with difficulty, had been driven off. Then, at the close of what is called the Fourteenth Dynasty, a fresh invasion completely overwhelmed the people of Egypt.

The newcomers were the Hyksos, or

15

'Shepherd Kings', fierce nomads who came raging out of the desert to carry fire and pillage through a helpless land. They brought with them a 'secret weapon' against which the Egyptians were powerless ... the horse-drawn chariot. They also brought a new weapon, the composite bow made of horn and leather and which had a far greater range than any known before.

During the period that the Hyksos ruled Egypt, the children of Israel settled in the land, Joseph and other Semites attaining high position during this period of alien control. The Hyksos were expelled by the Pharaoh Ahmose whose reign began the New Kingdom, in 1560 BC.

A ritual vessel (right) carved in the shape of the Minotaur, dated about 1500 BC, and (below) young Cretans bull-leaping.

c. 1700-1400 BC
The Building of Knossos

Heinrich Schliemann, who discovered Troy, had hoped to search for the palace of King Minos which, according to ancient Greek writers, had been built on the island of Crete. He died before he was able to do so and the archaeologist who was responsible for unearthing this legendary building was an Englishman, Sir Arthur Evans (1851–1941).

He began to dig in 1900 and continued, almost without pause, until his death. By then his discoveries had amazed the world, for he unearthed Knossos, 'the oldest civilization in Europe'. The 'palace' of King Minos was actually a mass of buildings set around a square courtyard, but to no apparent plan, for there was sometimes a difference of several storeys between the ground-floors in one building, with its roof serving as a terrace to the house behind it.

This seemingly haphazard building resulted in a great warren of twisting passageways which may well have given rise to the legend of the Minotaur, a creature half-man, half-bull which, according to the legend, lived in a labyrinth in Crete. This bull formed an important part of Cretan worship and was symbolized by an axe with two blades (a *labrys*). From this word most probably came the word 'labyrinth' to describe the maze-like world of Knossos.

Young Cretans – girls as well as boys – performed a sport called bull-leaping, in which the performer grabbed hold of a charging bull's horns and somersaulted over its back. Many paintings at Knossos depict this dangerous sport. Life at Knossos was civilized, and full of revelry and pleasure: Cretan art is lively and urbane.

Eventually the whole Minoan civilization was wiped out by a wave of barbarian invaders called Dorians, who burned the palace, as deep layers of ash and scorch marks on columns clearly show, although its final destruction may well have coincided with an earthquake which completed its ruin.

c. 1500 BC
The Book of the Dead

The ancient Egyptians believed that when they died they had to appear before Osiris, god of the dead, to be judged, before being given the blessing of eternal happiness if they were worthy. To save having to learn the necessary formulae, the spells and texts were inscribed on papyrus. The Book of the Dead, as it was called, was buried with the mummy.

c. 1500 BC
The Rig-Veda

The hymns of the Rig-Veda, the literature of ancient India, are purely religious in character but give a great deal of information about the life of the country during the second millennium BC.

There are 1,028 psalms addressed to various gods in the Rig-Veda, and as the first book of the Hindu scriptures, it is the oldest sacred scripture of a living religion.

c. 1500 BC
Rise of the Ganges civilization

During the second millennium BC, the Aryans had advanced as far as the Indian frontier. Faced with primitive, aboriginal inhabitants, they moved across the frontier and the struggle for possession of India began. The rudimentary civilizations soon gave way before the more advanced and vigorous Aryans, who moved onwards until they reached the Ganges and the Jumna rivers. This migration ended about 1500 BC.

During the next five hundred years these Aryan invaders developed strong monarchs who ruled over great tribes and vast kingdoms. This was not done without continual fighting, especially with the uncivilized aborigines who lived in the great Punjab plain, but also with the civilized and well organized Dravidians of India. Realizing that they were faced with an entirely different opposition, the Aryans changed their policy of usurpation to one of amalgamation.

c. 1500-1200 BC
The building of Mycenae

Mycenae was described by Homer as 'a strong-founded citadel rich in gold'. Knossos apart, it was the finest capital city of its time and truly 'golden'. It was built, in the first instance, as a small but heavily fortified citadel on the east coast of the Peloponnese, some six kilometres from the harbour of Nauplia.

A later dynasty enlarged the citadel, enclosing it within a strong fortress-wall. This wall contained the imposing Lion Gate, a magnificent gateway adorned above the lintel with a carving of heraldic lions flanking a sacred pillar.

Life in this Mycenean palace in the fifteenth and fourteenth centuries BC was an odd mixture of primitive simplicity and a luxury that was almost modern. Everything – buildings, furniture and clothing – was lavishly decorated in a riot of flowing forms; a design which also spilt on to the palace frescoes, where hunting, dancing and feasting scenes bring back the gay and active life of the times. These pictures show, however, that the men of Mycenae were quite different from those of Crete, being tall and bearded warriors whilst the Cretans were shorter, clean-shaven and far less agressive.

The industrious Schliemann (*see 2870 BC The settlement of Troy*) excavated the royal tombs at Mycenae to find death-masks, vessels, rings, wine-cups and necklaces, all elaborately worked in gold. It is believed that these treasures were actually the work of Minoan craftsmen who had settled in Mycenae.

The tombs were known as *tholos* or 'beehive' tombs because of their strange shape. Most of them had been shattered by time and raided by despoilers, although the largest, known as the Treasury of Atreus, still reveals something of its former splendour. It is a cupola of heavy masonry, some fifteen metres in diameter and with a door lintel that weighs more than forty tonnes.

c. 1362-1356 BC
The reign of Tutankhamun

A pharaoh of Egypt, Amenhotep IV, was a great religious reformer and not only tried to stop the worship of the old gods of his country but moved the capital from Thebes to Tell el-Amarna. This naturally upset the priests and civil war seemed inevitable when, in 1362 BC he suddenly died. His young son-in-law Tutankhamun moved the royal residence back to Thebes and restored the old religion.

Although not an important prince – he was only eighteen years old when he died – the grateful priests enriched his tomb with priceless treasures. His tomb remained hidden for three thousand years (*see 1922 Tutankhamun's tomb is discovered*).

c. 1230 BC
The Exodus

About 1750 BC many Hebrews settled in Egypt and were well treated, but when the Hyksos were driven out and Egyptian pharaohs again ruled the country, they were forced into labour. As the Bible says: 'they made their lives bitter with hard bondage in mortar and in bricks'. As they toiled for their Egyptian masters their one thought was of escape, but for that they needed a leader.

In time the ideal man appeared – Moses, a desert-toughened young man. He led out a great army of Hebrew men, women and children and evading the Egyptian troops who were ordered to bring them back by, it is believed, Rameses III, took them to the land 'flowing with milk and honey' that their god, Jahweh (Jehovah) had promised them. It was a long migration, taking some forty years, but at last they reached the river Jordan.

During their wandering they became a tough, independent people who lived

According to the Bible, Moses presented the Hebrews with the Ten Commandments which God had dictated to him. During their long migration, the Hebrews learned to live by the Mosaic law, the *Torah*.

by the *Torah*, the Mosaic law. Led by Moses' successor Joshua, they crossed the Jordan and entered the land of Canaan where, for the most part, they were content to let their neighbours live in peace in the cities whilst they preferred the freedom of an agricultural, tribal life.

c. 1200 BC
The rise of Phoenician seapower

For centuries the Phoenicians had lived in towns along the Mediterranean sea-board although, for much of that time, they were ruled by the pharaohs of Egypt. Round about 1200 BC, however, the Phoenician princes saw an opportunity to throw off this yoke and become fully independent, although they had to fight to remain so. The principal cities on the coast were Tyre and Sidon which became the home of the greatest seamen of antiquity.

They were far ahead of their time, building ships that sailed across the Mediterranean and through the Straits of Gibraltar. They navigated their ships by the Pole Star and the position of dawn and sunset. Indeed, the continent of Europe gets its name from the Phoenician word for 'sunset'. They were business men also, and invented a time-saving style of writing. This travelled to Greece, then Rome and thence to the rest of Europe.

c. 1193 BC
The destruction of Troy

Situated at the north-east corner of the Aegean Sea, stood the powerful city of Troy. It was very rich, for it levied a toll on all merchants travelling between Europe and Asia who preferred – as most of them did – to use the narrow sea-crossing near Troy itself (*see 2870 BC Settlement of Troy*).

Immensely thick walls surrounded the city, in some cases as much as six metres high and five metres thick: these, together with the bravery of the Trojan warriors, successfully resisted the armed forces of the entire Greek nation for many years.

How, then, had it fallen? Schliemann, digging patiently through the debris of ages to find nine towns, could only guess that on the lowest level was but a village, but each successive town became larger until a considerable city with a great gated wall and fine houses was unveiled. It had obviously suffered terribly from an earthquake but had been rebuilt in an even more ornate style. This was the city that had been destroyed by the Greeks, and although it was rebuilt on a far smaller scale, it disappeared about the fifth century BC.

c. 1122-249 BC
The Chou dynasty

The five-hundred-year-old Shang dynasty ended when the country was overrun by the fierce Chou people from the west. They intermarried with the former inhabitants of China and began a settled dynasty of another five centuries. During that period they made several great advances in science.

The prototype of the astronomical observatory was erected by Wen Wang, founder of the Chou dynasty. Constant observation by his wise men led to the creation of the almanac and the establishment of the date of the New Year. They also kept careful records of eclipses of the sun and moon. During this period also, great advances were made in medicine, especially in the study of healing drugs, and in acupuncture.

The Chinese at this time were magnificent artists and the maps they produced for the captains of their sea-going junks were highly decorative as well as very practical. A number of excellent pieces of literature were also written during the Chou dynasty. Taoism came into being and a dictionary, regarded as the world's first, was also produced during this period of great scientific and cultural progress.

c. 1100 BC
Founding of the Assyrian empire

At the time when the kings of Ur ruled the 'land between the two rivers', one of its cities was Assur, home of a Semitic people called Assyrians. They spoke a dialect of the Akkadian language which

The Assyrians maintained their empire by military prowess, despite continual harassment by Israelites and Phoenicians.

was quite different from that of their Babylonian cousins of the south.

They were mainly merchants, trading in textiles and metals, sending great caravans of camels and asses across Mesopotamia until they reached their trading colony at Kanesh, hundreds of kilometres from Assur.

As the Assyrians relied for survival upon these trade routes, they always sent strong companies of armed soldiers on horseback to defend them against attack by desert tribesmen. Sometimes these skirmishes developed into small-scale battles but, for the most part, the Assyrians were always victorious.

For a time their nation was governed by Hammurabi, King of Babylon and then by the powerful Hittites. When this empire collapsed about 1200 BC, the Assyrians resolved to make themselves independent. With their superior iron weapons and skill acquired from centuries of desert fighting, they soon proved themselves invincible. Led by their king, Tiglath-Pileser I, they stormed and captured Babylon and by 1100 controlled a vast empire.

c. 965 BC
The temple built at Jerusalem

Abraham left Ur about 1900 BC as one of a small group of Hebrews. Nine hundred years later, under King David, the Israe-lites had become rich and powerful, with an empire that stretched from the Euphrates to the frontiers of Egypt and down to the Red Sea. Its capital was at Jerusalem.

Preparations for the building of a temple were made by David and his son Solomon, and on the former's death, the building began. It was designed to house the Ark of the Covenant and other sacred objects which had been carried during the forty years of the Exodus. The Phoenician Hiram, King of Tyre, provided cedars of Lebanon for the building of the temple which in plan and adornment resembled those of Babylon. The Ark was brought into the inner chamber and placed between two great winged figures of gilded olivewood.

c. 850 BC
The works of Homer

Homer, an Asiatic Greek, is traditionally pictured as a blind old man, wandering from village to village, reciting his poems which were later written down. The two major works credited to him are the *Iliad*, which tells of the siege of Troy, and the *Odyssey* which relates the many adventures of Odysseus (Ulysses) on his voyage home from the Greek wars.

A bust of Homer, the great Greek poet.

c. 813 BC
The founding of Carthage

With the passing years, the fame and riches of the Phoenicians grew (*see 1200 BC The rise of Phoenician seapower*). Their settlements, the largest of which were Tyre, Tripoli and Arvad on offshore islets, and Sidon on the mainland itself, hummed with continual activity. Their ships waited in these harbours whilst desert caravans arrived from Egypt, Babylon, Arabia and even China, bringing precious burdens of spices, incense, ivory and ebony, ready for shipment to almost every part of the known world, including West Africa and Britain.

In 813 BC the Phoenicians founded Carthage in North Africa, building it in a bay not far from modern Tunis. Legend tells of Queen Dido arriving at the site and being allowed by the local inhabitants to have as much land as could be covered by the hide of a bull. She cunningly ordered the hide to be cut into very small strips which surrounded a very large area on which she built the city. Its citadel was called Byrsa (from the Greek for 'bull's hide') and the city grew up around it.

In time Carthage, with its advantageous situation, became one of the largest and most powerful cities of the ancient world.

c. 776 BC
The first Olympics

The Olympic Games, which today are held every four years, were revived after a very long interval in 1896, more than two and a half millennia after the first. The original Games were held amid the mountains of north-western Asia in the sacred city of Olympia in Greece, taking place every fifth year at the first full moon after the summer solstice. During the festival month of the Games, a truce was in operation throughout all Greece and no one, going as a competitor or spectator, was allowed to bear arms.

The ancient city of Carthage, near modern Tunis in North Africa, the centre of Phoenician trade and maritime power.

Olympia lay beneath the conical height of Kronos where the holy grove, or *altis*, soon became surrounded with temples, many containing exquisite works of art including Pheidias' statue of Zeus, which was to become one of the seven wonders of the ancient world. Near the *altis* was the stadium or foot race course, where 45,000 spectators could watch the events.

c. 753 BC
Foundation of the city of Rome

About 1000 BC, a wave of invaders of Indo-European stock moved through the Alpine passes and occupied parts of central and southern Italy. They were mainly of four tribes – Sabines, Samnites, Umbrians and Latins.

The Latins settled in central Italy and built small villages for themselves. By 800 BC, when forty such villages existed, they resolved to build a city. They chose a site beside the river Tiber, a dismal, malaria-ridden swamp for the most part, and began to clear the area and drain the marshes.

As they worked they were under constant threat from their neighbours the Etruscans who were on the north side of the Tiber. Realizing that their enemies could only cross the river at one point, and that the gentle slope of the Palatine Hill overlooked this ford, they chose that as the site for their new city.

Two legends tell of its founding. One legend credits Aeneas, the Trojan warrior. The other and more popular one gives the credit to his descendants, twin brothers Romulus and Remus who were raised by a she-wolf.

The date fixed for the founding, the legend goes, was in April 753 BC and according to custom, brushwood fires were lit and every man leaped through the fire to cleanse himself of evil. Then, having harnessed a snow-white cow and bull, Romulus ploughed a furrow along the lines of the future walls. In those days such lines were held to be sacred and it was desecration to enter other than at the place left for the gates. But Remus, jealous of his brother, leaped over the furrow exclaiming, 'Shall such defences as these keep your city?' For his impiety he was struck down and Romulus commented, 'So let it happen to all who pass over my walls.'

Seven kings were to rule Rome until 509 BC when it became a republic.

c. 621 BC
The laws of Athens

During the seventh century BC Greece was going through a period of great unrest. A situation had arisen where the aristocracy treated the freemen as slaves.

A kind of ruler called a 'tyrant' had also appeared and the freemen were even more oppressed.

To avoid civil war, it was decided to give the freemen of Athens a voice in the government similar to that which they had enjoyed in the days of their Achaean ancestors. A noble called Draco was asked to provide a set of laws that would protect the poor against the rich. He began work in 621 BC but when completed his Draconian Laws, although impartial, contained such harsh penalties that they were impossible to enforce.

Twenty-five years later a more humane man called Solon was appointed chief magistrate in Athens in the hope that he might be able to resolve the situation. He did this by a number of reforms which were to improve the lot of the freemen and peasants without affecting the prosperity of the nobles. In effect, by his treatment of the common people (the *demos*) he may claim to have introduced 'democracy' (rule by the people).

Aesop's fable *The Tortoise and the Hare*.

c. 620 BC
Aesop writes the *Fables*

The Greek writer Aesop is said to have been a Phrygian slave owned by Iadmon of Aamos who, recognizing his genius, freed him. Aesop is remembered for his fables, although he never wrote them down in his lifetime. In them the characters are nearly always animals. Stories such as *The Wolf in Sheep's Clothing* and *The Frogs Asking for a King* are all witty illustrations of a moral point.

c. 604 BC
Birth of Lao-Tse

The Chinese philosopher Lao-Tse was the first of the three great religious leaders of the East, the others being Confucius and Buddha. He taught that life had to be spent in searching for *Tao* (or 'the Way') which was the virtue of individuality, offering eternal life through the understanding of the secret processes of nature. His treatise the *Tao Teh King* was later to form the basis of the Taoist religion.

Everyday life in the streets of Athens.

c. 600 BC
The teachings of Zoroaster

Zoroaster (or Zarathustra) was a great legislator and prophet of ancient Persia. We know little about his life. He saw life as a battle in which good and evil constantly struggle for mastery. Fire, the symbol of cleanliness, was an important part of the Zoroastrian form of worship which, however, received its death blow in the middle of the seventh century AD with the Moslem invasion.

c. 600 BC
The Celtic migrations

The Celts, whose name derives from the Greek term for all who lived in Northern Europe – *keltoi*, or savages – were a warlike Indo-European people who had settled in Western and Central Europe during the New Stone and Bronze Ages. Their civilization gradually developed, centred upon north-east France, south-west Germany and Bohemia.

Aggression from northern Germanic tribes forced them to migrate southward to Greece and Italy, and westward to western France and Spain. Successive waves of Celtic tribes brought the Iron Age to Britain, where their power was supreme until the Roman conquest in AD 43.

Celtic civilization in the British Isles, pushed ever westward by Anglo-Saxon and Norman, survives today in Wales, Scotland, Ireland and the Isle of Man, and also in France, in Brittany. The modern Celtic languages fall into two main groups: 'Goidelic', including the Scots Gaelic and the Irish Erse, as well as Manx (the former language of the Isle of Man); and 'Brythonic', which includes Breton, Welsh and the now extinct Cornish language.

Although warlike and quarrelsome, the Celtic tribesmen were successful farmers and outstanding craftsman, producing ornaments of rare beauty and intricate design. Their priests, or druids, engaged in philosophy and poetry, but also practised human sacrifice. The Celtic migrations were to change the face of Europe and introduce a unique civilization.

586 BC
Nebuchadnezzar burns Jerusalem

Nebuchadnezzar (*d.* 562 BC), a Chaldean, had already gained much fame as a warrior before he succeeded his father, Nabopolasser, to the throne of Babylon in 605 BC. A rebellion in Tyre caused him to lead an army against the Phoenicians' stronghold which he was forced to besiege for thirteen years.

When he had captured the city he went on to deal with another revolt, this time in Jerusalem, led by King Jehoiakim of Judah. In 597 BC he captured the city and placed a new king on its throne – Zedekiah. But he also rebelled against his overlord and a furious Nebuchadnezzar returned to assault it once again. This time, however, it held out against him for eighteen months. Life for the besieged became very hard, for the food stocks ran low and famine broke out in the city.

At last in 586 BC the walls were breached and the Chaldeans swept in. Zedekiah's sons were killed while he was taken in chains to Babylon where he died in prison. Jerusalem's stout walls were pulled down, the temple, palace and homes of the nobility were looted and then burned and many of the Hebrews taken off to captivity in Babylon.

c. 560 BC
Birth of the Buddha

Gautama Buddha (*c.* 560–483 BC) was born Sīddhartha, the son of a nobleman who lived in Northern India. He was the pampered son of a very rich man. As he grew older, however, he saw three moving sights which, it is said, were to change his life. They were a man enfeebled by age, another crippled with leprosy, and a corpse. These brought home to him the realities of life and he decided to find a way to help his fellow men. He turned his back on his home, his wife and young son, and set out on his search.

At first he tried to live as a strict Brahman who believed that a man could only reach a state of perfection if he neglected his body and fasted continuously, but Buddha nearly died from the results of such self-denial. He went on to develop a religion which was contrary to the prevailing Brahmanism. It was pure, moral and humane in its origin although it subsequently became mixed with the idolatrous worship of other deities. As it included a protest against the caste system, it was eagerly adopted by the non-Aryan inhabitants of India.

A statue of Buddha made of sandstone.

c. 553 BC
The work of Pythagoras

Pythagoras was a Greek who settled in Crotona in southern Italy and founded the school of 'Pythagoreans'. He is regarded as one of the greatest of early Greek philosophers although much of his early work was based on the vast accumulated knowledge of the ancient world, reintroducing astronomical facts to his own time that had been known to the ancient Egyptians and Babylonians.

His great discovery was in music, being the first to determine that an octave has eight notes.

His famous theory of the 'square on the hypotenuse' came from a study of ancient Egyptian engineers who constructed a triangle with the sides in the ratio of 3 : 4 : 5 in order to make a right-angle. By mathematics he proved that the earth was a sphere; previously it had always been thought flat. He also believed that the souls of dead people returned to earth, sometimes in animals.

Confucius teaching his disciples.

c. 550 BC
Birth of Confucius

The third great religious movement of the East was Confucianism, named after its Chinese founder, Kung-fu-tse, or Confucius (*c.* 550–*c.* 479 BC). Whilst still a young man he established a school of learning and the principles he taught appealed to 'practical' men. It was basically a system of morality and as it did not involve worship of a god, cannot really be called a 'religion' in the accepted sense of the word.

It praised the present world, was inclined to doubt the existence of a future one, and called upon all who practised Confucianism to cultivate all the virtues that seemed worthy – industry, modesty, sobriety, gravity and thoughtfulness towards others. He attracted a great number of disciples who, when he died, buried him with great pomp. On his death, in *c.* 479 BC, Confucianism rapidly became the state religion of China.

538 BC
Cyrus takes Babylon

Cyrus the Persian (*d.* 529 BC), later to be known as 'the Great', was one of the greatest warriors of the ancient world. He was destined to forge a band of ill-equipped men into a great army which was to establish the first truly great empire in history. The *Book of Ezra* quotes Cyrus as saying, 'The Lord God hath given me *all the kingdoms of the earth.*'

He first led his men against Astyages of Media (551 BC) and then against Lydia (546 BC), the city of King Croesus whose name, even today, is synonymous with great wealth. He then moved to attack Babylon, then ruled by Nabonidus who had offended the priesthood of the god Bel Marduk by bringing in other gods.

Cyrus appeared before the mighty walls of the great city (538 BC), there was a brief skirmish and then, with the help of the priests, he and his men entered the city without fighting.

He proved to be a very humane ruler, respecting local customs and religions, even allowing the long-exiled Jews to leave Babylon and return to Jerusalem.

Cyrus the Great, one of the most remarkable of the Persian kings.

c. 520 BC
Shwe Dagon Pagoda, Burma

It is said that two rich Burmese merchants had occasion to pass through Buddha's village. They offered him a gift and, in return, the prophet gave them eight hairs from his head. They decided to build a temple to house them and the result was the Shwe Dagon Pagoda, the most revered shrine in Indo-China and the most beautiful in the world.

c. 517 BC
Hecataeus' map of the world

Hecataeus was an early Greek historian who travelled widely and then decided to write a book about his experiences. Giving it the grand sounding title of *A Tour of the World*, it was fascinating because he illustrated it with a map. This showed the world as a disc divided into two equal parts, Europe and Asia.

Two officials of the Roman Republic: the praetor (left) and the lictor (right), who carried the *fasces*.

509 BC
Founding of the Roman Republic

In 509 BC Tarquin the Proud, last of the Roman kings who reigned 534–510 BC, was expelled from the city for a disgraceful deed. The rising against him had been led by the heads of the Roman family clans and as the very name 'king' had become a hated word, a republic was formed, the leaders being formed into a Senate with two of their number appointed as consuls.

The consuls were the virtual rulers of Rome, but so that they did not assume too much power, they had to vacate their office after one year.

Thus, the Republic was ruled by the consuls and Senate and also by the people themselves (*senatus populusque romanus*). The citizens of Rome were divided into the *patricians* (or aristocracy) who assumed public office automatically, and the *plebeians* who formed the majority of the free citizens who elected their own representatives.

About 506 BC the people of republican Rome began work on the Capitol, building a temple to Jupiter on the Capitoline Hill to house their Senate. This was to lead to the great architectural glories of later Rome when the great temples, baths, circuses and triumphal arches were built.

c. 500 BC
Building of the theatre at Delphi

The first 'man of the theatre' was a Greek called Thespis who lived about 500 BC. He was said to have travelled round Greece with a group of strolling players and a wagon used as a stage. He was also the first to introduce an actor (instead of just using the traditional chorus) so it was in ancient Greece that the modern theatre was founded.

Plays were first performed as part of the religious festivals in honour of the god Dionysus (Bacchus) and they often lasted for several days.

Greek theatres such as the famous one at Delphi were built on hillsides in the open air. The theatre at Epidaurus (built *c.*340 BC) is a perfect example and is often still used for performances of ancient Greek masterpieces. These include *Antigone* by Sophocles (486–406 BC), the *Oresteia* by Aeschylus (525–456 BC) and the *Bacchae* by Euripedes (480–406 BC).

490 BC
The Battle of Marathon

Cyrus the Great *(see 538 BC Cyrus takes Babylon)* was followed by Cambyses *(d.*522 BC) who added Egypt to the already vast Persian empire. Darius I *(c.*549–486 BC), the Mede, and third of the Persian rulers was, almost literally, the monarch of the world. The Greek colonies along the Aegean which paid a yearly tribute, began a revolt against their Persian overlords and Darius decided to subjugate not only the colonial Greeks but also the European Greeks as well.

In *c.*490 BC his troops were landed at Marathon to the north of Athens, where they were totally defeated by an Athenian army which sent the remnants of the once great Persian army scrambling back into their boats. Heartbroken, Darius died soon afterwards and his son and successor, Xerxes *(c.*519–465 BC), resolved to avenge this defeat. When it was heard that the Persian emperor was assembling the greatest army the world had ever seen, the kingdoms of Greece forgot their rivalries and joined together to meet the threat to their homeland.

A number of battles were fought including the battle of the Pass of Thermopylae and Salamis (both 480 BC) and then Plataea (479 BC) which marked the final defeat of the Persians in Greece. The end of the war was marked in 478 BC by a confederation of all the Greek states which was known as the Delian League.

490-429 BC
The age of Pericles

The Delian League marked the beginning of the Golden Age of Greece which for thirty years was dominated by one of the most outstanding men in history – Pericles (490–429 BC). He was the son of noble parents who provided him, when

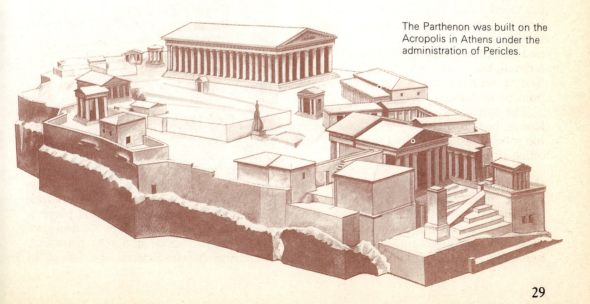

The Parthenon was built on the Acropolis in Athens under the administration of Pericles.

a youth, with the finest and most advanced teachers of the day.

By 461 BC he had become one of the leaders of the democratic party, assuming control when its leader, Ephialtes, was assassinated. He carried the democratic system further, insisting that every officer of state, except the generals and judges, were to be chosen by lot. Also, any person carrying out such civic duties was to be paid accordingly, thus allowing even the poorest citizen to become an office-holder.

His work was interrupted by war with Athens' great rival, Sparta, which broke out in 456 BC, Pericles becoming one of the Athenian generals. War ended in 451 BC and Pericles was able to devote himself to the rebuilding of his capital city. Much of it had been burned by the enemy during the Persian wars and Pericles resolved to make Athens the most beautiful city in the world. He engaged the greatest architects (Ictinus and Callicrates) and sculptor (Pheidias) and these men produced the magnificent Parthenon, high on the Acropolis.

He did more than rebuild Athens architecturally, he also did much to rebuild men's minds. In addition to the architects and sculptors he gathered together a number of men whose influence has lasted to the present day – Sophocles and Euripedes, the great dramatists, Anaxagoras who spoke about the solar system and Herodotus, the greatest historian of the ancient world, who gave lectures on his travels.

He again led his country to war against the Spartans in 431 BC, the time of the Great Peloponnesian War during which, dissatisfied with his strategy, he was deposed by the Council but reinstated before his death two years later.

399 BC
Death of Socrates

Socrates (c. 469-399 BC), a controversial figure in Athenian society, was to become one of the greatest philosophers the world has ever known. He was continually surrounded by men of all ages who wished to learn from him. His own particular style of teaching was by 'question-and-answer', whereby wisdom could be learned by recognizing one's own ignorance.

With 'Socratic irony' he often exposed the pompous and pretentious as shallow and stupid and although, through this, he gained a great following amongst the young, he also acquired a number of enemies from those whose bubble of self-importance he had pricked.

In 399 BC he was brought to trial, charged that he did not worship the state gods and that he corrupted the young men of the city with his lectures. He was condemned to death and died by drinking a draught of poison called hemlock. His teachings were preserved by Plato, Xenophon and Aristotle.

Socrates drinks poison.

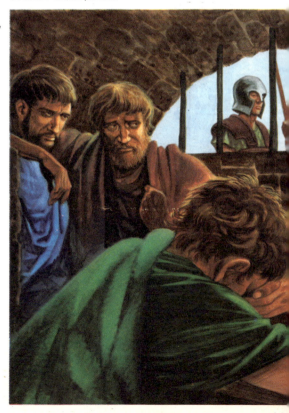

387 BC
Plato founds the Academy

Plato (*c.* 427–347 BC) was a noble Athenian who, not wishing to attain high office like others of his family, chose to become a disciple of Socrates. On his master's death he assumed leadership of the group of urgent enquirers and founded a philosophical school in Athens known as the 'Academy'.

He intended that this should produce philosopher-statesmen, for he criticized the Athenian form of government whereby men with no special training were allowed to fill important political posts.

He dealt with this in one of his early works – *The Republic*, in which he outlined his ideal – an aristocratic elite. His message was simple – all can live in another and wiser fashion if they choose to think and work everything out for themselves, and become fully aware of their

Plato addresses pupils from his Academy.

own potential. He was working on an important work called *Laws* when he died in 347 BC.

338 BC
Philip of Macedon invades Greece

Lying between Thrace and Thessaly was the small kingdom of Macedon. It was peopled by tough mountaineers who were very independent but, as a nation, Macedonia was little regarded by its neighbours, the more powerful Greek states.

Philip II, King of Macedon (382–336 BC), however, was to make them change their minds. He was a brilliant diplomat and strategist and managed to weld his independent warriors into a disciplined army. In a style new to warfare, he armed them with four metre-long pikes and drilled them in an equally new tactic of warfare – the *phalanx*. His foot soldiers held the enemy at bay with their long pikes, leaving the Macedonian cavalry free to charge at the enemy's weakest point.

The Greek states of Athens and Thebes joined together to fight him, meeting at the Battle of Chaeronea in 338 BC where Philip scored a great victory, which opened the frontiers of Greece to his army.

336 BC
Accession of Alexander the Great

After the battle of Chaeronea *(see 338 BC Philip of Macedon invades Greece)* Philip II was preparing to lead a Greek and Macedonian army into Persia and put an end to their empire. Before he could do so he was murdered by one of his nobles, and his son, Alexander (356–323 BC) took over the command.

He was only twenty-two when he set out with his army, and was never to see his homeland again. Indeed, he was destined to make himself master of the world during the next eleven years and to earn himself the title of 'the Great'.

He marched into Syria and defeated King Darius III of Persia (reigned 336–330 BC) at the battle of Issus (333 BC) then swept on to capture Tyre after a siege of seven months, before invading and conquering Egypt. He next led his army into Mesopotamia to defeat Darius III yet again at the battle of Arbela (331 BC) then pushed on, despite grumblings from his weary army, until he reached northern India. He finally made his way down to the Indus and then, satisfied at last, he agreed to lead his world-conquering warriors home again. He reached Mesopotamia once more but became stricken with fever and died in Babylon at the early age of thirty-three.

335 BC
Aristotle founds School

One of Plato's finest pupils at his Academy was the Greek philosopher

A mosaic portrait of Alexander the Great, conqueror of a vast empire.

Aristotle (*c*. 384–322 BC). He left Athens when Plato died in 347 BC, to wander the world, teaching as he went. One of his pupils was the future Alexander the Great, whom Aristotle educated for three years.

Returning to Athens he founded the Lyceum school. His followers were known as Peripatetics, because his school had a garden in which he would walk about with his pupils, engaging in philosophical dialogue – 'peripatetic' means 'walking about'.

Aristotle remains one of the most influential philosophers of all times. His work forms the basis of modern deductive logic, and his work on ethics and aesthetics has had an incalculable influence on western civilization.

For political reasons Aristotle had to flee to Athens and he died in Chalcis in Euboea in 322 BC.

c. 300 BC
Euclid active in Alexandria

In 332 BC, Alexander founded the great city which was named after him – Alexandria at the mouth of the Nile. He built a great library within the city and this, a centre of learning known as the Museum, attracted scholars from every part of the ancient world.

One of these was Euclid, probably the most famous mathematician of all time. The dates of his birth and death are unknown but he had studied under Plato in Athens before going to Alexandria where he founded a school during the reign of Pharaoh Ptolemy I (306–283 BC).

His great work was the *Elements*, contained in thirteen books, in which he drew upon the work of his predecessors, but of which much was entirely original; he opened up a new world of geometry and of mathematics. This work is the oldest scientific text-book in the world, having been in use, almost unchanged, for more than two thousand years.

c. 300-280 BC
The Colossus of Rhodes

One of the seven wonders of the ancient world was an immense statue placed at the entrance to the harbour of Rhodes. Formed in the likeness of Helios (Apollo), the sun god, it was designed by Chares. It was only in position for little more than fifty years when in 224 BC an earthquake brought it toppling down to crash in pieces.

279 BC
Completion of the Pharos Lighthouse

Another of the seven wonders was a huge lighthouse erected at Alexandria. Built of white marble to the design of Sostratus of Cnidus, it stood some 180 metres high. Its beacon was constantly burning and the light was increased in range by a clever system of mirrors. It stood until the fourteenth century AD.

c. 279 BC
Aristarchus' Theory of the Universe

Aristarchus of Samos, a Greek astronomer who was active between 280 and 264 BC, was the first to maintain that the earth, instead of being the centre of the universe as formerly believed, actually was one of several planets which revolved around the sun. Some of his theories anticipated the findings of later astronomers, such as Copernicus, who lived in the fifteenth century AD.

275 BC
Defeat of Pyrrhus at Beneventum

King Pyrrhus (*c*. 318–272 BC) proved to be a fighting man from a very early age. He occupied much of Macedonia but was

In 280 BC Pyrrhus defeated the Romans at Heraclea, terrifying his enemy with elephants that thundered against the Roman flanks.

defeated at Edessa and forced to return to his own kingdom of Epirus. In 281 BC he fought against Rome, leading an army of twenty-five thousand men; had he received support from other Greek cities Rome's history might have been vastly different.

Pyrrhus relied upon his cavalry and elephants to defeat the Roman army at Heraclea but the slaughter on both sides was so severe that, in reality neither side was the winner. From this battle has come the phrase 'a Pyrrhic victory'. Finally, at Beneventum in 275 BC, he was defeated by a combined army of Romans and Carthaginians. He returned to Epirus and continued to fight until his death. He wrote a history of the art of war which became a classic of the ancient world.

c. 264 BC
Asoka becomes Emperor of India

According to one story, Asoka, ruler of a vast empire in India from c. 264–224 BC, was a cruel monster, coming to the throne after the massacre of all his brothers. As he later became a devout Buddhist, it is believed that he was himself responsible for this story as he wished to show the beneficial effect his religion had upon his original blood-thirsty nature.

Indeed, his nature had changed so much that he suppressed all hunting and sent a number of Buddhist priests around his kingdom talking of the sanctity of life, even of animals, birds and insects. He also sent missionary priests to the farthest parts of his vast empire and to countries beyond, telling them of the blessings of Buddhism. One such country which accepted his religion was Ceylon (Sri Lanka).

Asoka was also one of India's greatest rulers, expanding trade, encouraging the arts, and stabilizing his empire.

264 BC
The beginning of the Punic Wars

With Carthage becoming the richest and largest trading nation of her time (*see 813 BC The founding of Carthage*), and Rome becoming master of Italy (*see 509 BC Founding of the Roman Republic*), it was inevitable that the two nations should come into conflict. In 260 BC a long series of wars began which were to become known as the Punic, or Carthaginian, Wars.

The first (264–241 BC) was fought over the possession of Sicily, and ended in a Roman victory. The defeat of his country rankled with Hannibal, a Carthaginian general (247–*c.*183 BC) and he swore to take revenge.

This began the Second Punic War (218–201 BC). Hannibal invaded Italy from Spain, crossing the Alps in extreme hardships with soldiers and elephants. Although he scored outstanding victories in Italy, culminating in the Battles of Lake Trasimene and Cannae, he had to leave eventually when he learned that a Roman army under Scipio Africanus (237–183 BC) was attacking Carthage. This war ended with the defeat of Hannibal at Zama. Carthage was compelled to withdraw her army from Spain and surrender her great navy.

Yet Carthage became powerful again, causing Cato, the Roman senator (234–149 BC) to warn the Senate with the words, '*Delenda est Carthago*' ('Carthage must be destroyed'). At the end of the Third Punic War (149–146 BC) Carthage was conquered and completely razed to the ground.

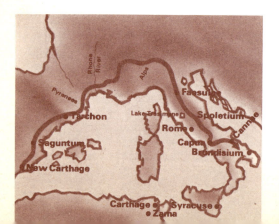

(Left) A map showing Hannibal's march to Rome across the Alps.

c. 255 BC
The Septuagint

Alexandria in the third century BC was a great centre of learning. Ptolemy Philadelphus (*d.* 247 BC) arranged the translation of the Old Testament from Hebrew to Greek. The High Priest Eleazar sent seventy learned Jews to Alexandria to start the long task – hence the title, from the Latin word for seventy (*septuaginta*). This work was to have great influence on Jewish and, in later years, Christian scholarship.

c. 250 BC
Archimedes' Principle

One of the many scientists who studied at the Museum of Alexandria was Archimedes (*c.* 287–212 BC), a Greek from Syracuse. He had already made at least one discovery before he arrived.

It is said that the King of Syracuse suspected that a jeweller had cheated him and asked Archimedes to determine whether his purchase was of pure gold. Later, whilst in his bath, Archimedes noticed that his body displaced some of the water and at once realized a way of solving the king's problem. Thrilled with the discovery he is said to have run home without bothering to dress shouting '*Eureka!*' ('I have found it!') His principle, in simple terms, was that when a solid is weighed in air and then in liquid, the apparent loss in weight in the liquid is equal to the weight of the liquid displaced.

Archimedes researched in the fields of geometry, mechanics and hydrostatics, and his theories were to prove of great help to Galileo, Newton and other scientists who followed.

c. 215 BC
The Great Wall of China

It has been said, with considerable justification, that the Great Wall of China is the most stupendous example of human endeavour. Known in China as the *Wan-Lich'ang Ch'en*, the Wall of Ten Thousand Miles, it formed the northern boundary of the Chinese Empire and was actually some 2,400 kilometres long, varying in height from four-and-a-half metres to nine metres.

It was built at the command of Shih Huang Ti, of the Ch'in dynasty (221–

206 BC) who pressed every third able-bodied man in his kingdom into its building. The result was truly the eighth wonder of the world. It was built across northern China, over high mountains and through very difficult country. In terms of human suffering and futility a writer once said, 'The Chinese never got over it . . . but the Tartars did!'

Shih Huang Ti was a brutal ruler who cared little for art and learning, and who ordered that every book in China should be burned with the exception of religious, medical and agricultural works. In 206 BC, Liu Pang led a revolt against the Ch'in and, changing his name to Kao Tsu, became the first ruler of the Han dynasty.

It is said that in his bath one day Archimedes discovered that the weight of a body in water is equal to the weight of the water it displaces.

c. 200 BC
The Rosetta Stone

For centuries men had puzzled over Egyptian hieroglyphs. Then in 1798, a black slab of inscribed stone was unearthed in Egypt. It had fifty-four lines in Greek, thirty-two in demotic Egyptian, whilst the rest was in hieroglyphs. It dated from 200 BC. A Frenchman, Jean-François Champollion began work on the inscription and by 1822 had discovered how to decipher hieroglyphs.

c. 200 BC
The *Mahabharata*

One of the great epic poems of the Indian nation is called the *Mahabharata* meaning 'the great poem of the Bharates'. Actually it is not a single work but a collection of poems which tell of the heroes of two great houses of ancient India and of their deadly rivalry. The *Mahabharata* is divided into eighteen separate books.

167 BC
The Maccabean Revolt

Antiochus IV of Syria (*d.* 163 BC), sometimes called Epiphanes the 'Madman', had crushed a rising by the Jews of Jerusalem. He allowed his troops to plunder the Temple and had all the copies of the Law of Moses burned, while altars to Greek gods were erected throughout Palestine.

A Syrian officer, sent to the city of Modin, ordered Mattathias, the city headman (*d.* 166 BC), to worship at a hastily erected altar and for the rest of the Jews to follow. When Mattathias refused, the officer called to some of his guard to punish him, but Mattathias summoned his five stalwart sons to support him and within minutes the Syrian and his men were dead.

This incident provoked a great revolt against the armies of Antiochus. The leadership passed to Mattathias' son Judas Maccabeus (the 'Hammer') and ended in the defeat of Antiochus in 167 BC and independence from Syria.

The Gracchi brothers, Tiberius and Gaius.

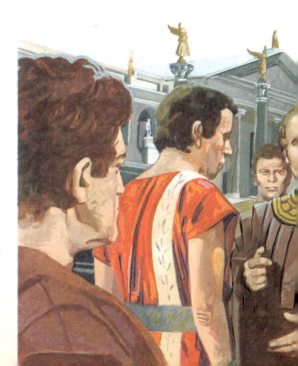
Gaius Marius after an election. He was elected consul seven times in all.

---

c. 140 BC
Venus de Milo

Venus (Aphrodite) was an important Greek goddess and a continual source of inspiration to Greek sculptors. Indeed, perhaps the most famous piece of sculpture in the world depicts Venus de Milo (or Aphrodite de Melos). Although her arms were broken off when found, it is believed that one held an apple, symbol of the island of Melos where the statue was found.

---

133 BC
The reforms of the Gracchi

Two Roman brothers, Tiberius and Gaius Gracchus, were to become known to history as political reformers. When their father died, their mother, the noble Cornelia, devoted her life to their education.

Tiberius Gracchus (168–133 BC) saw service in Spain then, on his return, pressed for the re-establishment of ancient laws which forbade the rich to possess great estates. This roused the anger of the wealthy and Tiberius and many of his supporters were assassinated.

Gaius (c. 159–121 BC) who was in Spain at the time of the murder, returned to Rome and continued his brother's social reforms. The rich senators and others were alarmed and, once again, a Gracchus and his supporters were murdered. As a token of the people's love and appreciation, however, in later years a statue was erected in the Roman forum which bore the simple words, 'To Cornelia, the Mother of the Gracchi.'

106 BC
Marius elected consul

The death of the Gracchi marked the beginning of a century of civil war. From that day in 121 BC when Gaius died, armies, not votes, were to determine events.

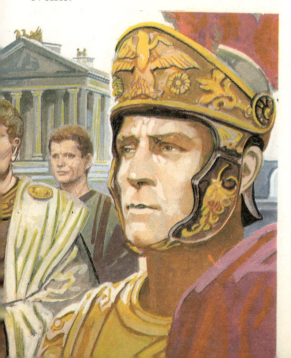

Two powerful men succeeded the Gracchi, Gaius Marius (c. 156–86 BC) and Lucius Sulla (138–78 BC). Marius, who had gained popularity when he defeated Jugurtha, King of Numidia, took advantage of Sulla's absence to march on Rome with his army – an unprecedented happening.

Sulla returned and began a reign of terror, slaughtering some eight thousand of Marius' party. By his orders lists of people to be executed were published and often the lists exceeded two hundred names.

Many Romans, including a young Julius Caesar, had to flee for their lives, until Sulla, who made himself dictator of Rome, was dead.

73 BC
The Slaves' Revolt

During the Jugurthine War (111–106 BC) slaves owned by Roman masters broke into revolt. This was the second so-called Servile War in Rome's history and like the first was quelled with very little trouble.

The slaves, for the most part, were incapable of standing up to the men of a Roman legion. However, the third Servile War, in 73 BC, was quite different. It began when two hundred trained gladiators in Capua killed their guards and escaped.

They were joined by others and put themselves under the command of a young gladiator, Spartacus. They defeated a strong Roman force and the rebel army grew daily until it reached a hundred thousand desperate men.

Spartacus led his force towards the Alpine passes in 71 BC but was met by the praetor Marcus Lucinius Crassus (c. 115–53 BC), leading a large Roman army, at the Battle of Lucania. After a terrific struggle, Spartacus was killed and Crassus took six thousand of the survivors to crucify them along the road between Rome and Capua.

63 BC
Cicero and the Catiline conspiracy

Marcus Tullius Cicero (106–43 BC) was educated in Athens and Rome and soon became recognized as the greatest orator of his time, although he was looked on as a 'new man' because none of his ancestors had reached high office.

In 63 BC an impoverished aristocrat named Lucius Catiline (c. 108–62 BC) planned to seize power in Rome and free himself from the burden of his debts. His plans were disclosed and Cicero, one of the consuls for the year, acted with urgency. He attacked Catiline in the Senate in a speech so vigorous that his opponent was forced to flee from Rome. The next day Cicero made an even more forceful oration in the Forum and in consequence Catiline was declared an outlaw and an army sent to deal with him. Catiline was killed and, mainly thanks to Cicero's silver tongue, the threat to Rome was over.

Gnaeus Pompeius Magnus, known as Pompey.

60 BC
The First Triumvirate

The rivalries and bloodshed of Marius and the Third Servile War left Rome in a state of collapse, its people anxious for a settled peace. It finally came when the three most powerful men in Rome formed the First Triumvirate (or three-man rule). They were Crassus (c. 112–53 BC) an immensely rich man and the general who had defeated Spartacus, Pompey (106–48 BC) a very popular general who had crushed the slave rebellion in the Second Servile War, and Julius Caesar (102–44 BC) a man destined for greatness. Pompey married Julia, Caesar's daughter, and the pair seemed very united.

In 58 BC Caesar was elected consul and proposed some very popular laws. The next year he was appointed governor of Transalpine Gaul (or Gaul beyond the Alps) to command three legions. With this small army, about 18,000 men, he began a series of conquests that astonished everyone in Rome. Pompey was made governor of Spain and Crassus sailed for Asia and war with Parthia but was soon to die in battle. Pompey, on the other hand, remained in Rome and then, becoming jealous of Caesar's continual triumphs, began to plot against him.

58-51 BC
The conquest of Gaul

Soon after Julius Caesar arrived in Gaul as governor, the Helvetii, a Celtic people, decided to migrate and pass across Roman territory. Although greatly outnumbered, Caesar brought them to battle and defeated them utterly. Realizing Caesar's mettle, some Gallic chieftains appealed to him to aid them against the Germanic King Ariovistus and he fought and destroyed that king's army also.

He then went on to crush other tribes, soon becoming master of almost the whole of Gaul. His last great battle before returning to Rome was against the Arverni. In 51 BC Vercingetorix, their leader, surrendered, riding into Caesar's camp to announce that he was prepared to surrender himself if his followers were allowed to disperse. This showed unusual courage – and optimism. Vercingetorix was thrown into prison and a million Gauls were deported to Rome as slaves. Caesar's brilliant campaign in Gaul was over.

Julius Caesar's second invasion fleet approaches the coast of Britain in 54 BC.

55 BC
The invasion of Britain

Late in the summer of 55 BC, a fleet of eighty ships commanded by Julius Caesar arrived off Dover. His men struggled ashore, and after a brief clash with British tribesmen, established a camp. But an unusually high tide wrecked many of his ships and after a few more skirmishes, Caesar was glad to return to Gaul.

He returned in July of the following year, in command of eight hundred ships bearing five legions and two thousand cavalry. This large force was landed somewhere near Sandwich and soon began to move inland. A brisk action was fought near Canterbury and another against the British leader Cassivelaunus, in which the Roman legionaries had to

contend with the fast-moving British chariots.

Caesar moved north, crossing the Thames somewhere near Brentford and then, re-crossing the river, returned to the coast and sailed away leaving an un-conquered country behind him.

Rome at the time of Caesar was the centre of the known world, the heart of a mighty empire of which the civilization was to last for centuries.

(Right) Julius Caesar is murdered by conspirators led by Brutus and Cassius.

49 BC
Caesar crosses the Rubicon

As Caesar was finishing his ten years' campaign in Gaul, the Senate, urged by Pompey, sent a messenger ordering him to give up his command. Knowing that

this would mean his political ruin he re-fused and led his army to the banks of the river Rubicon. It was a grave offence to cross into Roman territory with an army, as it was considered an invasion; but with the words 'The die is cast', Caesar led his troops onward. Hence the saying 'to cross the Rubicon' meaning to take an irrevocable step.

As Caesar advanced, so Pompey retired, finally sailing for Greece. On June 6, 48 BC, the two armies met at Pharsalia in a battle to decide the fate of the Roman world. Pompey rode from the field a defeated man and made for Egypt. As he landed he was seized and beheaded. And that irrevocably ended the First Triumvirate.

44 BC
The murder of Caesar

The Battle of Pharsalia made Caesar lord of Rome. He then had to deal with Africa which was in revolt. A short campaign ended in the victory being announced in the Senate as *Veni, vidi, vici* (I came, I saw, I conquered). He returned to Rome and took supreme command; the Repub-

lic was at an end. Now the head of the army controlled the empire.

Unlike Marius and Sulla, Caesar proclaimed a general pardon for all his former opponents, not one was put to death. He then instituted a number of popular reforms, but some jealous men who wished to restore the Republic waited for him in the Forum and stabbed him to death.

A Second Triumvirate was formed consisting of Marcus Antonius (Mark Antony), Lepidus and Octavius, Caesar's heir.

43 BC
Accession of Cleopatra

Regarded as the most famous woman in history, Cleopatra (c. 68–30 BC) was the daughter of Ptolemy V although, like her father, she was entirely Greek, not Egyptian. In 51 BC she became joint ruler of Egypt with her young brother but they quarrelled and she was forced to leave and go into Syria. At this time Julius Caesar arrived in Alexandria and Cleopatra, using her charms, persuaded him to make war on her behalf. Her brother was killed and she became Queen of Egypt once more.

Caesar took her to Rome with him, but following his assassination she returned to Egypt. She then became the mistress of Marcus Antonius (Mark Antony, c. 83–30 BC) and added her fleet to his at the Battle of Actium (31 BC), where she

Caesar Augustus (Octavian, 63 BC–AD 14) became sole ruler of the Roman world by the Battle of Actium, inaugurating an era of stability and peace.

fought against Octavian (later to become Caesar Augustus). Realizing all was lost, she poisoned herself with an asp; the line of Ptolemies ended with her death and Egypt became a Roman province.

---

c. 38 BC
The Laocoön sculpture

Laocoön, according to Greek legend, was a priest who tried to warn the Trojans of the Greek wooden horse. An angry Apollo destroyed him and his two sons with serpents. This legend was a popular one in ancient times and in 38 BC Agesander, a Rhodian sculptor, produced a wonderful group showing the three victims in agony as the serpents tightened about them.

---

37 BC
Herod captures Jerusalem

The Jewish King Herod the Great (c. 73–4 BC) had a stormy early life, being constantly at war with the various factions fighting in Palestine and Syria after the assassination of Caesar.

In 39 BC Mark Antony put the Roman troops in Palestine at his disposal and with them he laid siege to Jerusalem. The Holy City was taken by storm, although Herod did his best to restrain the butchery of his people and the plunder of the temple. He later rebuilt much of the city, including the temple, and went on to build other great cities and fortresses.

On Antony's fall Herod allied with Augustus. His reign as King of Judaea was marked by suspicion, intrigue and cruelty. He ordered the death of his wife Mariamne and his two sons by her, and is said to have ordered the massacre of the innocents referred to in the Bible. He was succeeded by his son Herod Antipas, who died sometime after AD 40.

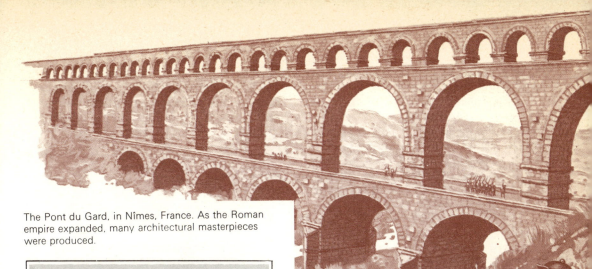

The Pont du Gard, in Nîmes, France. As the Roman empire expanded, many architectural masterpieces were produced.

c. 20 BC
Virgil completes *Aeneid*

Publius Virgil (70–19 BC) is considered the greatest poet of ancient Rome. He was born near Mantua which earned him his title of 'The Mantuan Swan'. He was a master of epic, didactic and idyllic poetry, his finest work being the *Aeneid*, an epic poem which tells of the wandering of Aeneas and of the fall of Troy.

c. 14 BC
Agrippa builds the Pont du Gard

Marcus Agrippa (c. 63–12 BC), was a great general yet is best remembered for his building works. The Pantheon, for example, begun by him in 27 BC is still the chief Roman building more or less intact. His greatest work (c. 14 BC) was the Pont du Gard in Nîmes, France, an aqueduct which is still impressive today.

9 BC
Livy writes *History of Rome*

Titus Livius, or Livy (59 BC–AD 17) was a Roman historian born in Padua. He went to Rome when still a young man and gained the favour of Caesar Augustus and his successor, Tiberius. Although he wrote books on several subjects, his favourite was history, his masterpiece being the *History of Rome* in one hundred and forty-two books, of which only thirty-five have survived.

c. 6 BC
The birth of Jesus Christ

The actual year of the birth of Christ is still in doubt. The main indication of the

year is contained in St Luke's Gospel, which states that Caesar Augustus issued an order that every member of his empire should return to his own city to be counted. St Matthew also states that Christ was born in the reign of Herod the Great (*see 37 BC Herod captures Jerusalem*), who at some period not more than two years afterwards ordered a massacre of all infants at Bethlehem.

The Bible story is well-known: amongst the thousands who travelled for the census was Joseph, a carpenter of Nazareth, who returned to his family home in Bethlehem. By the time he arrived in the small city he found that all the accommodation had gone, but through the good services of an innkeeper, he and his wife Mary were allowed to stay in an outhouse. Here, in humble surroundings, Jesus Christ was born.

The crucifixion of Jesus Christ.

c. 2 BC
Ovid writes *Ars amatoria*

Publius Ovid (43 BC–AD 17) was a fashionable poet and one of the leading figures in Roman society. In AD 8 he offended Augustus Caesar and was banished to Tomis (Costanza) a dismal frontier town on the Black Sea. The reason given was that his book *Ars amatoria* ('Art of Love'), offended public morality.

to move from the safety of the camp and into the neighbouring thick forests. The ruse was successful and the legion began to march. As they did so Arminius summoned all the Germanic tribesmen for miles around and in September AD 9 the legions were ambushed in the Teutoburger Wald.

Although they fought bravely and desparately, the legionaries were hopelessly out of formation and were slaughtered where they stood. Varus, realizing the inevitable, fell on his sword. This battle was a great turning point in history for it proved that Rome's dreaded legions were not invincible.

AD 9
Arminius defeats Varus

During the early part of the first century AD, three Roman legions were stationed on the German frontier. Lulled into security by the local chief Arminius (18 BC–AD 19), P Quintilius Varus (d. AD 9) the Roman general, did not heed the massing of the Germanic tribes all about him.

Arminius, who had been educated in Rome and well understood the working of the Roman military mind, arranged for a local rising that would tempt Varus

AD 28
Execution of John the Baptist

In the fifteenth year of the reign of Tiberius Caesar, John, son of Zacharias, began to preach 'in all the country about Jordan', baptizing and announcing the coming of the Messiah. He baptized Jesus Christ, recognizing his identity. John was later imprisoned by Herod Antipas whose wife, Herodias, persuaded the king to have the prophet beheaded.

c. AD 29
Crucifixion of Jesus Christ

When Jesus Christ was about thirty years old he was baptized by John, and then entered upon his life's work. After forty days' meditation in the wilderness, he walked along the shores of Galilee until he had gathered twelve disciples around him.

With them as companions he spent the next three years teaching and giving sermons, wandering from place to place, and healing the sick. The New Testament tells of many miracles he performed. Although he was careful not to offend Jewish religious laws, speaking mainly of the love of God and of man's duty to his neighbour, he was continually harassed by the Scribes and Pharisees.

The officials finally decided to stop his activities, the religious authorities being jealous of his growing following, and the political authorities wary of more unrest in Judaea. He was seized and brought before Pontius Pilate, Roman Procurator from AD 26 to 36, who sentenced him to death. He was taken to a hill outside Jerusalem called Calvary and crucified between two thieves. Christians believe he later rose from the dead and ascended into heaven.

In the years after the death of Jesus Christ, his teachings spread rapidly; within three hundred years Christianity was the state religion of the Roman Empire.

AD 32
Conversion of Saul of Tarsus

Saul was born at Tarsus in Asia Minor but was trained as a rabbi in Jerusalem. As a young Pharisee he energetically persecuted Christ's followers but when on his way to Damascus he saw a vision and was converted to the new faith. It is due to the intense missionary activity of Paul – as he became known – that Christianity established such a firm foothold, first

throughout the Roman Empire and subsequently throughout the world.

His journeyings took him to Ephesus, Philippi, Corinth and the cities of Galatea, and his letters to the converts in these places form a large part of the books of the New Testament. He was tried at Caesarea for causing a disturbance and, as a Roman citizen, appealed to Caesar. He was sent to Rome and after two years' captivity, was executed in AD 64.

AD 41
Assassination of Caligula

Caligula's real name was Gaius Caesar (12 BC–AD 41) but when as a small boy he accompanied his father Germanicus on a Syrian campaign, he wore a specially made legionary's uniform. With it he wore soldiers' boots (*Caligae*) to earn him the nickname of Caligula.

He was adopted by Tiberius as his co-heir and succeeded him in AD 36. He then had a terrible illness and when he recovered, his character had changed completely. He became a monster of cruelty and vice, confessing that he hated the people of Rome so much that he wished they all had but one head so that he could

taken to Rome. Here his manly bearing and an inspired speech caused Claudius to pardon him and his family and allow them to live on in Italy.

AD 61
Revolt of Boudicca

Boudicca (sometimes known as Boadicea) was the Celtic Queen of the Iceni, a tribe living in what is now Norfolk. For some reason her elderly husband, Prasutagus, had willed half his kingdom to the Emperor Nero and half to his two daughters. On his death in about AD 60 the Romans moved in and began to loot the palace. When Boudicca objected, she and her daughters were roughly handled.

She swore revenge and soon, not only her own Iceni were in arms, but many tough warriors of other tribes. Erupting into sudden revolt, the blood-crazed tribes swept southwards descending upon Colchester, London and Verulamium (St Albans) to leave ruin and corpses behind them.

Only Suetonius Paulinus, with two under-strength legions, stood against the British army of 100,000 men. His hard-won victory brought peace and civilization to Britain that lasted for four centuries and changed the history of the world.

chop it off with a single blow.

He managed to rule for four years until an officer of the guard named Chearea, whom he had insulted in public, struck him down when he was on his way to the Games, and all Rome rejoiced.

AD 43
Second Roman invasion of Britain

Julius Caesar had come and gone (*see 55 BC The Invasion of Britain*) and it was to be nearly a century before Roman soldiers again invaded Britain. The second invasion came in AD 43 when the Emperor Claudius sent four legions to Britain, this time to conquer and to stay. Britain was a country of small kingdoms, a confederation of which, paying allegiance to King Cunobelinus (Cymbeline, *d. c.* AD 43), were to meet the first attack.

It was delivered by the legions of General Aulus Plautius, who defeated the British and then marched stolidly northwards, crushing all who opposed them.

In AD 50 Caractacus (Caradoc, *d.* AD 54), chief of the Silures, led his tribe against the Romans but was defeated and

AD 64
The burning of Rome

The Roman emperor Nero (AD 37–68), like his predecessor Caligula, became completely mad. His reign began with much promise, but he was weak and too easily influenced by his mother and he soon plunged into tyranny and de-

bauchery. It is possible that the great fire that almost demolished Rome was begun on his orders even if he did not, as legend would have it, stand watching the holocaust whilst plucking at a lyre.

The fire broke out in a number of shops and was soon blazing with great fury. Tacitus, the historian (*see AD 120 Tacitus writes Annales*) has described how the fire raged throughout the city and how nearly everyone was involved in the conflagration. The fire continued for six days and when it was finally quenched, only four of the fourteen quarters of the city remained. Nero, seizing the opportunity, began a building scheme which was to result in a far more beautiful and stately city than the Rome which had vanished in smoke and ashes. He did not live long to enjoy it, however, for four years later he committed suicide during a revolt.

AD 78
Agricola becomes governor of Britain

Gnaeus Agricola (*c.* AD 37–93) arrived in AD 78 to become governor of Britain. He was to prove himself the greatest of them all. One of his first tasks was to conquer Scotland and he met and defeated the Highland tribes at the battle of Mons Graupius in AD 84. Soon after this conquest he was recalled to Rome.

AD 79
The destruction of Pompeii

The little town of Pompeii, facing the beautiful Bay of Naples, was a popular holiday resort in ancient times, yet other-

News of the burning of Rome is brought to the capricious and tyrannical emperor, Nero.

wise was of little importance. It has since attained immortality.

One pleasant morning in August, AD 79, the volcano Vesuvius, which had been showing signs of activity for some days, suddenly erupted and began to bury the town with fine volcanic ash. The eruption lasted for forty-eight hours, and when it was over no trace of Pompeii was left; it was buried beneath seven metres of ash and lava. The survivors tried to recover their buried treasures but had little success. They drifted away and the world forgot the place.

In 1710 it was again located and since then excavations have uncovered a town that seems frozen in time. It is easy, when strolling round its streets today, to visualize what life was like in Pompeii some 1,900 years ago.

AD 114
Trajan's Column

A magnificent column, nearly forty metres high, still stands in Rome and marks the many victories of the Emperor Trajan (AD 53–117). During his reign the empire reached its greatest extent, for he made Armenia, Assyria, Dacia and Mesopotamia Roman provinces. More than a victorious general, however, he built roads, bridges and libraries and the magnificent Forum Trajanum.

c. AD 120
Accession of Kanishka

The country now known as Afghanistan was ruled by the Parthians for some three hundred years until they, in turn, were expelled by the Yue-chi, an Asiatic tribe. At first the Yue-chi had been a loosely knit federation of five tribes, but in about AD 80 they were formed into one powerful nation which went on to conquer the Kabul valley and remove the remains of Greek domination.

It was ruled by Kanishka who became famous as a patron of Buddhism, convening a great Buddhist council and establishing that religion throughout his empire, which eventually included the whole of northern India and considerable stretches of central Asia.

The reign of Kanishka is regarded as the turning point in the intellectual life of India, for he introduced many western ideas into his empire which, in time, resulted in the decline of Buddhism and the rise of Hinduism.

c. AD 120
Ptolemy's experiments

Ptolemy (Claudius Ptolemaeus) of Alexandria (c. AD 90–168) was one of the cleverest men of antiquity – mathematician, astronomer, and geographer.

One of his interesting discoveries lies in his theory of refraction of light. In pure mathematics he was outstanding, especially in his exposition of trigonometry. He also wrote several books on music, including *Harmonica*.

In his book *The Almagest* Ptolemy sets down the ancient Greek view of the universe, which placed the Earth at the centre of the universe, with the Moon, Mercury, Venus, the Sun, Mars, Jupiter and Saturn revolving around it, followed by a sphere containing the fixed stars – a theory that was accepted for more than 1,300 years.

He is perhaps best remembered for his cartography. His great work was the construction of a series of twenty-six maps and a general map of the then known world.

c. AD 120
Tacitus writes the *Annales*

Tacitus was born about AD 55 and lived through the reigns of ten emperors before dying some three years after Trajan. He became a first-class historian, his two most important works being the *Historiae* and the *Annales*. Through Tacitus we have been provided with knowledge of some eighty years of important Roman history.

AD 122
Hadrian builds wall

Southern Britain became settled and prosperous under Roman rule but the northern frontiers were continually ravaged by tribesmen from Caledonia (Scotland) called Picts, and the tribe of Brigantes occupying what is now Yorkshire. Consequently, in AD 122, the Em-

Hadrian's Wall, northern outpost of the Roman empire.

peror Hadrian (AD 76–138) ordered a barrier to be built to keep out the Pict raiders, a wall to stretch some 110 kilometres, with detached forts every six kilometres, from the Tyne to the Solway. It served its purpose well, although the legionaries guarding it could never relax.

In AD 197 the Governor of Britain withdrew the legions in an unsuccessful attempt to gain the empire. The northern tribes immediately swarmed over the wall until the new emperor, Septimus Severus, bought them off. In AD 367 the northern tribes again crossed the wall, aided by Saxons, and order was only restored when legions were brought in from the Continent.

AD 164
Galen active in Rome

Galen (c. AD 130–200) was a Greek physician who arrived in Rome about AD 164. His skill in healing brought him imperial favour and he was made personal physician to the emperors Marcus Aurelius and Commodus. He wrote of his work, and those of his writings that survived were studied by other physicians for centuries.

AD 212
Constitutio Antoniniana

When the Emperor Caracalla (AD 188–217) succeeded Severus his great sprawling empire was running short of cash. One great burden was the vast sums paid to keep barbarian chieftains at peace. In AD 212, therefore, he decided to grant citizenship to every free man in his empire to increase his tax revenue. His decree was called the *Constitutio Antoniniana*. For the first time in history men from Asia to Spain could proudly claim 'I am a citizen of Rome'.

AD 220
End of the Han dynasty

It has been said that more inventions occurred during the Han dynasty (202 BC–AD 220) than at any time in the history of the world.

One of these was the compass, the Chinese realizing that magnetized strips of iron would always settle along a north–south line when hung from a cord. They also discovered an explosive powder made from potassium nitrate, charcoal and sulphur (gunpowder) but only used it to make fireworks for celebrations.

Ink and paper also made their first appearance during the Han dynasty, the latter being used in the first century AD as a substitute for silk cloth.

Astronomical instruments were greatly improved; an astronomer of the time first used water power to run an 'orrery', from which has grown the modern clock.

All these inventions were set against a period of great expansion. A steady trade was carried on with the Roman Orient, both by land and sea. At this time also, Buddhism was introduced into China to become the state religion. But the imperial line became weak and although the great dynasty came to an end in AD 220, its influence was to last for centuries.

Constantinople, eastern capital founded by Constantine on the site of Byzantium (now Istanbul).

AD 224
The Sassanid dynasty founded in Persia

The Sassanid (or Sassanian) dynasty was founded by Ardashir I (*d.* 241), a ruler of one of the small kingdoms into which Persia had been divided. Its name came from Sassan, an ancestor of the founder.

Ardashir had to fight hard for his new country. It was ruled by the Parthian King Artabanus, but when he died Ardashir marched at the head of a large army and slowly began to overrun Mesopotamia, to form a national Persian empire once more.

His activities, however, brought in the Roman legions – it was the reign of Alexander Severus (AD 205–35) – who, despite heavy losses, managed to regain much of the recently taken territory. Then the Roman empire seemed to collapse after the defeat of Decius by the Goths in AD 251, and the legions, in a continual state of mutiny, kept electing one emperor after another.

Ardashir's son Shapur I (*d.* AD 272) continued the war, plundering Antioch and conquering Armenia. One of the emperors elected by the legions, Publius

Valerian (AD 193–260), marched against him, and was heavily defeated at Edessa (AD 260). He was taken prisoner and tortured to death. The Sassanid dynasty was to continue for four centuries until it was destroyed by the Arabs in AD 637.

AD 320
Gupta empire founded in India

The classical age of Indian civilization began with the Gupta dynasty, and with Chandragupta I who founded it in AD 320 after a series of foreign invasions. His son, Samudragupta (*c.* AD 340–80) enlarged his father's empire whilst *his* son, Chandragupta II Vikramaditya proved to be a most energetic soldier, extending the empire until it was one of the largest of the ancient world, leading his armies far to the south in search of fresh kingdoms. It eventually included Nepal, Assam and the kingdom of the Punjab.

The Gupta empire was to last for about one hundred and fifty years although

members of the family still ruled areas long after this. The whole era is remarkable for the advances made in art, science, medicine, mathematics and Sanskrit literature.

AD 330
Constantinople becomes the new capital

During the early part of the fourth century AD, Rome was continually under attack from barbarian tribes striking from the east. It had also become an old and inconvenient city in which to live. These factors encouraged the Roman Emperor Constantine (c. AD 280–337) to move his capital to the eastern city of Byzantium which in AD 330 was nearly one thousand years old, having been founded about 657 BC by Byzas the Greek.

Constantine chose Byzantium because he was attracted by the city's position – with any attack coming only from the west as the other three sides were protected by the sea. He was baptized as a Christian in AD 337 by which time his architects and engineers had transformed the old city into a new and magnificent fortress. In AD 395, when the empire was divided into two, it became the capital of the Eastern Roman – or Byzantine – Empire.

AD 410
Sack of Rome by Visigoths

In AD 410 a host of fierce barbarians, followed by their women, children and cattle, poured across Europe in a great, all-engulfing flood. The barriers of the Roman empire were down and the savage tribesmen of the northern forests joined up with Visigoth warriors; led by an able commander, Alaric (c. AD 370–410), they first poured into Greece. Athens, Sparta and Corinth all fell and were thoroughly pillaged, and the inhabitants carried off into slavery.

With Greece and then the Balkans thoroughly devastated, Alaric began the march upon Rome and soon appeared at the foot of the Julian Alps, the first invader to threaten the city since the days of Hannibal, five hundred years earlier. Stilicho, a gallant Roman general, did his best to stem the relentless tide, but to no avail. In August AD 410 the hordes assembled before the city of Rome and were soon inside the walls of the doomed city. After three days of looting, Alaric gathered his men together and faced with a food shortage, led them off again, leaving behind a city in ruins. He took them south but died shortly after in Sicily.

AD 413
St Augustine writes 'The City of God'

Augustine (AD 354–430) was born of Roman parents in Tunis. Although they were Christian he did not profess any faith during his early years. When thirty-four, however, he accepted Christianity, was baptized and studied to become a priest. Amongst his greatest works were *Confessions* (AD 397) and *De Civitate Dei* ('The City of God', AD 413–26).

AD 428
Foundation of the Merovingian dynasty

One Frankish tribe was the Salians who occupied a region near the Meuse river. In the fifth century when Roman legions were withdrawn to fight the barbarian invasion, the Frankish Salians became an independent people, giving their name to France. An early Salian king was Merovech, founder of the Merovingian dynasty, the first to rule over France: his son was Childeric I (AD 457–81) and his grandson was Clovis.

AD 432
St Patrick's mission to Ireland

St Patrick (c. AD 385–461), the patron saint of Ireland, was born in Britain near the river Severn. He was educated as a Christian but when he was sixteen years old he was carried off by a band of Irish pirates and forced to become a shepherd until he managed to escape in a ship which landed him in Gaul.

After religious training he returned home to Britain for a while, then had a vision in which he was asked to return to Ireland and carry the Gospel to that mainly pagan land. In order that he might prepare for his work, he returned to Gaul to study at Tours, and was later consecrated as a bishop by Pope Constantine I in AD 432. The same year he took a ship for Ireland to begin his missionary work and despite early opposition, he persevered, bringing Christianity to the island.

St Patrick

c. AD 435
Britain invaded by Jutes, Angles and Saxons

For centuries Britain had been a settled land, backed by the power of Rome, but about AD 410 the legions were withdrawn and soon, apart from those men left behind who were prepared to band together to protect their homes, the coasts of Britain were wide open to attack.

The first invaders were a pagan Teutonic tribe known as the Angles, coming from north-west Denmark. They first came to pillage and then to stay, giving their name to East Anglia.

Their neighbours were also a Teutonic tribe, the Saxons, and like the Angles their influence on the development of early England was very great. Yet another Teutonic tribe descended on Britain's coasts. These were the Jutes, but the other two tribes seem to have been the more dominant. The Anglo-Saxons gradually conquered the Britons, pushing Romano-Celtic civilization to the west (see c.AD 500 The Battle of Mount Badon).

AD 451
Attila the Hun invades Gaul

Attila the Hun (c. AD 406–53), was a man whose very name brought a sudden chill to thousands of people during the fifth century, being aptly named 'The Scourge of God'. He was born about AD 406 and on the death of his uncle, became the ruler of the race that came from the easternmost edges of the great plains of Europe – the Huns.

In AD 447 he led them across the Danube and was soon compelling tribes living on the fringes of the Roman empire to flee him. Pillaging, burning and killing as they went, the Huns swept across Germany and in AD 451 crossed into Gaul.

Aetius, a Roman, and Theodoric, a Vandal, combined to stop them and a battle fought near Châlons-sur-Marne ended in the complete rout of the Huns. Forced to retreat, their battered army invaded and devastated Italy. Attila died in AD 453 and without his guiding hand, the Hun hordes began to drift apart.

c. AD 500
Clovis and the Franks accept Christianity

The Merovingian dynasty, founded in AD 428, steadily became more and more powerful, advancing across France to establish their capital at Tournai. In AD 481 they had a new king, a young warrior named Clovis (c. AD 466–511). One of his first actions was to fight a battle with Syagrius, a Roman general who had created a kingdom for himself nearby, and heavily defeated him.

Clovis then led his Salian Franks to a new capital he built in Soissons and slowly extended his kingdom until it was almost an empire. In AD 493 he married Clotilda, a Burgundian princess and a Christian. He allowed his children to be baptized but continued as a pagan until, in battle against the Alemanni, he swore to become a Christian if victory were his. He triumphed and he was accordingly baptized in AD 496 in Rheims, with three thousand of his fellow Franks.

c. AD 500
The Battle of Mount Badon

The Anglo-Saxon invaders of Britain eventually conquered most of Britain except Scotland, Wales and Western Cornwall, yet they often found very stiff opposition. Although the Romans had gone, many retired legionaries were left behind, and a blend of Roman-Christian and Celtic civilization lingered on in the villas of important Britons.

These families maintained the Roman knowledge of warfare, and resisted the Saxons. These troubled times are described in Gildas's *De Excidio et Conquestu Britanniae* ('On the Destruction and Conquest of Britain', *c.* AD 540).

One hero from this period is a British general, Arthur, who seems to have collected a band of warriors about him, and fought at least twelve battles against the Saxons, the last and greatest being at Mount Badon, probably near Swindon, in *c.* AD 500.

Arthur soon became a legendary figure in Celtic folklore, and one of the favourite subjects of later medieval literature, in which he is transformed into a great king at the head of a chivalrous court.

The Mayan heritage in Mexico: (left) pyramid and temple at Palenque and (right) ceramic figure from Campeche.

c. AD 500
Chichen Itzá flourishes

One great civilization occupying South America was that of the Mayas who, about AD 300, began to migrate northwards to search for a more suitable place in which to build again. Such migrations were frequent in olden times because they had not learned how to enrich the soil and were forced to move on when crops failed.

One of the eighteen Mayan clans chose a site in Mexico called Chichen Itzá

which, unlike most cities which were founded on or near a river, for a large part of the year was dry and arid. They obviously knew what they were doing, however, for their city was built upon limestone through which the annual rains percolated to collect in pools beneath. The Mayans built large reservoirs assuring themselves of cool sweet water throughout the year.

The city was very large with several massive buildings of white gleaming sandstone and, towering above all a huge pyramid topped with a temple, twenty-six metres high. All these buildings were covered with rich carvings. There was also a sacred well used for the sacrifice of maidens. In its heyday Chichen Itzá was regarded as a holy city.

AD 523
Boethius: 'On the Consolation of Philosophy'

Anicius Boethius (AD 480–524) has been described as 'the last of the Romans and the first of the Scholastics'. In AD 500 he was made a consul and soon proved himself a fair but determined man. Without justification he was accused of treason and sent to prison where he wrote his great work, *De Consolatione Philisophiae* ('On the Consolation of Philosophy', AD 523).

AD 532
Building of St Sophia

The ancient name of Byzantium (*see AD 330 Constantinople becomes the new capital*) was changed in honour of the emperor to Constantinople. After Theodosius had divided the Roman Empire into two, the Eastern Empire, with Constantinople as its capital, became very powerful.

It also became very beautiful, for it developed into a fortress-city of palaces

Justinian and his court. Mosaic from Ravenna, *c.* AD 540.

and theatres, circuses and churches, the whole of Rome's great empire being ransacked for treasure with which to decorate the capital. Within six years of Constantine founding the city the work was completed and Constantinople dedicated to Christianity.

It reached the zenith of its glory during the reign of the Emperor Justinian (AD 483–565) who had two main aims. One was to win back the Western Empire from the barbarians (in which he was only partially successful), and the other was to give his empire a new code of laws. His *Codex constitutionum* was produced in AD 529 to clarify and bring up to date all previous Roman laws.

Amongst the fine buildings erected during his reign, the most beautiful was (and is) the Church of St Sophia, a masterpiece of beauty and grandeur, where the sweep of curve upon curve rises to a height of fifty-three metres at the apex of its great dome. It is now an Islamic mosque.

AD 540
The first Welsh poets

As the Anglo-Saxons pushed the Celtic peoples westward, we see the flowering of poetry in the region of Wales, much of which found inspiration in Irish myths and legend. The songs of bards such as Taliessin (c. AD 540), Aneirin (sixth to seventh century AD), and Llywarch Hên (c. AD 700) were later written down in the middle ages. Aneirin's main work, the *Gododin* laments British heroes killed in battle with the Saxons.

c. AD 563
St Columba founds Iona

One of the Hebrides is the small island of Iona. It is remarkable as the cradle of Christianity in Scotland. When St Columba landed on the island to found a monastery, it became one of the most famous in the country and a centre of Christianity in the north. Iona itself also became the see of a bishop.

AD 570
The birth of Mohammed

Mohammed (AD 570–632) was born in Mecca, the son of a poor merchant of the powerful Koreish tribe. There was at this time considerable dissatisfaction with the traditional pagan religions, and after periods of meditation Mohammed had a vision of the archangel Gabriel in which he was commanded to preach a new faith – that there was but one invisible god, Allah.

For a time Mohammed was forced to flee from Mecca, and this flight (the *hegira*) in AD 622 is the date from which Moslems reckon their calendar. Mohammed fled to Medina, where he and his followers became increasingly influential; he declared a holy war on the Meccans and defeated them. Peace was made in AD 628 and his missionaries were allowed to travel throughout Arabia.

Mohammed made his last pilgrimage to Mecca in AD 632 and died shortly after. The influence of the new faith, Islam, and its holy book, the Koran, soon spread far and wide, carried by victorious armies throughout the middle east to Africa, the Mediterranean and Spain: Islam became, and remains, one of the major religions of the world.

AD 602
St Augustine founds Canterbury Cathedral

The second St Augustine (*see AD 413 St Augustine writes The City of God*) was originally the prior of a Roman monastery. In AD 597 he was sent to England by Pope Gregory I with about forty monks. King Aethelbert of Kent allowed them to settle in Canterbury, and was later baptized by Augustine. In AD 602 work was begun on the magnificent Cathedral. Augustine died in AD 604.

AD 618
Foundation of the T'ang dynasty

When the great Han dynasty, that had ruled China for more than four centuries, collapsed in AD 220, nomads invaded from the north and for another four centuries China was without a stable government.

In AD 618 the T'ang dynasty came to power. From that date the country was to become large and prosperous, T'ang armies extending the frontiers of China to make it the greatest empire in the world. The next three centuries of T'ang rule are today regarded as China's golden age.

The greatest of all T'ang emperors was Li Lung-chi who proved to be well worthy of his title 'Son of Heaven', for his reign was one of great artistic achievement. He founded academies of music, dancing and poetry and also took a great interest in scientific problems, even ordering the building of history's first iron suspension bridge.

Glazed earthenware horse and rider, T'ang dynasty.

AD 638
Jerusalem captured by Moslems

Within two centuries of Mohammed's death his followers conquered an empire which was larger than the former Roman empire. The first great warrior of Islam was Caliph Omar who came to power in AD 634 to continue Mohammed's original policy of 'conversion by force'. One of his first triumphs was the capture of Jerusalem, then a Christian city. The inhabitants resisted for four months and only surrendered when Omar promised that life and property would be spared on payment of tribute. This promise he faithfully kept.

Omar died in AD 644 but the Moslems swept on, besieging Constantinople (AD 673–8) and swarming into Carthage (AD 698) and Spain (AD 711) until stopped at Tours by Charles Martel (AD 732) in a battle which saved Christendom.

c. AD 650
Invention of wood printing blocks

The most important invention to come out of China at this time was that of printing, using simple wooden blocks, which was developed during the T'ang dynasty (AD 618–907). Wood around the design to be printed was carved away so that the design was in relief. The block was then inked and applied, under pressure, to the material and later, on to paper.

AD 664
The Synod of Whitby

From the year AD 597 when Augustine and his small band stepped ashore, England had steadily become converted to Christianity. Missionaries went out from Canterbury and St Columba's isle of Iona and the Gospel was taken throughout England. Within a century paganism had virtually disappeared, even though the fierce old Saxon gods took a lot of killing off.

Because the missionaries came from two different centres, however, a problem had arisen. Was England to adopt the Roman form of Christianity as preached by the followers of St Augustine, or the Celtic form as practised in Iona, Ireland and Northumbria?

Finally King Oswy called a great ecclesiastical council, or Synod, in the Yorkshire town of Whitby in AD 664. The outcome was a victory for those supporting Rome, the date of Easter was established, and the Celtic church agreed to accept the same doctrines and control as the Roman Church.

AD 700
Lindisfarne and its *Gospels*

Lindisfarne, a small island some three kilometres off the Northumberland coast, was the home of St Aidan, a monk who had sailed from Iona to build a monastery there in about AD 635. Aidan used the island as a base from which to reconvert Northumbria which had lapsed into paganism about AD 633 and, helped by King Oswald, the country was soon Christian once more.

Aidan died in AD 651 and one of his successors was St Cuthbert who was bishop of the see until his death in AD 687, travelling constantly over all Northumbria, baptizing vast numbers of men and women. About AD 700 the artist-monks of the island's monastery produced what is now known as the *Lindisfarne Gospels*, one of Europe's finest illuminated manuscripts. When in AD 875 the island was attacked by Vikings, the monks fled, taking with them the body of St Cuthbert and their priceless possession – the *Lindisfarne Gospels*.

The *Book of Kells*

c. AD 715
Beowulf

Beowulf is the hero of the oldest epic poem in the English language, which tells the story of his fight with a grim monster and a dragon. The phrases and the style of writing used are identical with those of the monks of the seventh century and experts consider that the poem was first written down early in the eighth century, about AD 715.

AD 731
Bede writes his *History*

Bede (known as the Venerable) (c. AD 673–735) was the greatest of all early English historians. When a child he entered the monastery of Wearmouth, and then moved to the monastery of Jarrow. He was a brilliant scholar and his *Ecclesiastical History of the English Nation* has proved of inestimable value to subsequent historians. He died in AD 735.

AD 750
The *Book of Kells*

The eighth century produced several masterpieces of illuminated manuscript art such as the *Lindisfarne Gospels* and the Irish *Book of Durrow* of AD 750. Perhaps the finest early Christian art is contained in the magnificent Irish *Book of Kells*. This manuscript of the gospels in Latin is decorated with intricate design in the Celtic manner and fine illustrations.

AD 778
The death of Roland

The famous French epic poem about the warrior-knight Roland (*see AD 1200 The growth of medieval literature*) seems to have been based on historical fact. In *c.* AD 820 the Frankish historian Einhard wrote a history of the life of his patron Charlemagne (*see AD 800 Charlemagne becomes Holy Roman Emperor*), in which he mentions the death of Roland, or Hruodland, the prefect of the Breton marches, at the Battle of Roncesvalles.

In AD 778 Charlemagne invaded Spain. He captured Pamplona, but failed to take Saragossa. News came to him of a Saxon revolt on the Rhine, and he was forced to return to France through the passes of the Pyrenees. Charlemagne's rearguard was cut off from the main army by hostile Basques, who destroyed them.

The epic's dramatic tale of a great

Offa's Dyke, the great defensive earthwork built by the King of Mercia, in AD 782.

Saracen army, the blowing of the horn, and the friendship of Oliver and Roland, is purely part of the legend that grew up around the Battle of Roncesvalles.

AD 782
Offa's Dyke

Offa (*d.* AD 796) became King of Mercia in AD 757 and immediately set out to restore his kingdom to its former greatness. He finally controlled almost all of Britain south of the Humber. To protect his northern frontiers, in AD 782–3 he built a great earthwork, now known as Offa's Dyke, which ran from sea to sea between the Severn and the Dee.

AD 793
The first Viking raid on Britain

The Vikings who first attacked Britain in AD 793 earned themselves a reputation for bloodshed and destruction. They were tall, bearded warriors who swept in from the sea to murder and ravage and then disappear over the horizon before reinforcements could be rushed to the spot. Despite this, they were far from being a barbaric people, their way of life and culture being as advanced as that of their victims.

At home, after a raid, they would return to being farmers, traders or craftsmen. They were great travellers, sailing southwards to Byzantium or northwards to Russia, which is called after them – 'men of Rus'.

They were particularly famous for their ships – long, beautifully designed craft which did not butt their way through the water but slid over it like a sea-bird. Fortunately several Viking boats have been unearthed in a remarkably good state of preservation. Three of these, the Gokstad, the Oseberg and the Tune, together with their contents, are now on view for all to see in the Viking Ship Hall near Oslo, Norway.

AD 800
Charlemagne crowned Holy Roman Emperor

Christmas Day, AD 800, can be regarded as one of the most important dates in history, for it was on that day that Charles, King of the Franks, was crowned by Pope Leo III and was to become known as Charles the Great, or Charlemagne (c. AD 742–814). This date is often looked on as the beginning of the Middle Ages.

Charlemagne was the grandson of Charles Martel, who defeated the invading Saracens at the battle of Tours (AD 752), and his father was Pepin the Short who seized the Frankish kingdom from Childeric, the last of the Merovingian kings. On Pepin's death in AD 768 his kingdom was divided between his two sons, Charles and Carloman, but the latter died three years later and Charles became king of all France.

He faced a grim world. Europe was torn apart by dissension, ignorance, greed and superstition which surrounded him on all sides. With a cross in one hand and a sword in the other he began his great work. He conquered the Saxons and the Lombards, subdued the barbarian Avars on the Danube, fought in Spain against the Moslems and in Germany against the Magyars. By the time of his death he ruled an empire that stretched from the Baltic to the Spanish marches, from Brittany to the Lower Danube.

He was not only a soldier, however. He encouraged scholarship and music and also built many churches and palaces. At his death only one of his sons, Louis the

be in danger, Egbert took refuge first at the court of Offa, King of Mercia, and then at the court of Charlemagne.

Here he was able to study the ways of the great king and when in AD 802 he became King of Wessex on Bertic's death, he was able to follow Charlemagne's example, deciding to win superiority over England as the other had over the continent of Europe.

England's southern kingdoms accepted his rule without question but he had to fight and defeat Mercia (AD 823) until, in AD 828, he was finally acknowledged overlord of all England with the title of Bretwalda or 'Wealder of Britain'. He died in AD 839.

AD 844
Coronation of Kenneth I of Scotland

Kenneth, son (Mac) of Alpin is considered to be Scotland's first king. He had become King of the Scots in AD 832 and as his grandmother had been a Pictish princess, he considered that he should have the throne of the Picts as well, Scotland then being divided between Picts and Scots. War was declared between them and dragged on until AD 843 when a final battle brought death to the King of the Picts and most of his nobles.

Thus Kenneth MacAlpin became ruler of both nations and was the first to call his kingdom Scotland. He proved to be a good king, treating his joint subjects justly, and occasionally leading a combined army of Picts and Scots over the border into England. He invaded Northumbria on six occasions before his death in AD 860.

'Pious' (AD 814–40) was living. By the Treaty of Verdun (AD 843) Louis divided his empire between his two sons, to split it into quarrelling fragments.

AD 828
Egbert recognized as Overlord of England

In AD 784 Cynewulf of Wessex died, and Egbert, son of a King of Kent, laid claim to the throne. His rival Bertic was elected, however, and fearing that his life might

AD 850
Acropolis of Zimbabwe

In the thirteenth century Bantu tribes drove out the Bushmen from South-Central Africa and gave the area now known as Zimbabwe Rhodesia the name of Zimbabwe – or 'house of stones' – for there they found a number of large stone buildings. The largest of these, a great fortified mound of stone and cement is about ninety metres high, and was probably built by eastern traders in about AD 850.

AD 868
The first printed book

The earliest printed book we know of is a copy of the Buddhist scripture the *Diamond Sutra*, found in a Turkestan cave in 1900. A five-metre scroll, it is made up of six pages of text printed from wood blocks and one page of woodcut illustrations glued together. Printed by one Wang Chieh in AD 868, it was distributed free in memory of his parents.

AD 871
Accession of Alfred the Great

Alfred (AD 849–99) was born at Wantage, the youngest son of Aethelwulf of Wessex. When still in his teens he helped his brother Aethelred fight an invading army of Danes, winning fame at the battle of Ashdown in AD 871. His brother died in the same year and Alfred became King of Wessex in his stead. In time he was to be acknowledged as the overlord of all England.

He was defeated by another Danish army and was forced to take refuge in Somerset, but it was not long before he had gathered an army to defeat the enemy at Edington in AD 878.

This was followed by a treaty in which it was agreed that Alfred and the Danish leader Guthrum should divide the country between them, Alfred taking the south and west. He had to fight further hordes of invaders in AD 884, but held his own. He died in AD 900 and was buried at Winchester.

c. AD 900
The building of Angkor Wat

The great city and temple complex of Angkor was little known to Western travellers until the present century. It lies buried deep in the jungle to the north of Cambodia. In spite of some thirteen centuries and the ravages of the encroaching forest, Angkor has changed very little, and even its earliest buildings are intact.

The city of Angkor became the capital of a nation known as the Khmers at the end of the ninth century AD. Its finest temple, still a place of pilgrimage, is the Angkor Wat, built for the worship of Buddha, a vast building some two and a half kilometres from the original royal city and surrounded by a moat measuring more than five thousand metres. The building is in the shape of a pyramid, rising in three stages, with profusely decorated walls showing gods, men and animals.

AD 950
First reference to chess

The earliest written reference to chess is by Masudi, an Arabic author writing about AD 950. The word 'chess' is the modern English equivalent of the Persian *shah* or king and the term 'checkmate', used in the game, is from *shah mat* or 'the king is dead'. Chess is believed to have originated in India.

AD 982
Erik the Red colonizes Greenland

The Viking settlement of Iceland, known as the 'Land-taking', had been colonized by farmers and fishermen from Norway and from Norse settlements in Britain. One of these settlers was Erik the Red who, having killed two men in a quarrel, was outlawed for three years. Thinking where he should go he remembered a tale told of a strange land some three hundred kilometres to the westward which had been sighted by Vikings but had never been revisited.

He followed their route across the Atlantic and after some days' sailing saw a great land mass rising out of the morning mist. He landed and spent most of the three years of his exile exploring the coast and then, satisfied that it would make a fine place for colonization, gave it the unlikely name of Greenland to attract others to settle there.

AD 987
Founding of the Capet dynasty

Since AD 800, the kingdom of the Franks had been ruled by the descendants of the house of Charlemagne (*see AD 800 Charlemagne crowned Holy Roman Emperor*) – the Carolingians – whose kings became steadily weaker whilst other men, rendering great service to their country, were coming steadily to the fore. One of these was Eudes, son of Robert the

Alfred the Great (*see AD 871*) built a fleet which for the first time managed to fight off Danish raiders from the English coast.

Strong, who was elected king because of his gallant defence of Paris against the Vikings, the Carolingian king, Charles 'the Fat', having been deposed. He headed a new dynasty known as the Robertians.

A long struggle began, the Carolingians and the Robertians seeming to alternate with each other on the throne. Finally, in AD 987, Hugh Capet (c. AD 938–96) came to the throne to found the celebrated Capet dynasty to which, for nearly nine centuries, the kings of France (including the Valois and Bourbons), and many of their most powerful nobles belonged.

AD 991
Battle of Maldon

Edward, King of England, later known as 'the Martyr', (c. AD 963–78) was murdered at Corfe Castle by his step-mother Elfrida who wanted her son, Aethelred (AD 968–1016), to be king. Her plan succeeded and her ten-year-old son came to a throne he was to occupy for nearly forty years.

England was soon in great difficulties, for the Danes took advantage of the fact that the country was now ruled by a weak and cowardly young king. The beginning of his reign coincided with the third period of the Danish invasion, with the Danes determined to conquer England for their own.

In AD 991 they went plundering through Essex and were met at Maldon by Brihtnoth, alderman of the East Saxons, with a hastily gathered army. The English fought courageously but, terribly outnumbered, were finally defeated by the better armed and more battle-tried Danes.

AD 1000
Leif Eriksson discovers North America

Leif, son of Erik the Red (see AD 982 Erik

the Red colonizes Greenland) was living in the new colony when he heard a strange story from a Viking who had newly arrived in the island. The man, Bjarni Nerjolfsson, had sailed from Iceland for Greenland, but missing his landfall, had sighted a range of low-lying islands. Not bothering to explore he turned his boat's bows around and headed eastwards.

In AD 1000 Leif hired Bjarni's boat, gathered thirty-five comrades and set off to find the unknown land. The first landfall was a low, barren coast with high mountains that shone like glass. His boat grounded on the stony shore and Leif jumped down, the first European to set foot on the shores of the New World. Where he landed was, centuries later, to become known as Frobisher Bay, North Canada. He sailed southwards, following the coastline, then decided to overwinter before returning home.

1007
Aethelred pays Danegeld

Despite signs of his subjects' courage as revealed by the Battle of Maldon, Aethelred II, soon to become known as the 'Redeless' or 'Unready', began the short-sighted policy of trying to buy off the invaders, levying a new tax called Danegeld. This merely encouraged Danes to come and collect 'easy' money.

In AD 994, Sweyn, King of Denmark and Olaf, King of Norway appeared together and harried Kent, Sussex and Hampshire. They, too, were bought off but others followed and the country was rarely free from the invaders.

In 1002, when the country was briefly at peace, the stupid Aethelred ordered all Norsemen and Danes who had settled in the country to be slaughtered. Furious, Sweyn returned to ravage and slay with hardly any resistance and Aethelred was forced to flee to Normandy. He returned on news of Sweyn's death but died himself soon afterwards, in 1016.

1014
The Battle of Clontarf

Brian Ború (*c.* AD926–1014) was the son of one of the chieftains of Munster, in Ireland, then a loose collection of tribes. He was a tough young man who lived for fighting and was soon kept fully occupied with the Danes who constantly tried to ravage his father's lands.

On his father's death his brother, Mathgamhain became chieftain, but was murdered. After avenging the deed, Brian became chieftain. Partly by force and partly by persuasion he forced the other tribes of Munster and Leinster to acknowledge him as overlord.

With a greatly enlarged army he attacked the Danes who were surrounding Dublin, defeated them, and overthrew the chief king of Ireland to become king himself.

He fought the Danes again, almost annihilating them at the Battle of Clontarf in 1014, but after the battle the old king, aged nearly ninety years, was assassinated.

Canute is said to have publicly demonstrated that the power of kings is not divine by showing that he could not control the waves.

1016
Accession of Canute

On the death of Aethelred (*see AD991 The Battle of Maldon*) his son, Edmund Ironside (*c.* AD981–1016) who was quite the opposite of his cowardly father, was elected king by the citizens of London. But it was Canute, claiming what had been won by his father, Sweyn, who was supported by most of the leading men of the realm. Their two armies met several times in battle, the last being fought at Assandune in Essex, where Canute (*c.* AD994–1035) won a crushing victory.

The two kings then met on the island of Olney where it was agreed that Edmund should be overlord and possess the southern shires whilst Canute should have Mercia and Northumberland. Edmund did not live to enjoy his new kingdom for he died seven months later.

Canute found a rival in Edwy, Edmund's brother, but the council (Witenagemot) decided that England should be united under one strong king. This made Canute king over all England as well as Denmark and, later Norway; he finally proclaimed himself overlord of Sweden. He put away his Danish wife to marry Emma, widow of Aethelred and daughter of Richard, Duke of Normandy, a union which was to cause much trouble later.

1040
Macbeth slays Duncan

Our view of eleventh-century Scotland has been coloured by Shakespeare's play *Macbeth*, which does not present an accurate picture. When Duncan came to the throne in 1034, he was to face a number of serious defeats by the Northumbrians and the Norsemen. In 1040 an unsuccessful raid into England sparked off a civil war at home. The Scottish general Macbeth, Mormaer of Moray, who had a claim to the throne, both in his own right and through his wife Gruoch, slew Duncan and became king in 1040.

Macbeth's rule was efficient and stable, helped by the support of Thorfinn, the Norwegian Earl of Caithness and Sutherland, a cousin of Duncan. Scotland was at this time an entirely Celtic society and culture, and Macbeth's accession marked a reaction against the influence of England and the south. Macbeth was finally killed by Duncan's eldest son Malcolm Ceanmor in 1057, who became Malcolm III.

1050
The *Rubáiyát* of Omar Khayyám

Omar Khayyám was considered, in his time, as the greatest mathematician in the Middle East. His treatise on algebra made him famous even in the western world and he also reformed the Moslem calendar. He is, however, best remembered as a poet, his famous *Rubáiyát* being translated by Edward Fitzgerald to give delight to millions. He died in 1123.

1050
The *Mabinogion*

For a time the principal language in the north-western and south-western corners of Wales was Irish. This area became the centre for a number of poets (*see AD 540 The first Welsh poets*) and their influence was considerable. Eleven mythological Irish romances became popular with later Welsh poets, especially young bardic aspirants. They were later collected into one work to be called the *Mabinogion*.

c. 1063
The building of St Mark's, Venice

Dominating one end of the Piazza, Venice, is St Mark's Cathedral, begun about 1063 by Doge Contarini and consecrated about thirty years later. The wealth of the East was used to beautify it – columns from Byzantine basilicas, rare marbles from the Indies and four antique bronze horses brought from Constantinople in 1204.

1066
The Battle of Stamford Bridge

On the death of Edward the Confessor in January 1066, there emerged three main claimants for his throne – William, Duke of Normandy; Harald Hardrada, King of Norway, a son of Edmund Ironside; and Harold Godwinson, Earl of Wessex.

It was Harold that the Witan elected. He was soon aware that the two others were raising armies with which to claim their inheritance. In September it was learned that Harald Hardrada had landed and was advancing south, having joined forces with Tostig, Harold's own brother. The king set out to meet them and the two armies met at Stamford Bridge. By evening both Harald Hardrada and Tostig were dead and their armies utterly defeated. As Harold began to move south again his other rival, William of Normandy, had already set sail and was making for England.

Harold meets his death from a Norman arrow.

1066
The Battle of Hastings

Learning that William of Normandy had already landed in Pevensey Bay, Harold led his tired host on the long march southwards. He reached a small hill called Senlac and waited for further troops from the southern shires to join him. Not all came and Harold was forced on to the defensive. His army consisted of housecarls (the king's personal body-guards), magnificent troops, but the rest was composed of peasants equipped only with spears and farming implements.

The battle began and it was soon obvious that the Norman knights, despite their horses and armour, were being beaten, so William tried a ruse, ordering some of his men to pretend to retreat. Excited by this, some of the Saxons broke their ranks and followed, only to be cut down. Harold stood in the centre of his housecarls but their numbers were growing less, especially when William ordered his archers to fire into the air. Harold was shot in the eye and his two brothers were also killed and the Saxon army was thrust from the hill and slaughtered. This battle was later portrayed in the famous Bayeux Tapestry, the work of Matilda, wife of William, and her ladies.

1072
Defeat of Hereward the Wake

William had been crowned in Westminster Abbey but resistance to his rule continued for many years. One Saxon rebel was Hereward the Wake, a Lincolnshire land-owner who made his headquarters on the Isle of Ely and gathered many supporters. In 1072 he was betrayed but it is not certain what became of him.

1077
The humiliation of Canossa

The Holy Roman Emperors guarded men's bodies, whilst the Popes – the Bishops of Rome – guarded their souls. Sometimes, however, a belligerent emperor and an energetic Pope would clash, as in 1077.

The former was Henry IV (1050–1106), the latter Hildebrand (c. 1020–85), Pope Gregory VII who, immediately upon his accession began to put in hand a number of urgent reforms, asserting his authority over mere temporal power. The two men fell out and when, at the Diet of Worms (1076) Henry decreed that

Gregory was deposed, he in turn was excommunicated.

Henry was forced to yield in the end when his subjects began to throw off their allegiance to him, and he had to travel to Canossa in Calabria. Here he was forced to wait at the gates, dressed humbly as a penitent, craving the Pope's pardon. He was kept waiting for three days before Gregory finally saw him and lifted the ban of excommunication.

1086
The Domesday Book

By order of William the Conqueror (*see 1066 The Battle of Hastings*) a survey was taken of all holdings through his new lands and this record is known today as the *Domesday Book*. It gives details of holdings in every shire, except those of the north, their value and the names of the holders, their possessions and other details.

1094
El Cid takes Valencia

Ruy Diaz de Bivar was born near Burgos in Spain about 1040. He was to become the hero of the struggle between Christian and Moslem in the eleventh century but his deeds are so obscured by legend it is difficult to tell fact from fable. He was born at a time when Christian and Moor were struggling for mastery of Spain. His deeds won him his Spanish title of *El Campeador* – 'the Champion' – when he defeated the enemy's champion in single combat. His enemies, who respected a hero, gave him the more familiar title of *El Cid*, the 'Lord'.

Whilst on one campaign, however, he found himself banished from the Spanish court, whereupon he fought for Christian

El Cid before Valencia.

or Moor indifferently. He captured the city of Valencia in 1094, reigning there until his death in 1099.

1095
Proclamation of the First Crusade

For many years in Europe and the Middle East, Christians and Moslems had fought each other until, by the eleventh century, the Moslems had conquered the whole of Asia Minor. Then came the startling news; in 1071 the Seljuk Turks had captured Palestine and with it the holy city of Jerusalem. This was not only an insult to Christendom, but also made things very difficult for the thousands of Christian pilgrims who had been flocking to the Holy City for years.

In 1095, Pope Urban II spoke to a great gathering in France to urge that a Christian army of nobles and commoners should go to Palestine and win back Jerusalem from the Turks. Every man who took part would be pardoned from all his sins. The response was overwhelming. Spurred by the promise of absolution and the possibility of loot, volunteers assembled in every Christian country in Europe.

Because each man wore a cross as a badge, the enterprise was known as a crusade (from the Latin *crux*, or cross). After much fighting, which included a battle at Antioch which lasted for seven months, the Crusaders finally reached Jerusalem which they captured in 1099.

1100
Death of William Rufus

William I died in 1087 and his second son, also a William, succeeded him. The Conqueror chose him as his successor rather than his heir, Robert of Normandy, who was too weak to be king of a

73

still-troubled land. William II (reigned 1087–1100) became more familiarly known as William Rufus, or the Red King, because of his red hair and violent and cruel temper.

He was determined to crush remnants of Saxon resistance that still persisted and to bring peace to the land, for many of the nobles, in support of Robert of Normandy, were also up in arms. Rufus soon dealt with them, arming his Saxon subjects to aid him when necessary. He made a great deal of enemies and no one was very surprised when in 1100 he was found dead in the New Forest with an assassin's arrow in his breast.

placed upon good manners, art, poetry and calligraphy. The new capital was at Heian-kyo (on the site of present day Kyoto) but as the years passed, so the power of the provincial barons grew.

Soon these nobles began to assume power, forming themselves into groups of fighting men which, in turn, offered their services to the great lords. Thus a form of feudal system was born. These free-lance warriors became known as the *Samurai*. They had a strict code of honour and in many ways resembled the mediaeval knights of Europe. In time they were to bring down the Heian dynasty, in 1160.

c. 1100
The *Samurai* are formed in Japan

The Heian dynasty of Japan lasted for nearly four centuries. At first it was an era of gentleness, with great store being

c. 1100
The first known Inca

The beginnings of what was to become the great Incan empire are related in legends. According to them, a small band

(Left) William Rufus is killed by an arrow.

(Right) Japan's warrior knights, the *Samurai*.

of migrants calling themselves the Children of the Sun were looking for a suitable place in which to settle. They were led by Manco Capac and finally chose the fertile valley of Cuzco.

A later leader of the band, Sinchi Roca was either the son or descendant of Manco Capac. In any case, he was the first to call himself *Sapa Inca* (the Only Inca) and was to found a long line of kings who ruled the golden land until their unique civilization was destroyed by Spaniards in the sixteenth century.

By then the empire of the Incas had grown to more than half a million people living in what is now Peru, Ecuador, Bolivia and Northern Chile. This vast territory was ruled by the Inca aided by thousands of officials who looked after people's welfare and collected the taxes. The Incan people were clever farmers, engineers (they built massive buildings and suspension bridges) and were wonderful craftsmen, their work in gold and silver being magnificent.

1121
Turlough O'Connor becomes Ireland's High King

For many years Ireland had consisted of a number of independent kingdoms, the last great king who had exercised some control over them all being BrianBorú (*see 1014 The Battle of Clontarf*). He was followed by a number of kings, many of whom claimed to be king of all Ireland – or *Ard Rí* – but with little justification.

During the early part of the eleventh century, Turlough O'Connor, who was King of Connaught, one of the four kingdoms of Ireland, put forward his own claim when the King of Ulster, Domhnall O'Lochlainn died in 1121. He gave a vast amount to the church at Armagh to support his claim but despite this, he had to spend the rest of his long reign (he was seventy-seven when he died) fighting for supremacy. He was, as it happened, Ireland's last great king.

1138
Civil War in England

Henry I of England died in 1135, having nominated his daughter, Matilda, as his successor. Her husband was Geoffrey, nicknamed 'Plantagenet' from a sprig of broom (*planta genista*) he wore in his helmet.

The Council, however, put aside the dead king's wishes and chose Stephen, the Conqueror's grandson. Furious at the decision, Matilda began a civil war which was to last for eight weary years. The war gave the great barons an opportunity to wage war on their own account, first on one side, then on the other. Soon conditions in England were so terrible that a chronicler of the time wrote 'Men said that Christ and His Saints slept.'

The war ended tamely, Matilda agreeing that Stephen should reign until his death and then be succeeded by her son, Henry Plantagenet. A year later Stephen was dead and Henry II reigned over England.

1140
The Council of Sens

Few religious teachers have had such an enthusiastic following of young people as the French scholastic, Pierre Abélard (1079–1142). Although Abélard greatly influenced the minds of his contemporaries and the course of medieval thought, he is better known in modern times for his tragic love affair with Héloïse. The two lovers were married in secret, but Héloïse, fearing that she would hinder Abélard's career, ran away to a convent. Her furious uncle broke into Abélard's home, attacked him savagely and castrated him. Abélard became a monk.

For many years Abélard had been the opponent of Bernard of Claivaux (1090–1153). Bernard's eloquence and studious life made him the oracle of Christendom, but he rejected Abélard's teachings; he upheld the principle of unhesitating faith and Abélard's rational inquiry seemed to him sheer revolt.

In 1141 the two men met at the Council of Sens. Sens, a town in northern France, was the meeting place of six great highways and was frequently used for international councils. The meeting held in 1141 was concerned with matters of religious doctrine and Abélard was to plead his cause on a charge of heresy. He appealed to Rome but he was condemned nonetheless and died two years later.

1145
Proclamation of the Second Crusade

When Jerusalem fell during the First Crusade (*see 1095 Proclamation of the First Crusade*) the Latin Kingdom of Jerusalem was established, a kingdom that was to last for many years. Nevertheless, the Moslems began to win back much of the territory they had lost and the fall of Edessa on Christmas Day, 1144, sparked off the Second Crusade.

It was begun, as before by the urgings of a Pope, this time Eugenius III, and was immediately supported by King Louis VIII of France and the Emperor Conrad III of Germany. But there was little unity between the Crusaders themselves and, indeed, Conrad's men of northern Germany never reached the Holy Land at all, stopping on the way to attack southern Germany, whilst Crusaders from England and the Low Countries plundered Lisbon on the way. They began a siege of Damascus which was unsuccessful and soon afterwards the whole crusade collapsed, the two kings returning home separately.

1152

Frederick Barbarossa becomes emperor

Frederick (*c*. 1123–90) was born into the powerful Hohenstaufen family about 1124 and in 1147 became Duke of Swabia. Soon afterwards he accompanied his uncle, Conrad III, on the disastrous Second Crusade. Conrad was so impressed with him that he urged that he should be Germany's next king.

Frederick was accordingly crowned at Aix-la-Chapelle in 1152 as Frederick I, but was commonly known as 'Barbarossa' or 'Red-beard'. As Holy Roman Emperor he set to work to create unity and order in the Empire. He led six campaigns into Italy in the hope of restoring the Empire's power, but he was opposed both by the rich Italian cities and the Pope.

Frederick Barbarossa drowns whilst on the Third Crusade.

Frederick had a magnetic personality and his reign both as king of the German people and Holy Roman Emperor marks one of the most brilliant periods in the Empire's history. At the height of his power he led the Third Crusade against Saladin, but was drowned on his way to the Holy Land.

1154

Accession of Henry II

Henry II (1133–89) who gained the throne of England through his mother (*see 1138 Civil war in England*) was, at the time of his coronation, by far the richest prince in Europe. From his mother he gained the throne of England, through his father the Duchy of Anjou. Two years before he came to the throne he married Eleanor of Aquitaine who brought with her as dowry the whole of south-western France.

Henry began his reign by restoring order from the chaos left by years of civil war. In 1155 he prepared to invade Ireland, but his scheme was not carried through. However, Malcolm of Scotland was forced to restore the northern counties of England, and Wales was finally conquered. He also began to reform the English system of law, founding a tribunal of the *Curia Regis* which grew into the courts of King's Bench and Common Pleas.

c. 1155

Foundation of the University of Paris

Europe's oldest university is the University of Paris. It is the most famous of all medieval seats of learning and one on which most others have been modelled. The original name for a university was *studium* (place of study) but was later changed to university because it was controlled in Paris by the guild (*universitas*)

of teachers and the name survived.

This guild became very powerful and was the first to free itself from the control of the Church, especially from the Chancellor of Notre Dame Cathedral. It also gave teachers the right to grant licences, *Licentia docendi* (the right to teach), to their pupils which would enable them to be teachers also.

The University of Paris was probably founded about 1155, the actual date being unknown, but it is recorded that King Philip II granted it certain privileges in 1200 and Pope Innocent III in 1215.

1163
Foundation of Oxford University

Oxford University began in a very modest way. About 1120, Theobald of Etampes, under the patronage of Henry I, was teaching 'sixty to one hundred clerks' outside the city, but it was not until 1163 that a university (*studium generale*) came into being. It began to attract many pupils and soon its teachers were claiming it as second only to Paris. The first colleges to be founded were University College (1249) and Balliol (*c.* 1263).

Cambridge University was founded a little later. In 1209 a body of students moved to Cambridge from Oxford where they had been expelled and some even hanged for murder. In 1214 they were allowed to return but some stayed to begin the foundation of the University. Its earliest colleges were Merton (1274) and Peterhouse (1284). The college system in both universities came from the friars, who influenced their future in the thirteenth century.

Richard I of England was victorious over Saladin at Arnif and captured Acre for the Crusaders. He abandoned plans to capture Jerusalem.

1170
The murder of Becket

Thomas Becket first joined the household of Theobald, Archbishop of Canterbury, becoming archdeacon and then Chancellor of the Cathedral. He also became a close friend of Henry II, hunting and feasting with him. When Theobald died in 1162, he made him Archbishop in his stead.

By this act, Henry hoped to bring the church under his control and he was surprised and angry when he realized that his *protégé* had changed, becoming withdrawn and austere.

The two men, no longer friends, became bitter opponents until, in 1170, Henry is said to have asked in a fit of anger if there was no one 'that will free me from this quarrelsome priest?'

Four knights heard the remark, rode straightaway to Canterbury and murdered Becket within the Cathedral. The murder shocked the Christian world and Becket became a saint. The Pope ordered Henry to make a public penance at the altar of Canterbury Cathedral, where he was scourged by the monks, and Canterbury became a place of pilgrimage.

1189
The Third Crusade launched

After the fiasco of the Second Crusade a new and more powerful Moslem army had come into being. Led by Saladin it captured one Crusaders' stronghold after another and in 1187 Jerusalem itself.

Consequently the Third Crusade was launched, three armies led by three kings – Richard I of England, Frederick Barbarossa of Germany and Philip II of France. They set out separately for the Holy Land. Barbarossa died before he reached Palestine, Philip became ill and returned to France, and Richard of England was left in command. His victory over Saladin at Arnif earned him the title of 'Lion Heart' (*Cœur de Lion*). He captured Acre and Jaffa but not Jerusalem.

In 1192, on his way home, he was taken prisoner in Germany and held captive for two years until a large ransom was paid for his release. He died in battle in 1199.

1194
Building of Chartres Cathedral

'Gothic' architecture began during the middle of the twelfth century. It was a slender and graceful style and its finest example is Chartres Cathedral, southwest of Paris. It was begun in 1194 and compared with the dim interiors of former churches, it was ablaze with many-tinted lights from its stained glass windows, regarded as the world's finest.

12th century
The growth of medieval literature

In the early middle ages, Latin was the literary and ecclesiastical language used throughout Europe. The twelfth century

Troubadours

saw the birth of modern European literature, as courts developed a taste for spoken or sung poetry in the language of the country.

Written in about 1100 the French epic the *Chanson de Roland* presents a legendary version of Roland's death in AD 778. The medieval epics were stories of heroic battle and feudal bonds, often revealing glimpses of an older epic tradition, as in the German *Nibelungenlied* (*c.* 1200), which has elements inherited from old Scandinavian sagas.

Singers and poets travelled the rough roads of Europe at the time of the crusades, seeking patronage at castles. In Provence a new convention developed among these *troubadours*: the idea of 'courtly love'. For the first time woman was exalted and ideal love pursued. This new verse spread with the *trouvères* of northern France and the German *Minnesänger*. Notable troubadours included Bertrand de Born (*c.* 1140–*c.* 1215); the greatest *Minnesänger* was Walther von der Vogelweide (*c.* 1170–1230).

Much of the best literature concerns tales of Arthur and his knights, and associated legends originating from Brittany. Authors of Arthurian romance include Thomas, Chrétien de Troyes and Marie de France in the twelfth century, and Wolfram von Eschenbach and Gottfried von Strassburg in the thirteenth.

1204
The Fourth Crusade

Innocent III, who became Pope in 1198, decided that the best way to revitalize religion would be to begin a new Crusade in the traditional medieval manner. He hoped to lead it himself, but the actual leader was to become Boniface, Marquess of Montferrat, whose aims had little to do with religion, but with loot.

Montferrat's army never reached the Holy Land. He made an agreement with the Venetians to help them capture and loot the Christian city of Constantinople.

They then proceeded to alter the map of Europe. Count Baldwin of Flanders was made the first 'Latin Emperor of the East' whilst Venice took over a quarter of Constantinople and captured most of the trade that had formerly gone through that city.

1206
Temujin proclaimed Genghis Khan

For centuries the people of China had tried to keep out the fierce tribes of barbarians that threatened the borders of their sacred soil. The wildest of these tribes was the Mongols who, although utterly ruthless and completely savage, continually fought amongst themselves and thus presented little danger.

Then in 1162 a Mongolian was born called Temujin. He succeeded his chieftain father and began to fight the neighbouring tribes. Finally, after many years of struggle, he brought every Mongolian tribe under his control to earn himself the name of Genghis Khan ('Mighty Warrior'). Within five years he had assembled an enormous army of 200,000 horsemen which easily burst through the Great Wall to conquer the whole of northern China, then went on to overrun the Turks of Asia Minor and the small kingdoms of Russia. Nothing could stop these fierce warriors who seemed part of the small, sturdy horses they rode. When the Khan died in 1227 he had carved out the largest empire then known to history.

The Fourth Crusade turns against Constantinople.

1208
The Albigensian Crusade

During the twelfth century, a new sect began in Southern France. Its followers were known as the Albigenses after the town of Albi, not far from Toulouse. Its members were considered heretics although they lived austere lives which contrasted with the laxity of most of the clergy of the time.

They grew in numbers until Pope Innocent III was forced to send missionaries amongst them to 'bring them back to the accepted Church', but when in 1208 his legate was murdered whilst in their country, he declared a Crusade against them.

His call was eagerly answered by many northern barons who saw an opportunity of plunder and they were led by Simon de Montfort whose son (*see 1265 De Montfort's Parliament*) of the same name, was to play a large part in English history.

The Albigenses were exterminated after the capture of their fortress of Montsegur in 1244, and their sect disappeared.

1210
Francis of Assisi founds the Franciscans

Born in 1181, Francis was the son of a cloth merchant of Assisi in central Italy. When he was young he wished to become like the heroes of chivalry he had heard of in the *chansons de gests*, but experience of fighting soon changed his mind.

Later he felt the urge to wander about the world doing good and, travelling to Rome, received the Pope's blessing on his idea. By 1223 he had gathered an army of several thousand disciples and his converts became known as Franciscan friars.

They did not live in monasteries like other monks but spent their lives travel-

St Francis renouncing his inheritance – a fresco from the school of Giotto.

The barons force John to sign Magna Carta.

82

ling from country to country working and preaching and, when necessary, begging for food. They practised total poverty and were the poorest of the poor. Their leader (later to become Saint Francis) died on October 3, 1226 in the 'Chapel of the Little Portion' which still stands outside Assisi.

1215
Magna Carta

King John (1167–1216) came to the throne on May 27, 1199 following the death of his brother, Richard I. Even during Richard's absence at the Crusades, John had proved himself wicked and tyrannical.

On ascending the throne he seemed to become worse. He lost a great part of the English lands in France, became involved in a struggle with the Pope over the appointment of Stephen Langton to the see of Canterbury and then in a series of quarrels with his barons.

Finally England had had enough. He was not deposed, as one would have expected, but at Runnymede in June 1215 he was forced to sign *Magna Carta* ('The Great Charter') which stated that the

king was beneath the law, not above it. The spirit of *Magna Carta*, with its sixty-three sections, has influenced the law of England ever since.

1240
Alexander of Novgorod is called 'Nevsky'

In 1224 the Tartar Mongols appeared in the southern steppes of Russia and were soon ravaging central Russia itself, laying waste to the south and sacking Kiev. Their domination of Russia was to last for over two centuries.

One part of Russia which had suffered less than other cities was Novgorod which, however, had other enemies – the Swedes and the German Knights of the Teutonic Order.

In 1240, under Prince Alexander (1220–63) the men of Novgorod attacked the Swedes in the Neva region and defeated them, giving their leader the title of Alexander Nevsky (of the Neva). Two years later he smashed the German knights in a battle fought on the frozen surface of Lake Peipus.

He was realistic enough to know that his army could never defeat the seemingly limitless Mongol hordes and after paying tribute and homage to the Great Khan, his country was left unmolested.

1254
End of the Hohenstaufen dynasty

The Hohenstaufen were a princely family whose members were emperors or German kings from 1138–1254. The empire became particularly powerful when Frederick Barbarossa (1123–90) became Holy Roman Emperor in 1152. The last emperor was Frederick II (1212–50) and the last king was Conrad IV (1250–54). The execution of Conrad's son in 1268 brought an end to the male line of the Hohenstaufen.

1257
Llywellyn becomes Prince of Wales

During the 1250s, a Welsh battle of power was won by Llywellyn ap Gruffydd (d.1282) who soon made himself lord of north and south Wales. At the time of his accession his country was overrun with English barons and his first task was to rid Wales of the foreign invaders. In this he was successful and in 1257 Henry III (1207–72) of England acknowledged him as Prince of Wales and Overlord of his country.

Henry's successor, however, was Edward I (1239–1307) who was determined to rule over an undivided kingdom. In 1277 he led a powerful army into Wales, forcing Llywellyn to come to terms. In a further rising the prince was killed in a skirmish near Builth Wells in 1282. Two years later, at Caernarvon Castle, Edward offered his own son, a baby, as the first English Prince of Wales.

1260
Kublai Khan becomes the Great Khan

The great Genghis Khan left an empire that stretched from the Yellow Sea to the Persian Gulf and the Black Sea. His son Ogdai sent armies into most of the northern countries and it was only his death, which recalled the Mongol leaders to dispute the succession, that saved Europe.

The new leader was Kublai, a grandson of Genghis who, becoming the Great Khan, completed the conquest of China and founded the Yuen dynasty, becoming the ruler of more subjects than any man in history.

Yet he was a far more civilized person than the earlier Mongols and it was during his reign that reports of 'far Cathay' were received in Europe, finally resulting in the appearance of Marco Polo at his court (*see 1271 Marco Polo's journey*).

On Kublai's death his empire fell apart, although his successors continued to rule over many conquered territories.

Kublai Khan, ruler of the immense Mongol empire, presided over a magnificent court whose fame spread to Europe.

c. 1264
Aquinas writes *Summa Theologica*

Thomas Aquinas was born in Aquino near Naples in 1225, joining the Dominican order to work in Cologne and become known as the greatest scholar in Christendom. He began his *Summa Theologica* about 1264, a work intended to be the sum of all known learning. He died in 1274 and was made a saint in 1323.

1265
De Montfort's Parliament

Before the Norman Conquest the Saxons had no parliament but a Witanagemot (Assembly of the Wise). In Norman times there was a Great Council but this did very little and kings did as they pleased until King John was checked by his barons and forced to sign the Magna Carta (*see 1215 Magna Carta*).

John's son, Henry III (1207–72) was little better with a great idea of his own importance, but little ability. Within four years he had bankrupted his kingdom and finally his powers were wrested from him by the nobles who were tired of helping finance his foreign wars. In 1258, led by the idealistic Simon de Montfort, Earl of Leicester, the barons governed the country by committee.

In 1265 de Montfort formed England's first Parliament with nobles and commoners. The first true or 'Model' Parliament was called together in 1295 by Edward I and was the pattern for later legislatures.

1266
Bacon's *Opus Majus*

Roger Bacon (*c.*1215–*c.*1292) was a scientist who was far ahead of his time. The Western discovery of gunpowder as an explosive, for example, is attributed to him. He wrote three books – *Opus Majus*, *Opus Minus* and *Opus Tertium* in which he developed many of his astounding theories.

Roger Bacon

1271
Marco Polo's journey

In 1260, Nicolo and Maffeo Polo, two Venetian merchants, left Constantinople to travel towards the east, hoping to find new areas in which to trade. They finally reached the court of Kublai Khan, the great Tartar emperor, who treated them most kindly. They set out for the east again in 1271, this time accompanied by Marco, Nicolo's fifteen-year-old son.

After a long and arduous journey, they arrived at Kublai Khan's court at Peking where the Khan took young Marco into his service, showing him many favours. The Polos were to stay at the court for some twenty years until 1292. Finally they sailed to Persia by Sumatra and southern India, the first Europeans to take this route.

They reached Venice in 1295 but not long afterwards Marco was captured in a sea battle and imprisoned for a while. He used the time to good advantage, getting a fellow prisoner to write the stories of his many adventures, although many did not believe them, they were so incredible. He died aged seventy about the year 1324.

1291
The Everlasting League of Uri

For centuries there was no such country as Switzerland. As early as the first century BC, the territory of two tribes, the Helvetii and the Rhaetii were conquered by Julius Caesar and taken into the Roman Empire.

When that crumbled they were over-run by Germanic tribes from the north. The eighth century saw the territory as part of Charlemagne's Holy Roman Empire and it later came under the rule of the Hapsburgs.

This royal family of Austria was ruled by Rudolph of Hapsburg and on his death the inhabitants of the valleys of

Uri, Schwyz and Nidwalden, determined to be an independent people, banded together and on August 1, 1291 formed the 'Everlasting League' for mutual defence. From this, the Swiss nation slowly and painfully achieved complete independence by 1648.

Robert Bruce defeats the English at Bannockburn in 1314.

1298
The defeat of Wallace

Scotland was facing dark days indeed. Edward I of England had stripped Baliol, the Scottish king, of all his powers, and he and his nobles were forced to pay homage. Edward also carried off the sacred Stone of Scone to place it in Westminster Abbey. Then, when the country's fortunes seemed at their very lowest, a patriot came forward – Sir William Wallace.

He quickly gathered an army of the people about him and after turning them into a reliable fighting force, stormed and captured stronghold after stronghold.

He fought a pitched battle at Stirling Bridge in 1297, utterly routed the English and for a year reigned in Scotland as Baliol's deputy.

Edward was forced to lead another army to Scotland. He met Wallace at Falkirk on July 22, 1298 and defeated him. Wallace escaped but was treacherously handed over to Edward who had him executed in 1305.

1306
Robert Bruce crowned at Scone

Six months after Wallace's death, Robert Bruce and John (the 'Red') Comyn met to decide who should assume leadership of Scotland. There was a quarrel and Bruce stabbed his rival in an outburst of anger. Assembling his vassals Bruce now asserted his rights, and in 1306 was

crowned at Scone.

Fully committed now, Bruce began to gather an army to combat the English remaining in Scotland after Falkirk but in March 1306 he was decisively beaten at Methven. By the spring of 1307 he had raised another army and Edward was again forced to march north, but died on the way, his son, Edward II (1284–1327) taking command.

The two armies met on June 24, 1314 at Bannockburn and the English were completely defeated. The treaty of Northampton recognized Scotland as an independent country in 1328, but Bruce died in the following year.

1309
The Papacy moves to Avignon

The fine city of Avignon in France, standing high above the river Rhone, is dominated by a great palace which, for many years, was occupied by the Popes rather than Rome, their home of centuries. This came about when a new king Philip IV (1285–1314) known as 'The Fair' and the founder of modern France, sought to bring the Papacy under his control, the Pope of the time being Boniface VIII.

Agents of the king seized Boniface who died soon afterwards and from 1309 Avignon became the home of the Popes until 1378, a period sometimes called the 'Babylonian Captivity'.

After this Pope Urban VI and his successors ruled from Rome whilst an 'anti-pope', Clement VII, set up his court at Avignon. Called the Great Schism, this lasted until 1417.

1310
Giotto's *The Ascension*

Giotto di Bondone was an Italian artist born near Florence about 1266. Cimabue, a great artist of the time,

quickly recognized the young Giotto's skill and made him his pupil. Much of Giotto's work is lost but his campanile at Florence, his frescos at Assisi and Padua and his magnificent painting of Christ's Ascension reveal his genius.

1314
Dante writes *La Divina Commedia*

Dante Alighieri was born in Florence in 1265 and eighteen years of his later life were occupied in writing his immortal work *La Divina Commedia* ('The Divine Comedy') which tells of a soul's pilgrimage, guided by Virgil representing philosophy and Beatrice (Dante's ideal love) representing religion. Dante died in 1321.

Dante Alighieri

c. 1327
The Aztecs found Tenochtitlán

The great nation that was to become that of the Aztecs, came originally from somewhere in North America. From similarities of language with the Piman, a Red Indian tribe, it may well have been from what is now Arizona. Several tribes linked together to begin a great migration southwards about 1100 and reaching the kingdom of the Toltecs, settled there.

At first they were happy to be fishermen or simple farmers, paying allegiance to their Toltec overlords, but as the power of the latter steadily declined, their

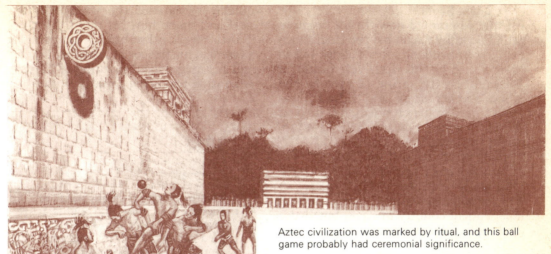

Aztec civilization was marked by ritual, and this ball game probably had ceremonial significance.

own increased. About 1327 a number of them formed a settlement on a marshy island near a lake called Tenochtitlán, the site of modern Mexico City, where the Toltecs were unable to dislodge them. From this first settlement grew the great and powerful nation of the Aztecs. Within fifty years they had elected their own king, although their greatest was to be Itzcoatl (*c.* 1430) who made them the premier nation of Mexico with boundaries that extended over most of southern Mexico as far south as the isthmus of Tehuantepec.

They were conquered by Cortes (*see 1521 The conquest of Mexico*) and their existence as a great empire was over.

1338
Start of the Hundred Years' War

Known to history as the Hundred Years' War, the long struggle between England and France started in 1338 and, with brief truces, was not to end until 1453.

The Kings of England were also hereditary Dukes of Aquitaine and for two centuries had paid homage to the King of France for this duchy, an act they resented. Things came to a head when Philip VI of France took over Edward's

land in France and war began.

The first major encounter was a naval battle in 1340 when two hundred and fifty English ships fought a French fleet at the mouth of the river Sluys and at the end of the day only twenty-four French ships escaped.

Edward III (1312–77) later won the famous victory of Crécy, fought on August 23, 1346. Masses of heavily armed French cavalry attacked the lines of English archers only to fall to their deadly arrows, some 60,000 French troops being annihilated. The supremacy of long bow over heavy armour was decisively proved.

During this action Edward, the Black Prince, 'won his spurs'. He was to die, still a young man, in Spain in 1376.

1348
Black Death reaches Europe from the East

Since the early part of the fourteenth century, a terrible disease had been ravaging Egypt, China and India. Today it is realized that it was bubonic and pneumonic plague, but to the people of Europe it was a curse of the pagan 'savages' of those distant lands. For England was at peace, thanks to her warrior king Edward III, and she was thriving on her large exports of wool and cloth, and even reports that the plague had moved to Europe carried by caravans bearing silks and spices from Oriental bazaars, caused little concern.

Then, on a summer's day in 1348 a French sailor stepped ashore on England's south coast. All unknown he carried bacillus of the pestilence that was to become known as the Black Death.

Once a victim had contracted the disease he died soon afterwards, usually after a few hours of terrible pain. No one knows how many victims the Black Death claimed although a conservative estimate gives the number of deaths in England alone at half a million, a large percentage of the population.

The pestilence reached its peak in the spring of 1349 and died out during the autumn, having ravaged Europe, dislocating society and ruining trade.

c. 1350
Sir Gawain and the Green Knight

This long alliterative poem was written by an anonymous English poet of the fourteenth century who used the language of northwest England. It describes the exploits of Gawain, a knight of Arthur, who undergoes a series of temptations in his quest for vengeance on a giant dressed in green.

1353
Boccaccio writes the Decameron

The *Decameron* (Greek for 'ten days') was written by an Italian, Giovanni Boccaccio (1313–75). It is a collection of one hundred short stories related over ten days by a party of young people who have left Florence for the hills during the plague. The *Decameron*, which includes tales that are both bawdy and full of pathos, greatly influenced European literature.

1356
The expansion of the Hanseatic league

During the twelfth century a number of important towns in northern Europe, especially those on the Baltic Sea and along the Rhine, found themselves coming into conflict with each other over trade.

Some of these towns soon realized that, by forming themselves into some kind of union, they could secure many trading privileges when developing commerce with foreign countries. The members became known as *Hansa*.

In 1356 the various *Hansas* united for even greater strength and led by the maritime towns of Lübeck, Hamburg and Bremen, the great Hanseatic League was created which became richer and more powerful than many important European states.

Hanseatic merchants settled in England and soon became the most important group of foreign merchants in the country. They had special privileges which were later confirmed by Richard III, after some difficulty had been experienced with jealous English merchants.

c. 1362
Langland writes Piers Plowman

One of the most important books to come from late medieval England is *The Vision of William concerning Piers Plowman*. An allegory, written by a priest named William Langland, the story is centred around the Malvern Hills and provides invaluable glimpses of rural life in fourteenth-century England.

Chu Yuen-Chang seizes Peking to become Hung Wu, first of the Ming emperors.

1366
Petrarch writes the *Canzoniere*

Francesco Petrarca, known as Petrarch (1304–74) went to live in Avignon where in 1327 he began to write prolifically in verse and prose, especially in the type of sonnet to which he gave his name. He became infatuated with a girl named Laura and wrote about her in a series of poems called *Canzoniere* (1366).

1368
Foundation of the Ming dynasty

Following the return of the Polo family from the court of the Great Khan (*see 1271 Marco Polo's journey*) the news of 'far Cathay' compelled others to follow, especially merchants and missionaries. When the great Mongol Empire collapsed, however, the trade routes became dangerous and when an anti-foreigner campaign began in China, few Europeans dared return.

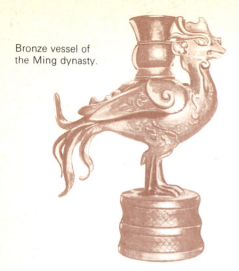

Bronze vessel of the Ming dynasty.

After the Mongols a wholly Chinese dynasty came into being in 1368 – the Ming. The first emperor was Hung Wu and his dynasty was to last until 1644. The country became settled and prosperous, the capital being established at Nanking. The third emperor, Yung Lo, was one of China's greatest builders and many of the palaces, temples and pagodas that exist in China today were built during his reign and those of his Ming successors.

A new kind of blue-and-white porcelain ware was developed during this dynasty which also saw a very high standard of textiles, brocades and embroideries and especially beautiful Chinese rugs and carpets. Realizing the settled nature of the Ming dynasty, Europeans began to return to China, some Portuguese being the first, reaching the country in 1514.

1377
Wycliffe and the Lollards

John Wycliffe (*c.* 1329–84) was an English religious reformer who was born near Hipswell in Yorkshire about 1324. He became Master of Balliol College, Oxford about 1360 and in 1374 became a priest in the rectory of Lutterworth where he was to stay until his death in 1384.

He spent the latter part of his life in attacking the worldly power and evil lives

John Wycliffe, English religious reformer.

of the clergy and soon collected a large number of followers who became known as Lollards (from the Dutch *lollen* 'to sing in a low voice'). The first complete translation of the Bible is credited to him and he did much to influence the Protestant Reformation.

The leadership of the Lollards was taken over by Sir John Oldcastle, originally a soldier and friend of Henry, Prince of Wales, afterwards Henry V. He was imprisoned for heresy in 1413, escaped from the Tower but was later recaptured and burned to death.

1381
The Peasants' Revolt

It is said that Wycliffe's Lollards did much to increase discontent amongst English peasants and artisans by their teaching. They had fertile ground, certainly, for the peasants were still little more than serfs whilst the labourers were forced by law to work for near starvation wages.

In 1381 this discontent reached a climax when the government passed a poll-tax (so much tax per head) to pay for the French war (*see 1338 Start of the Hundred Years' War*) and a leader appeared. He was Wat Tyler, a tiler from Kent, who had killed a tax collector and then gathered an army of ill-armed peasants to march on London. They burned the houses of officials and grasping landlords as they went. One priest took as his text the rhyme:

'When Adam delved and Eve span,
Who was then the gentleman?'

Others joined them on their way and by the time they had reached Smithfield, where they were met by young King Richard II (1367–1400) they had grown into a force of thousands.

Richard granted them everything they asked and they then dispersed quietly. Tyler, however, stayed until the following day for another interview at which he was stabbed by the Lord Mayor because, he said, Tyler had insulted the king.

c. 1388
Chaucer writes *Canterbury Tales*

The *Canterbury Tales* is the last, longest and most famous work by the English poet, Geoffrey Chaucer (*c.* 1340–1400). The *Prologue* to the tales describes thirty pilgrims who agree to tell each other stories on their way from London to Canterbury and is particularly noteworthy. The tales range from the romantic *Knight's Tale* to the bawdy *Miller's Tale*.

Geoffrey Chaucer

1397
Scandinavian Union of Kalmar

King Haakon VI of Norway (1355–80) married Princess Margaret of Denmark. Their son, Olaf V, who had become King of Denmark in 1375, became King of Norway in 1381, but died seven years later aged eighteen.

His widowed mother, Margaret, then became the 'right sovereign' of all three Scandinavian kingdoms although, for a time, the real power lay in the hands of the nobles. By 1396, however, she had forced them to destroy their strongholds and renounced their newly acquired privileges, including freedom from taxation.

Margaret's triumph was to present her great-nephew Erik of Pomerania (1389–1440) as her successor and ruler of the three kingdoms by the important Union of Kalmar of 1397. Nevertheless she remained Regent of Norway, Sweden and Denmark until her death in 1412.

However, in 1436 Erik III was deposed and Norwegian nobles made his nephew Christopher of Bavaria their king in 1442.

1398
Timur conquers North India

Timur of Samarkand (1336–1405) had the nickname of *Timur i Leng*, 'the lame Timur', from which has come his more familiar name of Tamberlaine or Tamer-

The invincible Timur defeated the Ottoman sultan Bayazid II at Ankara in 1402.

lane. Lame or not, he soon proved himself to be a doughty warrior and the greatest world conqueror since Alexander the Great. Son of a tribal chieftain, he fought some khans and supported others until his army had occupied Moscow and conquered a huge territory.

The following year (1381) he took an army into Persia and smashed aside all opposition. In 1398 he invaded India, crossed the Indus and attacked Delhi which he left in ruins.

1399
Henry of Lancaster usurps the throne

For a long time the crown of England had been handed down from father to heir without break. Then the custom of 'primogeniture' suddenly stopped when King Richard II proved to be a weak and unreliable king.

His two most powerful barons, Henry Bolingbroke, Earl of Lancaster, (1367–1413) and the Duke of Norfolk became enemies and the king commanded that they should meet in mortal combat. A huge crowd turned out to watch the duel but at the last moment Richard stopped the fight sending Norfolk into exile for life and Henry for ten years, while confiscating their estates.

Alarmed at his action the other great nobles rose in Lancaster's favour and in 1399 Richard was forced to resign the crown in favour of his cousin Lancaster, saying, 'I present and give to you this crown, with which I was crowned King of England, and with it all the rights dependent on it.' He died a few months later in Pontefract Castle.

Lancaster's claim to the throne was through his father, John of Gaunt, third son of Edward III which, although somewhat slight, at least showed he had royal blood in his veins. His reign began the rule of the House of Lancaster.

1400
Welsh War of Independence

Owen Glendower was born to a noble Welsh family about 1359. He studied law at Westminster and then in 1385 fought for Richard II against the Scots. It was partly his association with the deposed king that encouraged him to fly the banners of revolt soon after Henry IV came to the throne. Claiming descent from the old Welsh princes, he gathered an army.

Henry, in turn, led an army against him on several occasions but with little success. Soon Owen was intriguing with another rebel, Henry Hotspur (*see 1403 The Battle of Shrewsbury*) and hoped that a simultaneous rising would topple the new English king. But it was not to be, and both were defeated. Glendower retired to Wales to carry on the fight which he was to maintain for another ten years, dying a natural death in 1415. He was the last independent Prince of Wales.

1401
De Haeretico Comburendo

On becoming king, Henry IV sought the support of the Church to regularize his claim to the throne. Knowing that the Lollards were violently opposed to the Church he had Parliament bring in a law – *De Haeretico Comburendo* – which allowed civilian authorities to burn heretics, even priests, who held views 'contrary to the truth of Holy Church' and had been condemned in a spiritual court.

Owen Glendower presides over the Welsh parliament at Machynlleth.

1403
The Battle of Shrewsbury

The most powerful noble in England during Henry IV's reign was Henry Percy, nicknamed 'Hotspur' (1364–1403). He had played an important part in the rebellion that had deposed Richard and had made himself a hero by defeating the Scots at Homildon Hill in Northumberland. But he and the king quarrelled and Hotspur, aided by his father the Earl of Northumberland, rose in rebellion, calling the king a usurper and hinting that Richard II had been taken from Pontefract Castle and was still alive. Hotspur gathered his own large army and made a pact with Owen Glendower (*see 1400 Welsh War of Independence*) to bring another against the king and to join forces. But before the junction had been made, Henry's own army arrived and the Battle of Shrewsbury was fought on July 21, 1403.

The armies were well matched but by nightfall Hotspur lay dead on the field of battle and his army was routed.

1415
The Battle of Agincourt

When Henry V (1387–1422) came to the English throne in 1413 his country was still suffering from the troubled years of his father's reign. To distract his subjects from problems at home he sailed for France laying siege to Harfleur. Then, with an army weakened by sickness, he marched for Calais, but his passage was blocked by a French army which outnumbered his by four to one.

One the morning of October 25, 1415 the two armies faced each other and when the heavily armed French knights began their lumbering advance, the air was suddenly filled with the deadly hiss of English arrows. As at Crécy (1346) and Poitiers (1356) the English archers proved their supremacy and the chivalry of France lay dead or was driven from the field.

By the Treaty of Troyes (1420) Henry was made Regent of France and married Catherine, the French king's daughter.

1427
Hussites rise in Bohemia

John Huss, born about 1370, was a Bohemian reformer. He became a priest and then, in 1402, Rector of Prague University. He began to preach similar doctrines to Wycliffe and was charged with heresy. By then he had collected a large following and despite excommunication he continued to preach.

In 1412 he retired from active work to write his opus, *De Ecclesia*, and three years later, despite a promise of safe conduct, was arrested when attending a Council and was burned as a heretic.

His martyrdom made his followers more fanatical and for several years they made war on the Emperor Sigismund (1368–1437) who had been responsible for Huss's death, winning several battles including Aussis and Tachau, in Germany. Peace was made in 1431 by one of the two Hussite parties but it was to be several years before the other party followed suit.

1434
Van Eyck: *Giovanni Arnolfini and his wife*

It was in the fifteenth century, through the work of Jan van Eyck (*c.* 1385–1441) that Flemish painting developed a deliberately new, realistic style. The portrait *Giovanni Arnolfini and his wife* illustrates van Eyck's attention to detail and his psychological observation. Other paintings by van Eyck include the *Adoration of the Lamb*, a masterpiece in Flemish art, and the *Annunciation*.

1431
The burning of Joan of Arc

The Hundred Years' War, begun in 1338, was ending at last. Henry V, England's great warrior king, had died in 1422 and a few months later France's Charles VI followed him. Now France was ruled by counsellors, who were jealous of each other, and possessed a demoralized army.

Then, with dramatic suddenness, a raw peasant girl arrived at the royal court. She had come from a small village in Lorraine and claimed that she had heard heavenly voices telling her to go and free Orleans from the besieging English. Although most of the nobles mocked her, the army, inspired by her courage, followed her into battle. She drove the English from Orleans and stood at his side whilst the Dauphin was crowned Charles VII in Rheims Cathedral.

Although she was later betrayed, sold to the English and, found guilty of sorcery and heresy, burned at the stake, she had helped unify France – leaving behind a symbol of hope and of courage.

Joan of Arc is burnt at the stake, accused of heresy

1434
The rise of the Medicis

The name 'Medici' first appeared in a Florentine chronicle of the twelfth century, but it was to be Giovanni dei Medici (1360–1429) who should be considered the founder of the family's vast fortunes. He was basically a trader and created his family's fortune with a number of banks he opened in Italy and elsewhere.

On his death his business was shared between his two sons, Lorenzo and Cosimo (1389–1464). When Cosimo's political rivals were exiled, he became in fact, though not in name, ruler of Florence in 1434. He was not only a brilliant businessman but a most astute politician. He insisted on being regarded as a private citizen and refused to accept any public office yet, with his wealth, influence and connections, was the absolute ruler of a very republican country.

Cosimo was a great patron of the arts and a great builder and many of his palaces, churches and villas were truly magnificent. He saved priceless Greek and Latin manuscripts for posterity and opened public libraries where students and others could study them.

He died in 1469 leaving his two sons, Lorenzo and Giuliano to continue the fortunes of the Medici family.

Prince Henry the Navigator.

could learn navigation, mathematics and have instruction in map-making.

He then began to send out expeditions which, in time, were to discover the Azores, Madeira and the Canaries; Cape Verde was rounded by Birnil Diaz in 1445 and the African coast was explored as far as Sierra Leone by Alvaro Fernandez in 1446. One of his 'ex-students', Bartolomeu Diaz, was the first European to round the Cape of Good Hope in 1488.

1437
Henry the Navigator founds Institute

Prince Henry (1394–1460) was the son of John, King of Portugal and Philippa, daughter of the English John of Gaunt. He first made his name as a courageous soldier but whilst warring in Africa he became interested in the Continent and excited by the possibilities of unknown lands beyond. Returning to Portugal in 1437 he founded a Colonial and Naval Institute at Sagres where young men

1438
Albert becomes Holy Roman Emperor

The Hapsburgs were an Austrian imperial family who took their family name from the castle in which they lived near the junction of the Rhine and the Aar rivers. The founder of the family was Albert, Count of Hapsburg, who together with his son, made his family the most powerful in Swabia.

In 1273 Rudolph of Hapsburg became not only King of Germany but also Holy Roman Emperor, having wrested Upper and Lower Austria, Styria and Carniola from Ottokar of Bohemia. This greatly increased the power of his family.

In 1356 the Golden Bull issued by Emperor Charles IV made the imperial throne elective; emperors were to be chosen by a majority vote of seven German electors. However, in 1438, Albert, Archduke of Austria, another Hapsburg, became emperor and although the imperial power remained elective it passed permanently to the Hapsburgs. It remained with their family until the end of the empire in 1806.

1448
Fra Angelico paints the Vatican frescoes

Guido da Fiosole (1387–1455) entered a monastery and was called Fra (*frater*) and Angelico because of his lovable and humble nature. A brilliant artist, he did much work in Rome and in the Vatican, in the Chapel of Nicholas V (SS. Stephen and Lawrence) and also frescoes in Florence, Orvieto and elsewhere.

1453
The Turks capture Constantinople

Mahomet II having taken Constantinople.

In 1451 a new Sultan, Mahomet II, came to the Turkish throne and swore to capture Constantinople. He trained an army of fighters called 'janissaries' and engaged a Hungarian engineer to cast guns which proved to be the world's largest; one was nearly eight metres long and fired a 545 kilogram ball. Within two years he was ready and by April 1453 his army was ready to attack.

Within the great walls the garrison, weakened and impoverished, could only muster seven thousand men, whereas Mahomet II had an army of over eighty thousand.

The big Turkish guns began a bombardment which was to continue, without pause, for six weeks. The garrison fought bravely, filling up breaches in the walls, fighting off attack after attack. But the end was inevitable. On May 29 the final assault began. Wave after wave of Turks poured into the city, the Emperor Constantine XI died a hero's death and by nightfall the city had fallen. Its conquest was to alter history for its scholars had already fled, taking their manuscripts and documents with them to spread a new interest in learning throughout Western Europe.

1454
Gutenberg sets up his printing press

Johann Gutenberg (*c.* 1398–*c.* 1468) was born in the German city of Mainz but lived for part of his early life in Strasbourg. Here he worked as an artisan but spent all his free time working on an idea that had come to him . . . printing.

He returned to Mainz and in partnership with a Johann Fust, from whom he borrowed money to continue, began work on a large Latin Bible. It was similar to the work of the monks, for the wooden printing type was large whilst

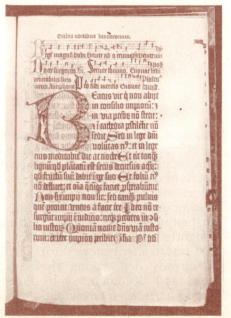

spaces were left at the beginning of some lines in order that a hand-illuminated letter might be inserted. This work was finished about 1456 with some smaller books and folios.

Gutenberg soon realized that due to the difficulty of carving, wooden type was inefficient, so he developed a technique of casting type from metal.

In 1462 Mainz was stormed and sacked and a number of printers fled to other cities. Within fifty years, printing was going on in more than two hundred places in Europe and books and leaflets were becoming available to far more people than before.

1455
Alfonso becomes Pope Calixtus III

Borgia (the Italian form of Borja) was the name of an ancient noble family who came originally from the Spanish province of Valencia. The family (who came to Italy in 1443) achieved great prominence, power and notoriety in the fifteenth century.

In 1455 Alfonso de Borja (1378–1458) who was a bishop, became Pope as Calixtus III. He made his nephew, Rodrigo (1451–1503) a cardinal who also ascended the papal throne in 1492 as Alexander VI.

The most powerful of them all, however, was Cesare Borgia (1476–1507), son of Alexander, who exercised royal power and steered the fortunes of his country at that time. Another member of the family was Lucrezia (1480–1519), Cesare's sister, who was later accused of all manner of evil things including assassination, but who in later life, became a patron of art and learning and a supporter of charitable works.

(Above left) Gutenberg working at his Press
(Left) A page from Gutenberg's Bible.

101

1455
The Wars of the Roses

One of Britain's worst civil wars was that known as the Wars of the Roses, beginning in 1455 and lasting until 1485. It was so called because the two rival parties each chose a rose as a symbol: York (white) and Lancaster (red). It began when Henry VI (1421–71) became insane and Richard, Duke of York claimed the throne.

A number of battles followed (beginning with that of St Albans in 1455) with periods of truce between them. At the battle of Northampton (1460) Henry was captured and at Wakefield (1461) York was killed. The Lancastrians were defeated at Towton in the same year and their position seemed hopeless until the powerful Earl of Warwick, the 'King-maker', and hitherto a Yorkist supporter, changed sides.

Henry was released from prison and again made king, but the Lancastrians were defeated at Barnet (1471) where Warwick was killed and the Battle of Tewkesbury placed York's son Edward IV (1442–83) firmly on the throne. He was succeeded by Richard III (his own son Edward V dying mysteriously in the Tower) who reigned for two years until he died on Bosworth Field fighting the Tudor prince who was to become Henry VII (1457–1509).

The struggle between the Yorkists and Lancastrians came to an end with the Battle of Bosworth Field, fought on August 22, 1485. Richard III was killed and Henry Tudor came to the throne.

c. 1460
Development of Japanese Nō theatre

About the middle of the fifteenth century, a new style of acting and music was created in Japan which, quite unchanged, is still to be seen in Japanese theatres today. From about 1460 the language, costumes and setting have been exactly as they were at the outset and the drama and music combine to form Nō theatre.

The plays are performed on a square stage, the audience sitting on three sides whilst the fourth leads to the dressing rooms. The players are all male, the principal actor wearing a succession of masks to mark his changing moods, which are also reflected by traditional movements of a fan. The orchestra is usually composed of three drums and a flute. A small chorus, housed in a balcony, comments on the events of the play, while the actors dance and chant in a formal, traditional style.

1461
Villon writes *Le Grand Testament*

François Villon (1431–c.1463) a French poet, led a turbulent life and frequented disreputable society when young. When he murdered an ecclesiastic he was finally forced to leave Paris where he had just completed his *Petit Testament*. Later he wrote *Le Grand Testament*, a melancholic poem which reviews the poet's life, his disappointments and regrets.

1469
Malory writes *Le Morte d'Arthur*

The shadowy world of the historical Arthur bore little resemblance to the many fine chivalrous epics of the middle ages (*see 1200 The growth of medieval literature*). Malory's classic presents the complete legends of King Arthur and the Knights of the Round Table, Merlin, Lancelot and Guinevere. Sir Thomas Malory died in 1471, and *Le Morte d'Arthur* (The Death of Arthur) was first published by Caxton.

1469
Lorenzo the Magnificent rules Florence

Cosimo dei Medici (*see 1434 The rise of the Medicis*) was succeeded by his two sons, Lorenzo and Giuliano. It was soon obvious that the stronger character was Lorenzo who fell out with another powerful family, the Pazzi. When the two brothers were at mass in Florence cathedral, they were attacked by assassins and Giuliano, stabbed in the back, fell dying. Lorenzo was able to escape, gather his men and storm the palace of the Pazzi. Some of his enemies were cut down, others hanged from the palace windows, others sent into exile.

The Pazzi family disposed of, Lorenzo became the most powerful man in Florence which although technically a republic, was ruled by him until his death in 1492. His rule proved beneficial, commerce and art flourishing equally. Lorenzo himself was a brilliant writer and poet.

1476
Caxton sets up his press

Kentish-born William Caxton was originally apprenticed to a London mercer but in 1441 went to Europe to study the new craft of printing. In 1474 he set up a printing press at Westminster – the first in Britain – where he was to print ninety-six books including *The Canterbury Tales* and *Le Morte d'Arthur*.

1479
Aragon unites with Castile

As early as AD 711 the Moors had been grimly holding on to southern Spain and there were times when it seemed as if they would overrun the whole country. Spain's weakness lay in the fact that, for most of the time, it was not a united nation but a number of small kingdoms who maintained their independence in the northern mountains while, for most of the eight hundred years, the Moors controlled the south. The main Spanish kingdoms were Navarre, Castile, Leon and Galicia.

William Caxton demonstrates his press to Edward IV.

Towards the middle of the thirteenth century, Castile and Leon were united, whilst eastern Spain formed the kingdom of Aragon. In 1469 Isabella, the heiress of Castile married Ferdinand, son of the King of Aragon and on his father's death in 1479 Aragon and Castile became one powerful kingdom under united sovereigns: Spain was now to be reckoned as a major political force in Europe.

c. 1480
Inquisition becomes active in Spain

The Inquisition was founded as early as the thirteenth century by Pope Gregory IX in France in order to stamp out heresy, and was initially under the control of members of the order of St Dominic. The first court of inquisition (or tribunal) was set up at Toulouse. In 1252 Innocent IV introduced torture and those who were guilty, or pleaded guilty to stop the pain, were then handed over to the secular laws of the land, usually to be burned.

From France the system spread to Italy, Spain, the Netherlands, Portugal and later to the Catholic countries of the New World. It reached its peak of infamy during the fifteenth century in Spain where the court was presided over by an Inquisitor-General, the most notorious of whom was Torquemada (1420–98).

The accused was heard in secret session and often had no knowledge of his accuser; such tortures as the rack and an ingeniously horrific device known as the Iron Maiden were used to extract the 'truth' from him.

Columbus sets foot in the New World.

1487
Pretenders to the English throne

Henry VII (1457–1509) came to the throne after the Battle of Bosworth Field (1485) and was to reign over England for fourteen years. He was a Lancastrian. His claim to the throne was a vague one, based on the fact that his mother was a descendant of John of Gaunt. Inevitably there were a number of pretenders to the throne, the two greatest being Lambert Simnel (*c.* 1477–*c.* 1534) and Perkin Warbeck (*c.* 1474–99).

Simnel claimed to be the Earl of Warwick, son of the 'Kingmaker' at the time in the Tower. He was crowned in Dublin as Edward VI (1487) but Henry soon dealt with him and, to show his contempt, made him a scullion in the royal kitchen. Warbeck (1492) was a more dangerous pretender. He was treated well at first but when he tried a further attempt in 1499 Henry had him executed.

1492
Columbus discovers the West Indies

In 1492 Christopher Columbus (*c.* 1451–1506), an Italian captain in the service of Spain, sailed across the Atlantic Ocean in a ship not much bigger than a modern racing yacht. He was the first man to cross the 'green sea of darkness', as the Arabs called the unknown Atlantic. Sailors then never willingly sailed out of sight of land, and Columbus was taking a dangerous gamble.

Unlike many people at that time, Columbus knew that the world was round, and he calculated that by sailing toward the west he would find a valuable new trade route to the riches of the Far East. It was a good plan, except for two details.

First, Columbus believed that the world was much smaller than it really is. Second, he did not – and could not – know that the two great continents of North and South America lay in his way. So when he sighted land after a ten-weeks' voyage he believed he had reached the outlying parts of Asia, and he called the islands he had discovered the Indies.

Columbus made three more voyages to the West Indies, still hoping they were part of Asia. He died in 1506, not knowing that the Spaniards who followed him to the New World would soon discover riches greater than those he had ever hoped to find in Asia.

1497
John Cabot discovers Newfoundland

Like Columbus, Cabot was an Italian sailor in foreign service, and while Columbus was trying to get support for his voyage of discovery in Spain, Cabot was doing the same thing in England. The news of Columbus's successful voyage must have been a heavy blow to him. But in 1497 he gained the support of King Henry VII and sailed from Bristol in the *Matthew*. He took with him his son Sebastian, later a great explorer himself.

Following a more northerly route than Columbus, Cabot had a rougher voyage, but when the water was running low and the food beginning to stink, land was sighted. Cabot called it the 'New Found Land' and it has kept the name to this day.

The English were disappointed by Cabot's discovery. Although the fishing was good, there were no gold, silks or spices. Unlike the Spaniards, who were building an empire in Central and South America, the English waited over one hundred years before they began colonies in North America.

1498
Savonarola burned in Florence

Girolamo Savonarola (1452–98) was an Italian monk who tried to reform politics and religion in Florence. A spell-binding preacher, he attacked the vices of the ruling class and fiercely denounced opponents as powerful as the Pope and the Medici princes who ruled Florence. He feared nobody, and never minded making himself unpopular. When the French king Charles VIII (1470–98) invaded Italy, Savonarola boldly hailed him as the instrument of God sent to punish the Italians for their sins.

The invasion caused a revolt against the Medici in Florence and Savonarola became the real ruler of the city. He made fun-loving Florence a solemn city with psalm-singing instead of drunken feasts; but he gave it many wise laws. Savonarola's rule was severe and his tongue was bitter. Believing himself inspired by God, he would tolerate no criticism, and at last even the ordinary people, for

Renaissance Florence, home of the Medicis and the stern monk Savonarola.

whom Savonarola had fought many battles, turned against him. He was thrown into prison, tortured, and hanged from a burning cross in the market place.

Girolamo Savonarola

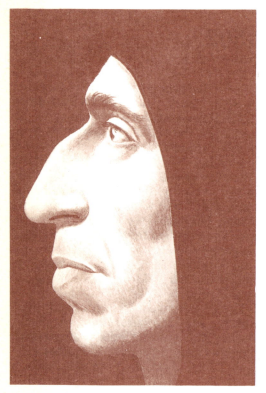

1498
Erasmus visits Oxford

Like Savonarola, the Dutch scholar Desiderius Erasmus (1466–1536) was a severe critic of the Roman Catholic Church. He attacked the ignorance, superstition and greed of the clergy, and his writings, especially his translation of the New Testament, prepared the way for the Reformation of Luther and others.

Erasmus himself never became a Protestant, although he lived nearly twenty years after Luther had nailed his paper to the church door at Wittenburg. He accused the Reformers of being as rigid and narrow-minded as the Church they attacked.

Erasmus travelled to many centres of learning throughout Western Europe. A wise and kind man, he had many friends among the scholars of all countries. In 1498 he visited England, but refused an offer to teach at Oxford. On a later visit he stayed in the house of his friend Thomas More, and it was there that he wrote his most famous book, *Praise of Folly* (1509).

1498
Dürer: *The Apocalypse*

Albrecht Dürer (1471–1528) was perhaps the greatest artist of the Renaissance in northern Europe. His greatest gift lay in drawing, rather than painting, and he is most admired for his engravings, and the fifteen large woodcuts of *The Apocalypse*, published as a book in 1498. They show the strong influence of the Gothic style of his native Germany. Dürer's later work was influenced by the ideas of the Italian Renaissance.

Dürer: *Self Portrait*

1499
Vasco da Gama reaches India

The Portuguese, the greatest sailors of the fifteenth century, were the first to search for new trade routes to Asia. They followed a route to the south, down the long coastline of Africa. Over many years

Portuguese ships ventured farther to the south, rounding the great bulge of West Africa only to find that the coast turned south again. Lopo Gonçalves crossed the equator, Diogo Cão discovered Zaïre, and finally Bartolemeu Diaz passed the tip of South Africa in 1488.

Nine years later the work was completed by Vasco da Gama. Leaving Lisbon with four ships in July, 1497, he sailed south through the Atlantic, saving time by not following the coast. After rounding the Cape, he sailed up the east coast of South Africa and visited the rich cities of the Arab merchants from Moçambique to Mombasa. From the coast of Kenya he crossed the Indian Ocean, and in April, 1499, he landed in India at the trading port of Calicut.

Although it was so long a voyage, many Portuguese ships soon followed the route that Vasco da Gama had pioneered. Portuguese trading posts, and later colonies, were founded in East Africa and on the western coast of India. Goa became Portugal's chief colony, and it remained in Portuguese control until the Indian government took it in 1961.

1499
Amerigo Vespucci's voyage to America

After Columbus, other captains sailed across the Atlantic on voyages of discovery. One of the most important was the voyage of Amerigo Vespucci and Alonso Ojeda in 1499.

Vespucci was an Italian merchant, who settled in the Spanish port of Seville in 1492 and probably invested money in Columbus's second voyage (1493). He was a member of an expedition that discovered the coast of Central America in 1497, and in 1499–1500 he and Ojeda explored hundreds of miles of the northern coasts of South America. On a later voyage in 1503, Vespucci sailed farther south along the coast of Brazil.

Amerigo Vespucci was one of the first to realize that Columbus had discovered a huge 'New World', quite separate from any known continent. His name will never be forgotten, because it was after him that the New World was called 'America'.

1502
Safawid dynasty established

The Safawid, or Sufi, dynasty, founded by Shah Ismail, ruled Persia (Iran) from the beginning of the 16th century to the middle of the 18th. The Safawids were the first true Persian rulers of Persia for nearly nine hundred years. The most able of them was Abbas the Great (1586–1628), who fought several successful wars, added Iraq to his empire, and with British help took the island of Ormuz from the Portuguese. He raised splendid buildings and encouraged trade and the arts, especially the art of carpet-making. But he had his children blinded, fearing them as rivals.

Later rulers were less successful than Abbas, and the attacks of Afghans, Turks, Russians and other old enemies brought chaos to Persia. The last Safawid shah, a little child, died in 1736.

1504
Raphael: *Marriage of the Virgin*

Raphael (1483–1520) was one of the greatest painters of the Italian Renaissance. He completed *The Marriage of the Virgin* in 1504, and it marks a turning point in his life. In that year he went to Florence, where he came under the influence of Leonardo and Michelangelo. Four years later he went to Rome, where he lived until he died, producing, with the help of assistants, an enormous amount of work for Pope Julius II.

1504
Leonardo da Vinci: *Mona Lisa*

The most famous painting in the world now hangs in the Louvre in Paris. It is a portrait of a young woman, faintly smiling, by Leonardo da Vinci (1452–1519). At first sight it appears a rather simple painting, but, looking harder, the subtle mystery of the woman's expression seems more extraordinary. It is hard to imagine how Leonardo could make such an effect with paint on a flat surface. Unfortunately, few of Leonardo's paintings have survived, partly because he was always experimenting with new materials, which did not last, and partly because he left so much work unfinished.

A true 'Renaissance man', Leonardo was interested in everything. Once he made a mechanical lion for a play – and designed the actors' costumes as well. His mind was full of ideas and his notebooks full of drawings and plans of machines and engines of war, even a submarine and a flying machine. Few of them were built, and they might not have worked anyway, but certainly Leonardo was an inventive genius far ahead of his time.

Leonardo spent his early life in Florence, later moving to Milan where there were few rival artists and good opportunities to study mathematics. He spent his last years in France.

Michelangelo

1508
Michelangelo paints the Sistine Chapel

While Raphael was painting his great frescoes in the Pope's apartments, not far away Michelangelo (1475-1564) was standing on a high platform painting Bible scenes on the vault (ceiling) of the Sistine Chapel. This tremendous work, most beautiful of religious paintings, covered an area of 1,500 square metres;

Michelangelo suffered pain in his neck, from bending his head back, for years after he had finished it. Much later, he also painted *The Last Judgment*, a grimmer masterpiece, on the wall behind the altar.

The greatest artist of his time, Michelangelo was not only a painter but also an architect, a poet and, above all, a sculptor. One of his most beautiful marble sculptures, of the Virgin Mary holding the body of Jesus, stands in the church of St Peter's, Rome, the great dome of which was also designed by Michelangelo.

The genius of Michelangelo, whose long life spanned the greatest years of the Renaissance in Florence and Rome, sprang from marvellous natural ability combined with a superhuman drive towards perfection. When he was at work, not even the Pope could get a polite word out of him. Yet his greatest work was a failure. He spent forty years on the tomb of his patron, Pope Julius II, and never finished it to his satisfaction.

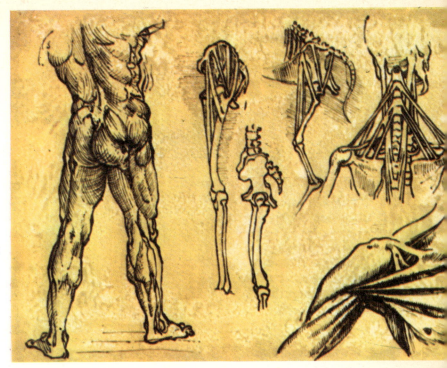

Leonardo da Vinci: impressions of this great artist's sketchbooks reveal a mind fascinated by anatomy, mechanics, and technological inventions.

1509

Accession of Henry VIII

As a young king, Henry VIII (1491–1547) was well-educated, good looking and adored by his people. He left the management of his kingdom in the hands of Wolsey (see 1530 Death of Wolsey) but when Henry wanted to divorce his queen, Catherine of Aragon, Wolsey failed to get permission from the Pope. This marked the beginning of the Reformation which gave England a national church.

Thomas Cranmer (1489–1556), Archbishop of Canterbury, pronounced the annulment of Henry's marriage and allowed him to marry Anne Boleyn. The Pope immediately excommunicated Henry who declared himself Supreme Head of the English Church; the king now had absolute authority both in spiritual and temporal matters.

Henry was ruthless not only to his wives, but also to his nobles. (He had six wives in all. They were Catherine of Aragon, Anne Boleyn, Jane Seymour, Anne of Cleves, Catherine Howard and Catherine Parr.) In his old age he grew grotesquely fat and despite the support he had from his people, all England sighed with relief at his death.

1513

Bellini paints *Feast of the Gods Gods*

Giovanni Bellini (c. 1430–1516) was one of a family of artists in Venice. In his own time he was no more famous than his brother, Gentile. He had many assistants and pupils, including Giorgione and Titian, and art scholars think that Titian may have helped to paint *The Feast of the Gods* (1513), one of Bellini's last works.

1513

Machiavelli writes *Il Principe*

Niccolo Machiavelli (1469–1527), a civil servant in Florence, wrote his book *Il Principe* ('The Prince') as a guide to rulers of his time. It was a practical handbook, not concerned with ideas, nor questions of right and wrong, only with methods that governments use to make themselves strong. Machiavelli discussed politics as they really are, not as they should be, and although his book contained much good sense, many people were shocked by its advice that rulers should tell lies and use violence if necessary.

1514

Castiglione writes *Il Cortegiano*

Conte Baldassare Castiglione (1478–1529) was born near Padua and whilst still a youth was attached to the court of the Duke of Urbino. An early mission was as the Duke's emissary to Henry VII in 1506. He later became a priest and bishop. In 1514 he wrote *Il Cortegiano* ('The Courtier'), a collection of dialogues on courtly ideals and manners.

1516

Ariosto writes *Orlando Furioso*

The Italian poet Ludovico Ariosto (1474–1533) spent most of his life in the service of the d'Este family, rulers of Ferrara. His fame rests on this one long poem, which he expanded in later editions. It is an epic of chivalry and romance, love and adventure – one of the great poems of the world.

Thomas More

1517
Luther's Theses at Wittenberg

When a thick-necked Saxon monk named Martin Luther (1483–1546) angrily posted his Ninety-five Theses (arguments) on the church door at Wittenberg, it was not the first time that the Church and the Pope had been criticized. Others had condemned the practice of 'indulgencies' – offering forgiveness of sins in return for cash – and some had been burned as heretics.

But Luther's action proved decisive in starting the events that led to the Reformation, when half Europe broke away from the Roman Catholic Church and set up separate Protestant Churches.

Martin Luther posts his theses on the church door at Wittenberg.

1516
Thomas More writes *Utopia*

The Greek word *utopia* means 'nowhere', and *Utopia* by Sir Thomas More (1478–1535) was a description of an ideal state, where life is based on reason and tolerance. It caused great argument, and it is still studied today. But it did not make life in sixteenth century England less unreasonable or intolerant.

By the time *Utopia* was published, More was well-known as a brilliant humanist scholar (the humanists were interested in the study of humanity – mankind and all his works). He conducted wars of words with reformers like Tyndale, and held minor posts in Henry VIII's government.

When Cardinal Wolsey fell from power in 1529, More became Lord Chancellor. While sympathizing with some of the ideas of the Reformation, he remained a Roman Catholic and refused to recognize the king as head of the English Church. For that he was condemned as a traitor and executed in 1535. He was canonized as a saint by Pope Pius XI four hundred years later.

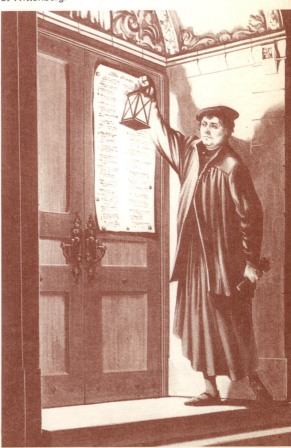

Martin Luther

Many of Luther's supporters wanted to go much farther than he, and in later years he spent much of his time restraining their zeal for destruction. Meanwhile, he helped to bring God nearer the people by translating the whole of the Bible into German.

1518
Titian paints *The Assumption*

This is one of the finest religious paintings of Titian (*c.* 1490–1576), the greatest master of the school of Venice, who became court painter to the Emperor Charles V and Philip II of Spain. Titian lived to a great age but never stopped developing his technique. He achieved rich and brilliant effects by applying many, thin, transparent layers of colour.

Earlier critics had attacked the behaviour of the Roman Church, but Luther attacked its beliefs. A man, said Luther, is saved by his religious faith, not by indulgencies. He condemned the power and wealth of the Pope and the influence of priests over the people.

Luther was condemned by the Pope, and when he refused to renounce his beliefs at the Diet (parliament) of Worms in 1521 he risked death as a heretic. But he was saved by politics. Powerful princes protected him, partly because they agreed with his ideas, partly because they wished to increase their own power by reducing the power of the Church.

1521
Conquest of Mexico

After Columbus's discovery in 1492, many Spanish adventurers travelled to the West Indies seeking their fortunes. One of them was Hernán Cortés (1485–1547), who in 1518 was given command of an expedition to Mexico.

The rulers of Mexico were the Aztecs, a race of warriors who controlled the longer standing inhabitants of the region by force. Aztec society was a strange mixture: they made beautiful fabrics and pottery, but had few metal tools; they built grand cities with huge palaces and temples, but the highlight of their religious ceremonies was the bloody sacrifice of hundreds of human beings.

When Cortés landed at San Juan de Ulua in 1519, Aztec power was not fully established, and Cortés gained support from some of their rebellious subjects. Cortés had other advantages unknown in Mexico, like guns and horses. His small force captured the capital, Tenochtitlán (Mexico City), and took the Aztec king, Montezuma II, prisoner. Later, while Cortés was absent, a rising took place in the city. Returning, the Spaniards were allowed to enter, but fighting began again. Montezuma was killed and Cortés's small band narrowly fought their way out to safety. They raised a new army among the native people and in April, 1521, renewed the attack on the Aztec capital. After a four-months siege in which the splendid city was ruined, the Aztec empire was destroyed, and Cortés became captain-general of the province of New Spain.

Montezuma welcoming Cortés to Tenochtitlán. Cortés made the Aztec king a prisoner.

1522
Magellan's voyage around the world

The search for a new trade route to the east continued after Columbus had discovered America blocking the way (*see 1492 Columbus discovers the West Indies*). Ferdinand Magellan (*c.*1480–1521), a Portuguese veteran who had fallen out of favour in Portugal, volunteered to find a route for the Spanish government.

He sailed with five worm-eaten ships and crews from many countries in August, 1519. By the end of the year he was off South America, where his men mutinied on learning of his plan to look for a strait in the far south of the continent. Magellan crushed the mutiny, and in October–November, 1520, he sailed through the strait now named after him, into the Pacific.

After a terrible voyage across the Pacific with no fresh supplies, Magellan reached the Philippines. There he was killed in a local war. Under Sebastian del Cano, Magellan's one remaining ship, the *Vittoria*, returned safely to Portugal in September, 1522, the first ship to sail around the world.

1525
Zwingli's reformation in Switzerland

Ulrich Zwingli (1484–1531), a priest at Zurich cathedral, was the leader of the Reformation in German-speaking Switzerland. Influenced by Erasmus and Luther, Zwingli in turn influenced the English Reformation. His success sprang from his willingness to co-operate with the local government, as long as it recognized the need for reform in the Church and the authority of the Bible. He is thought by many to have been the most open-minded and liberal of the reformers.

1526
Tyndale's Bible

Protestant reformers upheld the authority of scripture against the rules and rituals of Rome. Luther made scripture available to ordinary people, who could not read Latin, by translating the Bible into German, and William Tyndale produced his English New Testament in exile in 1526. Later he translated part of the Old Testament also. He was executed as a heretic in Germany in 1536.

1526
Pizarro's expedition to Peru

From Panama, Francisco Pizarro (1475–1541) set out to conquer the Inca empire, an area larger than modern Peru. With 170 men and three muskets he succeeded, capturing and killing the Inca (or king) Atahualpa by treachery, taking away fabulous treasure, and enslaving the people to work the silver mines. Pizarro himself was later murdered during a quarrel among the conquerors.

Baber, founder of the Moghul empire in India. He was a brilliant warrior, but it was his descendant Akhbar the Great who permanently established Moghul rule.

1527
Baber and the Moghul Empire

During the thirteenth century, Afghanistan was invaded by the Mongols (*see 1206 Temujin proclaimed Genghis Khan*) and the greater part of the country was later to become part of the vast empire of Timur (*see 1398 Timur conquers North India*).

In 1504 Baber (1483–1530) a descendant of both Timur and Genghis Khan was expelled from his small country in Afghanistan by more powerful neighbours and was forced to seek refuge in the mountains. He had one great ambition – to regain Timur's empire and to seat himself on the golden throne of Samarkand.

He had many setbacks but at last, in 1526, he led an army through the Khyber Pass and his cavalry made a great victory possible. At a subsequent battle near Patna the other Afghan chiefs were completely crushed. With all opposition overcome he attempted to create a Moghul Empire but only lived two more years, thus being unable to consolidate it.

1530
Death of Wolsey

Henry VIII (*see Accession of Henry VIII*) was greatly assisted by Thomas Wolsey (*c.*1471–1530) in the early part of his reign. Wolsey became a royal chaplain in 1506 and his rise under the king was so rapid that he became Archbishop of York and then, in 1515, both Cardinal and Lord Chancellor.

Wolsey was a brilliant administrator and one of Europe's leading diplomats, carefully balancing the rival powers of France and Spain. He gathered a large personal fortune, some of which he used to found Christchurch College, Oxford, and also to build Hampton Court. His downfall began when he failed to obtain a divorce for his royal master from

Catherine of Aragon. In 1529 he was deprived of his offices and then arrested for treason. He died whilst on his way to trial.

1532
Rabelais writes *Gargantua*

François Rabelais (*c.* 1494–*c.* 1553) was born in Chinon, France, and became a monk, a teacher, a professor of anatomy and finally a priest. His lively imagination is shown in his two books written between 1532–64 – *Gargantua* and *Pantagruel* which both reveal a love of humanity and culture. Both these bawdy and witty books show Rabelais to be one of the world's great satirists.

Ivan the Terrible besieges a fortress.

1532
Calvin becomes a Protestant

John Calvin (*c.* 1509–1564) was a theologian who was born in Noyon, France. He first studied for the priesthood but about 1532 became a Protestant and lived in Geneva, where he became a very active social reformer.

In 1538 he was banished by the city authorities and went to Strasbourg, but being recalled to Geneva in 1541, lived and preached there. He was determined to make the city a place of complete righteousness, and all who transgressed were punished, one man being burned after Calvin had denounced him.

He nevertheless greatly improved the city, education being encouraged whilst trade flourished and increased. His great work was *The Institute of Christian Religion* which he wrote in Latin in 1536 and which, translated into English, be-

came the second 'Bible' of the Protestants in Britain, especially Scotland.

1533
Accession of Ivan the Terrible

Ivan III (1440–1505) started the growth of Muscovy, the small principality around Moscow which developed into Russia, when he expanded his territory northwards and eastwards as far as the Arctic Ocean and the Ural Mountains. He even started to build the Kremlin, which has housed Russia's government for centuries.

In 1533 Ivan's grandson Ivan IV (1530–84) became Grand Duke of Muscovy and in 1547 he was crowned first emperor (czar) of Russia. For years Ivan was dominated by the powerful nobles or 'boyars', but he soon took over the government and made himself head of the

Eastern Orthodox Church.

Ivan determined to bring as much European influence to his lands as possible. However his cruel and barbarous treatment of his subjects and the boyars (earning him the name 'Ivan the Terrible') horrified Western countries who refused to trade with him. When the tyrannical czar died, Russia fell into chaos.

1534
Cartier explores Canada

The first explorer to attempt to settle in Canada was a Frenchman from Brittany, Jacques Cartier (1491–1557). In 1534 he set off on a voyage of exploration, hoping to find a North-West passage to India.

Cartier sailed along the north shore of Newfoundland and entered what is now the Gulf of St Lawrence, taking possession of the country in the name of Francis I of France. Having spent five months away from France he then returned to Brittany.

The following year Cartier set out again to explore the St Lawrence river, sailing up it as far as an Indian village on a hill which he named *Mont Réal* (Mount Royal). In 1541 Francis I decided to colonize New France, as he called Canada, so Cartier set off on a third expedition. But no colonists would settle there for they disliked the winter cold and the wilderness. Fifty years later another French expedition was sent to colonize New France.

1534
Loyola founds the Jesuits

Ignatius Loyola (1491–1556) was a Spanish nobleman who spent his youth at the court of Ferdinand and Isabella. He became a great soldier until the siege of Pampeluna (1521) where his leg was shattered by a cannon ball.

Whilst recovering from his wound, he began to read the lives of the saints and when he was well enough began to devote his life to the service of Christ.

Despite many hardships, including imprisonment by the Inquisition, he persevered and finally in 1534 he and six companions took vows in a church in Montmartre to found a 'Society of Jesus' (Jesuits).

Six years later his Society received the blessing of the Pope who appointed Loyola its first 'general', or commanding officer. He spent the rest of his life in Rome organizing his Society which, within a few years, was to become very influential. He died in 1556 and was canonized in 1622.

1537
Vesalius becomes professor of surgery at Padua

Galen, the great pioneer of medicine (*see AD 164 Galen active in Rome*) set standards that were unequalled for thirteen hundred years. During the Middle Ages, so-called doctors had little knowledge and much of their art of healing depended on Galen, leeches and even magic.

The father of modern medicine was a Belgian, Andreas Vesalius (1514–64). His research was greatly assisted by the epidemics of the time, which afforded him a number of corpses upon which to work. He was appointed professor of surgery at Padua and began to write his major work: *De humani corporis fabrica* ('On the fabric of the human body'). It turned anatomy into an exact science and his enthusiasm attracted others to Padua which was to become the centre of medical research in Europe.

1540
Copernicus publishes treatise

Nicolaus Copernicus (1473–1543) was one of the most original thinkers of his time. Born at Thorn, Poland, he studied mathematics, optics and perspective at Cracow, astronomy and law at Bologna and medicine at Padua.

From 1507 until 1513 he worked on his treatise *De Revolutionibus Orbium Coelestium* ('Concerning the Revolutions of the Heavenly Spheres') which showed the relationship of the earth to the sun and the planets. At first he was reluctant to publish his theories but the summary aroused such interest that in 1540 he agreed to the publication of the whole work.

Copernicus's theory contradicted the Ptolemaic theory adopted by the Church (*see c. AD 120 Ptolemy experiments with refraction*). Ptolemy believed that the earth was the centre of the universe, but in his treatise Copernicus suggested that the sun is a star, that the planets revolve around it and that the earth is simply one of these planets.

A diagram from Copernicus's treatise clearly shows his belief that the sun was at the centre of our solar system, and not the earth.

1540
Execution of Cromwell

The fallen Wolsey (*see 1530 Death of Wolsey*) was replaced by Thomas Cromwell (*c*.1485–1540) who had been Wolsey's secretary. He was admitted to the Privy Council and soon became Henry VIII's principal adviser.

Cromwell was to be the architect of the English Reformation, supporting the king in his break with Rome, arranging Catherine of Aragon's divorce and the dissolution of the English monasteries. He was so active in this latter work that he earned himself the name of *malleus monachorum* ('hammer of the monks').

He also played a large part in Protestantism by encouraging the translation and printing of the Bible and, by his Act of Supremacy (1534) confirmed the king as head of the English church.

He arranged Henry's marriage with Anne of Cleves (1540) but when the king recoiled from his choice, Cromwell's days were numbered. He was arrested on June 10, 1540 and charged with high treason, quite without cause. Found guilty, he was beheaded six weeks later. Henry soon realized his mistake and until his own death in 1547 spoke of the loss of 'the best servant I ever had.'

1549
Edward VI's Book of Common Prayer

An important step taken during the Reformation was the provision of a book for services held in the new Church of England. It was printed in English (earlier books being in Latin) and was condensed and simplified. Much of the preparatory work was done by Archbishop Cranmer (executed by Mary Tudor in 1556) and it was issued in January 1549, an Act of Uniformity making its use compulsory in all churches on and after the following Whit-Sunday.

It was produced during the reign of the young Edward VI (1537–53) and three years after its publication another edition was introduced. This edition lasted for only eight months for Mary Tudor came to the throne (1553) and reintroduced the old Latin services. She died in 1558 and by another Act of Conformity, Elizabeth reverted to the second Prayer Book which was in use until a revised edition was printed.

1551
Suleiman the Magnificent conquers Persia

The Turk Suleiman I (1494–1566) proved a prince of good fortune from childhood. From his father, whom he succeeded in 1520, he inherited a well-trained and disciplined army, a full treasury and a prosperous and contented

Suleiman I

country. He was also surrounded by wise councillors and although he listened to them, he preferred the company of his generals. With their help he set out on a number of campaigns of conquest, thirteen of which he led himself.

In turn he was to conquer Belgrade, Rhodes, Budapest, Baghdad, Aden and Algiers and soon his Ottoman empire was the most powerful in Europe. Although regarded as a great warrior, he was also a very just man, organizing a new set of laws that gave him his Turkish name of 'Lawgiver'. To the rest of the world, and to history, however, he is known as Suleiman . . . the Magnificent.

1553
Lady Jane Grey's brief rule

Lady Jane Grey was born in 1537 and by the will of Henry VIII, her great-uncle, had been placed next in succession after his daughters Mary and Elizabeth. Her unscrupulous uncle, Duke of Northumberland, caused her to be married to his son, Lord Guildford Dudley, hoping that he himself could continue in power after the death of the ailing Edward VI.

The king died on July 6, 1553 and Lady Jane was immediately proclaimed Queen of England on July 10. The supporters of Mary Tudor, however, proved too strong and by July 19 Lady Jane was in the Tower after the shortest and most pathetic reign in English history. She was later tried and sentenced to death for high treason and, preceded by her young husband, the unfortunate 'queen' was beheaded on Tower Hill (1554).

Henry VIII

1554
Palestrina composes *Missa ecce sacerdos*

During the sixteenth century, composers within the Catholic church were creating outstanding music for their formal services. One of the most gifted was Giovanni da Palestrina (1526–94) who devoted his life to creating new and beautiful religious music including masses which have never been surpassed, especially his *Missa ecce sacerdos* and *Missa pro defunctis*.

1554
Cellini: *Perseus with the head of Medusa*

Benevenuto Cellini (1500–71) is regarded as the world's finest goldsmith. He studied in Rome and Paris then moved to Florence. His works include the bronze statue of *Perseus with the head of Medusa* (1554). His *Autobiography* is a very candid book, revealing him as a brawling soldier of fortune and a braggart, but nothing can dim his exquisite craftsmanship.

1555
Nostradamus writes *Centuries*

Nostradamus (1503–66) was the assumed name of Michel de Notredame, a French astrologer. In 1555 he wrote a book entitled *Centuries* which brought his name to the notice of the powerful Catherine de'Medici. He attended her court and for a time was employed in casting horoscopes. He also became physician to Catherine's son, Charles IX.

1555
Burning of Latimer and Ridley

When Mary I (1516–58), daughter of Henry VIII, came to the throne in 1554 a major question was that of the queen's marriage. In spite of the protests from the nation she obstinately set her heart on Philip of Spain. Their marriage in 1554 caused the Protestants to turn from Mary and to regard her sister, Elizabeth, as their champion.

Mary altered much of what had been done in her father's time, especially doing her best to stamp out the new Protestantism and to bring back the Roman Catholic Church. She then began to persecute the Reformed Clergy; married clergy were ordered to abandon their wives and those who would not conform she expelled, putting Catholic priests in their pulpits.

Mary sent two leaders of the English Church – Latimer and Ridley – to the

Tower and in April 1554 they were taken before a court and offered their freedom if they would recant. Both refused and on October 16, 1555, they were burned together.

(Above) Mary Tudor married Philip of Spain in 1554; (below) Mary's reign saw the Roman Catholic church re-established in England.

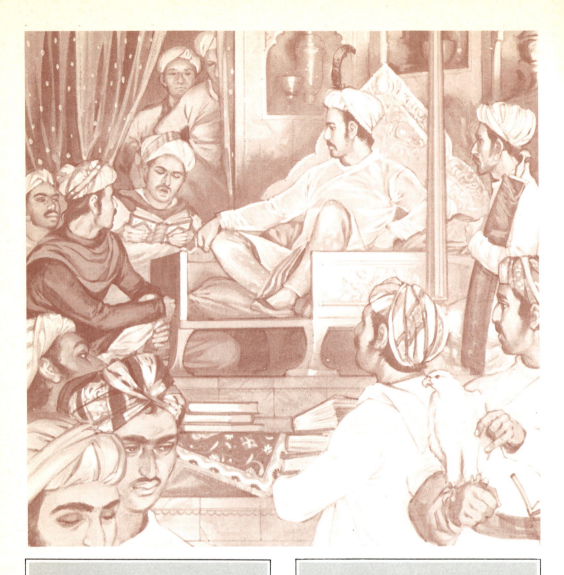

1555
Tintoretto paints *St George and the Dragon*

Born in Venice in 1518, Jacopo Robusti studied under the great artist Titian. He then changed his name to 'Tintoretto' (or 'Little Dyer') a popular name from his father's trade, and began to produce a number of masterpieces. These include *St George and the Dragon*, *Belshazzar's Feast* and *The Last Supper*. He died in 1594.

1555
Formation of *La Pléiade*

Pierre de Ronsard (1524–1685) spent his youth at the French court but later, becoming deaf, he turned to writing, especially poetry. He formed a group with du Bellay (1522–60) and other poets which endeavoured to improve French verse. The group was called *La Pléiade* and was directly responsible for the increase in classical influence in their country's poetry.

(Left) Akhbar the Great established the power of the Moghul empire in all northern India, and proved himself to be an excellent ruler.

1556

Akhbar the Great creates an empire

When Baber died in 1530 (*see 1527 Baber and the Moghul Empire*) he had tried, but failed, to establish an empire, an achievement to be left to his descendant Akhbar (1542–1605).

Akhbar was the son of Humayun, King of Delhi, a minor kingdom, and on becoming king himself he determined to complete what Baber had begun and create a great Moghul empire.

He led an army against his neighbours in 1556 and within six years his kingdom consisted of the Punjab and other large areas of India together with Kabul in Afghanistan.

He had created his empire but was not satisfied. Another fourteen years of constant warfare followed until he was ruler of the whole of northern India. He then marched into the Deccan and added further vast territories to his already huge empire which was to consist of fifteen great provinces.

He was more than a warrior, however. He was a great and just ruler who attempted to create a united India out of its jumble of warring races and religions. As the 'Great Moghul' he corresponded with England's Queen Elizabeth I.

1558

Accession of Elizabeth I

It is incredible that Elizabeth I (1533–1603) ever reached England's throne at all. Soon after she was born her father, Henry VIII, executed her mother, Anne Boleyn and declared his daughter illegitimate. Later, as a young princess, many people tried to draw her into plots against her half-sister Mary (*see 1554 Burning of Ridley and Latimer*) and during the nine days' reign of Lady Jane Grey (*see 1553 Lady Jane Grey's brief rule*) she pretended to be ill until the luckless Jane was imprisoned.

With Mary on the throne, Elizabeth was constantly the hope of the Protestants, especially when it was learned that Mary intended to marry the Catholic King Philip of Spain. Although she had no part in the uprising that followed this news, Elizabeth was thrown into the Tower and her later release was due to her keeping a cool head.

Back at court she was always conscious that a moment's indiscretion might see her back in the Tower, perhaps kneeling in the same place where her mother had died under the headsman's axe. Then a great cloud seemed lifted from her mind when she learned that Mary had died on November 17, 1558, and that she, at twenty-five, was the new and undoubted Queen of England.

Elizabeth I

125

1561
Mary, Queen of Scots, returns from France

Mary Stuart (1542–87), the daughter of King James V of Scotland (1512–42) became that country's queen when only a week old, her father being killed at the Battle of Solway Moss (1542). She went to the French court when a girl and married Francis II, to become Queen of France as well. She was also heiress to the English throne as next of kin to Elizabeth.

On the early death of her husband she returned to Scotland as queen. Being a Catholic she was opposed by the Protestant Calvinist movement and especially their leader, John Knox. She married her cousin, Lord Darnley who, jealous of her Italian secretary Rizzio, had him murdered before her in 1566. Darnley was himself murdered soon afterwards. She then married Lord Bothwell; her nobles turned against her and she was forced to flee to England (*see 1587 Execution of Mary, Queen of Scots*).

John Knox, the Scottish Calvinist, upbraids the Roman Catholic Mary, Queen of Scots.

1562
Hawkins commences the slave trade

Devon-born John Hawkins (1532–95) had the unenviable reputation of being the first Englishman to engage in the terrible slave traffic, in 1562 taking goods to the African coast where he bartered them for kidnapped negroes, whom he carried to the Spanish settlements in America in exchange for pearls, sugar and ginger.

On one privateering voyage, with a fleet that included two ships financed by Queen Elizabeth herself, Hawkins fell foul of a Spanish fleet in the Bay of San Juan de Ulua. After a fierce fight, all but two of the English ships were sunk and Hawkins barely escaped with his life. He afterwards rose to high rank in the navy but died at sea in November, 1595.

He is also credited with a more honourable innovation, being the first Englishman to introduce the potato into England, in 1563, Sir Walter Raleigh showing it to the queen some twenty years later.

1564
Birth of Shakespeare

William Shakespeare (1564–1616) one of the world's greatest dramatists, was born in Stratford-on-Avon, England, on or about April 23, 1564. When he was eighteen he married Anne Hathaway and had a family of three children.

In 1587, leaving his wife and family behind, he went to London and was immediately attracted to the theatre. At first he had quite menial jobs – small parts and, as a writer, a patcher of old scripts – but in time he became the head playwright and part-owner of the Globe Theatre, Bankside, in Southwark.

By the 1590s Shakespeare's reputation as a writer was growing steadily; he wrote some of the most beautiful sonnets in the English language and by the end of his

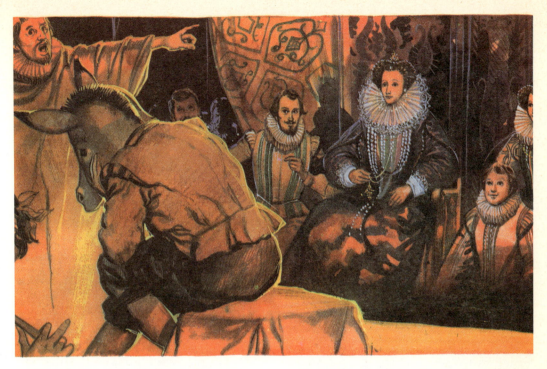

A private performance of *A Midsummer Night's Dream* before the court of Elizabeth I; (below) William Shakespeare.

The rich poetry of Shakespeare's plays allows his characters to speak with a vividness and variety that have perhaps never been equalled. It reveals the innermost thoughts of his characters, creates atmosphere and sets scenes. Some of the most famous plays by him include *Macbeth*, *A Midsummer Night's Dream*, *Hamlet* and *As You Like It*.

life he had written thirty-seven plays, including histories, comedies, romances and tragedies. His drama appeals to all tastes, for it contains poetry, action, love, excitement and humour.

1566

Breughel paints *The Wedding Dance*

Pieter Breughel (*c.* 1525–69) was the son of a Flemish peasant and although he was to travel in France and Italy, visiting Rome and Naples, he never forgot the scenes of his youth. His paintings, such as *The Wedding Dance* are full of humorous, high-spirited peasants, all obviously enjoying life. His two sons, Pieter and Jan also became outstanding artists.

1570
Palladio's treatise on architecture

Italian-born Andrea Palladio (1518–80) was one of the outstanding architects of his time. He showed great promise as a child and his patron, Count Trissino, made it possible for him to study art and architecture in Rome. In 1547 he returned to Vicenza, his birthplace, where he was to design some very fine buildings, including several ornate palaces for Italian noblemen. He later built some stately churches in Venice and some further palaces, this time on the Grand Canal.

He was a student of classical works and much of what he designed reflects that admiration, giving the name 'Palladian' to his grandiose style. His *I quattro libri dell' architettura* ('Four Books of Architecture') were translated into many languages, the English version being published by the great architect Inigo Jones, and his influence spread throughout Europe.

greatest naval battles took place. The fighting ended at dusk when the Turkish fleet of two hundred and seventy-five galleys was virtually destroyed and the naval power of the Sultan was ended. Lepanto was the last great sea battle in which galleys were used.

1572
Camoens writes *Os Lusiados*

Luis Vaz de Camoens (*c.* 1524–80) was a poet who was banished from his native country of Portugal in 1546. He became a soldier of fortune, fighting against the Turks and travelling to the East Indies. Whilst there he wrote his great epic poem *Os Lusiados* ('The Lusitanians') which relates the history of the Portuguese nation in verse.

1571
The Battle of Lepanto

The Turks had been capturing many of the finest harbours in the Middle East, their fleets sailing from Constantinople which had become their capital. They were ruled over by Suleiman the Magnificent (1494–1566) and then by his son Selim II, who was most ambitious. For a time things went his way for the Christian powers were jealous of each other, but at last Pope Pius V called Venice and Spain together to form a Holy League to fight the Turks.

By the summer of 1571 a fleet of more than three hundred ships, commanded by Don John of Austria (1547–78), a young man of twenty-four, was ready. It sailed for the Greek harbour of Lepanto and on October 7, 1571 one of the world's

1572
The St Bartholomew's Day Massacre

For a considerable time there had been a great deal of friction between Catholics and Huguenots (Protestants) in France. Clashes were frequent but the bloodshed was not too severe. Then, overnight, things changed dramatically. In August 1572 Henry, King of Navarre and Marguerite, sister of the French King Charles IX were to be married and many nobles, Catholic and Huguenot, had gathered in Paris for the celebrations.

With so many of both factions gathered together it was not long before rioting began. Taking advantage of the situation, Catherine de' Medici, the queen mother, persuaded her son Charles IX to organize a massacre of the Huguenots. Some 30,000 were killed, mostly in cold blood, not only in Paris but in other cities throughout France. This terrible massacre took place on the feast of St Bartholomew, hence its name.

It was to affect Charles's brain and he died soon afterwards in his twenty-fourth year.

1575
Tasso writes *Jerusalem delivered*

Torquato Tasso was a poet born in Sorrento, Italy, in 1544. For a while he was attached to the court of the Duke of Ferrara and whilst in his service wrote a magnificent poem, *La Gerusalemme Liberta* ('Jerusalem Delivered'), and a pastoral play, *Aminta*. Soon afterwards he became mentally ill and had to enter a hospital, dying in 1595.

The massacre of French Huguenots on St Bartholomew's Day.

1576
Tycho Brahe builds Uraniborg observatory

Danish-born Tycho Brahe (1546–1601) specialized in astronomy and was invited by Frederick II of Denmark to build a magnificent observatory at Uraniborg. Although he was a brilliant astronomer (he discovered Cassiopeia) he was in opposition to Copernicus, maintaining that the earth was the centre of the universe and remained still, whilst the other planets revolved around the sun.

His chief astronomical work was concerned with improvements in the art of observation of the universe and also a catalogue of fixed stars which he assembled in 1576. He gave the position of 777 although this number was increased by Kepler in 1605 to 1,627.

Brahe also published several books including *De Nova Stella* ('The New Star') in which he recorded his observations of the galactic supernova he had seen in 1573.

(Left) Medals struck to commemorate Drake's epic voyage; (right) Sir Francis Drake, first Englishman to sail around the world. Terror of the Spanish Main, he became a hero at the time of the Spanish Armada in 1588.

1577
Drake sets out in the *Pelican*

On December 13, 1577, Francis Drake (*c*. 1540–96), a seaman from Devon, set sail with a fleet of five ships and a hundred and sixty-six men from Plymouth. He reached the Brazilian coast on April 6, 1577 and on August 21 entered the Straits of Magellan. His ships became separated in a storm and he carried on alone in his ship, now renamed *Golden Hind,* capturing many unsuspecting Spanish ships.

By July 1579 he was in the Moluccas and then eleven months later he was rounding the Cape of Good Hope, homeward bound. On September 26, 1580 he sailed triumphantly into Plymouth harbour, the first English captain to sail around the world, a journey which took some two years and ten months. Soon afterwards Queen Elizabeth went on board the *Golden Hind* and knighted him for his achievement.

1578
Hilliard paints *Queen Elizabeth I*

Nicholas Hilliard (*c*. 1537–1619) brilliantly portrayed the personalities who thronged the court of Queen Elizabeth. He was apprenticed to a London goldsmith and almost immediately began to produce beautiful miniature portraits. One of his earliest, dated 1572, is of the queen herself. During half a century he created some of the most exquisite works of art ever produced.

1579
The Union of Utrecht

During the Middle Ages, what are now Belgium and the Netherlands were small feudal counties and duchies. They gradually passed into the control of the Burgundian dukes, Charles the Bold (*d.* 1477) seeking to weld them into one country, but without success. His daughter Mary married Maximilian of Austria and the 'Low Countries' (or Netherlands) passed quietly into the realms of the Hapsburgs.

When Charles V abdicated in 1555 they passed to Philip II of Spain, a Catholic, although the seven northern provinces were Protestant. A revolt broke out and in 1579 the Protestant provinces formed the separate Union of Utrecht, sometimes called the Dutch Netherlands or United Provinces, controlled by William, Prince of Orange. By the League of Arras (1579) the ten southern provinces, which were Catholic, recognized Philip II as their sovereign but retained their independence.

1586
Creation of the *kabuki* theatre

The traditional Japanese, all-male theatre, *kabuki*, is said to have started in 1586 when a woman called O Kuni performed parodies of Buddhist prayers. With her troupe of men and women dancers it was the first theatrical presentation of any stature that had been specifically aimed at the masses. Previously such entertainments had been the prerogative of the rich with the *nō* dramas and *kyōgen* comedies.

In 1629 the *kabuki* was banned as it was said to be vulgar and frivolous but it managed to continue as *wakashū* in which young boys played all the roles, including those of the women. This, too, was frowned upon by the authorities and eventually outlawed. But this time the theatre, as *yarō kabuki*, continued to thrive with an all-male cast. It is this form of all-male, highly stylistic, and traditional theatre that remains popular to the present day.

Kabuki, the popular theatre of Japan, with its stylized acting, music and dancing, has remained popular up to modern times.

1587
Marlowe writes *Tamburlaine*

Christopher Marlowe (1564–93), a brilliant dramatist, has been called the father of English tragedy and the creator of dramatic blank verse. He was born in Canterbury but soon moved to London where he associated with Shakespeare, Ben Jonson and others of their brilliant circle.

Between 1587 and 1593 he wrote four plays: *Tamburlaine the Great, Dr Faustus, The Famous Tragedy of the Rich Jew of Malta* and *Edward the Second*. The first three are concerned with power and the effect it has on men; heroes of the plays are tragic figures, villains battling against their fate. His *Tamburlaine the Great* was the first poem to be written in English blank verse.

Little is known of Marlowe's life, but he was known as a free-thinker and suspected of atheism. In 1593 he was stabbed at Deptford in a tavern brawl, possibly in Queen Elizabeth's service as a secret agent.

1587
Execution of Mary, Queen of Scots

Queen Mary escaped to England (*see 1561 Mary, Queen of Scots, returns from France*) only to be imprisoned by Elizabeth for nineteen long years. For a time she kept quiet and then, encouraged by promises of support from outside, she allowed herself to be involved in a plot to rescue her, whilst soldiers from Spain and Catholic supporters in England would be ready to beat down any opposition and escort her to her coronation.

Called the Babington plot, after one of

Mary, Queen of Scots, prepares to meet the executioner at Fotheringay.

the conspirators, it was easily revealed by Walsingham, Elizabeth's minister. Mary Stuart stood trial and was condemned to death, Elizabeth signing the death warrant on February 1, 1587.

By then Mary had been moved to Fotheringay Castle and a high scaffold had been built in its great hall. Dressed in black, Mary knelt down at the block and at the second blow her head was severed from her body.

1588
Defeat of the Spanish Armada

In 1585 England was at war with Spain and Drake took a fleet to the Spanish Main where he sank a large number of Spanish ships and plundered several of their rich cities. Two years later he sailed into the Bay of Cadiz and sank a number of ships he found assembled there. He called this enterprise 'Singeing the King of Spain's beard.'

The following year Drake was at Plymouth when news was received by him and his fellow captains that a great Spanish fleet had been sighted in the Channel. Known later as Spain's Invincible' Armada, its lumbering galleons were chased by the lighter and more active ships of the English fleet along the Flanders coast and into the North Sea where they were left to the violence of a fierce storm. Few of that once great Armada returned to Spain.

1590
Spenser writes the Faërie Queene

Edmund Spenser (c. 1552–99) was born in London of humble parents and was educated as a 'poor scholar' at Merchant Taylors' School and then at Cambridge. He began to write, his first important poem being The Shepheardes Calendar (1579). He later took up a post in Ireland and continued to write, his best known

work being *The Faërie Queene,* an allegorical poem which was to glorify his country and show the behaviour of the ideal courtier.

A swinging lamp in Pisa Cathedral is said to have inspired Galileo's observations on the pendulum.

1590
Galileo publishes De Motu

Galileo Galilei (1564–1642) was born in Pisa, Italy, and when only nineteen discovered the isochronism (regularity) of the pendulum; in 1587 he formulated the law of falling bodies ($h = \frac{1}{2} gt^2$) proving his theory by dropping leaden and wooden balls of the same size and watching them hit the ground at the same time. His theories were published in *De Motu* in 1590.

In 1592 he became professor of mathematics at Padua where he conducted some important experiments and firmly stated that the Copernican theory of the planets moving round the sun was true. For this he was imprisoned by the church authorities but, being released by the Pope, continued laying the foundation of modern experimental science.

In 1609 he constructed the first astronomical telescope with which he discovered the valleys of the moon, the phases of Venus and the four satellites of Jupiter. Nevertheless, the church authorities kept him under forced residence until his death.

1590
Jansen invents the microscope

A Dutch spectacle maker, Zacharias Jansen, is credited with the invention of the microscope about 1590. It was a somewhat unwieldy piece of equipment, about the same size as a telescope. Nevertheless it worked, an observer of the time remarking, 'With this long cannon you can see flies which appear to be as big as sheep.'

1591
The death of Grenville

In 1591 a squadron of six English ships were watering in Flores Bay in the Azores when a pinnace raced in with the warning that a large Spanish fleet was approaching. The commander of the squadron, Sir Richard Grenville (c. 1542–91) ordered the rest of the ships to escape but stayed himself to pick up half of his crew who were lying ill ashore. By the time he had tacked out of the bay it was too late – he was surrounded by fifty-three tall Spanish galleons.

For the next fifteen hours, Grenville's flagship, the *Revenge*, kept them at bay until she was an absolute wreck, her masts shot away, her hull and upperworks riddled with the shot that kept crashing into her from at least six ships at a time. At last, with his ship sinking beneath him, Grenville was reluctantly forced to surrender, dying soon afterwards of his wounds.

1596
Caravaggio paints *Boy with a Fruit Basket*

Michelangelo Amerighi Caravaggio (1569–1609) was born in Lombardy and founded a revolutionary school of painting in Naples, teaching his students to paint subjects in a natural way and not idealistically as formerly. Most of his sitters were young boys and his masterpieces include *Boy with a Fruit Basket*, *Fortune Teller* and *A Music Party*.

1598
The Edict of Nantes

For many years France had been torn apart with religious and civil wars, the Catholics fighting the French Protestants (Huguenots), first one side and then the other gaining the advantage. Finally, in 1598, King Henry IV of France decided to end the useless, self-destroying struggle for ever. He passed a law, to become known as the Edict of Nantes, which gave virtual religious liberty to the Huguenots.

It offered them liberty of conscience throughout all France; the right to hold public worship where they had held it previously; the grand nobility could hold Protestant services in their *châteaux*, and lesser nobles could do the same, but the gathering was limited to thirty persons. Full civil rights were granted to Protestants, including access to all official positions. Many other concessions were granted, whilst a committee of ten Catholics and six Protestants was established to deal with any religious disputes.

1600
English East India Company founded

For some years the Dutch had maintained a monopoly of the spice trade with Indonesia and the Moluccas and as the prices soared, the merchants of London became very concerned. On the last day of the sixteenth century, Queen Elizabeth granted a Charter to a new company giving permission to trade in 'all parts and places in Asia, Africa and America between Cape Cod and the Strait of Magellan'.

Four ships of the company sailed from the Thames in 1601 bound for the East by way of the Cape of Good Hope. Soon other ships followed and in time the East India Company grew into an organization which rivalled the British navy for ships and men. It continued until 1874.

Europe was quick to trade with the East and the new colonies of America. This map shows the New Colonies in the reign of James I, and portrays English adventurer, John Smith.

Inspired by the success of the 'John Company', as it was called, other companies, both British and European, were formed to trade with North America and Canada.

1602
Monteverdi composes *Arianna*

Claudio Monteverdi (1567–1643) was an Italian composer whose patron was the Duke of Mantua. In 1613 he became *Maestro di capella* at St Mark's, Venice, where his religious compositions restored the musical reputation of the church. In 1602 he wrote his first opera *Arianna* in which he used unaccompanied madrigals. His next, *Orfeo*, made an even greater impact and established him as a great composer.

1603
Power passes to the Stuarts

By the year 1603, Elizabeth had reigned for forty-five of her seventy years. Although she knew she could not live much longer, she refused to name her successor until, a few days before her death in March 1603, her chief minister Robert Cecil sent a messenger spurring northwards to inform James Stuart that he would be the next King of England.

He was already James VI of Scotland (1566–1625) having ascended the throne in 1567 at the age of one, on the abdication of his mother, the ill-fated Mary Stuart (*see 1561 Mary, Queen of Scots returns from France*). His father was the unfortunate Lord Darnley, whilst he was Elizabeth's cousin twice removed.

He came to the English throne to form the Stuart dynasty and to be known as James I of England, having descended from Henry VII. He prided himself on his 'kingcraft' but actually was so inexperienced in diplomacy that a French statesman described him as 'the wisest fool in Christendom'. He left behind a poor country for a rich one and his extravagance upset many of his new subjects. Nevertheless, he was the first king to rule over both England and Scotland, the Union being ratified in 1707.

1604
Lope de Vega writes *Peregrino en su Patria*

During the sixteenth century, Spanish writers stopped imitating those of France and Italy and a new style of Spanish writing was developed. A great innovator of this style was Lope de Vega (1562–1635) who wrote about two thousand plays. *Peregrino en su Patria* ('A Pilgrim in his own Land') is a romance which illustrates de Vega's flowing, easy, musical verse.

1605
The Gunpowder Plot

Despite his mother's Catholicism, James I had been brought up as a strict Protestant and soon after his accession in 1603 a plot was laid by a group of fanatical Catholics to kill him.

One of their number, Thomas Winter, persuaded Guy Fawkes (1570–1606), then fighting in Flanders, to join them. They evolved a plan: to blow up the king and his ministers when Parliament reassembled on November 5, 1605, then take over control during the confusion which was bound to follow.

At the last moment, however, one of the plotters warned his brother-in-law of the plot; he in turn alerted the officials and the cellars were searched on November 4. Fawkes was discovered near some barrels of gunpowder with a slow fuse in his pocket. Fawkes and seven others were executed on January 31, 1606, but he has been remembered every year since.

Guy Fawkes

1608
The Plantation of Ulster

The English conquest of Ireland began in 1169 during the reign of Henry II and had been carried on for more than four centuries. During the reigns of Elizabeth I and James I both monarchs believed that they could conquer the country, not only by armed forces, but also by more subtle means; the national costume was to be abolished together with the Catholic religion, whilst whole territories were to be cleared of the Irish natives and re-

placed by English and Scots settlers.

The turning point came when the great Irish chiefs were defeated at the battle of Kinsale (1602) and fled from the country. This 'Flight of the Earls' marked the end of the Irish chieftains and their vast estates. The confiscation of their lands began and the six northern counties were added to the English crown by the 'Plantation of Ulster' of 1608, only the three counties of Monaghan, Antrim and Down being excluded.

1608
Lippershey invents the telescope

The first telescope, it is believed, was made by another Dutch spectacle maker of Middleburg (*see 1590 Jansen invents the microscope*) called Hans Lippershey. Holding up a pair of spectacle lenses he directed them towards a steeple and found that it appeared nearer. Mounting them in a tube, some distance apart, he produced . . . the telescope. Galileo took the idea and improved upon it.

1609
Kepler's *Planetary Movements*

Johann Kepler (1571–1630) was born in Weil, Germany, and succeeded Tycho Brahe as Professor of Mathematics and Astronomy at Prague University, previously having published his *Prodomus* in 1596 when he was only twenty-five.

At first he relied a great deal upon Brahe, his master, and his great and most significant discovery, published in 1609, was that every planet follows an elliptical rather than a circular orbit. He also stated that the line drawn from a planet's centre to the sun takes the same time to move over equal areas of the ellipse, and that the square of a planet's period of revolution is proportionate to the cube of its mean distance from the sun. These laws are basic to modern astronomy.

1612
Donne publishes *Songs and Sonnets*

John Donne (1573–1631) was the first of the English metaphysical poets. Love-poetry of his predecessors had been formal and artificial but Donne wrote in a passionate, harsh and mature tone. He expressed both his passion and man's relationship to God in *Songs and Sonnets* in the language and rhythms of ordinary speech, but the exciting similes and metaphors he used gave his poetry an added depth and beauty.

1613
The first of the Romanovs

Poles invaded Russia in 1609 and in the following year Vladislav, son of the King of Poland, made himself czar, whilst the Swedes seized several Russian cities. The people of Russia united to drive out the invaders and in October 1612 regained control of their country. Fifteen-year-old Michael Romanov was chosen to be czar, thus founding a new Russian dynasty, which lasted until 1917 (*see 1917 Outbreak of Russian Revolution*).

1615
Inigo Jones becomes Surveyor General

Inigo Jones (1573–1651) was the son of a cloth-worker, yet was to become one of Britain's finest architects. His talent as an artist soon became apparent and he was sent by his patron, the Earl of Arundel, to study in Italy. He changed from landscape-painting to architecture and was particularly influenced by the work of Andrea Palladio (*see 1570 Palladio's treatise on architecture*).

Jones acquired such a reputation that he was invited to Denmark to design the two royal palaces of Rosenberg and Frederiksborg for King Christian IV. In 1604 he was appointed architect to England's royal court where he also designed sets and costumes for the court masques. He was later appointed Surveyor-General and designed such magnificent works as the Banqueting Hall, Whitehall and Greenwich Hospital. Under Cromwell he was forced to pay heavy fines for being a courtier of Charles I, and he died in poverty.

1615
Cervantes writes *Don Quixote*

Miguel de Cervantes (1547–1616) lived an adventurous life, being a soldier who was taken prisoner by Barbary pirates. Returning to Spain he began to write, and created his immortal 'hero', the Spanish knight, Don Quixote de la Mancha, whose mind was turned by tales of the medieval knights. In his book Cervantes was mocking both sixteenth century Spanish society and its romantic literature.

1617
Jonson becomes first Poet Laureate

In recognition of his services to poetry and drama, Ben Jonson (c. 1573–1637) was awarded in 1617 a royal pension by James I and thus became the first Poet Laureate, though not in name. His plays record contemporary scenes and are a shrewd criticism of mankind. Famous plays by Jonson include *The Alchemist* (1610) and *Bartholomew Fair* (1614).

The Battle of Lützen: Gustavus Adolphus (above) defeated the brilliant Wallenstein (right) but lost his life.

1618
Outbreak of Thirty Years' War

Since 1555 Germany had been divided into two religious camps – the Lutherans (Protestants) and Catholics, forming a Catholic 'League' and a Protestant 'Union'. Then, in Bohemia, an event occurred which was to begin the Thirty Years' War.

It began when the Czech leaders in Prague, protesting against the strict rule of the Catholic Hapsburgs, threw out their state officials and elected as king Frederick, the Elector of Palatine, a Protestant prince. Soon afterwards, however, a battle was fought at White Mountain in 1620, Frederick was defeated and, it seemed, the revolt was over.

But the war that had begun in Bohemia soon became a European conflict. Christian of Denmark (1577–1648) led a Protestant Union against a powerful army of the Catholic League led by Count Tilly and the Imperial General Wallenstein. Christian was defeated to be replaced by Gustavus Adolphus of Sweden (1594–

1632). They next met at Breidenfeld (1631) where Adolphus almost destroyed Tilly's forces and revenged his sacking of the city of Magdeburg four months earlier.

Wallenstein was beaten the following year at Lützen and after that the war lost its religious character to become a political struggle. Battle followed battle and much of Europe was plunged into chaos and brutal strife until the war was ended in 1648 by the Treaty of Westphalia.

1618
Van Dyck becomes a Guild Member

Dutch-born Anthony Van Dyck (1599–1641) was only nineteen years of age when he became a full member of the Antwerp Guild of Painters. When he visited England he became court painter and was knighted by Charles I. His paintings include an equestrian portrait of Charles, and another of the king, Queen Henrietta Maria and their children.

1618
Execution of Raleigh

Walter Raleigh was a Devon man, born near Sidmouth in 1552. He became a member of Elizabeth's court and, as legend says, came to her attention when he gallantly spread his cloak before her on the muddy ground.

He soon became her favourite courtier and in 1585 sent a fleet to America to found the colony of Virginia, named after the 'virgin queen'. He was supplanted by the Earl of Essex and for a time he went to Ireland, although he was later restored to the queen's favour.

On her death Raleigh realized that there was no place for him under a Stuart king. He was actually imprisoned for a while on a charge of treason during which he wrote his *History of the World* and *A Discourse of War*.

He was allowed his freedom to search for *El Dorado*, a land of gold, but was unsuccessful and on his return was condemned and was beheaded in 1618.

1620
The voyage of the *Mayflower*

'Puritans' was a name given in Elizabethan England to those who wished to see simpler and more devout worship than that existing after the Reformation, where many of the old rituals of the Catholic church still remained.

The Established Church and James I were hostile towards them and following a number of persecutions, many were forced to leave England and settle in Leyden, Holland, in 1608. They found, however, that the industrial life they had to follow was not to their liking and decided to begin a new life – in the New World.

They finally obtained permission from the Virginia Company to settle in North America and eventually, on September 6, 1620, their ship, the *Mayflower*, sailed with one hundred and two men, women and children who looked forward to a new life, and freedom to worship as they wished, in America. It was a difficult and dangerous passage. The weather was rough and, soaked and miserable, the Pilgrims huddled together with only their faith to sustain them. During the storm one of the main beams cracked but it was repaired, and at last, on the evening of November 19 they anchored in the sheltered but bleak harbour of Cape Cod, Massachusetts.

1624
Richelieu becomes chief minister

Armand de Richelieu (1585–1642) became a cardinal in 1622 and chief minister to Louis XIII (1601–43) in 1624. His ambitions were clear; to quash the Huguenots (*see 1627 Siege of La Rochelle*); to increase France's greatness; and to secure all power in the hands of the king and himself. He achieved all this (although he oppressed the people, overwhelmed them with taxation and denied them many of their local liberties) and can be regarded as the founder of absolute monarchy that reached its height under Louis XIV.

Richelieu's first task was to curb the power of the nobles who enjoyed virtual independence from royal authority. Their conspiracies to depose Louis and kill Richelieu led him to destroy their castles and to forbid private warfare. In 1630 he foiled an attempt by the Queen Mother, Marie de Medici, and leading nobles to arrange his downfall; Marie de Medici fled to Brussels and several nobles were imprisoned or executed.

In his foreign policy Richelieu was equally aggressive, and determined to combat the threat of the Hapsburgs. By the Treaty of Westphalia in 1648 (*see 1618 Outbreak of Thirty Years' War*) he had made France capable of dominating the peace negotiations.

the centre of French Protestantism. As soon as his troops appeared the Huguenots appealed to England for help and the Duke of Buckingham arrived with a strong fleet of forty-two warships and seven thousand troops, both infantry and cavalry, to deal with the situation. When he arrived, however, the people of La Rochelle refused him permission to land, declaring that they did not want to show any hostility to their king.

Buckingham then turned his attention to the Isle of Ré but the French threw in a superior force and he was completely defeated, more than half of his men being slaughtered. He returned to England soon afterwards to face the contempt of the people.

Richelieu besieges La Rochelle.

1625
Rubens: *Adoration of the Magi*

Peter Paul Rubens (1577–1640) was perhaps the greatest of all Flemish painters. In 1600 he went to Italy where he studied the works of Titian and Veronese; it was here that the foundations of his style were laid. Amongst his most well-known paintings are the *Adoration of the Magi* and *The Assumption of the Virgin*.

1627
The siege of La Rochelle

During Richelieu's campaign against the Huguenots (*see 1624 Richelieu becomes chief minister*) he began a siege of La Rochelle, then a great maritime city and

1628
The Petition of Right

During his reign, Charles I (1600–49) often did not wait for Parliament to agree, but ordered money to be raised by a Commission. When at last his Commissioners shrank from collecting money without Government approval, he issued an order on February 28, 1628 putting a duty on merchandise. This brought the merchants against him and the people of England sent as many strong men as possible to the next Parliament.

When the four hundred men of the Commons assembled they included such as Cromwell, Hampden and Pym, men who would stand against the king if he acted unconstitutionally.

Parliament drew up a limiting Petition of Right and forced the king to sign, but in 1634 and 1635 he broke this statute when he ordered other than maritime towns to pay 'ship money'. This act was to become a great issue between king and Parliament.

1628
Harvey discovers circulation of the blood

In 1628 Englishman William Harvey (1578–1657) published an account of how the heart works as a pump, circulating blood to every part of the body. He deduced this by actually measuring the output of blood from the ventricle (a chamber of the heart) and inferring that it returned via the auricle (another chamber). From this has grown the whole science of physiology.

1628
Piet Heyn captures the silver fleet

During the early part of the seventeenth century, Holland became a powerful and prosperous nation, her great trading colonies in the West and East Indies bringing in huge revenues. There had been an uneasy truce with Spain who, for a time, had ruled Holland, and in 1621 war again broke out between the two countries.

Dutch fleets went into action, sinking every Spanish ship they met, their greatest success being when in September 1628 one of their admirals, Pieter ('Piet') Heyn captured the entire Spanish fleet carrying bullion from the silver mines in America.

Another triumph of the Spanish–Dutch war was the Battle of the Downs in 1639 when a Dutch fleet under the great admiral Marten van Tromp (1597–1635) crushed the Spanish fleet to establish Dutch naval supremacy.

1632
Taj Mahal begun by Shah Jehan

The mausoleum of Taj Mahal standing by the Jumna River outside Agra in India is regarded as the finest example of Islamic architecture. Standing on a rectangular platform 580 metres by 304 metres, the highly decorated 'onion' shaped dome of the octagonal tomb in white marble is flanked by four smaller domes. At each corner is a slender minaret, and a pool lined with cypress trees reflects the whole edifice.

The mausoleum was commissioned by the Moghul emperor Shah Jehan in 1631 for his beloved wife who died in childbirth. The construction began the following year, took twenty-two years to complete and employed twenty thousand workers. The inside of the building is just as ornate as the exterior, with semi-precious jewels set into the marble. At the centre is an ornate cenotaph and in a vault below this lie Shah Jehan and his wife.

The magnificence of the Moghul empire: Shah Jehan built the Taj Mahal as a mausoleum for his wife.

1633

Bernini: the Tomb of St Peter

Giovanni Bernini (1598–1660) was the last of the universal geniuses produced by the Italian Renaissance. Architect, painter and dramatist, he is most renowned for his exquisite sculptures and his work on St Peter's Basilica, Rome.

A church had existed in some form over St Peter's Tomb since Emperor Constantine's reign (*d.* AD 337), though this 1000 year-old edifice was de-molished in 1506 for the construction of the present St Peter's. The cathedral was enlarged constantly and in 1624 the twenty-six year-old Bernini designed the *baldachin*, an immense canopy in gilt-bronze over the Tomb of St Peter at the heart of the building.

This masterpiece, completed in 1633, consists of four twisted columns and a canopy richly decorated with carved cherubs, laurels, bees and papal insignia. Bernini was later to design the impressive 'key-hole' shaped colonnade surrounding the piazza in front of the cathedral,

and to sculpt many famous pieces for the interior.

1635
Foundation of *L'Académie Française*

L'Académie Française (the French Academy) was established by order of King Louis XIII in 1635, the same year as Richelieu declared war on Spain. The Academy had begun several years earlier when a small group of writers and poets agreed to meet once a week and read and discuss their latest works.

The meetings were supposed to be secret but Richelieu, who missed very little, soon heard of them and, convinced that they were strictly non-political, offered to form the group into a properly recognized society. He also informed the king and in consequence, letters patent were granted on January 29, 1635.

A committee was formed with a chancellor at its head, Richelieu himself being appointed its chief patron to secure freedom from interference by similar bodies. One of the great achievements of the new Academy was begun in 1639, a dictionary of the French language, the first edition appearing in 1694.

1637
Corneille's *Le Cid* is produced

The French dramatist Pierre Corneille (1616–84) was one of the 'Five Poets' employed by Cardinal Richelieu to write plays under his direction. His most famous play, a tragedy called *Le Cid* (first produced in 1637) marks an epoch in the history of French drama. It introduced a favourite theme of Corneille's, that of the conflict in a human soul between passion and honour.

1637
Descartes: *Discours de la Méthode*

The French philosopher René Descartes (1596–1650) said in his *Discours de la Méthode* that everything should be doubted in the quest for absolute certainty. He argued that the senses deceive us, but there was one thing of which he was certain: *Cogito, ergo sum* (I think, therefore I am). Methodical thought, wrote Descartes, was to be the foundation of all knowledge.

1638
Death of Jansen

Cornelius Jansen (1585–1638) was a Dutch clergyman and teacher of theology. After studying and then teaching at a number of universities he went to Louvain (Leuven, now in Belgium) to take charge of a theological college. Although a Catholic, he was violently opposed to the Jesuits and did everything he could to discredit them.

He began work on *Augustinus*, a study of the theology of St Augustine, which was to occupy the rest of his life. In it he outlined his religious beliefs, putting forward a doctrine that would reform Catholicism. His principles were to become known as Jansenism and were to rend France during the rest of the seventeenth and early eighteenth centuries.

1642
Outbreak of Civil War in Britain

The struggle between King Charles I and his Parliament was reaching a climax, for he believed in the divine authority of kingship whilst his Parliament believed in the democratic right of Englishmen to be governed by their elected representatives. Charles's tax called Ship Money (*see 1628 The Petition of Right*) further widened the gulf between king and Parliament.

The near-penniless king was forced to recall Parliament but when he tried to arrest five members, England was thrust into a Civil War that was to last from 1642 until 1649. At first the victories were all Royalist ones, the dashing cavalry led by Charles's nephew Rupert, sweeping aside the poorly armed, mainly peasant soldiers.

But his opponent, Cromwell, slowly developed a new breed of fighting men, psalm-singing but tough and well-drilled 'Ironsides' and with them he won a series of important victories – Marston Moor (1644), Naseby (1645), Preston and Colchester (both 1648).

Charles sought refuge in Scotland but was handed over to his enemies (*see 1649 The execution of Charles I*).

1642
Tasman discovers Van Diemen's Land

In 1606 Willem Jans sailed along the coasts of northwest Australia and New Guinea, believing them to be the same stretch of land. In 1616, Luis de Torres sailed through the straits to which he has given his name, while part of southwest Australia was discovered by two more Dutchmen, Dirck Hartogszoon (1616) and Cornelis de Houtman (1619).

Then, in 1642 came the greatest of them all – Abel Tasman (*c.*1603–59). He sailed from the Dutch settlement of Batavia along the coast of New Guinea and discovered both New Zealand and Tasmania on the way. The latter island he named Van Diemen's Land after the governor of the Dutch East Indies, but in 1853 the British renamed it after its discoverer, calling it . . . Tasmania.

1642
Rembrandt paints *The Night Watch*

Rembrandt van Rijn (1606–69) is considered to be one of the world's greatest artists. He was born in Leyden, Holland, but settled in Amsterdam where he was greatly influenced by Italian art and more especially by the work of Caravaggio. His masterpieces include *The Night Watch, Pilgrims at Emmaus* and many paintings of people in old age.

1643
Mazarin becomes chief minister

When Louis XIII died in 1643 his son, Louis XIV was only five years old and his mother, Anne of Austria, became regent. A year earlier the great Richelieu had died and in almost his last breath begged the king to appoint Jules Mazarin as his successor.

Richelieu's wishes were carried out and it was not long before Mazarin was the real ruler of France, the regent wisely leaving the running of the country to him during her son's minority.

Mazarin (1602–61) was never a popular man; originally a Sicilian who had been entrusted with several delicate missions by Pope Urban VIII, he was mistrusted by the French. He became a naturalized Frenchman, however, and accepted Richelieu's suggestion that he join the French court.

His first important act on Richelieu's death was to bring the Thirty Years' War to an end with the Treaty of Westphalia in 1648 although war continued between France and Spain.

1644

The foundation of the Manchu dynasty

The great Ming dynasty came to an end when fierce bands of invaders from the north called Manchus swept into China and drove the weakened dynasty before them. Originally they had been a loose collection of tribes but they were welded into one fighting force by Nurhachu.

Soon after Nurhachu's death in 1626 there were internal troubles in China when a usurper seized the throne and the last Ming emperor, Chung-Chang (1627–44) committed suicide. The Manchus joined forces with a Ming general to throw out the usurper and when this was done a Manchu prince was made emperor in his stead. A period of rebellion followed but by 1662 the Manchus had made themselves secure and were to rule China until 1912.

The most significant event during their dynasty was the increasing number of Europeans who visited China, although only one port, Canton, was open for foreign trade – silks, tea and pottery, mainly – the European traders being confined to 'factories' or trading centres.

1648

Outbreak of the Fronde

The name 'Fronde' comes from a game in which slings (*frondes*) were used by boys in their mock street 'battles' in Paris. The name was given to two uprisings in France which occurred after Mazarin (*see 1643 Mazarin becomes chief minister*) had imposed heavy taxes on the French at a time when his unpopularity was growing.

The *Frondeurs*, or rebels, had no united programme and their leaders were divided by rivalries. The First Fronde (1648) was an alliance of the middle class and the nobility led by the *Parlement*; when their leader was arrested, the mob rose in anger and set up barricades, but peace was restored in 1650.

The Second Fronde (1651–53) began when Mazarin imprisoned Condé, a rebel from the nobility. The intrigues of other nobles made Mazarin flee from Paris, but soon the nobles lost their popularity and the movement came to an end.

1649

The Execution of Charles I

When Charles I was returned to London it was decided to bring him before a Court of Commissioners. The trial opened on January 20, 1649, and when the king was brought in he was blamed

Charles I on the scaffold.

The Anglo-Dutch Wars: commercial rivalry led to a number of clashes between the English and Dutch navies.

for causing all the misfortunes that had befallen the nation since the beginning of the Civil War. For his part, the king claimed that the court was illegal, because the House of Commons was not a court of law.

Charles refused to plead 'not guilty' when brought before the court again on January 27 and was then declared guilty.

He was kept under close guard for three days although he was allowed to say goodbye to his children and then, on January 30, the king left St James's Palace, walking on foot with a large escort. Taken to the Banqueting House in Whitehall, he stepped out onto a scaffold that had been erected in the street and after a brief speech he said, 'I shall say but very short prayers, and then thrust out my hands.' The king knelt with his head on the block and soon stretched out his hands. The axe fell and a groan rose from the thousands who thronged the street. Then, with many weeping, the crowd silently dispersed.

1651
Hobbes publishes his *Leviathan*

Thomas Hobbes (1588–1679) was educated at Oxford and became tutor to Prince Charles, (later Charles II). He managed to live quietly during the time of the Commonwealth, then was awarded a pension on Charles's return. His major work is *The Leviathan* which argues the importance of absolute sovereignty, the lumbering Leviathan (a huge sea-monster) being the State.

1652
Outbreak of the Anglo-Dutch War

Unlike so many other wars which had been fought for religious reasons, that between England and Holland which broke out in 1652 was purely commercial, each nation being jealous of the other's trading successes, particularly in the North Sea and the East Indies.

The war began when a Dutch fleet in English waters refused to salute the English flag, and hostilities broke out soon afterwards. The first action was fought off Dover when Van Tromp (1629–91) attacked a fleet commanded by Admiral Blake (1599–1657) who captured two Dutch ships.

These wars were the First (1662–4) and the Second (1664–7) Dutch Wars which ended with the Treaty of Westminster and the Peace of Breda respectively. The Third War (1672–4) saw the Dutch actually sail into the Medway and tow away England's latest warship and ended when the Dutch leader, William of Orange, forced England to make peace.

1652
Cape Colony founded

The Portuguese navigator, Bartolomeu Diaz, (c. 1450–1500) returned from his voyage in 1488 and showed the king of Portugal a map with a headland marked, 'Cape of Storms'. However, the king changed it to *Cabo da Boa Esperance* ('Cape of Good Hope'). Cape Town was founded in 1652 by Dutch colonists, but was captured by the British in 1806. It became a Republic in 1961.

1653
Caldéron's *Life is a Dream*

Pedro Caldéron (1600–81) was one of Spain's greatest dramatists, who after ten years' soldiering became superintendent of amusements to King Philip IV. Caldéron wrote with perfect fidelity to the Spanish thought and manners of his day. His most famous work is *La Vida es sueno* ('Life is a Dream').

1653
Cromwell becomes Lord Protector

Charles I was executed in January 1649 and in the following May Oliver Cromwell (1599–1658) established the Free Commonwealth of England with himself at its head. He next crushed rebellious Royalist and Irish forces, sending an army into Ireland with orders that 'no quarter' should be given.

In December 1653 Cromwell was formally installed as Lord Protector of England, Scotland and Ireland, taking the oath in Westminster Abbey. Then, almost immediately, he dissolved Parliament. For the next eighteen months the country was governed by his major-generals.

During Cromwell's period of power, England became a very gloomy place. Sunday sports, horse-racing, even dancing round the maypole which had been enjoyed since medieval times, were all banned. Cromwell later assembled another Parliament which offered him the throne but his army objected so strongly that he did not even consider the idea.

Oliver Cromwell

He proved to be an able ruler, with a great love of his country. His foreign policy especially was aimed at making Britain respected overseas.

Cromwell's health began to suffer and during the night of September 3, 1658, to the accompaniment of a great storm that was sweeping across England, he died.

1655
Verbiest's steam carriage

The first steam powered vehicle is credited to Father Verbiest, a Jesuit missionary in China, in 1655. The motive power was an aeolipile, a primitive steam reaction turbine first described by Hero of Alexandria in 130 BC. It is said that Verbiest's vehicle could move at a 'good speed' for as long as the steam lasted.

1653
Izaak Walton's *The Compleat Angler*

Izaak Walton (1593–1683) was an accomplished writer of biographies and treatises on the monarchy. However, his fame rests on his modest little book, *The Compleat Angler*, in which he describes the sport of angling as a simple, gentle and contemplative rural pastime. Later republished as *The Universal Angler*, it was over one hundred years before it achieved the true recognition it enjoys today.

1656
Velasquez paints *Las Meninas*

Court painter to the King of Spain, Diego de Silva y Velasquez (1599–1660) began painting in a naturalistic style but, greatly influenced by Titian, developed a flowing style demonstrating less awareness of form than of impressions. His painting is distinguished for its unflattering realism and his wide choice of human subjects including *Las Meninas* ('Maids of Honour', 1656) and *Las Hilanderas* ('The Spinners').

1654
Vondel writes *Lucifer*

The greatest of Dutch poets, Joost van den Vondel (1587–1679), employed his intense religious fervour and self-taught skill in Latin translation to produce poetry, prose and plays based on stories from the Old Testament and classical mythology. A devout Roman Catholic, his greatest achievement was his trilogy of plays: *Lucifer, Adam in Exile* and *Noah*, all written late in his life.

1659
Samuel Pepys's *Diary*

On January 1, 1659 Samuel Pepys (1633–1703) began his famous *Diary*. Written in his own shorthand, undeciphered until 1825, it provides an intimate picture of his character, official and social life of his time, and eye-witness accounts of the Plague and the Fire of London (*see 1666 Great Fire of London*). On May 31, 1669 he discontinued the *Diary* owing to his failing eyesight.

1660
Restoration of the monarchy

The dark days in England seemed to come to an end with the death of Oliver Cromwell (*see 1653 Cromwell becomes Lord Protector*) and, with the return of Charles II (1630–85) in 1660, everyone (with the exception of the Puritans) looked forward to happier, brighter days. As the king rode through the streets of London on May 26, the whole city seemed to be caught up in a frenzy of wild enthusiasm.

Charles, too, was glad to be home. He had lived, surrounded by exiles, in the courts of France and the Netherlands, often hungry and always in need of money. Now that was all over and, from the faces of his people and his ministers, he would want for nothing in the future. A London wit wrote of him: 'We have a very pretty king, Whose word no man relies on; He never said a foolish thing, And never did a wise one,' a sentiment with which the cynical Charles would have agreed.

Louis XIV and the glories of Versailles.

In the same year Louis decided to develop the small hunting lodge at Versailles. It was here that the glories of *le Roi Soleil* (the Sun King) were to be reflected and by 1682 the fantastic palace was completed and Louis moved in with his dazzling court. Everything there was grand (the symbol of *le Roi Soleil* was repeated in the decoration and furniture) and the nobility of every country in the world flocked to see Louis, who had made Versailles the symbol of his and France's power.

Although Versailles with its rituals, masques, ballets and fountains was the envy of every prince, the real France was to suffer miserably from Louis' heavy expenditure and his aggressive foreign policy.

1661
The building of Versailles

When Louis XIV (1638–1715) came to the throne in France, the government was largely in the hands of Mazarin (*see 1643 Mazarin becomes chief minister*). In 1661 Mazarin died and Louis took complete control declaring *'L'Etat, c'est moi'*, (I am the state).

1661
The Clarendon Code

Charles II relied a great deal upon his ministers, encouraging them to govern the country on his behalf so that he had more time for his many amusements. His chief adviser was the Earl of Clarendon who had shared Charles's exile and, two years before the Restoration had been made Chancellor of the Exchequer. On their return in 1660 he became his principal minister but, forced to resign in 1667, went to France and stayed there until his death seven years later.

Whilst in power Clarendon forced four laws through Parliament (known as the Clarendon Code) which were intended to strengthen the position of the Church of England. They were the Corporation Act (1661), the Act of Uniformity (1662), the Conventicle Act (1664) and the Five Mile Act which forbade all expelled clergymen to live within eight kilometres of a town unless they had taken an oath to be loyal to the established order.

1663
Milton writes *Paradise Lost*

John Milton (1608–74) revealed his genius very early, his *Lycidas* (1637) being one of the most moving elegies in the English language. For a while he was secretary to Cromwell but became blind about 1652 and retired from public life to write *Paradise Lost* and *Paradise Regained*. The former is one of the world's great poems and placed Milton second only to Shakespeare.

1665
The Great Plague

Plague had recurred frequently throughout Europe for many centuries but London had been unusually free of it during the years before the Great Plague. It really began in 1664, when a few isolated cases were observed but in 1665 sixty-eight thousand people died of it in London alone.

The situation in London grew so desperate that Parliament moved to Oxford and the Court to Salisbury. Meanwhile the capital had become a wilderness of closed doors as people tried to protect themselves and their families. Infected rats carried the disease from street to street; buildings were daubed with red crosses and the words 'Lord have Mercy on us' to show that they housed dying or dead and ringing bells announced the arrival of carts to take away the corpses.

From London the terrible disease spread across the country, but by 1667 the epidemic had died out. The disappearance of the Great Plague in London has been attributed to the Great Fire but it died out in other cities without such a cause.

1666
The Great Fire of London

At 2 am on September 2 a fire was discovered in the house of John Farynor, the king's baker, in Pudding Lane, a narrow street east of London Bridge. Fanned by a strong east wind, the flames spread rapidly through the city. For four days the fire raged. Even the king, Charles II, and his brother turned out to fight it.

The Great Fire

First it reached London Bridge, which had wooden buildings upon it, and then it spread northward to Lombard Street and Cornhill. On the third day it destroyed Cheapside and Fleet Street before continuing on to the Inner Temple and Newgate.

Over 121 hectares, containing more than thirteen thousand houses, were destroyed. The fire was not, however, a complete disaster for it destroyed many of the main areas of infection remaining from the Plague and made it possible to create a new city with wider streets and brick buildings to replace the cramped medieval streets and wooden buildings.

1666
Stradivarius makes his first violin

Antonio Stradivarius (1644–1737) made stringed instruments from 1666 to 1737. Although best known for his violins, the best of which were made between 1700 and 1725, he also made violas and 'cellos. Stradivarius made more than a thousand instruments, many of which still exist – and are extremely valuable.

1667
The War of Devolution

Louis XIV of France instigated several wars in his efforts to become dictator of Europe. In 1667 he claimed Spain and her possessions through his Spanish-born wife, the Infanta Maria Theresa. The queen had renounced all rights to the Spanish throne in 1659 but this was conditional upon the payment of a marriage dowry. Eight years later Louis asserted his wife's claims on the grounds that the agreement was invalid because the dowry had never been paid.

Fifty thousand French troops marched into the Spanish Netherlands in May, 1667. In 1668 England, the United Provinces, and Sweden formed the Triple Alliance to prevent French expansion and Louis prudently made peace with Spain with the Treaty of Aix-la-Chapelle.

Louis never forgave the Dutch for checking his advance and in 1672 he invaded many areas of Franche-Compté and Belgium. Fighting continued until 1678 when Louis, magnanimous in victory, dictated the peace terms at Nijmegen.

1667
First public performance of *Tartuffe*

A three-act version of Molière's *Tartuffe* was performed before the king, Louis XIV, at Versailles on May 12, 1664 but it was not until August 5, 1667 that it received a public showing. It was immediately banned as it was felt that Molière was being irreligious and in 1669 a new five-act version was produced.

Jean Baptiste Poquelin Molière (1622–73) is regarded as the greatest of French comedy playwrights. Born in Paris, he studied law before joining his father as an apprentice upholsterer. In 1643 he was one of the founders of *L'Illustre Théâtre* and eventually became its leading actor. His first play, *L'Etourdi*, was written in 1655 and was followed by some forty comedies including *Les Précieuses ridicules* (1659), *L'Ecole des femmes* (1662), *Le Misanthrope* (1666), *Le Bourgeois gentilhomme* (1670), and *Le Malade imaginaire* (1673).

1670
Origins of Hudson's Bay Company

This famous trading company, the oldest chartered company in the world, began in 1670 when Charles II gave a charter to the 'company of Adventurers of England trading into Hudson's Bay'.

The company traded in fur with the Indians but faced bitter rivalry from French traders until 1713 when, under the Treaty of Utrecht, France ceded Hudson's Bay to England.

In 1783 the North-West Company was formed, but in 1821 the two were amalgamated to form the Hudson's Bay Company. In 1869 the company surrendered a large portion of its land holdings to Canada to form three new provinces, but retained sufficient land for development and sale.

Even to this day the company operates as a fur trading company but is now better known for its large department stores in the principal towns and cities of Canada.

1670
Vermeer paints *Artist in his studio*

Jan Vermeer (1632–75) was born in Delft, Holland. When he was thirty he became master of the Guild of Painters of Delft but on his death was 'forgotten'. He was 'rediscovered' in the 1860s and heralded as a true Dutch master. Amongst his fine works are *Street in Delft*, *The Lacemaker* and *Artist in his studio* (1670).

1670
Publication of Pascal's *Pensées*

Blaise Pascal (1623–62), the French philosopher and mathematician, was born at Clermont-Ferrand. Educated by his father he soon revealed a precocious genius for mathematics but later became more interested in religious philosophy. In 1670 he published his *Pensées* ('Thoughts') a fragmented apology for Christianity written in 1657, but not published until after his death.

Eskimos trading skins with a ship of the Hudson's Bay Company.

1674
Henry Morgan is appointed lieutenant-governor of Jamaica

During the seventeenth century many pirates operated in the Caribbean attacking and looting the ships of Spain, who then ruled the West Indies. One of the most notorious of these buccaneers was the Welshman Henry Morgan (*c.* 1635–88).

In 1668 Morgan commanded an expedition to capture Puerto Principe (now Camaguey) in Cuba and the following year he attacked Maracaibo in South America. In 1671 he captured Panama.

As Spanish power declined the British, French, and the Dutch began to settle in the West Indies and in 1670 Spain acknowledged Jamaica as an English possession. At the same time many pirates were being captured and punished for their crimes. In 1672 Morgan was sent under arrest to England but he managed to gain the favour of Charles II who, in

January 1674, awarded him a knighthood and the post of lieutenant-governor of Jamaica.

1675
Rebuilding of St Paul's

Within a week of the Fire of London (*see 1666 The Great Fire of London*) Christopher Wren (1632–1723), at that time assistant surveyor general, presented plans for rebuilding the entire city. The plans were approved by Charles II but the high cost led to their ultimate rejection. Included in the plans was a new design for St Paul's Cathedral which had been damaged in the fire. Soon after receiving a knighthood in 1672 Wren presented a second plan for St Paul's but this, too, was turned down.

Several other designs were submitted, and eventually one received official blessing, so work began in 1675. Luckily Wren was allowed to make such alterations as he saw fit and so many of his original ideas were incorporated into the new building which was completed in 1716.

Wren also designed fifty-four other London churches but several were destroyed by bombing during the Second World War.

1675
Leeuwenhoek describes blood corpuscles

Anthony van Leeuwenhoek (1632–1723), the Dutch maker of microscopes, made several important scientific advances. These include the discovery of protozoa (1675), the first accurate description of red blood corpuscles (1675) in support of the theory of blood circulation, and the observation of spermatazoon from dogs and other animals (1677). A drawing by Leeuwenhoek published in 1683 shows the first representation of bacteria.

1677
Racine's *Phèdre*

The first performance of the classic tragedy *Phèdre* (Phaedra) by the French playwright Jean Racine (1639–99) took place on January 1, 1677. *Phèdre* is a powerful drama based on the Greek legend of Hippolytus. Its subject, Phaedra's illicit love for her stepson, shocked audiences at the time, but it was written with a boldness and verve that has never been equalled.

1678
Publication of *Pilgrim's Progress*

This famous book is a religious allegory that relates the adventures of Christian and Hopeful on their journey from the City of Destruction to the Celestial City. Written by John Bunyan (1622–88) whilst in Bedford gaol, the book was such an instant success that a second book describing the pilgrimage of Christina, Christian's wife, and Mercy was published in 1684.

1678
Titus Oates and the 'Popish Plot'

In September 1678 it was revealed that Roman Catholics in England were plotting to murder Charles II and to set the Duke of York (later James II) on the throne. The informant was Titus Oates (1648–1705), a man whose activities had already caused him to be sent down from Cambridge, thrown out of the Royal Navy, and dismissed from two religious colleges.

In spite of the man's dubious background many people believed in the 'Popish Plot' and a wave of anti-Catholic hysteria resulted in the execution of thirty-five Catholics and the imprisonment of many more.

In 1685 Oates was found guilty of perjury; he was flogged, imprisoned for life and ordered to be exposed annually in the pillory. After William III (1650–1702) came to the throne Oates was released and granted a pension.

1682
Accession of Peter the Great

Peter the Great (1672–1725) acceded to the czardom of Russia jointly with his rather weak half brother Ivan in 1682, although neither was old enough to assume power.

In 1689 Peter ousted the regency of his sister Sophia and took control of the government. Following the death of Ivan in 1696 Peter ruled alone and started on his plans to extend the borders of Russia to the Baltic Sea in the north and the Black Sea in the south.

A campaign against Turkey won him the port of Azov on the Black Sea and the chance to build a Russian navy. To this end he visited Holland and England, working in the shipyards of both countries. On his return to Russia, with European engineers and scientists, he began to reorganize the country along western lines.

Peter immediately attacked all outward signs of oriental life. Russian nobles were made to wear European dress and to shave off their beards which were considered an eastern fashion. Anyone who refused received Peter's personal attention. He cut off their beard himself!

During a lull in the Great Northern War of 1700 Peter began building his new capital, his 'window on the west', at St Petersburg on the newly acquired Baltic coast.

1685
The Battle of Sedgemoor

On February 6, 1685 Charles II died and the throne of England passed to his brother the Duke of York (1633–1701) (James II). Four months later the Duke of Monmouth (James II's nephew) formed an army to assert his claim to the throne. He had himself proclaimed king at Taunton, Somerset and on July 6, 1685 he attacked the king's forces on the plain of Sedgemoor, near Bridgewater.

Monmouth decided upon a night attack but an accidental pistol shot alerted the king's men. Hopelessly outnumbered and inadequately armed, Monmouth's men were no match for the royalist troops.

Monmouth escaped from the battlefield but was later captured and beheaded at Tower Hill, London on July 15, 1685. His supporters were tried by the notoriously cruel Chief Justice Jeffreys and were hanged or deported. As a result of the harsh sentences the trial became known as the 'bloody assize'.

1687
Publication of Newton's *Principia*

With Cambridge University closed because of the plague, the young mathematician, Isaac Newton (1642–1727), was sent home to Lincolnshire where he could work at his leisure. His experiments in optics here, showing that white light consists of many colours, are famous but his work into gravitation had a far deeper effect.

Newton's notion was that the force of gravity is not limited to terrestial objects but acts everywhere and can even be extended to heavenly bodies like the moon. It is said that this idea was suggested to Newton by the fall of an apple, but this story is probably a legend.

Newton used his invention the 'cal-culus', to show mathematically that the moon was held in its orbit by gravity; otherwise it would move in a straight line at a tangent to its orbit. He went on to describe mathematically the shape of the earth, the tides and even the motion of the whole universe, using his theory of universal gravitation which stated that every body attracts every other with a force that depends on their masses and decreases with the square of their distance apart.

Newton only disclosed these ideas much later in 1687 in his book – the *Principia* – probably one of the most influential scientific works ever written.

Isaac Newton

1688
The Glorious Revolution

James II, who succeeded to the English throne on the death of Charles II, was so unpopular because of his strong Catholic beliefs that in 1688 he was forced to flee to France. The government had already invited the Dutch leader William of Orange (1650–1702) and his wife Mary (1662–94), James II's daughter, to take the throne and William landed in England from Holland on November 5, 1688. The strength of the government was such that William and Mary had to agree to the Declaration of Rights which effectively placed the monarchy within the control of parliament.

William and Mary were declared joint sovereigns on February 13, 1689. The ousting of James II became known as 'The Glorious Revolution' for it was achieved without bloodshed and because it had such a profound effect on the conduct of the monarchy in England.

The declaration prevented any Catholic or anyone married to a Catholic from reigning, ruled that the sovereign could no longer raise taxes, could not keep a private army, and formed the basis for the system of constitutional monarchy that applies in Britain to this day.

Support for the Jacobite cause was strong in Scotland, and also in Ireland, where the former king, James II, was defeated by the Protestant forces of William III (below) at the Battle of the Boyne, in 1690.

1689
Purcell writes *Dido and Aeneas*

Dido and Aeneas by Henry Purcell (1658–95), the greatest English-born composer, is one of the classics of musical drama. Written originally for a performance at a girls' school in Chelsea, London it is the first English opera entirely without spoken dialogue.

1689
Locke's *Treatises on Government*

In his two *Treatises on Government* the English philosopher John Locke (1632–1704) stated that all governments ultimately derive their authority through the consent of the populace. He also claimed that any government that threatens the fundamental rights of the people is liable to be ousted from power. Such democratic principles have since formed the basis of the political ideals of many Englishmen.

1692
The Glencoe Massacre

Following the suppression of the Jacobite insurrection of 1689 the Scottish government declared an amnesty to everyone who swore an oath of allegiance by December 31, 1691. Lord Stair (1648–1707) made plans for severe military action in case of refusal.

When the time came all had sworn with the exception of the chief of the MacIans (a branch of the Macdonald clan) of Glencoe, an old enemy of Stair. The

MacIans took the oath on January 6 but Stair concealed this fact from William III and obtained an order for the total destruction of the Macdonalds.

The Campbells, also old enemies of the Macdonalds, were instructed to carry out the order. First they feigned friendship with the Macdonalds, and accepted their hospitality. But during the early hours of February 13, 1692 the 120-strong Campbell force rose up and attacked their hosts, murdered most of them, seized their possessions, and burnt their homes.

1700
Great Northern War

In 1697 Charles XII (1682–1718) acceded to the Swedish throne. He was only fifteen and this prompted Peter I of Russia to ally with Denmark and Poland to capture land from Sweden. Charles, however, a born soldier, reacted in 1700 by attacking the Danes and then dictating his terms in the Peace of Travendal.

During Sweden's war with Denmark Russia was laying siege to Narva in Livonia. Charles turned to relieve Narva with only eight thousand men against Russia's sixty thousand and scored a resounding victory. Next he became concerned with Poland, thus giving Peter time to retrain his army and to begin building St Petersburg.

Charles's fortunes began to change in 1709 when, after a crushing defeat at Potlava, he took refuge in Turkey until 1714. Following his death in December 1718 whilst besieging Frederiksten, Norway, the Swedes were forced to accept the Peace of Nystadt in 1721.

1700
Leibnitz founds Prussian Academy of Sciences

Gottfried Wilhelm Leibnitz (1646–1716), the great German philosopher, in 1700 persuaded Frederick I of Prussia to form the Prussian Academy of Sciences. Leibnitz, whose contributions to science, mathematics, philosophy, and law were of considerable importance, was elected perpetual president of the Academy.

1701
Execution of Captain Kidd

On May 23, 1701, the Scottish pirate William Kidd (b. 1650) was hanged at Execution Dock, London. It is said that

Charles XII of Sweden died on his Norwegian campaign of 1718.

his ship, the *Adventure*, engaged in piracy until 1699, when he was captured in Boston, Massachusetts, but there is now some doubt as to his guilt.

1701
Act of Settlement

Passed by parliament in June 1701 this Act ruled that should the reigning monarchs William and Mary fail to have children the crown would pass to Sophia of Hanover and her heirs. It was formulated in order that the Stuarts could not again ascend the English throne and to prevent the creation of a Catholic monarch. The Hanovers were of course Protestants.

The Act, which contained eight clauses in addition to those concerning the succession, also applied to Ireland. Scotland accepted its provisions under the Act of Union (*see 1707 Union of England and Scotland*). It stated that all future British sovereigns had to be members of the Church of England; wars entailing the defence of lands not owned by England could not be engaged upon without the consent of parliament; judges could not be dismissed from office except by parliament; and that the sovereign could not prevent an impeachment.

1701
War of the Spanish Succession

This war was fought by France, Spain, and Bavaria against Britain, Austria, the Netherlands, Denmark, and Portugal. It was caused by Louis XIV's acceptance of the Spanish throne on behalf of his grandson Philip of Anjou although he had renounced all such claims under the Partition Treaty of 1700. This treaty ruled that, upon the death of Charles II of Spain (1661–1700), the Spanish throne

should pass to the Archduke Charles of Austria.

Although the French had the largest army in Europe their power was weakened by the fact that they had to fight on several fronts. In 1704 they attempted to march on Vienna but were cut short by a crushing defeat at Blenheim on August 2. The French retreated, followed by their adversaries under the command of the Duke of Marlborough (1650–1722) and Prince Eugene of Savoy (1663–1736).

Most of the war, however, was fought on Belgian soil where Marlborough scored decisive victories at Ramillies (May 23, 1706) and Oudenarde (July 11, 1708). It was not until the Treaties of Utrecht (1713) and Rastadt (1714) that the bitter, fierce fighting eventually ceased.

1707
Union of England and Scotland

At the end of the seventeenth century there was growing dissension, particularly in Scotland, regarding the relationship between Scotland and England. William III was more interested in England because of its value to him in his European affairs and so Scotland was relegated to second place in the affairs of the two countries.

Many people advocated that the two kingdoms should become separate states, but William and his advisers were more in favour of an incorporated union, although Scottish feeling was of the opinion that such a union would stifle Scotland even further.

In 1706 Queen Anne (1665–1714) set up a commission to draw up a treaty for union. The resultant Act guaranteed freedom of trade, religious practices, and law making for Scotland and decreed that the two countries be united as Great Britain under one parliament and one flag. It became law in May 1707.

1712
Publication of *The Rape of the Lock*

In May 1712 the English poet Alexander Pope (1688–1744) published the first version of *The Rape of the Lock*, a mock-heroic poem based upon a true incident. In many of his works such as the *Dunciad* (1728), Pope made fun of public figures and the stupidity of man.

1714
Fahrenheit's mercury thermometer

Gabriel Daniel Fahrenheit (1686–1736), a German instrument maker, invented the mercury thermometer in 1714. At the same time he introduced a new temperature scale in which the zero is equal to a temperature thirty-two degrees below the freezing point of water (32°F) and the highest point (212°F) is the temperature of boiling water (*see 1742 Introduction of the centigrade scale*).

1715
The Jacobite Rebellion

The name 'Jacobites', from the Latin *Jacobus* for James, describes those people who continued to support James II after his dethronement in 1688 (*see 1688 The Glorious Revolution*).

After the accession of George I (1660–1727) in 1714, the Earl of Mar, a Scottish nobleman, proclaimed James Edward Stuart (1688–1766), the son of James II, as James III, the rightful king. On September 6, 1715 Mar (1675–1732) raised the flag of James III, 'the Old Pretender', at Braemar to mark the start of the rebel-lion. Many nobles joined the earl and within a month he controlled Perth and the ports on the east coast. But his attempts to gain Edinburgh, Dumfries, and Fort William resulted in failure.

At this point the earl, nicknamed 'Bobbing John' because of his hesitancy, could not make up his mind what to do next and the rebels became disunited. One group moved south to England and got as far as Preston before they were forced to surrender on November 13. On the very same day Mar was defeated at Sheriffmuir, near Stirling. In January 1716 James Edward arrived to support Mar but the rebellion, known as 'the fifteen', was already lost and he returned to France a month later.

1715
Handel composes the *Water Music*

In 1711 the opera *Rinaldo* by the German composer George Frederick Handel (1685–1759) was performed in London. Soon afterwards Handel decided to settle in England and in 1715 he composed his *Water Music* in honour of King George I for a royal procession on the Thames. Handel wrote all kinds of music including over forty operas and almost thirty oratorios.

George Frederick Handel

1717
First inoculations against smallpox

In the western world today not many people get smallpox, but up until the eighteenth century it was extremely common. Many people caught it and many died as a result. Those that lived to tell the tale bore 'pock marks', unsightly holes in the skin where the smallpox scabs had been.

Smallpox, or variola, is a very infectious and contagious disease that starts as a rash which develops into blisters. Within a few days the blisters fester and then start to crack and dry up.

In 1717 Lady Mary Wortley (1689–1762) noticed that people in Turkey, where her husband was an ambassador, sometimes used the fluid from smallpox blisters to protect people who had not been infected. Four years later she introduced the practice, known as variolation, into Britain where it was quickly accepted. Although the inoculation itself killed some people, the overall death rate was dramatically reduced (*see 1796 The first cowpox inoculations*).

1717
Watteau admitted to the French Academy

After many years as an unknown painter Jean Antoine Watteau (1684–1721) finally gained the recognition he deserved when, in 1717, he was admitted to the French Academy. He submitted *Embarquement pour Cythère* ('Embarkation for Cythera') as his diploma picture. Many of Watteau's paintings depict the world of courtly pleasures, the best known being *The Music Party* and *Conversations*.

1719
Publication of *Robinson Crusoe*

On April 25, 1719 the English novelist Daniel Defoe (*c.* 1660–1731) published the first volume of *Robinson Crusoe*. A second volume was published later the same year and a sequel issued in 1720. Defoe based his tale on the adventures of Alexander Selkirk who lived alone for fifty-two months on the island of Más-a-Tierra, Juan Fernández Islands, in the South Pacific.

1720
The South Sea Bubble

In 1720 The South Sea Company, formed in 1711 to trade with South America, offered to take over the national debt (money borrowed by the government). The company offered an advance of £7,567,000 to the government in return for certain commercial concessions.

Although, in fact, the trade with South America never materialized the public were given the impression that the company would make enormous profits and people from all walks of life rushed to buy shares.

In February 1720 the £100 shares were worth £130, but by June they were changing hands at £1,050.

Unscrupulous businessmen, anxious to cash in on the boom, sold shares in suspect companies. The directors of the South Sea Company called for the government to make eighty of these companies illegal (including one formed for the importation of jackasses from Spain) and in so doing burst the 'bubble'. People rushed to sell their shares, their values tumbled drastically, and thousands of people lost a great deal of money.

Walpole had entered Parliament in 1701 and very quickly became renowned for his wizardry with figures, his accurate judgement of people, and his shrewd capability. In 1708 he became secretary of war in the Whig administration but four years later was sent to the Tower on a charge of corruption. He returned to office in 1714 when George I came to the throne.

Walpole's premiership, the longest in British history, lasted until he became the Earl of Orford in 1742. He was knighted in 1726.

1721
Walpole becomes first prime minister

When the South Sea Bubble burst in 1720 the task of sorting out the financial tangles fell to Robert Walpole (1676–1745) who was appointed First Lord of the Treasury and Chancellor of the Exchequer in 1721.

Walpole held this post from April 3, 1721 to February 12, 1742 and is generally regarded as the first British prime minister although the post was not officially recognized until 1905. The office evolved as a result of George I's unwillingness to attend cabinet meetings because of his difficulties with the English language.

Swift's hero Gulliver, meeting a Lilliputian.

1726
Publication of *Gulliver's Travels*

Gulliver's Travels was originally published as a satirical work highlighting some of the foolishness and pomposity of the day. However, it is also an exciting adventure story and is read by both adults and children. Its author, Jonathan Swift (1667–1745), is also well known for his *Battle of the Books* and *Tale of a Tub*.

Sir Robert Walpole

1728
First performance of *The Beggar's Opera*

The first performance of this ballad opera was produced at Lincoln's Inn Fields, London on January 29, 1728. Based on popular tunes of the day, with music selected and arranged by John Pepusch (1667–1752) and with a libretto by John Gay (1685–1732), it is a lyrical drama of thieves and highwaymen.

1729
Founding of the Methodist Society

The Methodist Society was founded at Oxford in 1729 when a group of young men began to meet regularly for Bible readings and prayers. They became known as 'Bible Moths', the 'Holy Club', or, because they tried to live methodically in accordance with the tenets of the

John Wesley

New Testament, 'Methodists'.

The founder of the movement was John Wesley (1703–91), a tutor at the University. He was educated at Christ Church, Oxford and ordained in the Church of England in 1728. In the following year he returned to Oxford to teach. His brother Charles (1707–88), also one of the original Methodists, was the principal preacher and theologian of the movement. He was also a prolific writer of hymns.

The precepts of the movement are John Wesley's four volumes of sermons and his notes on the New Testament. Originally formed within the Church of England the Methodists did not become a separate body until 1795.

1733
Jethro Tull's *Horse-hoeing Husbandry*

Early in the eighteenth century several land-owners realized that the growing population would necessitate higher crop yields and more efficient methods of farming. As a result they began to experiment with new crops and improved techniques.

Jethro Tull (1674–1741) introduced new methods of cultivation and, in 1701, he devised a seed drill to furrow the soil and sow seeds mechanically. In 1733 he published his ideas in *Horse-hoeing Husbandry*.

Charles Townshend (1674–1738), a member of the House of Lords, retired from politics in 1730 and devoted his life to agricultural improvements. He introduced a system of crop rotation and advocated the use of artificial grasses and clovers. He was the first English farmer to plant turnips as a field crop and so was nicknamed 'Turnip Townshend'.

These men, and others, were responsible for the rebirth of agriculture in Britain and started an Agricultural Revolution that was as important as the Industrial Revolution that was to follow.

1735
Publication of The Rake's Progress

The Rake's Progress is a set of eight pictures painted by the English artist William Hogarth (1697–1764) in 1735. It depicts the downfall of a young man of fashion who lives loosely, gambles, is gaoled for not paying his debts, and ends up in a lunatic asylum. It followed the success of the artist's previous series of satirical pictures The Harlot's Progress (1731).

1735
Canaletto paints Regatta on the Grand Canal

Giovanni Antonio Canaletto (1697–1768) painted many scenes of the life and architecture of the Venice in which he was born, his best known work being Regatta on the Grand Canal (1735). In 1746 he settled in London and his paintings of the Thames are remarkable for their use of colour and perspective.

1735
Linnaeus begins Systema Naturae

Linnaeus (Carl von Linné, 1707–78), the Swedish botanist, began in 1735 his new system for the classification of plants. Although the method he used, grouping plants in orders and classes in accordance with the number of stamens and pistils in their flowers, was completely artificial, his system formed the basis for modern plant classification.

1739
Execution of Dick Turpin

Dick Turpin (1706–39), the notorious highwayman, was born at Hempstead in Essex. He was apprenticed to a butcher but after he was discovered cattle stealing he joined a band of outlaws who, under his leadership, robbed farms in the area.

In 1735 Turpin joined forces with Tom King, a highwayman, but he shot his partner by accident and then fled to Yorkshire. There, under an assumed name, he started in business as a horse dealer, but in 1739 he was arrested for stealing a black mare and a foal. Found guilty of the crime he was hanged at York on April 7, 1739.

Many of the heroic tales about Dick Turpin's exploits, including his famous ride from London to York, are nothing but folk legends. In the main they were created by the author William Harrison Ainsworth (1805–82) in his novel Rookwood.

1739
The War of Jenkins' Ear

On April 9, 1731 Captain Robert Jenkins was returning home from Jamaica when his ship, the Rebecca, was boarded by the Spanish coastguard. The Spanish commander cut off one of Jenkins' ears instructing him to carry it to the king with the message that if the king had been present he would have received the same treatment.

Jenkins related his story at the bar of the House of Commons on March 16, 1738 and the event created so much hostility towards the Spanish that it ultimately led to the war that broke out in 1739. Naturally enough the war became known as 'The War of Jenkins' Ear.'

There is, however, considerable doubt as to the truth of Jenkins' story. It is almost certain that he had lost an ear, or at least part of one, but he probably received the injury in a brawl.

1740
Accession of Frederick the Great

When Frederick II (1712–86), known as Frederick the Great, became King of Prussia in 1740 the country was prosperous, efficiently organized, and had a large and powerful army. These he used effectively to make his power and that of Prussia a force to be reckoned with.

One of Frederick's first actions on his accession was to claim Silesia from Austria and he fought two wars to assert this claim (*see 1740 War of Austrian Succession*).

In addition to great military power he also fostered the improvement of Prussia's industry and agriculture, established an educational system, encouraged religious tolerance, and reformed the country's judicial system. Although Frederick is regarded as one of the great soldiers of history he had a great passion for music and the arts, wrote prodigiously, and played the flute for relaxation.

In 1756 he attacked Saxony and in the Seven Years' War that followed suffered several defeats but eventually managed to retain his territories. He further enlarged Prussia in 1772 when, through a treaty with Russia, he forced Poland to give up some of its lands.

Although every inch a king, Frederick tended to dress sloppily and often wore an old battered grey hat, a snuff-stained, once blue, uniform, and dirty boots.

1740
The War of Austrian Succession

Emperor Charles VI had no son to succeed him, so in 1713 he issued a pragmatic sanction (a royal decree) stating that his possessions in Austria and its dependencies were to pass to his daughter Maria Theresa (1717–80) on his death. He succeeded in attaining the assent of other European rulers to his daughter's succession, but when he died in 1740 the agreements were ignored.

Frederick the Great invited the French philosopher Voltaire (left) to his court.

Maria Theresa and her heir

man's Fields Theatre, London, created a great sensation. His style of acting was natural and in great contrast to the staid delivery of previous actors. From 1742 to 1745 he performed at Drury Lane and eventually became its principal proprietor. He is still regarded as an actor of outstanding genius.

1741
Publication of Richardson's *Pamela*

Pamela, by Samuel Richardson (1689–1761), was one of the first English novels to be written in the form of letters. Richardson's second book, *Clarissa; or the History of a Young Lady* (1748) was written in the same form, the purpose being to give a clearer indication of the characters' thoughts and feelings.

Frederick II of Prussia claimed Silesia; France claimed the Austrian Netherlands; and Charles Albert of Bavaria, supported by France and Spain, claimed the Hapsburg lands. As a result war raged across Europe for the next eight years. Britain was already at war with Spain (*see 1739 War of Jenkins' Ear*) and in 1742 began fighting in support of Maria Theresa.

In 1743 an army of British, Austrians, and Hanoverians under the command of George II (1683–1760) beat the French at Dettingen and the Austrians entered Bavaria. (This was the last battle in which a British sovereign was personally involved.) But the French, under Marshal Saxe, defeated the British, Dutch, and Austrian troops at Fontenoy (1745), and Lawfeldt (1747). In the naval encounters of the war British naval strength proved to be superior. The war ended with the Treaty of Aix-la-Chapelle on October 18, 1748.

1741
Garrick appears on the London stage

David Garrick's (1717–79) appearance in Shakespeare's *Richard III* at Good-

1742
Introduction of the centigrade scale

The centigrade scale for thermometers was devised by the Swedish astronomer Anders Celsius (1701–44). The scale is divided into one hundred degrees, arranged so that 0°C is the freezing point and the upper fixed point of 100°C is the temperature of steam coming off boiling water (*see 1714 Fahrenheit's mercury thermometer*).

1745
Rebellion of the Young Pretender

In July 1745 Charles Edward Stuart (1720–88), son of the 'Old Pretender' James Edward Stuart sailed for Scotland to promote the Jacobite cause (*see 1715 The Jacobite Rebellion*). He had been advised not to attempt a second rebellion but when, on August 19, he raised his father's standard at Glenfinnan, near Fort William, many Highland clans rallied to his side.

Charles took Perth and Edinburgh almost without resistance and defeated the English at Prestopans, near Edinburgh on September 20. He then invaded England reaching Manchester at the end of November and Derby by December 4. Here his officers insisted that the invasion could not succeed and the army retreated on December 6.

Once he was back in Scotland Charles scored a victory at Falkirk, but pursued by the Duke of Cumberland and his troops, he was forced to retire to the Highlands where his army was completely routed at the Battle of Culloden Moor.

For the next five months Charles Edward, popularly known as 'Bonnie Prince Charlie' or the 'Young Pretender', hid in the Highlands with a price of £30,000 on his head. In spite of this enormous reward he was never betrayed and he eventually escaped to France. With his departure the Jacobite movement came to an end.

1749
Publication of *Tom Jones*

Tom Jones, the epic masterpiece by the English novelist Henry Fielding (1707–54), has been described as the greatest novel ever written. It relates the uproarious adventures of its hero with a reality and verve that some say has never been equalled. Fielding's other novels which include *Joseph Andrews* (1742), *Jonathan Wild the Great* (1743), and *Amelia* (1751) do not have the same sparkle.

1750
Publication of Gray's *Elegy*

Elegy Written in a Country Churchyard, the greatest work by the English poet Thomas Gray (1716–71), is probably the best known and perhaps the most beautiful poem in the English language. Inspiration for the elegy (a song of mourning) came from the churchyard at Stoke Poges in Buckinghamshire where Gray was, himself, buried.

1750
Publication of *L'Encyclopédie*

One of the world's most famous encyclopedias, *L'Encyclopédie*, was published in France in 1750.

Two publishers, Le Breton and Briason, decided to produce a translation of Ephraim Chambers' *Cyclopaedia* (1728) and they commissioned the French philosopher and scholar Denis Diderot (1713–84) to produce the work. Diderot persuaded them to produce a new work with wider scope.

The contributors to the new work included all of the brilliant French writers of the day such as Rousseau (1712–78), Voltaire (1694–1778), Buffon (1707–88), and Montesquieu (1689–1755). In addition to providing factual material on a wide variety of subjects *L'Encyclopédie* contained a great deal of current philosophical thought. It contained only subjects to which there could be offered a rational explanation and in so doing aroused considerable hostility from officialdom and the clergy and publication was prohibited in 1752 and 1759.

L'Encyclopédie captured the spirit of the new age of reason that was dawning in France – an age of enlightenment that was eventually to result in revolution. This spirit is also evident in the condemnation of the corrupt and poverty stricken society and the welcoming of a new freedom that features in other works produced by the Encyclopaedists.

1750
Walpole builds *Strawberry Hill*

In 1750 the English author Horace Walpole (1717–97) began converting his cottage, Strawberry Hill, in Twickenham into a mock gothic castle and that area of London is still known as Strawberry Hill. Fifteen years later he wrote the tale of terror *The Castle of Otranto*, but he is best known for his letters.

1752
Franklin invents the lightning conductor

The lightning conductor was invented by the American statesman, scientist, and writer Benjamin Franklin (1706–90) in 1752. He also invented a heating stove and bifocal spectacles, started a fire service, a subscription library, and the college that was to become the University of Pennsylvania.

Born in Boston of poor parents Franklin had only two years' schooling. He was apprenticed to his father as a soap and candle maker and then to his brother in a printing shop. He was so successful as a printer that in 1749 he retired to devote his energies to science. By flying a kite during a thunderstorm he was able to prove that lightning is a form of electricity.

In 1753 he was appointed postmaster general to the British colonies in North America and he was elected to the Pennsylvania Assembly. From 1776 to 1785 he was ambassador to France and for the next three years President of Pennsylvania.

1753
British Museum founded

A national lottery provided the money for the purchase in 1753 of the books, coins, medals, and natural history specimens collected by Sir Hans Sloane (1660–1753). In 1754 Montagu House was bought to house the collection together with those of Lord Oxford Harley, and Sir Robert Cotton, and the royal collections. The British Museum opened to the public on January 15, 1759.

Benjamin Franklin

1755
The Lisbon earthquake

On November 1, 1755 about thirty thousand people died in the earthquake that struck Lisbon in Portugal. As buildings collapsed people rushed to a nearby quay for safety but all were killed when a second shock wave destroyed the quay. A third shockwave caused giant waves to roll across the sea to complete the destruction of the city.

1755
Publication of Johnson's *Dictionary*

The English writer Samuel Johnson (1709–84) first proposed his *Dictionary of the English Language* in 1747, but it was not published until 1755. Johnson received £1,575 for the work which was the first standard English dictionary. It did much to consolidate the meanings of English words as we know them today.

1756
Founding of Sèvres porcelain factory

Sèvres porcelain includes classically designed decorative pieces, large vases, and dinner services. The factory at Sèvres, near Paris was opened in 1756 to produce 'soft paste', an artificial porcelain, but in 1768 hard paste made of kaolin (china clay) and feldspar, which was closer to the original porcelain invented by the Chinese, was introduced.

1756
The Seven Years' War

This was a renewal of the fight between Britain and France and between Austria and Prussia (*see 1740 The War of Austrian Succession*).

Between Britain and France the struggle concerned the colonies in India and America and resulted in the collapse of France as a colonial power and the founding of the British Indian Empire. The main issue of discontent between Austria and Prussia was Austria's resolve to recapture Silesia taken from them during the War of Austrian Succession.

The fighting started when the French captured Minorca in 1756 and, later the same year, Frederick, fearing that Austria was about to attack, attacked Saxony with a view to invading Bohemia.

Britain's part in the war was, in the main, confined to the colonies in India and North America. In India, where fighting had been continuous since 1748, the decisive incidents occurred at Plassey (1757) and Wandewash (1760). In North America the principal event was the siege and capture of Quebec (1759) (*see 1756 The Black Hole of Calcutta* and *1759 Wolfe takes Quebec*).

1756
The Black Hole of Calcutta

The outbreak of the Seven Years' War in Europe brought renewed fighting between the French and English in India.

On June 20, 1756 the Nawab of Bengal attacked the English settlement at Calcutta. He imprisoned 146 Europeans in a small dungeon, the Black Hole of Calcutta, but conditions were so cramped and airless that only twenty-three survived the night. Robert Clive (1725–74) and Admiral Charles Watson sailed from Madras and recaptured Calcutta on January 2, 1757.

Clive promised Mir Jaffir, the Nawab's commander-in-chief, that he would be given the throne of Bengal and in June he advanced to Bengal with one thousand troops and two thousand sepoys (native soldiers) and only ten guns. At Plassey in West Bengal, Clive attacked the Nawab's fifty thousand-strong force and scored a resounding victory. Mir Jaffir was made Nawab but the real power in Bengal belonged to the British.

Robert Clive achieved British dominance in Bengal at the Battle of Plassey in 1757.

1759
Wolfe takes Quebec

British victories in Canada during the Seven Years' War were brought about largely through the absolute co-operation of the sea and land forces. This was particularly illustrated by the taking of Quebec in 1759.

A fleet of ships carried James Wolfe (1727–59) and nine thousand men up the St Lawrence river to the Isle of Orleons. After waiting for several months Wolfe sent a contingent of men to make a mock attack against Quebec whilst he and the rest of the force were conveyed in boats further up the river. On the following day Wolfe engaged the French on the Plains of Abraham.

Both Wolfe and the French leader, General Montcalm (1712–59) were mortally wounded on the same day, September 13, 1759. Four days later Quebec surrendered to the British and thus paved the way for the complete British conquest of Canada in the following year.

1761
Opening of Bridgewater Canal

Transport systems in Britain were not sufficiently effective to cope with the new demands for increased communications brought about by the Industrial Revolution in the eighteenth century. The roads were extremely bad and the railway had not yet been invented.

Francis Egerton, third Duke of Bridgewater (1736–1803), found the answer to the problem. He wanted a cheap method of transportation to carry coal from his mines at Worsley to Manchester so he commissioned James Brindley (1716–72) to construct a canal to do the job. Within two years the sixty-seven kilometre-long canal was completed and was filled on July 17, 1761.

The building of this waterway marked the beginning of the canal era in Britain and very soon a network of canals covered much of the country. As a result of his initiative the Duke of Bridgewater is often regarded as the 'father of British inland navigation'.

1764
Hargreaves invents the spinning jenny

The second half of the eighteenth century marked the start of the Industrial Revolution in England, a period in which the economy changed from being primarily agricultural to an industrial based society. As the amount of industry increased new inventions emerged making work more automated and efficient.

One such device was the 'spinning jenny' invented by James Hargreaves (1720–78) in 1764. Turned by hand, the 'spinning jenny', which Hargreaves named after his wife, enabled one person to spin eight threads at the same time. Combined with the flying shuttle that John Kay patented in 1733, it revolutionized the cotton industry.

Cotton workers, worried that these machines would threaten their livelihood, raided Hargreaves's house in 1768 and smashed his equipment but they could not stop the wind of change that was sweeping the country.

1765
Robert Adam designs Kenwood

Robert Adam (1728–92) and his brothers John, James, and Charles brought about great improvements in architectural style in eighteenth century Britain. Robert, the most celebrated of the four, designed several notable houses including Lansdowne House, Luton Hoo, Harewood House, Syon House, and Kenwood House in Hampstead.

1765
Watt improves the steam engine

Contrary to popular belief, James Watt (1736–1819) did not invent the steam engine. He did, however, make it more efficient.

Earlier engines used steam travelling through a cylinder to push a piston within the cylinder. Cold water was then poured on to the cylinder to condense the steam and created a vacuum to pull the piston back before the operation was repeated. Watt reasoned that the system was inefficient: in condensing the steam, the cylinder also was cooled so that when steam re-entered a great deal of its energy was being wasted in reheating the cylinder.

Watt solved the problem by using a separate vessel as a condenser so that the main cylinder remained at an even temperature. He also encased the cylinder in a steam jacket to prevent heat loss and he used steam instead of a vacuum to push the piston down as well as up.

James Watt, pioneer of the age of steam.

1768
Royal Academy founded

This famous British art institution was founded by George III (1738–1820) on December 10, 1768 'for the purpose of cultivating and improving the arts of painting, sculpture, and architecture'. It provided for the appointment of a president and forty members, annual exhibitions of work, and the setting up of schools of instruction.

The first president of the Royal Academy was Sir Joshua Reynolds (1723–92), the English artist famous for many types of painting although he is generally associated with portraiture. His subjects · included many of the famous personages of the day including Goldsmith, Garrick, and Johnson. He was knighted in 1768.

One of the origi........
Academy was Thoma.......
(1727–88) whose reputa......
ground after his acceptance. ......
best known paintings are *The Blu*....
and *The Harvest Wagon*. He was pri....
cipally a portrait painter, that being the main requirement of his wealthy patrons, although he himself preferred to produce landscapes.

1768
Arkwright invents the spinning frame

The spinning frame of Richard Arkwright (1732–92) made possible the British cotton industry of today. Initially he met with the same resistance encountered by Kay and Hargreaves (*see 1764 Hargreaves invents the spinning jenny*). His machines were smashed, but his invention had already proved its usefulness and the cotton industry progressed rapidly as a result of its introduction.

1768
Cook's voyages of discovery

One of the greatest names in the history of exploration is that of James Cook (1728–79). He made three epic voyages during which he discovered many new places, charted coastlines, and paved the way for the British colonization of Australia and New Zealand.

During his first voyage (1768–71) in the *Endeavour*, he charted the coastline of New Zealand and surveyed the east coast of Australia, claiming it for Great Britain. The second expedition (1772–75) with the *Resolution* and *Adventure* covered over ninety thousand kilometres during which Cook became the first man to cross the Antarctic Circle.

With the *Resolution* and *Discovery* Cook commenced his third voyage on June 25, 1776. He sailed to New Zealand, discovered several of the Cook

...ands, rediscovered the Hawaiian or Sandwich Islands, and surveyed a large stretch of the American coastline. He returned to Hawaii in 1779 but was clubbed to death by natives on February 14.

1769
Cugnot builds his steam carriage

The first successful steam-powered road vehicle was invented in 1769 by Nicolas Cugnot (1725–1804), a French military engineer. Although the three-wheeled carriage had to be stopped every fifteen minutes to get up steam it could travel at up to about three kilometres per hour.

The French government was so impressed with the machine's possibilities that it ordered a similar vehicle for use by the army. Unfortunately it was never used by the army because it had several accidents and knocked down a wall during its trials and the government decided it was too dangerous to use.

Other inventors produced steam road vehicles with varying degrees of success. Principal among these was Richard Trevithick (1771–1833) but after some considerable success he decided that there was no future in road transport and he turned his attentions to the railway (*see 1804 The first steam railways*).

1769
Wedgwood opens Etruria factory

Prior to the time of Josiah Wedgwood (1730–95) English pottery was rather nondescript, but Wedgwood raised it to such heights that it became known and admired throughout the world.

Born at Burslem, in Staffordshire, Wedgwood was only nine years old when he started work in the family pottery. In 1754 he teamed up with Thomas Whieldon, a well known potter. During this partnership Wedgwood produced the melon and cabbage styles of earthenware. Five years later he became a master potter, set up on his own, and in 1762 was appointed queen's potter. In 1769 he opened his Etruria works at Stoke on Trent.

At Etruria Wedgwood made the green glaze and cream-coloured pottery known as Queen's Ware because Queen Charlotte liked it. Later he invented Jasper Ware, a coloured porcelain bearing cameo-type embellishments, for which he is best known, and which is still produced by the company he founded.

1770
Goethe starts work on *Faust*

These are several versions of the story of Dr Faustus, the sixteenth century German scholar said to have sold his soul to the Devil, but possibly the greatest is the

two-part drama by Johann Wolfgang von Goethe (1749–1832). He started part one of *Faust* in 1770 and it was published in 1808 but the second part was not published until 1831.

Goethe's earliest works were produced during a period of German literary tradition known as *Sturm und Drang* (storm and stress) which was a precursor of the romantic movement that swept Europe in the nineteenth century. From 1786 to 1788 Goethe visited Italy and was inspired to write classical dramas of formal purity and restraint. Goethe's poetry is the finest ever produced in the German language.

Goethe was also extremely interested in science. His life at the Weimar court marks a unique cultural achievement in many fields.

The American colonies' discontent with British legislation came to a head with the Boston Tea Party. Colonists dressed as Red Indians threw chests of tea overboard in protest against tea taxes.

1772
Priestley publishes his experiments

Although Joseph Priestley (1733–1804) was an English Nonconformist minister with views ahead of his time it is as a scientist that he is remembered. In 1767 he published a *History of Electricity* which was followed by several brilliant experiments in electricity and he proposed several suggestions that were not to be proved for another hundred years.

In 1772 Priestley published a paper in which he set out his discovery of hydrochloric acid, nitrous oxide, and outlined the possibility of forcing carbon dioxide into water – a product now known as soda water.

In 1774 Priestley discovered oxygen and showed its importance, and he also discovered sulphur dioxide and ammonia. His work, and that of his contemporaries, formed the foundations of modern chemistry.

1773
The Boston Tea Party

Trade in the American colonies was regulated by Great Britain and, as this inevitably meant the imposition of restrictions in trade, the settlers turned to smuggling. The British tried re-enforcing the Navigation Acts which controlled trading – but with little success.

In 1765 the British government passed the Stamp Act which required that all legal documents in North America had to bear an official stamp. The colonists objected so violently to this imposition that the Act was repealed a year later.

In 1767 tea and other imported goods were taxed in America. Although most of the taxes were later abolished, that on tea remained. In 1773 some of the colonists demonstrated their objection. Dressed as Red Indians they boarded British ships in Boston harbour and threw cases of tea overboard. As a result of this

'Boston Tea Party', Boston was placed under military control. The seeds of the American War of Independence had been sown.

1773
The Pugachev Revolt

Catherine II (1729–96), known as Catherine the Great, ruled Russia for thirty-four years after her husband Czar Peter III, an unbalanced weakling, had been deposed and murdered. During her reign Russia extended its territories to include parts of Turkey, Sweden, and Poland.

She was said to be in favour of better treatment for the serfs (peasants) but she did little to help them. In fact life for them became even more intolerable during her reign and they were taxed heavily. As a result there were several revolts, including the Pugachev Revolt in 1773.

Emelian Pugachev (*c.*1744–75) claimed that he was Peter III and, although others had made the same claim,

the people, to whom he had promised an end to serfdom, rallied to his side. They captured fortified posts, burned the homes of landowners, and headed for Moscow. As the peasants approached, a party of hand-picked troops attacked them and the rebellion was quashed. Pugachev was taken to Moscow in an iron cage and executed there in January 1775.

1773
First performance of *She Stoops to Conquer*

On March 15, 1773 the first performance of *She Stoops to Conquer* by Oliver Goldsmith (1728–74) took place at the Covent Garden Theatre, London. This five-act play concerns the hilarious adventures of a lady who dresses as a serving maid to win the man she loves. Goldsmith also wrote the humorous novel *The Vicar of Wakefield* (1766) and the poem *The Deserted Village* (1770).

1775
First performance of *The Rivals*

The Rivals, the five-act comedy by English playwright Richard Brinsley Sheridan (1751–1816), was not very well received when it was first performed at Covent Garden Theatre, London on January 17, 1775. However it soon achieved success and remains popular to this day as do *The School for Scandal* (1777) and *The Critic* (1779).

Catherine the Great, Czarina of Russia, an able yet ruthless ruler.

1775
First performance of 'The Barber of Seville'

Le Barbier de Séville ('The Barber of Seville'), a comedy by Pierre Augustin Caron de Beaumarchis (1732–99), was first performed in Paris on February 23, 1775. The italian composer Rossini used it as the basis for an opera and Mozart bestowed the same honour on Beaumarchis' other great work Le Mariage de Figaro ('The Marriage of Figaro').

1776
American Declaration of Independence

Great Britain regulated trade in the American colonies to such a great extent that the settlers began to grow annoyed at the controls imposed upon them. There were acts of rebellion (see 1773 The Boston Tea Party) and this hostility flared into war when, on April 19, 1775, shots were fired at Lexington.

The first battle of the war, fought at Bunker Hill, Charlestown, was won by the British who also scored decisive victories in New York (1776) and Philadelphia (1777). But the American Continental Congress had appointed George Washington (1732–99) to take charge of the untrained American soldiers and he inspired them to fight for their freedom. Further inspiration was provided on July 4, 1776 when the Congress issued the Declaration of Independence.

The Declaration renounced allegiance to the British throne and resolved 'that these United Colonies are, and of right ought to be, free and independent States'.

The Americans were aided in their fight by Britain's enemies in Europe and in 1777 the British general, Burgoyne

(1723–92), was forced to surrender at Saratoga. In 1781 General Cornwallis (1738–1805), cut off at Yorktown with French ships preventing aid reaching him by sea, surrendered and the fighting ended. America was granted its independence in 1783.

1776
Publication of The Wealth of Nations

The Wealth of Nations by the Scottish economist Adam Smith (1723–90) was largely responsible for the creation of economics as a separate science. Although many of its theories have now been superseded it remains the most famous work on the subject and is still required reading for political economists.

1777
Lavoisier's experiments with oxygen

Oxygen was discovered in 1774 by Priestley (see 1772 Priestley publishes his experiments) and given the name 'dephlogisticated air'. It was also discovered at about the same time by the Swedish scientist Scheele who called it 'empyreal' or 'fire air', but the French chemist Antoine Laurent Lavoisier (1743–94) gave the element its modern name. He considered it to be an essential constituent of acid and so he called it oxygène (acid former).

In addition to repeating the experiments conducted by Priestley, Lavoisier carried out several of his own. In one of them he showed that mercury, heated in a small amount of oxygen, was transformed into a red powder which he called 'mercury oxide'.

1779
Crompton invents the spinning mule

To help his mother the Englishman Samuel Crompton (1753–1827) spun cotton at home. But he found the job awkward so he tried to improve the equipment. The machine he invented combined features from Arkwright's jenny and Hargreaves' frame and because of this 'cross' was known as a mule.

1779
The first iron bridge

The first iron bridge in the world was erected in 1779 near Coalbrookdale, Shropshire, England. The whole of the surrounding area, which is rich in other reminders of the Industrial Revolution including a canal complex, coal mine, coking works, and furnaces, is at present being developed as an environmental museum of science and technology.

The Industrial Revolution introduced new technology in every sphere: the first iron bridge near Coalbrookdale, erected in 1779.

1780
The Gordon Riots

The Gordon Riots were an appalling explosion of violence in London in June, 1780. They began as an attempt to force Parliament to repeal an Act it had passed in 1778 to stop some forms of discrimination against Roman Catholics.

Lord George Gordon (1751–93) a fanatical young aristocrat, led a great procession of Protestants to Westminster in protest against the Act on June 2. The procession became a mob which, shouting furious cries of 'No Popery!', began attacking the Catholic chapels of foreign embassies. The mob soon extended its activities to the houses of well-off Catholics, then to prisons, the Bank of England and even to the home of the prime minister, Lord North.

For a week the 'No Popery' mob was in charge of London, until order was restored. The memory of those days and nights of fire and terror remained in men's minds for many years.

1780
The first Derby

The Derby, one of the five Classics of English horse racing, was first run at Epsom, Surrey, in 1780, and has been run every year since.

Named after the 12th Earl of Derby, it is a flat race for three-year-old colts and fillies. In the 1913 Derby, Emily Davidson, a Suffragette, was killed when she threw herself under George V's horse. Famous winners include Sir Ivor, Nijinsky and Hyperion.

1781
Herschel discovers Uranus

William Herschel (1738–1822) was born in Hanover but moved to England in

1757 and taught music. In his spare time he studied astronomy and, as he earned very little money, he had to make his own telescope.

His first (1774) was so successful that he devoted a great deal of the rest of his life to the improvement and manufacture of telescopes. By 1789 he was using for his observations a forty-eight-inch reflecting telescope, the largest in the world at that time.

Herschel made several important astronomical discoveries including several double stars and two satellites of Saturn. He raised the number of known nebulae from 180 to 2,500 and, in the field of physics, he was the first to discover infra-red rays. But his most spectacular achievement was the discovery, on March 13, 1781, of the planet Uranus. A year later he was appointed private astronomer to George III.

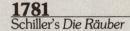

1781
Schiller's *Die Räuber*

Johann Christoph Friedrich von Schiller (1759–1805) was a great German dramatist, poet and historian. His first play, *Die Räuber* ('The Robbers'), published in 1781, caused a sensation with its strongly-worded, revolutionary call for freedom. Some of his most famous plays, including dramas based on the lives of Wallenstein, Mary Stuart, Joan of Arc and William Tell, grew out of his historical research.

1781
Kant's 'Critique of Pure Reason'

Kritik der reinen Vernunft ('Critique of Pure Reason') was the first of three books in which Immanuel Kant (1724–1804) expounded his influential idealist philosophy. Unlike other thinkers of his day who said that man could understand all things purely by reason, Kant suggested that there was certain knowledge, such as the existence of God, which men could not understand in this way because they could not experience it.

1782
Burke's Economic Reform Act

One of the great causes which Edmund Burke (1729–97) pursued throughout his outstanding career in British political life was that of economical reform. By this, Burke meant the freeing of the House of Commons from the influence and control of the king.

George III was able to influence the way the House of Commons voted by putting his own supporters and friends into certain government offices and places, including parliamentary seats.

The economical reform movement in the 1770s and 1780s, of which Burke was one of the leaders, demanded parliamentary, not royal, control of the choice of people to fill various positions and of the salaries they were paid. Burke's Economic Reform Bill, which became law in 1782, was one step on the way to fulfilling this demand. The Act regulated the pensions and payments of a number of posts in the royal household, and abolished about forty others.

1782
Laclos: *Les Liaisons Dangereuses*

Pierre Ambroise François Choderlos de Laclos (1741–1803) achieved fame with one novel. He was a soldier who, bored with life in French garrison towns, turned to writing. His novel in letter-form, *Les Liaisons Dangereuses*, was published in 1782. It was an instant success, not just because it told of the immoralities of a group of decadent aristocrats, but because Laclos wrote with compelling power and brilliant style.

The Montgolfier balloon

1782
Pitt the Younger becomes chancellor

William Pitt the Younger (1759–1806), so-called to distinguish him from his famous father William Pitt, Earl of Chatham, became Chancellor of the Exchequer in 1782. Although Pitt had shown great talent as an orator and politician, it was a very quick promotion for a young man who had entered Parliament less than two years before. In 1783 George III chose the twenty-four year old Pitt to be First Lord of the Treasury (the official title of the king's first minister) and Chancellor of the Exchequer.

Pitt held office until 1801, and was in power again when he died in 1806. No British prime minister since then has been so young when appointed to the office, and none has held office without a break for so long.

Pitt's time in office, much of it overshadowed by war with France, was distinguished by the wide-ranging administrative and economic reforms he introduced. It was Pitt who first made the British pay income tax, from 1799 to 1816.

1783
The Montgolfier balloon ascents

The Montgolfier brothers, Joseph (1740–1810) and Etienne (1745–99), from Annonay in France, made aviation history with their hot-air balloons in 1783. They were convinced that the same kind of heated air which sent pieces of paper wafting up the chimney from their home fire could also be used to lift men up into the air.

After several months' work, they felt confident enough to give a public demonstration of their experiments on June 4, 1783. They released a large balloon over the heads of the astonished citizens of Annonay. The balloon was made of linen lined with paper and filled with hot air from a straw and wool fire.

At Versailles in September, Louis XVI and Marie Antoinette witnessed the first flight by living creatures, when the Montgolfiers sent a sheep, a duck and a rooster into the air in a basket suspended from their balloon. A month later, the first person to fly, Pilâtre de Rozier, went up in a Montgolfier balloon.

1783
The *Pyroscaphe*

Several attempts had been made to propel boats by steam power before the Frenchman, Claude, Marquis de Jouffroy d'Abbans (1751–1832) achieved the first real success in 1783.

Earlier, he had had a boat built which carried paddles designed on a system similar to the paddling movement of water birds. When this proved unsuccessful, Jouffroy returned to the paddle wheels with which others had experimented before him.

His new boat, the 182-tonne *Pyroscaphe*, carried a double-acting steam engine, on the basis of James Watt's recent improvements, to activate the ratchet mechanism which turned the paddle wheels. On July 15, 1783 the *Pyroscaphe* steamed upstream on the river Saône near Lyons for fifteen minutes, the first boat ever to be propelled by steam power against a current.

Jouffroy did not have the capital to carry his experiments further, and the steamboat was perfected by men in the USA and Britain.

1786
Burns's *Poems*

Robert Burns (1759–96), a young farmer from Ayrshire, published his *Poems Chiefly in the Scottish Dialect* in Kilmarnock in 1786. The poems brought him immediate fame, which was consolidated by his magnificent narrative poem *Tam O' Shanter* (1790) and his many beautiful lyrics, including *Comin' thro' the Rye, A Red, Red Rose* and *Auld Lang Syne*. Today, Burns is revered as Scotland's national poet.

1787
Formation of the MCC

The Marylebone Cricket Club (MCC), the first international administrative body of world cricket, was formed in 1787. An historic meeting of the club in 1788 revised cricket's existing rules and laid the basis of the modern game. MCC first met on Thomas Lord's ground in Dorset Square, London. When Mr Lord moved to St John's Wood in 1809, MCC also moved there.

1787
Mozart appointed Chamber musician

Wolfgang Amadeus Mozart (1756–91), who was born in Salzburg, Austria, showed an extraordinary musical talent from his earliest years, and began composing when he was only five.

In his short life, often over-shadowed by poverty and illness aggravated by over-work, Mozart wrote some of the finest music ever composed. His work included symphonies, operas, concertos, sonatas, chamber pieces, and masses – over six hundred compositions in all. His operas, including *Le Nozze di Figaro*, ('The Marriage of Figaro') and *Die Zauberflöte* ('The Magic Flute'), are among the greatest of all his works.

Official recognition of his genius, in the form of an appointment as Chamber musician to the Emperor Joseph II (1741–90) in Vienna, came in December 1787. But it was too late to rescue Mozart and his loving wife, Constance, from poverty. He died in Vienna in 1791, and was buried in a pauper's grave.

1788
The impeachment of Warren Hastings

The trial of Warren Hastings (1732–

181

1818) for corruption and atrocities committed while he was Governor General of India from 1774 to 1785, began in Westminster Hall in February 1788.

Hastings had been a very able administrator in India, but had been high-handed in his efforts to raise money to defend British possessions there against the French. He had been forced to desperate measures because British resources were stretched to their limits by the War of American Independence. The English politicians, led by Edmund Burke, Charles James Fox and Richard Sheridan, who demanded Hasting's impeachment, had misunderstood his activities and greatly exaggerated their evils.

Hastings was found not guilty in 1795, seven years after the trial had begun. Although the impeachment had been unjust, it did draw attention to India's problems and awoke Britain to a sense of her responsibilities there.

1788
Hepplewhite's *Guide*

George Hepplewhite (d. 1786) was an English cabinet-maker who planned his book, *The Cabinet Maker and Upholsterer's Guide, or Repository of Designs for Every Article of Household Furniture* simply as a catalogue to attract buyers to his furniture designs. It was published in 1788, two years after his death, and is now regarded as a major expression of eighteenth-century English furniture design.

1789
The mutiny on HMS *Bounty*

The *Bounty* was a Royal Navy ship which in 1789 became the centre of the most famous mutiny in naval history.

Her captain, William Bligh (1754–1817), had been ordered to Tahiti in 1787 to obtain breadfruit trees and take them to the West Indies for cultivation. The ship had left Tahiti and was far out in the Pacific near Tofua when the majority of the crew, led by the master's mate Fletcher Christian, mutinied on April 28, 1789, probably because they wanted to stay in Tahiti and not return to England.

They set Bligh and eighteen members of his crew adrift in the ship's longboat. With only a compass to help him, Bligh arrived safely in Timor in June 1789 – a journey of nearly 6,500 kilometres in an open boat. It was a remarkable feat of navigation.

Bligh later became Governor of New South Wales. Some of the mutineers, led again by Christian, settled on remote Pitcairn Island. Others were caught and hanged.

1789
Louis calls the Estates General

Louis XVI (1754–93) ascended the throne in 1774 and by 1788 the public treasury was empty, the State was burdened with a huge debt, and the people were crushed under heavy taxes. Louis and his ministers were therefore forced to call together the Estates General – nobility, clergy, and Third Estate – for the first time since 1614 to try to find a way to pay the nation's debts.

The Estates General met at Versailles on May 5, 1789. The Third Estate hoped that this meeting would begin granting them the equality and freedom to take part in government which they had long been denied, but it soon became clear that they could expect no such results.

The Third Estate broke away and, joined by some of the clergy, on June 17, proclaimed itself the National Assembly, representing the majority of the French people. The alarmed king had the delegates locked out of their usual meeting

The people of Paris storm the Bastille at the start of the French revolution, assisted by mutinous troops.

1789
The fall of the Bastille

place, but the new National Assembly moved to a nearby indoor tennis court where, on June 20, they took the famous *Jeu de Paume* oath not to separate until 'the Constitution of this realm has been established on solid foundations'.

By the end of June most of the clergy and many nobles had joined the Assembly. On July 7 it became a Constituent Assembly and began planning a new constitution for France.

When Louis XVI dismissed his chief minister Necker on July 11, 1789, replacing him and other officials with aristocrats, the people of Paris rose in revolt. They were already discontented with soaring bread prices and unemployment, and were by now inspired by the activities of the Third Estate at Versailles. To fight the king and the troops he was placing round Paris, they needed weapons. One place which might provide them was the massive, brooding Bastille prison, where many people had been imprisoned without trial.

A mob demanding arms arrived at the Bastille early on July 14, and swarmed into the outer courts. The Governor, Launay, ordered his small garrison force to fire and many people fell dead. Provoked to fury by news of this, more people, including French Guards with cannon, surged to the Bastille. Late in the afternoon Launay surrendered. He was dragged off to prison but was beheaded by the mob on the way.

The Bastille held only seven prisoners. The real significance of its fall was symbolic: the king had been defeated by Paris. The people of Paris emphasized their victory over the king when a great crowd marched to Versailles in October and forced the royal family and the National Assembly to return to Paris.

1789
Discovery of uranium

Uranium, a heavy, radioactive metallic element, was discovered in 1789 by a German scientist, Martin Klaproth (1743–1817) who had no inkling of the momentous nature of his discovery. It was not until 1938 that scientists realized uranium's very special properties. It is the only element so far known to science which can readily be used in the creation of nuclear (atomic) energy.

1789
Bentham's theories published

Jeremy Bentham (1748–1832) was one of the most influential philosophers of his age. He constantly questioned and criticized the British law and constitution, saying they should be improved and that the purpose of law and government should be to create 'the greatest happiness of the greatest number'. He ex-

plained his theory in *Introduction to Principles of Morals and Legislation.*

1789
Blake's *Songs of Innocence*

William Blake (1757–1827) published his second book of poems, *Songs of Innocence*, in 1789. Although the poems were bright, fresh lyrics about innocence, they still contained the mystical, magical thoughts which were to set Blake's poems apart from the writings of most of his contemporaries. An engraver, he etched his poems and their decorative designs on copper plates himself.

William Blake was a mystic, a poet and a remarkable artist, as shown by this illustration for Dante's *Divina Commedia* (Tate Gallery, London).

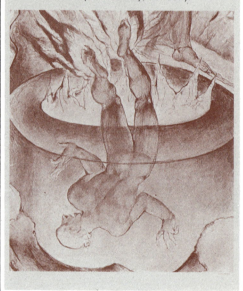

1791
Galvani's experiments on electricity

In 1786, Luigi Galvani (1737–98), anatomy professor at Bologna University, was using a steel scalpel to dissect a frog's leg when an assistant in his laboratory produced a spark with a static-electricity machine. The frog's leg twitched.

Galvani thought this phenomenon so intriguing that he tried other experiments. Once he went out in a thunderstorm to see if lightning would also cause a dead frog's legs, attached by a brass hook to an iron fence, to contract. It did.

Galvani thought he had discovered 'animal electricity' and that it was present in the material of an animal's nerve and its corresponding muscle. In fact, he was observing electricity in motion: the frog's legs were acting as electrolytes allowing electrons to flow from one piece of metal to the other, causing a momentary current.

The publication of Galvani's experiments in 1791 helped lead other scientists to the discovery of electric currents.

1791
Sheraton's *Drawing Book*

Thomas Sheraton (1751–1806) was, with Chippendale and Hepplewhite, one of the three major influences on English furniture design in the eighteenth century. His *Cabinet Maker's and Upholsterer's Drawing Book*, published in parts between 1791 and 1794, included designs for many types of furniture, much of it decorated with veneers and inlays rather than carving. He seems to have been a designer rather than a maker of furniture; nothing made by him is known to exist.

1791
Paine's *The Rights of Man*

Thomas Paine (1737–1809) was an English radical thinker who played a part in both the American and the French Revolutions.

He went to America in 1776, and was soon in the midst of the colonists' struggle for independence, writing a series of pamphlets encouraging resistance to the British (*see 1776 US declare independence*).

He returned to England in 1787, but was forced to flee, this time to France, to avoid being arrested because of the extreme language of his book *The Rights of Man*, published in two parts in 1791 and 1792. In the book, Paine supported the French Revolution and said that Britain, too, should rid herself of her monarchy and set up a revolutionary government. He also suggested a number of reforms to help the aged and poor in Britain which seemed revolutionary then, but which have since been adopted.

Paine was made a member of the Convention in France, and returned to the United States in 1802.

1792
France becomes a Republic

Growing political activity in Paris, a serious economic crisis, and a threat of war from other countries in Europe, combined to move the journeymen, craftsmen and wage-earners of the city, the *sans-culottes*, to revolt in 1792. Early on August 10, great crowds surrounded the Tuileries Palace, where Louis XVI and his family had virtually been prisoners since their attempted flight from France in June, 1791. They had been recaptured at Varennes and had been completely mistrusted by the French people since.

The king and his family took refuge with the Legislative Assembly, but the *sans-culottes*, armed with pikes, moved in and forced the Assembly to suspend the king from his duties. They also demanded that a National Convention be elected to plan a new constitution.

The Convention met on September 20, and the next day voted unanimously to abolish the monarchy. In December Louis was brought to trial and called upon to answer for repeated acts of treason against the Republic. A death sentence was passed and Louis was executed on January 21, 1793 at the Place de la Révolution.

1793
The Reign of Terror

The Reign of Terror (1793–94) took place in France at a time of great crisis, when exiled royalists were plotting against the government and foreign powers, including Prussia, Austria and Great Britain, were threatening invasion.

The makers of the Terror were the extreme republican Jacobins, dominated by Maximilien Robespierre (1758–94), who were swept into power by mob violence in June 1793. Working through the Committee of Public Safety which

Marie Antoinette, wife of Louis XVI, is led to the guillotine.

had been set up by the Paris revolutionary, Georges Jacques Danton (1759–94), the Jacobins imposed a dictatorship on France.

In the name of 'public safety', their Revolutionary Tribunal sent hundreds of people, including Queen Marie Antoinette, aristocrats, priests, officials and ordinary citizens to the guillotine. Those who protested, like Charlotte Corday (1768–93) were guillotined (she had stabbed to death the Jacobin Jean Paul Marat (1743–93) in his bath and eventually even Danton was executed.

It was not until July 1794 that anarchy in the provinces, financial and economic chaos and a general horror at the bloodshed, combined to bring Robespierre down. The French army had begun to win victories against their enemies, too, and Robespierre's repressive rule was no longer needed. He was executed without trial on July 28, as were many of his followers.

1795
Mungo Park explores Africa

In 1788 the African Association was formed to encourage exploration and promote British interests in the virtually unknown continent of Africa. One of its first objectives was 'to ascertain the course and, if possible, the rise and termination of that mysterious river – the Niger'.

A Major Houghton responded to the call in 1790 but, as nothing was heard from him after 1791, he was presumed killed. Mungo Park (1771–1806), a Scottish surgeon, requested that he be allowed to step into Houghton's place and the African Association accepted.

Park began his expedition in December 1795, and had several narrow escapes. But he collected the required information and published his adventures in *Travels in the Interior of Africa* (1799).

The book aroused so much interest that Park was commissioned to make another expedition in 1805. During this journey his canoe overturned and he and his companions were drowned.

1796
The first cowpox inoculations

Country people in England had long suspected that there was a connection between cowpox and smallpox. They had noticed that people who worked with cattle and who contracted cowpox never seemed to catch smallpox.

Edward Jenner (1749–1823), a doctor in Berkeley, Gloucester, set out to find if there was any truth in the belief. In May 1796 he injected liquid from cowpox sores into a young boy, James Phipps, who caught the disease but the sores soon healed. Later Jenner injected Phipps with smallpox but it had no effect on the boy's health: the cowpox had made him immune.

In spite of initial opposition the practice of vaccination gained steady support both in Great Britain and abroad, so that today smallpox has been virtually eradicated all over the world.

This drawing of a sculpture of Jenner shows the first cowpox inoculation.

1797
The Spithead Mutiny

The English writer Samuel Johnson described life at sea in the eighteenth century as follows: 'No man will be a sailor who has contrivance enough to get himself into jail; for being in a ship is being in a jail, with the chance of being drowned. A man in a jail has more room, better food, and commonly better company.'

Conditions in the navy were virtually intolerable and led the men to mutiny at Spithead and the Nore in 1797. Of the two mutinies that at Spithead was conducted in the most sensible manner; the mutineers put a deliberate plan into action and appointed delegates to negotiate. When their chief demands were met they returned to duty. The Nore mutiny, however, was little more than a dangerous and unnecessary brawl.

As a result of the mutinies several changes were made to Navy regulations. Conditions and pay were improved and the British sailor became a respected member of society instead of a social outcast.

1798
Publication of *The Ancient Mariner*

Lyrical Ballards (1798) published anonymously by the poets William Wordsworth (1770–1850) and Samuel Taylor Coleridge (1772–1834) contained one of the finest magical English poems – *The Ancient Mariner*. The poem was based on a dream related to Coleridge by a friend. At about the same time Coleridge wrote his magnificent *Kubla Khan* and the first part of *Christabel*.

1798
Publication of Malthus's theories

The publication of *Essay on the Principle of Population* by Thomas Robert Malthus (1766–1834) aroused considerable controversy – largely due to the fact that his theories were misunderstood. He stated that population increases at a faster rate than food supplies increase and that ultimately there would be insufficient food to go round.

1798
First performance of Haydn's *Creation*

The *Creation*, the popular oratorio by the Austrian composer Franz Joseph Haydn (1732–1809) was first produced in Vienna in 1798. Written to words from *Genesis* and a poem by Lidley, the work was first performed in London in 1800. It became so popular in England that several choral societies were formed specially to sing it.

1798
Rebellion in Ireland

In 1790 the Irish patriot Wolfe Tone (1763–98), inspired by the French Revolution, helped to form the United Irishmen. This society was devoted to the creation of a United Ireland and the elimination of English rule. Tone believed that armed rebellion was the only way to achieve these objectives and he enlisted the aid of the French.

In December, 1796 he sailed from Brest with French troops under the command of General Hoche, but bad weather forced them back.

Two years later an uprising was attempted in Dublin but the leaders were arrested and on June 26, 1798 Vinegar Hill, the headquarters of the United Irishmen, was stormed. A last attempt was made by Tone in October when he landed with a small force at Lough Swilly in the north, but he was captured by the British. He was sentenced to be hanged but on November 19 he took his own life.

1798
The Battle of the Nile

British attitude towards the French Revolution was largely sympathetic until the execution of Louis XVI (*see 1793 The Reign of Terror*). When the revolutionaries began interfering in the affairs of other countries, Britain and other nations declared war on France in 1793.

At the same time a young officer, Napoleon Bonaparte (1769–1821) was beginning to make a name for himself and in 1798 he invaded Egypt, capturing Malta on the way, with a view to threatening British power in India.

Prior to Napoleon's departure for Egypt the British became aware that he was preparing a fleet at Toulon and they sent a squadron under Horatio Nelson (1758–1805) to investigate. Unfortunately Nelson's ship, *Vanguard*, was damaged in a storm and whilst it was being repaired at Sardinia the French set sail.

Not knowing Napoleon's destination Nelson had to search for the French ships. It was to be two months before he finally caught up with them – at Aboukir Bay, near Alexandria.

On August 1, 1798 Nelson engaged with the French and all but four of the enemy ships were taken or destroyed in the battle at the mouth of the Nile. Napoleon's army was cut off in Egypt and all thoughts of advancing to India had to be abandonned.

1799
Publication of 'Sacred Songs'

Novalis was the pseudonym of the German writer and poet Friedrich Ludwig von Hardenberg (1772–1801). His *Geistliche Lieder* ('Sacred Songs', 1799) had great influence upon the development of symbolism and the Romantic Movement. His other works include *Hymnen an die Nacht* ('Hymns to the Night', 1800) written on the death of his betrothed Sophie von Kühn.

1800
Volta invents first battery

Count Alessandro Volta (1745–1827), the Italian physicist, made several important discoveries in electricity. Among them was that if two different metals placed in a salt solution are connected by a wire an electric current runs along the wire. In 1800 Volta took this a stage further by placing several pairs together to produce what is now known as the voltaic pile, or battery.

1800
Owen takes over New Lanark Mills

The British industrialist and social reformer, Robert Owen (1771–1858), was convinced that if working and living conditions were of a high standard the character of people would improve and they would work for the good of the community. In 1809 he moved to New Lanark, Scotland, to manage the cotton mills. By improving conditions and providing schools he created a model community and the mills prospered.

In 1817 he advocated the creation of self-supporting 'villages of co-operation' but people in England were not interested. He went to America to form such a community at New Harmony, but the project failed.

After returning to Britain he joined a working class movement which led to the formation of large trade unions, but they collapsed in 1834. Owen's concept of co-operation did, however, eventually lead to the formation of the co-operative movement that flourishes to this day.

1801
Union of England and Ireland

Following the unsuccessful rebellion of 1798 (*see 1798 Rebellion in Ireland*) the British prime minister William Pitt (1759–1806) decided that the only way to restore law and order was for Britain and Ireland to be united.

The Act of Union was passed by the British government on July 2, 1800. The Irish, reacting favourably to the promise of Roman Catholic emancipation (and a fair amount of bribery), passed the Act on August 1. The new Act became law on January 1, 1801. It formed the two kingdoms into one under the same flag, monarch, and parliament.

About a month later the cabinet began considering its promise to the Catholics. But George III heard of their proposals and flatly refused to accept the idea of allowing the Catholics any political rights and Pitt resigned in protest.

1801
Flinders circumnavigates Australia

James Cook called the continent 'New South Wales', the Dutch christened it 'New Holland', but it was the British sailor Matthew Flinders (1774–1814) who gave it the name by which it is known today – Australia.

Whilst serving as a surveyor in the Royal Navy at Sydney from 1795–1799, Flinders mapped the eastern coast of Australia and circumnavigated Tasmania which up to that time had been regarded as part of the mainland.

In 1801 he was sent again to Australia and spent the next two years charting the whole of the south and east coast and most of the north. In carrying out this survey he sailed all the way round Australia.

Returning home in 1803 he was captured by the French, remaining a prisoner for six years, so it was not until 1810 that he was able to announce his discoveries.

1803
Dalton develops his atomic theory

John Dalton (1766–1844), the English chemist, began work on his atomic theory in 1803. He proposed that all elements are made up of atoms, that atoms were so small they were indivisible, that elements combined because their atoms joined together, and he gave each element an atomic weight. His theories have been modified in the light of recent developments in nuclear physics.

1804
The first steam railways

The first iron railway was laid at Coalbrookdale, Shropshire and the trucks were pulled by horses. Richard Trevithick (1771–1833), a Cornish mining engineer, who had experimented with steam powered road vehicles (until one blew up!) was the first to use a steam engine to haul the trucks.

On February 11, 1804, at the Pen-y-Darren ironworks in Wales, the engine hauled a twenty tonne load from Merthyr Tydfil to Abercyon, a distance of over fifteen kilometres. In spite of the pessi-

mists' predictions that the wheels would slip on the iron rails, the trial was successful.

Trevithick was convinced that the railway could also be used for passenger travel and in 1808 he set up a small railway in London. The engine, the *Catch-me-who-can*, carried people around a circular track at one shilling a ride – until one day an engine wheel broke and Trevithick dropped the scheme.

1804
Napoleon becomes emperor

On May 18, 1804 Napoleon Bonaparte was declared Emperor of France. A coronation ceremony was held at Notre Dame in Paris on December 2 and the

(Left) Napoleon as First Consul; (right) Nelson, Britain's greatest admiral, killed at Trafalgar.

republican constitution for which the people of France had fought the revolution existed no longer (*see 1792 France becomes a Republic*).

Napoleon's meteoric rise to power began in 1785 when he received a commission in the La Fère artillery regiment. In 1793 he was put in charge of the artillery at Toulon which was being invaded by English and Spanish forces and he was largely responsible for the recapture of the city. Two years later he crushed the royalist rising in Paris with just 'a whiff of grapeshot' and soon after he set out on his Italian Campaign before proceeding to Egypt (*see 1798 Battle of the Nile*)

In 1799 Napoleon returned to France, overthrew the Directory (the executive group which held power from 1795–99), and set himself up as leader. By 1802 he had secured the consulate for life together with the power to name his successor. At the same time he secured peace with Britain, the first time France had been at peace since 1792. He could now concentrate on the reorganization of France: he established the Bank of France, simplified the law, encouraged trade and industry, and introduced a system of public education.

1805
The Battle of Trafalgar

Napoleon utilized the peace of 1802 to strengthen internal matters in France (*see 1804 Napoleon becomes Emperor*), but he also extended French influence abroad. Britain realized the danger inherent in Napoleon's increasing strength and decided to make the first move in 1803 by declaring war.

The French reasoned that the only way to defeat Britain was by invasion, so troops were made ready at Boulogne. But the British ruled the seas, so Napoleon had first to get the British fleet out of the

Channel.

French and Spanish ships were ordered to sail for the West Indies in the hope that Britain would give chase, but only thirty-three, under Admiral Villeneuve (1763–1806), managed to evade the British fleet that was laying in wait. Those that did escape were pursued by Admiral Horatio Nelson in the *Victory* and Villeneuve returned to Cadiz in Spain.

Napoleon then ordered the French and Spanish fleets to the Mediterranean and two days later, October 21, 1805, the British attacked off Cape Trafalgar. The French were completely defeated and Napoleon's invasion plans duly thwarted. But the victory was won at the cost of the life of Britain's greatest admiral, Nelson, who was killed during the battle.

Napoleon Bonaparte

October 22 he inflicted a serious defeat upon Austria at Ulm without even fighting a battle and he also took Vienna.

On November 28 he met with the combined Russian and Austrian forces at Austerlitz. There were three emperors on the battlefield: Napoleon of France, Alexander I (1777–1825) of Russia, and Francis II (1768–1835) of Austria.

Napoleon's army of 65,000 men was outnumbered by the Russians and Austrians who had some 83,000 troops at their command. Nevertheless the French were the overwhelming victors in the battle on December 2. They lost only about 7,000 men whereas some 35,000 Russians and Austrians were killed or captured. It was one of Napoleon's greatest victories.

As a result, Alexander's army was forced to retreat to the east, the Austrians signed the Peace of Pressburg, and the coalition ended.

1805
Wordsworth writes *The Prelude*

Some of the best loved English poems such as *Daffodils*, *On Westminster Bridge*, and *The Solitary Reaper* were written by William Wordsworth (1770–1850). In 1805 he wrote one of his longest poems, *The Prelude*, an autobiographical work, but it was not published until 1850. Wordsworth was made poet laureate in 1843.

1805
The Battle of Austerlitz

In July 1805 Britain, Austria, Russia, and Prussia formed a coalition against France. Napoleon's immediate reaction was to invade Germany and Austria. On

1806
End of the Holy Roman Empire

The Holy Roman Empire is sometimes regarded as originating with Charlemagne (*see* AD 800 *Charlemagne crowned Holy Roman Emperor*) although some claim it began with the coronation in AD962 of Otto the Great, King of Germany, as Roman Emperor. The last emperor, Francis II of Austria, abolished the title following the defeat at Austerlitz, so that it would not pass to Napoleon.

1807
Hegel writes *The Phenomenolgy of Spirit*

Georg Wiljelm Friedrich Hegel (1770–1831) was one of the most influential of German philosophers. His writings included *Logic, Encyclopaedia of the Philosophical Sciences, Philosophy of Right* and *The Phenomenology of Spirit*. Although his works were involved and often obscure, his followers included Karl Marx and other historians who used Hegel's works to prove the inevitability of radical change.

1808
The Peninsular War

In July 1808 the Spanish, ruled by Napoleon's brother Joseph, rebelled and defeated the French at Baylen. The British realized that this was an opportunity to attack France through Spain and sent Sir Arthur Wellesley (1769–1852), later Duke of Wellington, to Portugal. He defeated the French at Vimeiro and then returned to England.

Sir John Moore (1761–1809) then took command and advanced into Spain to cut French lines of communication but Napoleon was in Spain at the time and he forced Moore to retreat to Corunna on the coast, where Moore was killed in 1809.

Wellington took a new army to Por-tugal and marched towards Madrid. He beat the French at Talavera but then had to retreat and he remained on the defensive until he achieved a victory at Salamanca in 1812. Wellington then took Madrid and, by a victory at Vittoria in 1813, drove the French out of the country.

1809
Metternich becomes Austrian chancellor

Prince Clemens Wenzel Lothar Metternich (1773–1859) was the principal figure in European politics following his appointment as Chancellor and Foreign Minister of Austria in 1809.

It was largely through his efforts that the Austrian Empire remained intact for the next thirty-nine years until the revolution of 1848 (*see 1848 European Revolution*). The spirit of revolution had been rife in Europe ever since the French Revolution in 1789 and Metternich did his utmost to suppress it wherever it occurred. As foreign minister he raised the international status of his country and led the countries of Europe in a coalition that checked the career of Napoleon; as a dedicated Austrian he always put the interests of his own country first.

In many ways Metternich was not typical of the time in which he lived, for he represented an age that was almost past. Many people resented his methods of preserving that age, but in so doing he ensured peace in Europe during his period of office.

1810
Prizefight between Cribb and Molineux

The American boxer Tom Cribb (1781–1848) was the first of the bare-knuckled prizefighters to achieve everlasting acclaim. This reputation was gained principally through his two fights with Tom

Molineux (1784–1818), a freed Negro slave. Cribb won both although he received a sound beating in the first and only won the second because Molineux had eaten a boiled chicken and an apple pie washed down with half a gallon of porter for his breakfast.

1810
Northumberland miners' strike

Coal miners in Northumberland, England, ceased work in 1810 in support of their protest against an alteration of their terms of yearly binding.

This annual bond had been a cause of contention for many years and was largely responsible for a long-term strike in 1765.

In 1810 troops were called in but the strike was eventually settled through the intervention of a clergyman, William Nesfield.

Napoleon's retreat from Moscow.

1811
Kleist's *Prinz Friedrich von Homburg*

Heinrich von Kleist (1777–1811) was a German dramatist and poet. His best plays are still popular today, notably *Prinz Friedrich von Homburg*, for which the scene is Prussia under the Great Elector. He wrote some admirable short tales, the finest of which perhaps is *Michael Kohlhaas*, a tale set in the days of Luther.

1811
Luddite Riots

The first outbreaks of the Luddite Riots occurred in and around Nottingham, England, in 1811. They were possibly named after a workman, Ned Ludd. Historians have never agreed as to whether the riots were the result of a secret, national movement with branches throughout Britain, or whether they were a series of disconnected movements.

The members of the movement were factory hand-workers whose objective was to destroy new factory machinery. As the Industrial Revolution developed, men began to realize that the machines could work faster and more efficiently than they could. They felt their jobs were seriously threatened.

Masked members of the movement broke into factories in the middle of the night and smashed up the new machines. The movement soon spread, and by 1812 machinery was being destroyed in York-shire, Lancashire, Derbyshire and Leicestershire. By 1813 many Luddites had been brought to trial at York Assizes where many were sentenced to death or transported overseas.

1811
Nash designs Regent's Park

John Nash (1752–1835) had already gained a considerable reputation as an architect when he came to the notice of the Prince of Wales (later Prince Regent) who engaged him to plan the new Regent's Park in London in 1811. Nash's greatness lay in his ability to plan whole districts of London as though they were landscape gardens.

1812
Battle of Borodino

The Battle of Borodino is remembered chiefly for the tremendous loss of life incurred by both the French and Russian armies. But it is also remembered because it was Napoleon's ill-fated attack on Moscow and the beginning of defeat for the French emperor.

Napoleon invaded the vast land mass of Russia with a huge army, narrowly defeating the Russians at Borodino. But when his army finally reached Moscow he found the Russians had burned the city and deserted it. His army was cold, hungry and sick; and forced to retreat, his men suffered miserably from the effects of the harsh Russian winter. Only 32,000 of his 600,000 strong army were to survive and the Russians were to lose 42,000 men out of 121,000. Meanwhile Napoleon hurried back to Paris to raise new levies.

This humiliating expedition encouraged the nations of Europe, who now saw some hope in massing their armies against Napoleon.

1812
Grimms' *Kinder-und Hausmärchen*

The brothers Grimm, Jacob Ludwig Carl (1785–1863) and Wilhelm Carl (1786–1859) both studied law at Marburg in Germany and both were students of folk-lore. In 1812 they published their first edition of *Kinder-und Hausmärchen* ('Fairy Tales'), which includes *Rumpelstiltskin* and *Hansel und Gretel*. The tales have been translated into many languages, so that children from all over the world are familiar with them.

1813
Jane Austen's *Pride and Prejudice*

Jane Austen (1775–1817) was born in Hampshire, England, the daughter of a rector. She was a quiet, sensitive person and the author of six novels, the first of which, *Pride and Prejudice* did not appear until 1813. Her novels are wonderful documentaries of the English comfortable middle-class life in the nineteenth century, and her caustic wit and ability to depict rounded, three-dimensional characters have made her one of England's best-loved novelists.

1813
Battle of Nations

Encouraged by Napoleon's crushing setback in Russia, a new form of nationalism began to grow among the peoples of Europe. In Holland, Belgium and Italy, people increasingly wanted to be rid of Napoleon. Prussia reorganized its army, encouraging its people 'to defend the state.'

In October 1813 the combined armies of Prussia, Russia and Austria aided by Great Britain and Sweden defeated Napoleon near Leipzig, Germany, in the Battle of Nations. On March 21, 1814 Paris was taken and in April Napoleon abdicated. He was sent into exile on Elba, a little island off the coast of Italy.

Meanwhile the Bourbon monarchy was restored. Louis XVIII (1755–1824), brother of the executed Louis XVI was made king, but it was not long before he had made himself extremely unpopular by reversing some of the achievements of the Revolution. This opened the way for Napoleon's return from Elba (*see 1815 Battle of Waterloo*).

1813
Elizabeth Fry visits Newgate Gaol

Elizabeth Fry (1780–1845) was an English Quaker. In 1813 a friend told her about the miserable conditions of prisoners in London's Newgate Gaol. Elizabeth went straight to the Gaol where she found three hundred women, tried and untried, herded together with their children in filth and squalor. From that day she devoted herself to prison reform.

1814
Kean plays Shylock

Edmund Kean (1787–1833) was an extraordinary man who established a reputation on the English stage as the greatest tragic actor of his day. In 1814 he appeared as Shylock in Shakespeare's *Merchant of Venice* at Drury Lane. The supporting cast was poor, but Kean was an overwhelming success and for several years he dominated the English theatre.

1815
McAdam begins road construction

John Loudon McAdam (1756–1836) revolutionized road making in Britain. He first began experimenting in 1798 and concluded that roads should be made of successive layers of broken stone, for the weight of the traffic would bind them into a smooth surface. In 1815, as surveyor-general of Bristol roads, he began employing his method and it was soon in general use.

1815
Battle of Waterloo

When allied forces captured Paris in March 1814, the great French emperor, Napoleon Bonaparte was sent into exile on the Mediterranean island of Elba. Ten months later he escaped. He landed in France and advanced towards Paris. Old soldiers flocked to him and King Louis XVIII, so recently restored to his throne, fled abroad.

The allies gathered their forces. An Austrian force prepared to attack in the south, a vast Russian army advanced from the north. In Belgium, Marshal Blücher (1742–1819) commanded a Prussian army of over one hundred thousand while the Duke of Wellington had almost as many British, Dutch, German and Belgian troops assembled near Brussels. Napoleon moved fast. With 120,000 men he marched into Belgium to attack his enemies before they could unite.

Wellington had defeated most of Napoleon's best marshals during his campaign in Portugal and Spain (1808–14). He had not met Napoleon before the four-day campaign of Waterloo. The battle was a famous one, though neither general was at his best. Wellington did well to hold off the main French attack all day on June 18, forcing the Imperial Guard, the cream of Napoleon's army, to retreat.

Before sunset Blücher's Prussians began to arrive, and the French were doomed. Napoleon abdicated, and this time his enemies sent him farther away – to the island of St Helena in the South Atlantic. He did not return again.

Arthur Wellesley, 1st Duke of Wellington

1815
Congress of Vienna

The congress met in order to settle the affairs of Europe after the defeat of Napoleon in 1814. France was represented by the great Talleyrand (1754–1838), but the congress was dominated by Prince von Metternich (1773–1859) of Austria and Viscount Castlereagh (1769–1822) of Britain.

Both these men were strong conservatives, who believed that the revolutionary ideas released all over Europe after the French revolution of 1789 were responsible for the troubles throughout the continent since then, and ought to be suppressed. Napoleon's escape from Elba forced the congress to reach a settlement, which it did just before Waterloo.

Most of the representatives at Vienna wanted to restore the balance of power and to restore rulers to the thrones they held before the French Revolution. The settlement was therefore a victory for the big powers over small states and for the old form of kingly government over republicanism. It tried, and succeeded, to put the clock back in Europe, but it thus ensured that revolution would break out again. On the other hand, the settlement prevented a general war in Europe for a century.

1815
The Davy lamp

Sir Humphry Davy (1778–1829), the British chemist, was a brilliantly inventive scientist who suggested (among other ideas) laughing gas as an anaesthetic (first used long after his death). He invented the miners' safety lamp in 1815 and refused to patent, so that everyone might benefit quickly. Others invented similar lamps, notably George Stephenson, the railway engineer.

1816
Invention of the stethoscope

A stethoscope is the instrument used by doctors to listen to the sounds made by the heart, lungs or other organs inside a patient's body. Its inventor was a French doctor, René Laënnec (1781–1826), who first used a paper tube and later a wooden pipe. The modern stethoscope which hooks into both ears was developed later.

1818
Grillparzer's *Sappho*

Franz Grillparzer (1791–1872), Austria's greatest playwright, wrote chiefly poetic dramas, some of which are better read than acted. Grillparzer suffered intellectual persecution as a result of strict censorship in Austria, and he eventually

stopped writing plays altogether. *Sappho*, written very quickly, is about love doomed to disappointment and the impossibility of reconciling life with art – themes that troubled Grillparzer personally.

1819
Peterloo Massacre

The years after the Battle of Waterloo were turbulent times in Britain. High unemployment brought the poorest workers close to starvation; there were strikes, riots and cases of machine-breaking (machines were blamed for unemployment). Calls for reform of politics and society were loud and continuous; cities like Manchester and Birmingham had a special grievance because they were not

Troops are sent in to break up a political meeting in Manchester, in the incident known as the Peterloo Massacre.

1819
Voyage of the *Savannah*

The *Savannah* crossed the Atlantic, from Savannah, Georgia, to Liverpool, England, in twenty-five days. That was a very fast time, but what made her voyage important was that the *Savannah* was a steamship – the first to make the Atlantic crossing.

The *Savannah* was built in New York as an ordinary sailing ship with masts and, like all ships then, a wooden hull. But before she sailed she was fitted with steam power and two enormous paddle wheels. She still kept her sails and on her trans-Atlantic crossing she probably covered a greater distance under sail than steam. Her paddle wheels could be drawn up and laid on the deck when not in use.

All the early steamers were fitted with sails as well as steam-driven paddle wheels, because the early steam engines were not perfectly reliable. By the end of the century, using screw-propellors instead of paddles, steamers were crossing the Atlantic in one-fifth of the time taken by the *Savannah*.

represented in Parliament. The government was worried by the disturbances and feared violent revolution.

On August 16, 1819 a large meeting was held on St Peter's Field, Manchester, to organize a petition for reform. The local magistrates, hearing talk of military drill and revolutionary flags, sent in soldiers to arrest the chief speaker, Henry Hunt (1773–1835). The soldiers were jostled by the angry people, cavalry went in to help them, discipline broke down and in the panic eleven people were killed and several hundred injured. The incident caused great anger; opponents of the government called it the 'Peterloo Massacre', recalling the slaughter at Waterloo.

1819
Keats's *The Eve of St Agnes*

Though he died at twenty-six of tuberculosis, John Keats (1795–1821) is one of the greatest and most loved of British Romantic poets. He brought a sense of magic and delight to English verse hardly known since the Elizabethans. The *Eve of St Agnes*, written like most of his best works during his passionate love for Fanny Brawne, is (said the poet Swinburne) 'a perfect and unsurpassable study in pure colour and clear melody'.

1819
The British acquire Singapore

The island of Singapore lies at the tip of the Malay peninsula. In 1819 it was a swampy, unattractive place, where no one lived except a few fishermen. The Dutch, who were the chief European power in the region, had overlooked the island when they were taking over all the important points in the Malay archipelago.

Stamford Raffles (1781–1826), an official of the British East India Company, persuaded Warren Hastings, then governor-general of India, that the place was worth having. The East India Company bought it from the Sultan of Johore, Raffles was appointed governor, and within four years he had made the settlement so prosperous that its annual trade was worth £2,500,000.

Situated approximately midway between India and China, Singapore was one of the most important British bases on the Far Eastern trade route for over 130 years.

1819
The start of the *Zollverein*

At the settlement of Europe made at the Congress of Vienna (1814) after the defeat of Napoleon, Germany became a confederation of independent states. A contest began between Austria and Prussia, the two largest, to decide which should dominate the new Germany.

One major economic problem in Germany was the existence of so many customs' barriers, not only between the different states but also between different provinces. The Prussians decided on a major reform of the customs' system, abolishing or reducing most tariffs (taxes on trade).

It soon became obvious that if the system were to work well, the numerous small states around Prussia, or in some cases actually surrounded by it, would have to be included. Pressure was brought to bear on these states to join the Prussian *Zollverein* (customs' union). The first one to join was the tiny principality of Schwarzburg-Sondershausen.

Gradually, more and more German states were drawn into the *Zollverein*. In less than forty years, nearly all of modern Germany belonged, preparing the way for the foundation of the German Empire in 1871.

1819
Schopenhauer: *The World as Will and Representation*

According to Arthur Schopenhauer (1788–1860), the will (including emotion, ambition and instinct) is hostile to – and stronger than – intelligence. He published *The World as Will and Representation* at the age of thirty-one but, like later works, it was largely ignored at the time.

1820
Shelley's *Prometheus Unbound*

Percy Bysshe Shelley (1792–1822), friend of Keats and Byron, was full of boundless love for mankind, but contempt for most of man's institutions (church, government, etc.). Above all he was a brilliant Romantic poet, the equal of Keats and Wordsworth, perhaps for some people greater than either. *Prometheus Unbound* is a long, difficult, philosophical drama; the book also contains some of Shelley's sweetest lyrics.

1820
Lamartine's *Méditations* published

In his *Méditations poétiques et religieuses*, Alphonse de Prat de Lamartine (1790–1869) gracefully expressed feelings of love and despair, hope and melancholy, and man's affinity with nature. Lamartine was a politician as well as a poet, a stirring speaker and one of the leading spirits of the revolution of 1848. He later wrote many volumes of history in a vain attempt to pay off his debts.

1820
The Brontës settle at Haworth

The Rev Patrick Brontë had three extraordinary daughters, Charlotte (1816–55), Emily (1818–48) and Anne (1820–49), who passed almost their whole, sadly short, lives at Haworth parsonage. Charlotte wrote *Jane Eyre* (1847) and three other novels; Emily wrote *Wuthering Heights* (1847) and Anne *The Tenant of Wildfell Hall* (1848). Their brother Bran-

Charlotte Brontë in 1850

well showed talent as a painter, but drank himself into an early grave.

1821
Greek nationalist revolt

Throughout the nineteenth century the empire of the Turks, which included south-east Europe and the Middle East, seemed to be on the point of collapse. The first people to launch a major war of independence against their Turkish masters were the Greeks. The Greeks attracted much sympathy in Europe, but the situation was complicated by the conflicting interests of the major powers, and by the tendency of the Greeks to fight each other no less bloodily than they fought the Turks.

Russia supported the Greeks; Britain and France favoured a compromise. In 1827 these three powers joined in destroying the Turkish-Egyptian fleet at Navarino, when it refused to obey instructions to withdraw from Greek waters. Next year Russia attacked by land and the Turks were forced to yield.

The Greeks gained their independence in 1830, though within limited boundaries. The modern frontiers were not achieved until the Balkan wars of 1912–13.

1822

Ampère's *Observations electro-dynamiques*

The unit for measuring an electric current is called an 'ampere', or 'amp' for short. It is named after the great French physicist and mathematician, André Marie Ampère (1775–1836), who was one of the founders of the science of electro-magnetism. In 1822 he published his discoveries in a work called *Observations electro-dynamiques*.

1823

Beethoven's ninth symphony

The ninth and last symphony of Ludwig van Beethoven (1770–1827) was written when the composer was almost totally deaf and gloom was gathering about him. But there is no gloom in this noble and glorious choral symphony. Written for the London Philharmonic Society, it was planned as early as 1816, as the third of a group of three symphonies.

The great events of Beethoven's sad but heroic life are all musical. Born in Bonn of Flemish descent, he went to Vienna in 1792 to study with Haydn (who was too upset by the recent death of Mozart to be much help), and was soon very popular as a pianist.

Growing deafness made Beethoven feel depressed and persecuted, though his fame increased rapidly after about 1800. He never gave up: 'I will seize Fate by the throat', he swore, and for thirty years he produced a stream of marvellous works. He revolutionized most forms of orchestral and choral music; his influence on music is as impossible to measure as Shakespeare's influence on literature.

Ludwig van Beethoven

1823

The Monroe Doctrine

This principle of United States foreign policy declared that no interference by European powers would be tolerated in North or South America. It was proclaimed by President James Monroe (1758–1831) but its real author was John Quincy Adams (1767–1848), the secretary of state.

It was provoked by European threats to reconquer the Spanish colonies in South America, which had recently gained independence. The doctrine was supported by Britain, and in practice it could only be enforced by the British navy.

Since 1823 the Monroe Doctrine has been often modified, restated, and occasionally challenged. The most recent example was the construction of Soviet Russian missile bases in Cuba; the United States government forced the Russians to dismantle them in the 'Cuba Crisis' of 1962 (*see 1961 Kennedy becomes President of USA*).

1823
Babbage's calculating machine

Charles Babbage (1792–1871), 'father of the computer', was a professor of mathematics at Cambridge University. In 1823 he began work on a calculating machine. It was never completed, nor was his second machine, which he called an 'analytical engine'. Nevertheless, Babbage's 'engine' was the direct ancestor of the modern digital computer.

1824
Death of Byron

Many people were shocked by Lord Byron (1788–1824): 'mad, bad and dangerous to know,' someone called him. Extremely handsome, fearlessly outspoken, and determined to experience everything that life offered, he was a romantic man as well as a Romantic poet (*Childe Harold, Don Juan*). When the Greeks rebelled against their Turkish overlords (*see 1821 Greek nationalist revolt*) Byron threw himself into their struggle, but he died of marsh fever at Missolonghi.

1825
Opening of the Stockton and Darlington Railway

The Stockton and Darlington Railway was the first public railway in the world which carried goods and passengers by locomotive. But it was not much of a railway by modern standards. Its real

Part of Babbage's 'analytical engine'.

purpose was to carry freight, and for fifteen of its forty kilometres the carriages could run downhill without the help of the engine.

Few passengers used the railway, and most of those who did hired a carriage which was drawn by horses (half the line was already built before the company decided that a steam locomotive should be used at all). There was no regular passenger service until some years later.

Still, the little Stockton–Darlington Railway marked the beginning of the great age of railway-building: twenty years later Britain had a railway network of over three thousand kilometres of track.

1825
Stephenson's *Rocket*

This rugged little railway engine was built by George Stephenson (1781–1848) and is preserved in the Science Museum, London. Four years after it was built, it defeated its rivals in trials held to choose a locomotive for the Liverpool–Manchester Railway, winning the £500 prize. It reached a speed of 48 kph and triumphantly proved the efficiency of Stephenson's multi-tubular boiler.

1825
Portugal acknowledges Brazilian independence

When Portugal finally recognized Pedro I as emperor of its former colony of Brazil, the largest country in South America became an independent state. In the same year Bolivia, taking its name from the great liberator, Simón Bolívar (1783–1830), the 'George Washington of South America', declared its independence from Spain. The colonial era in South America was over.

Except for Brazil, all South America had been under Spanish control, and the eclipse of Spain during the Napoleonic period (1808–14) encouraged nationalists throughout the continent to fight for independence. Besides Bolívar, the liberators of South America included José de San Martín (1778–1850) and Bernardo O'Higgins (1778–1842). San Martín's leadership was especially important in Argentina (independent 1816), while O'Higgins took the leading role in Chile (independent 1818).

Simón Bolívar

1826
Menai Bridge opened

This 175 metre suspension bridge linking Wales with the island of Anglesey was the world's longest suspension span. Still in use, it was built by Thomas Telford (1757–1834), the most famous

British engineer of his day. Telford built the Conway Suspension Bridge at about the same time, but his greatest work was improving the roads, bridges and harbours of his native Scotland.

1826
Niépce prints photographic image

Joseph Nicéphore Niépce (1765–1833) was one of the French pioneers of photography. He discovered that an image could be permanently recorded by the action of sunlight on a metal plate coated with asphaltum – a substance used as a ground in etching. Such a plate was printed in Paris in 1826, when Louis Daguerre approached Niépce to form a partnership. The successful daguerreotype process was perfected after Niépce's death (*see 1839 Daguerre demonstrates daguerreotype*).

1827
Ohm's law is published

One of the basic laws of electricity was discovered through the experiments of the German scientist Georg Simon Ohm (1787–1854), and published in a pamphlet in 1827.

Ohm's law is concerned with the relationship of resistance to potential difference and current in an electrical circuit. It is sometimes written as $I = \frac{E}{R}$, in which I is the current measured in amperes, E is the potential difference, and R is the resistance. The unit used for measurement of electrical resistance is now called an ohm, in honour of the discoverer of this law.

1827
Mendelssohn's *Midsummer Night's Dream*

Felix Mendelssohn (1809–47) wrote this as an overture to Shakespeare's play but besides his own compositions, he was famous as a pianist, as a conductor, and for his revival of the music of Bach. He was especially popular in England, and once entertained Queen Victoria by playing *Rule Britannia* with his right hand, whilst his left played the Austrian national anthem.

1827
Manzoni's *I promesi Sposi*

Alessandro Manzoni (1785–1873) was the greatest Italian writer of the Romantic period and *I promesi Sposi* ('The Betrothed') was his greatest work, perhaps the greatest Italian work of the century. Manzoni was already well-known as a poet, but after the last volume of *I promesi Sposi* was published in 1827 he became a great national hero.

1828
Death of Chaka

Chaka was the warrior-king of the Zulus. He turned them from a humble little tribe into a powerful military nation. Under his rule, which began soon after 1800, the Zulu *impis* (regiments) controlled almost the whole of Natal.

Chaka introduced the 'buffalo's horns' formation (troops drawn up in a crescent) and the short-bladed *assegai* (spear) for fighting at close quarters. He liked Europeans and allowed the British to settle at Port Elizabeth (Durban). Chaka was eventually assassinated by his successor, Dingaan.

1829
Rossini's 'William Tell'

The last opera of the Italian composer Gioacchino Antonio Rossini (1792–1868), *Guillaume Tell* ('William Tell'), about the Swiss hero, was produced in Paris, where Rossini lived. Except for the marvellously comic *Il Barbiere di Seviglia* ('The Barber of Seville'), it is his most famous work. During the next few years Rossini wrote some religious music and songs.

1829
London Metropolitan Police founded

A criminal who got caught in the early nineteenth century was likely to suffer very severe punishment. But most criminals were not caught, because there was no regular police force. Law enforcement was carried out by two or three constables appointed by each parish. They had no training and did not wear uniforms.

Many people were afraid that a regular police force would allow the government too much power to suppress the freedom of ordinary citizens. But with crime so high, police seemed necessary.

When he became home secretary in 1821 Sir Robert Peel (1788–1850) decided that London had to have a system of police. After a long delay (eight years), a force of three thousand top-hatted constables was created to police the area within twenty kilometres of Charing Cross. Later, the system was introduced to the whole country.

1830

The French capture Algiers

King Charles X of France (1757–1836) hoped that a glorious imperial exploit would make his government less unpopular, but less than a month after the capture of Algiers he lost his throne (*see 1830 The July Revolution*).

The French had been quarrelling with the Dey of Algiers for some time. When the Dey lost his temper with the French consul and hit him in the face with his fan, an expedition was sent against the North African city.

Algiers had once beaten off an attack by the Emperor Charles V, ruler of half Europe in the early sixteenth century, but the French under the Comte de Bourmont (1773–1846) captured it without too much trouble. It took them much longer to conquer the surrounding country. The skilful Arab leader Abd-el-Kader (1807–83) was not captured until 1847.

1830
Berlioz's *Symphonie Fantastique*

This was the first major work of the great French Romantic composer, Hector Berlioz (1803–69), and its first performance in 1830 revealed an array of new musical ideas. It has always remained the most popular work of this devoted musician. Berlioz gained his musical education against fierce family opposition and earned a living for thirty years as a music critic.

Berlioz possessed a genius for large-scale orchestral work that made him one of the greatest French composers.

207

1830
The July Revolution

In 1814 the French monarchy was restored and French aristocrats returned from exile to their estates. But the French people did not forget the ideas of the French Revolution and the liberal reforms of Napoleon.

The Bourbon kings Louis XVIII (1814–24) and Charles X (1824–30) had led sheltered lives and felt little sympathy with the hopes and ideas of most of their subjects. Indeed, before he succeeded his brother, Charles was the leader of the party of fierce reaction. As king, he put extreme conservatives in charge of the government. Many feared that he was about to create a dictatorship.

Louis Philippe, King of France 1830–48, came to the throne as a result of the July revolution.

A general election in which the government lost its majority in the Chamber of Deputies brought matters to a head. The government prepared orders to dissolve the Chamber and change the rules in elections, and to enforce strict censorship of the press. The printers of Paris, threatened with unemployment, shut up shop, and others soon copied them. Angry crowds gathered in the July heat. The government was taken by surprise, and when the revolt began, there were not enough troops to control it. The tricolour (Revolutionary flag) flew again from the towers of Notre Dame cathedral.

Finally the king realized he would have to abdicate. The Chamber invited Louis Philippe, a member of the junior royal house of Orléans, to take the throne. So began the eighteen-year reign of the 'July Monarchy'.

1830
Belgium wins independence

When the Dutch gained their independence in the late sixteenth century, the southern provinces of the Netherlands (roughly equal to modern Belgium) remained under the rule of Spain, and later Austria. During the Napoleonic wars they were overrun by the French, and when Napoleon was defeated in 1814, they were reunited with the Netherlands as one kingdom.

The union with the Dutch was not popular in Belgium. Although the two peoples had much in common, some awkward problems arose out of differences in religion, language, and social customs.

Under the Dutch king, the Belgians felt – and with justice – that they were treated as second-class citizens. Riots broke out against Dutch rule in 1830 and quickly developed into a full-scale revolution. The Belgians declared their independence, and next year drew up a national constitution, inviting Leopold of Saxe-Coburg (1790–1865) to be their first king.

1830
Liverpool-Manchester Railway opens

This was the first public railway built specially to carry passengers in a train drawn by a steam locomotive. The chief engineer was George Stephenson, who had to build the line across the ten kilometre bog of Chat Moss – one of the great stories of pioneer construction engineering.

The line was opened at a great public ceremony on September 15, with the Duke of Wellington attending. But a horrible accident spoiled the occasion. William Huskisson, a former cabinet minister, was run over by the train and died soon afterwards.

The opening of the Liverpool–Manchester Railway marks the true beginning of the railway age. Until then, few people were certain that steam locomotives could provide a practical form of public transport. The success of the railway put all doubts to rest. Railway companies blossomed like flowers and steel tracks began to spread rapidly across Britain.

1830
Delacroix's 'Liberty Leading the People'

This famous painting by the very fine Romantic painter, Eugène Delacroix (1798–1863), was inspired by the July revolution. 'If I haven't fought for my country at least I have painted for her', Delacroix wrote to his brother, a soldier. His delight in rich colours and physical vigour brought a lively new spirit into painting, and his influence was perhaps even greater than his actual works.

1830
Palmerston becomes foreign secretary

It is as Whig foreign secretary that Viscount Palmerston (1784–1865) gained his reputation, although he did become prime minister of Britain twice (1855–58 and 1859–65). He started his political life as a Tory but in 1830 he changed sides to become foreign secretary under the Whig, Lord Grey.

In his later years Palmerston personified all that was aggressive about Victorian Britain's foreign policy. He was considered a tactless man; always intent on reminding other countries that Britain was a very powerful nation. This earned him the name 'firebrand Palmerston'.

He was nevertheless a great champion of Liberalism. His first major success was setting up Belgium as an independent state, and he later openly criticized the repressive policies of Austria, Prussia and Russia, aiding both Italy and Hungary during the 1848 revolutions that spread through Europe.

All his life he was a great orator, and he was liked even by those who disapproved of his policy.

1830
Sturt explores the Murray river

Captain Charles Sturt (1795–1869), an officer in the British army, was posted to Australia in the 1820s and became interested in exploring the unknown interior of New South Wales. On his first expedition in 1828 he discovered the Darling river.

Setting off again in 1830 Sturt followed the Murrumbidgee down to its junction with the Murray, the largest river in Australia. He traced the Murray down to Lake Alexandrina, though he failed to discover the mouth of the river. He suffered terrible hardships and was half-blind when he returned.

On his third expedition, 1844–5, he lost his sight completely, and never fully recovered it. He died in England in 1869, just before receiving the knighthood he had been promised.

1830
Hugo's 'The Hunchback of Notre Dame'

The funeral of Victor Hugo (1802–85) was a great ceremonial occasion in France. Hugo had become a giant figure in nineteenth century French literature. *Notre-Dame de Paris* ('The Hunchback of Notre Dame'), a marvellous recreation of medieval Paris, belonged to his first great period of work in the 1820s and 1830s.

1831

Faraday discovers electrical induction

Michael Faraday (1791–1867) once refused to become president of the Royal Society because he was afraid it would delay his research. He was the ideal scientist: calm, careful, clear, humble, but a genius. A blacksmith's son, he had very little education. Through Sir Humphry Davy (1778–1829) he got a job as a laboratory assistant in the Royal Institution, and rose to become professor of chemistry.

Faraday's greatest work was in electricity, not chemistry. From experiments, he deduced that a magnet is capable of producing electricity, and from this followed his famous report to the Royal Society in 1831 of his discoveries – electro-magnetic induction. From there it was a short step to the invention of the first electrical generator.

Faraday made many other discoveries in electricity and chemistry, including what is now known as electrolysis. He was the first scientist to emphasize the importance of the 'field' rather than the 'particle', and this connects him with Einstein and the theory of relativity.

1831
Pushkin's *Eugene Onegin*

The greatest work of Alexander Sergeievich Pushkin (1799–1837) was at last finished in 1831. Its author called it a 'novel in verse' and it owed much to Pushkin's study of Byron's poetry. He came from an aristocratic family, and married a silly though beautiful girl. Pushkin died from a duel against one of her admirers.

Faraday's laboratory at the Royal Institution, where he carried out his research into the nature of electricity.

1832
Morse invents the telegraph

The idea of an electromagnetic recording telegraph came to Samuel Morse (1791–1872) as he was on a ship returning to New York to take up his job as professor of painting. He also devised the system of dots and dashes, now called Morse Code, for sending messages.

Morse did not have much money and he was not able to spend all his time on his invention. It was not until 1844, after the US Congress had voted money to string a copper wire between Washington and Baltimore, that Morse, from the Supreme Court building in Washington, tapped out the first telegraph message: 'What hath God wrought'.

Although the US government refused to buy Morse's telegraph, he sold the system to private companies and, unlike most inventors, made a profit out of his invention.

A modern Morse Code operator. Samuel Morse's code is still used internationally for telegraphic communications.

1831
Stendhal publishes 'Scarlet and Black'

The inscription on the tomb of Stendhal (1783–1842) reads, 'He wrote, he loved, he lived'. His two great novels, *Le Rouge et le Noir* ('Scarlet and Black') and *La Chartreuse de Parme* ('The Charterhouse of Parma', 1839), illustrate his deep understanding of human psychology and beautifully clear style. Stendhal's real name was Marie Henri Beyle.

1831
Chopin settles in Paris

Like many great musicians, Frédéric Chopin (1810–49) showed his genius very early (he composed his first *Polonaise* before he was ten and died of tuberculosis while still young). Born in Poland of a French father, he was a brilliant pianist and perhaps played his own exquisite and lyrical compositions and lively dances (he wrote little orchestral music) better than anyone else.

1831
Schumann: *Papillons*

Papillons and *Carnaval* (1835) and several later works, mostly for piano by Robert Schumann (1810–56) are undoubted masterpieces; but in his own time Schumann was almost equally important for his championship of young composers and his brilliant musical criticism. His originality and daring delayed his fame until after his sad mental illness and early death.

1832
Great Reform Bill

The cause of 'reform' in Britain was the greatest subject of argument in the early nineteenth century. What people meant by reform was, first and foremost, reform of parliament.

Very few people were allowed to vote in parliamentary elections (about 435,000 out of a population of nearly 20,000,000), and the seats in the House of Commons were allocated in strange and unreasonable ways. A thinly populated county like Cornwall had twenty-four members, while booming industrial cities like Manchester and Birmingham had none. Some 'pocket' boroughs had only ten or twelve voters, while other constituencies had several thousand.

Reform had to wait until the Whigs, the party who supported it, formed a government in 1830. Then followed two years of crisis, including another election, two resignations by the prime minister, Earl Grey, and threats against the anti-Reform House of Lords.

The bill was finally passed in 1832. Its first effects were small: pocket boroughs were abolished, big cities gained parliamentary representation, and the number of voters was increased about fifty per cent. The real importance of the act was that it opened the way for more democratic reforms in the future.

1833
Factory Act

Most people in the early nineteenth century believed that industry would be profitable only if governments did not interfere with it. But some were shocked by the grim working conditions and long hours worked by labourers, especially children.

In England a parliamentary committee in 1832 revealed the horrible truth of child labour in textile factories and gave Lord Ashley (later Earl of Shaftesbury, 1801–85) the opportunity to begin his great career in defence of the poor and helpless.

The Factory Act of 1833 was a disappointment to Ashley, who had hoped to enforce a maximum working day of ten hours for all workers. However, it did stop the employment of children under nine, it limited hours of work for older children, and it introduced a system of inspectors to make sure the law was obeyed by the factory owners.

1833
Abolition of slavery

News of the passing of the act abolishing slavery in British colonies was brought to William Wilberforce (1759–1833) as he lay dying. Wilberforce had spent his entire political career fighting against the slave trade.

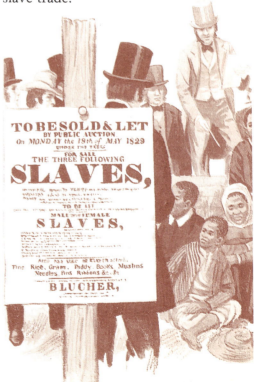

The cruel slave trade, campaigned against by Wilberforce.

Slavery had been illegal in England since 1772, but the slave trade continued in full flood. About 20,000 Africans were transported to America every year by ships from Liverpool, Bristol and London. The opponents of the trade, called 'Abolitionists', fought long and hard against it. Finally, a motion to declare it illegal was carried by Charles James Fox (1749–1806) through parliament.

The next step was to persuade other countries to abolish the trade, and to stop illegal trading (profits were so large that slave-traders could afford to lose two ships out of three). France, Spain and Portugal soon agreed to stop trading, but as long as slavery itself was legal, illegal slave-trading went on.

Britain's abolition of slavery cost the government £20,000,000 in compensation to slave-owners. But it was an important step towards ending an ancient evil.

1834
Hundred Views of Mount Fuji

Hokusai (1760–1849), the most famous of Japanese artists among Europeans, was born poor and, in spite of the number of his drawings (over thirty thousand) and the popularity of his prints, died poor too. He made plenty of money but spent it fast. His *Hundred Views of Mount Fuji*, the mountain whose beautiful shape might have been designed by Hokusai himself, were published in three volumes, in monotone (one colour).

1834
Tolpuddle Martyrs

Although trade unions were not illegal in 1834, they were closely restricted by laws against secret political societies. The 'Tolpuddle Martyrs' were a small group of farm labourers in Dorset who formed a union that was to become part of Robert Owen's Grand National Consolidated Trades Union (*see 1800 Owen takes over New Lanark Mills*).

The Dorset labourers, led by George Loveless, were prosecuted because they had a secret initiation ceremony, including the swearing of oaths. But their little society was against violence and law-breaking.

They were sentenced to seven years transportation in a penal colony in Australia, but two years later the sentence was remitted. Their case became a famous rallying cry for early trade unions.

1834
Balzac's Le Père Goriot

This is one of the most popular novels of Honoré de Balzac (1799–1850). Balzac, who is to France what Dickens is to England, regarded himself as 'secretary' to French society. His vast, detailed *Comédie Humaine* ('Human Comedy'), teeming with characters, was an attempt to portray every aspect of French history in his lifetime. *Le Père Goriot* is one of the most popular masterpieces in this collection.

1835
Mme Tussaud's opens in London

Marie Tussaud (1760–1850) was an expert modeller in wax. In Paris, she made many heads of people executed in the French Revolution, and was imprisoned herself for a short time. After a successful show in London (1802) she travelled around England and eventually settled in Baker Street, where she opened her permanent exhibition.

1835
Andersen's Fairy Tales published

Hans Christian Andersen (1805–75) had an unhappy childhood. A teacher treated him badly and fellow-students jeered at him. *The Ugly Duckling* was in a way about himself, for he became a famous writer of children's fairy stories, loved all over the world. He wanted to be a famous novelist and playwright, but there he was less successful.

1835
Colt patents revolver

The first successful revolver, the prototype from which all later revolvers are descended, was patented by the American gunsmith, Samuel Colt (1814–62). He also made rifles and shotguns with revolving chambers, but his first factory went bankrupt and it was not until the 1850s that Colt had a big success with his Navy revolver. His guns were used by the army and the navy in the American Civil War.

1836
The Great Trek

The British took over the Cape Colony, South Africa, from the Dutch in 1814. The settlers of Dutch descent were not happy under British rule and felt that native African peoples were too much favoured. Under Piet Retief and others about ten thousand Boers ('farmers') left Cape Colony and trekked with their ox waggons to the north-east, away from British influence. On the way they came into bloody conflict with the Zulus. Retief and many more were killed.

Victoria in old age. Her reign, which lasted into the twentieth century, saw Great Britain as the most powerful and industrially advanced nation in the world. Victoria's empire covered a quarter of the world.

When Natal was annexed by Britain to prevent the Boers establishing a republic, they moved north, across the Vaal river. Eventually the British acknowledged independent Boer republics in the Transvaal and Orange Free State.

In 1902, after the South African War, the Boer republics became British colonies, and later joined the Union of South Africa.

1836
Battle of the Alamo

In 1835 Texas was part of Mexico, but inhabited by many Anglo-American immigrants. When the Mexican government tried to stop immigration and refused various demands by the white settlers, rebellion broke out. Sam Houston (1793–1863) was appointed the Texan commander.

In February 1836 the Mexican general and president, Santa Anna (1795–1876) marched into San Antonio and besieged the Alamo, a thick-walled fortress covering just over one hectare which had once been a mission settlement. It was defended by less than two hundred men, including Davy Crockett (1786–1836), and was commanded by William Travis (1809–36) and James Bowie (1799–1836).

The siege lasted twelve days, then Santa Anna ordered his 2,400 men to make an all-out attack. Two assaults were beaten off, but the third succeeded, and all the defenders were killed.

Two months later Santa Anna was routed by Sam Houston at San Jacinto, where the Texan war-cry, 'Remember the Alamo!' was first heard. Texas became an independent republic, but nine years later it joined the United States.

Victoria R

1837
Accession of Victoria

The British people thought that the slight, eighteen year-old girl made a pleasant change after her two fat and foolish uncles who had reigned before her. She was to reign longer than any other English monarch, dying in 1901. Reigning over the richest, strongest country in the world for so long a time, Victoria (1819–1901) grew to be a more interesting person than perhaps she was by nature.

As a young queen she was helped by her first prime minister, the amiable, fatherly Lord Melbourne (1779–1848), and by her dedicated husband, the German prince, Albert (1819–61), whom she married in 1840. After Albert's death in 1861 Victoria retreated into gloomy widowhood, refusing to play her full part as sovereign.

Another prime minister, Disraeli (1804–81), flattered her out of her gloom in the 1870s and in her later years this dumpy, lame, little old lady in a cheap lace bonnet became a figure of huge prestige, before whom cabinet ministers trembled.

1837
Dickens publishes the *Pickwick Papers*

Publication of *The Posthumous Papers of the Pickwick Club* launched the career of the greatest English popular novelist, Charles Dickens (1812–70). For ordinary readers, his finest gift was his creation of vivid, often humorous characters. But he was also a powerful critic of the evils of Victorian society. Novels by Dickens include *Oliver Twist* (1839), *Nicholas Nickleby* (1839), *David Copperfield* (1850), *A Tale of Two Cities* (1859) and *Great Expectations* (1861).

1838
The People's Charter

The Chartist movement, a working-class movement for reform, grew out of disappointment at the results of the Reform Act of 1832 and the failure of Robert Owen's trade unionism. The Charter was drawn up by William Lovett (1800–77), founder of the London Working Men's Association, and Francis Place (1771–1854), a well-known radical. Most of the reforms it demanded – votes for all adult males, constituencies of equal size, salaries for MPs etc. – now seem moderate; but in 1838 they seemed too dangerously democratic.

Chartism also attracted more militant figures, like Feargus O'Connor (1794–1855), who was particularly active in the movement.

A national convention was held in 1839 and a Chartist petition with over a million signatures (some, it turned out, forged) was presented to parliament, which rejected it. O'Connor's call for violence resulted only in a few small riots and strikes. The Chartist movement remained very active and was revived in 1848. After that, its cause was taken up by other organizations.

1838
Archimedes is launched

Though not the first steamship to be built with a screw-propeller, the SS *Archimedes* proved that a propellor was more efficient than paddle-wheels. Built in England by the inventor Sir Francis Smith (1808–74), the 207-tonne *Archimedes* could maintain an average speed of 7·5 knots. She persuaded I K Brunel to fit a propellor to his great ocean-going steamer, the *Great Britain* (see *1858 Brunel launches Great Eastern*).

A scene from *Oliver Twist*.

1838
Wreck of the *Forfarshire*

On September 7, 1838 the *Forfarshire*, bound from Hull to Dundee, was wrecked on the rocks of the Farne Islands. The lighthouse keeper and his daughter, Grace Darling (1815–42), a frail girl, bravely set out in a small, flat-bottomed boat and succeeded in rescuing five people.

Grace's father made a second trip with two of the rescued, and took off four more people – the last alive out of sixty-three on board. The exploit made Grace Darling a national heroine.

1838
First Afghan War

Fear of Russian expansion caused some strange policies in British India, none more disastrous than the attempt of the governor-general, Lord Auckland (1784–1849), to replace Dost Mohammed (1793–1863) as emir of Afghanistan – he had made himself ruler in 1826.

The British expedition, though badly organized, took the Afghan capital of Kabul in April 1839, but foolishly remained in occupation after Dost Mohammed had surrendered. Communications across the North-West Frontier began to crumble and rebellion broke out in Kabul. Early in 1842 the British began a disorderly retreat, under constant attack by Afghan tribesmen. Only one man reached safety.

A subsequent campaign restored British prestige somewhat by recapturing Kabul to release British prisoners, before withdrawing to India.

The second Afghan War (1878–80) resulted in British occupation and control of Afghan foreign relations. The emirs kept internal self-government, and after the brief, third Afghan War, Britain recognized the full independence of Afghanistan in 1921.

1839
Daguerre demonstrates daguerreotype

With others, Louis Daguerre (1789–1851) had been experimenting for many years with methods of recording a picture, and in 1839 he displayed the method he had invented to the Paris Academy of Sciences.

A polished silver plate, coated with silver iodide, was exposed, in a camera, for three or four minutes. The image was developed by mercury vapour, which condensed on the plate in proportion to the amount of light that had reached it, and was 'fixed' by a salt solution. Prints could then be made from the plate.

The daguerreotype, as it was called, immediately became very popular. A number of improvements in the process were made by Daguerre and others. Modern photography, however, is more directly descended from the method of W H Fox Talbot (1800–77) who recorded images on paper and published his results a few months before Daguerre.

1839
Liszt's European tour begins

Franz Liszt (1811–86) was acknowledged, even by Chopin, as the world's greatest pianist. His European tour was a huge success, though the profits were soon dissipated by Liszt's open-handed generosity. As a composer he is probably best remembered for his Hungarian rhapsodies and symphonic 'tone poems', a form he virtually invented.

1840
McMillan's bicycle

The bicycle developed from the 'velocipede', which had no pedals and was propelled by the rider, sitting on a cross-bar,

217

pushing his feet against the ground. One variety, called a *draisine*, had a pivoting front wheel and primitive handlebar. It was to one of these machines that a Scottish blacksmith, Kirkpatrick McMillan, fitted pedals to drive the rear wheel.

1840
Proudhon's 'What is Property?'

Pierre Joseph Proudhon (1809–65) answered the question himself: property is theft. Son of a French workman, Proudhon became a brilliant political philosopher and one of the founders of anarchism. Karl Marx wanted to co-operate with him after reading *Qu'est-ce que la propriété* ('What is Property?') but Proudhon had moderated his views. He wanted peaceful reform, not violent revolution, and was against authority whether on the Left or the Right.

1840
Penny post is introduced

Although the British Post Office has benefited from many good ideas, it has usually resisted them as hard and as long as possible. That was certainly true of John Palmer's idea of using mail-coaches, which began (in 1784) only when the prime minister insisted. It was also true of the penny post, which Rowland Hill (1795–1879) had been urging for years.

Postage was so expensive that only a few people could afford to send letters. Hill said that a single, cheap, one-penny rate would actually be more profitable, because of the great increase in business that would follow. He also suggested using a postage stamp, previously unknown.

Of course he was right. The number of letters posted rose eight hundred per cent in twenty-five years, while the use of stamps and standard rates made the whole system much more efficient.

1840
First China War

This sordid war between Britain and China had complicated origins. It was fought over trade, and it is sometimes called the Opium War, because this drug was being illegally traded by British and Chinese merchants. All British opium was surrendered on the command of the Chinese government in 1839, but Britain spoiled its case by later demanding compensation. There were other grievances, including an attack on a British warship, which led to war.

At the Treaty of Nanking (1842), the Chinese made concessions to British and other foreign merchants, but neither side was happy, and war began again after the Chinese had imprisoned the crew of a British-registered ship. The British foreign secretary was Lord Palmerston, an aggressive patriot who believed in protecting British nationals at any cost. Although the men were released the Chinese refused to apologize and rejected other demands.

Britain and France, passively supported by other countries, then resorted to force, and the Chinese were compelled to give way when a military expedition reached Peking in 1860. The opium trade was reinstated on the grounds – true but cynical – that the Chinese authorities were incapable of stopping it.

1840
New Zealand becomes British

European settlement in New Zealand after Captain Cook explored the coasts in 1769 was slow and confined to the coast. Most of the immigrants were adventurers and criminals, who badly disrupted the native society of the Maoris.

Properly planned colonization began with the formation of the New Zealand Company in 1838, and in 1840 Captain William Hobson was sent out to make a treaty with the Maoris granting sovereignty over the two islands to Great Britain. The government was reluctant to take responsibility for New Zealand, but feared that otherwise the French would do so. It was also necessary to protect the Maoris from lawless Europeans though, as later events proved, the protection was not sufficient.

The colony became self-governing only twelve years after it was founded.

1840
Discovery of Antarctica

In 1775 Captain Cook (1728–79) had circled the Antarctic continent without sighting land. In his wake sailed many whaling and sealing ships, and it may have been one of them that first glimpsed the mainland of Antarctica. The long peninsula that points towards South America was certainly seen by an American sealer, Nathaniel Palmer, in 1820, but it had probably been marked down earlier by a British ship commanded by Captain Edward Bransfield. The Russian expedition of F B von Bellingshausen in 1819–21 may have beaten both of them.

However, nothing was known about Antarctica until the late 1830s, when three large expeditions sailed to explore it. The French under J C S Dumont d'Urville (1790–1842) planted their flag on an island off the coast of Adelie Land in 1840. The Americans under Charles Wilkes (1798–1877) discovered Wilkes Land in the same year. The third and most successful expedition was British. Commanded by James Clark Ross (1800–62), it discovered the Ross Ice Shelf and Mount Erebus, named after Ross's ship, in 1841.

1841
Browning's *Bells and Pomegranates*

This collection of the works of the English poet Robert Browning (1812–89), of which the first of eight parts appeared in 1841, contained some of his most popular lyrics as well as some of his well-written but unactable plays. Browning sometimes was – and is – a difficult poet, who did not earn popularity easily. Not the least of his achievements was rescuing (and marrying) fellow-poet Elizabeth Barrett (1806–61) from family tyranny.

1841
The British occupy Hong Kong

Hong Kong, place of 'sweet waters', is a rocky island, forty-eight square kilometres in area, lying off the south-east coast of China. Having an excellent harbour, it has long been an important place for trade. The British occupied it in the China War (*see 1840 First China War*) and the Chinese recognized British sovereignty at the Treaty of Nanking the following year. Later, more territory was added to the colony, and a lease was granted, which is due to run out in 1997.

1842
Ether is used as an anaesthetic

Anyone who had an operation in 1842 was cut up while still conscious, although with luck he or she would be doped with opium or some other pain killer. General anaesthesia (making the patient unconscious) was demonstrated in public by two American dentists, using nitrous oxide (1844) and ether (1846). But anaesthetics had been used earlier: probably the first use of ether for this purpose was by another American, Crawford Long (1815–78), in 1842.

Chloroform was developed for women in childbirth by the Scottish physician, Sir James Simpson (1811–70) in 1847. Many people were against its use, but Queen Victoria, who bore nine children, had no patience with them: 'That blessed chloroform!' she gratefully called it.

1842
Gogol publishes *Dead Souls*

This macabre but amusing satire of Nikolai Gogol (1809–1852), which relates an attempted swindle by a villain who buys dead serfs, is the masterpiece of the great Russian humorist. Less realistic and less optimistic about human nature than Dickens, he shared with him a teeming imagination that poured forth a gallery of grotesque characters.

1844
O'Connell imprisoned

Daniel O'Connell (1775–1847), the Irish statesman, was largely responsible through his Catholic Association, for ending political discrimination in Britain against Roman Catholics (Roman Catholic Emancipation Act, 1829).

Though it righted one wrong, the act did not end Irish dissatisfaction, and in the 1840s O'Connell led the call for a repeal of the Act of Union, which had joined Ireland to England in 1800. The movement was not supported by all Catholic Irish, but enormous mass-meetings were held to demand repeal.

The fiercer, more anti-English propaganda of the 'Young Ireland' movement, with which O'Connell was not in sympathy, made the situation very dangerous in the eyes of the government, and troops were moved to Ireland in case of rebellion.

In October 1843, a large meeting called by O'Connell was banned by the government. He obeyed the order but was arrested nevertheless and, after a very biased trial, sentenced to a year in prison. The verdict was reversed on appeal and O'Connell freed. But the few months he had been held in prison without bail harmed his health (he was sixty-eight), and his great influence over the Irish people had practically vanished.

1844
Turner's *Rain, Steam and Speed*

The later works of J M W Turner (1775–1851), to which this vibrant red-and-gold study of a train on a bridge belongs, were regarded as decadent, but are now seen as a striking development foreshadowing the French Impressionist school. Turner was the most gifted of artists and, with Constable, the greatest of English landscape painters.

1844
Dumas' 'The Three Musketeers'

This romantic story, full of colour and adventure, was written by a romantic French character, Alexandre Dumas (1802–70). He is often called Dumas *père*, to distinguish him from his son who, like the father, was a popular playwright. *Les Trois Mousquetaires* ('The Three Musketeers') was soon followed by *Le Comte de Monte Cristo* ('The Count of Monte Cristo'), eighteen volumes long.

A scene from 'The Three Musketeers'.

description of working-class conditions in England, where he lived most of his adult life, was written in the year that he began his collaboration with Marx.

1846
Lear's *Book of Nonsense*

Edward Lear (1812–88) was a funny, eccentric Englishman, who made popular the type of comic verse called a limerick. He was also a talented artist, and was hired by the Earl of Derby to draw the animals in his private zoo. He became a great favourite of the Earl's family and wrote his first *Book of Nonsense* for the Earl's grandson.

1845
Poe's *Tales of Mystery and Imagination*

This was a vintage year for the American writer of grisly and ghostly stories, Edgar Allan Poe (1809–49). His poem *The Raven* (that grim bird for ever croaking 'Nevermore!') appeared the same year. Poe's literary reputation now stands very high. Although Poe became famous, he remained poor, ruining his health and killing himself with drink.

1845
Engels: *The Condition of the Working Class in Britain*

The German socialist, Friedrich Engels (1820–95) is best remembered as the partner of Karl Marx, although his clear style makes him a simpler guide to Marxism than Marx himself. Engels's

1846
Repeal of the Corn Laws

The greatest argument in Britain after the Reform Act of 1832 was: 'free trade' versus 'protection' (high duties on imports). At the centre of that argument lay the Corn Laws. The Corn Laws attempted to protect British farmers by keeping the price of wheat – and therefore bread – high, by duties on imported corn. The Tory party, representing landowners and farmers, favoured the Corn Laws. The Whigs, representing manufacturers and businessmen wanted to abolish them, to make bread cheap and thus keep wages down.

Sir Robert Peel (1788–1850) although head of a Tory government, had come to believe in free trade. The failure of the potato crop, causing famine in Ireland, convinced him that cheap bread was necessary, and he brought in a bill to repeal the Corn Laws. With the help of Whig votes, the bill was passed, although a majority of Peel's party voted against it. Soon afterwards, the Tory government fell, and Peel's career was finished.

Repeal of the Corn Laws made very little difference to the immediate situation, but it represented the decisive victory of free trade over protection.

1848
The Communist Manifesto

The Communist Manifesto was in fact written by Marx, although he often described his friend Engels as its joint author. A masterpiece of political propaganda it summoned the working classes of Europe to rebel against their capitalist masters. Its argument is clearly stated, neatly summed up in the sentence: 'The history of all hitherto existing society is the history of class struggles.'

1848
California gold rush

In the great gold rushes of the nineteenth century, many people made their fortunes, but many did not. The discovery of gold in California sent thousands of Americans rushing westwards; the population soared and California was on its way to becoming one of the world's richest – and most violent – places. Other great gold rushes include those in Victoria, Australia (1851), on the Witwatersrand, South Africa (1886) and the Klondike in Alaska and north-west Canada (1897).

1848
Pre-Raphaelite Brotherhood

The name was chosen by a group of English artists, including Dante Gabriel Rossetti (1828–82), John Everett Millais (1829–96) and W Holman Hunt (1827–1910). Reacting against early Victorian standards of academic painting, they wanted to get closer to Nature, and identified themselves with what they regarded as the ideals of artists before the Renaissance (or 'pre-Raphael'). The PRB (formed *c.*1848) had very great influence; the brilliant detail of early disciples achieved a striking realism.

The ideas of the PRB later became associated with the 'arts and crafts' movement – a reaction against industrialism of which the leading advocate was William Morris (*see 1884 William Morris forms the Socialist League*). It was in this field – design rather than painting – that the ideas of the PRB proved most fruitful.

The Death of Ophelia, by Sir John Everett Millais, is in the Tate Gallery, London.

1848
February Revolution

Louis Philippe (1773–1850) came to the French throne via revolution (1830) and left it the same way. The February Revolt grew out of protests against the government's suppression of the cause of liberal reform. Faced with a hostile combination that included many of the middle class, on whom his monarchy relied, Louis Philippe abdicated.

Left-wing leadership plus working-class pressure ensured that the monarchy would not this time be restored. A republic was declared and an election held in which all males were allowed to vote (previously, only about one in thirty could vote). The result, however, was a thoroughly conservative Chamber of Deputies. The Left wing was defeated, and the barricades went up in the streets again in June. This second rising was suppressed by troops, with many dead and wounded, and socialism was repressed.

The constitution of the Second Republic was ratified in November, and the difficult question of finding a suitable president was solved by the election of Prince Louis Napoleon (1808–73), a nephew of the emperor, who appealed to a sufficient number of people.

Hardly anyone was satisfied with the Second Republic, and it lasted less than four years. As his elected spell neared its end, Louis Napoleon carried out a *coup d'état* which made him, in effect dictator. In 1852 he proclaimed himself emperor as Napoleon III.

1848
European Revolutions

In 1848 every important country in Europe, except Britain, was shaken by revolt. The frustration of popular liberal and national ambitions formed the background; an economic slump, with failed harvests and rising unemployment, provided more immediate causes. The revolts were not planned, though they took place as a chain reaction following outbreaks in France and the Austrian empire. Revolutionaries like Marx were taken by surprise; *The Communist Manifesto* had little effect.

The first outbreaks occurred in northern Italy and Sicily. The French revolt followed in February, and it was promptly echoed in Belgium, Holland, and various German states, including Prussia. Within the Austrian empire, the Hungarians and the Czechs rebelled, and Metternich fell from power after almost forty years. Venice seized brief independence, and the Papal States gained constitutional government.

None of these revolutionary movements was wholly successful, and in two years the old systems of government were restored nearly everywhere.

1848
Millet's *The Winnower*

Jean François Millet (1814–75) was one of the leaders of the Barbizon school, so-called after the French village where these painters lived. They wanted to depict, realistically, the natural landscape, though Millet, the son of a peasant family, was more interested in the hard life of the peasants who inhabited that landscape. His best-known works include *The Winnower* (1848), *Peasants Grafting* and *The Gleaners*.

1851
The Great Exhibition

Housed in a glass palace so large it enclosed several elm trees in Hyde Park, London, the Great Exhibition was at once a celebration and an advertisement of British trade and industry, both of which at that time were at a peak.

The chief organizer of the Exhibition was Prince Albert, Queen Victoria's husband, who may have damaged his health by his immensely hard work. The 'Crystal Palace', one of the few Victorian buildings planned on what we should call functional principles, was designed by Sir Joseph Paxton (1801–65), a gardener by trade who had previously designed only greenhouses.

The Great Exhibition of 1851, organized by Prince Albert, Queen Victoria's husband.

The basis of the Exhibition was machinery and raw materials from Britain, the empire and other countries; but it included some oddities, like rhubarb champagne, stuffed frogs and a garden seat made of coal. The Exhibition was a tremendous success, and in memory still symbolizes Britain at the height of its greatness.

1851
Melville's *Moby Dick*

One of the greatest of American novels, this story of the struggle between a man and a fierce white whale can be read in many different ways. On one level, the contest stands for man's struggle with fate. The author of *Moby Dick*, Herman Melville (1819–91), was never particularly successful during his lifetime; recognition did not come until about thirty years after his death.

1852
Giffard's aero-engine

The French inventor Henri Giffard (1825–82) was the first man to control the movements of a flying machine in the air. All previous airships could not be properly steered or propelled because they had no suitable engine. Giffard mounted a steam engine to drive a propellor in his forty-five metre-long airship and flew it at nine kph, steering his own course.

1852
Stowe's *Uncle Tom's Cabin*

This novel about slaves in the American South helped to rouse opposition to slavery. Today it seems sentimental, and 'Uncle Tom' has become an insulting name for a black man who humbles himself in white society. Harriet Beecher Stowe (1811–96) became famous through this book. She wrote many others, and some poems, but few people read them now.

1852
Wells Fargo founded

Henry Wells (1805–78) and William George Fargo (1818–81) founded Wells, Fargo and Company to provide safe banking and fast communications for California gold-miners. Their fast overland stage-coaches began to run a few years later.

Although their long-distance business was affected by the building of railways, as late as 1916 Wells Fargo and other similar companies covered well over sixty-thousand kilometres of western routes.

1852
Independence of the Transvaal

The Transvaal was first settled by the descendants of Dutch colonists from the Cape Colony in 1838, anxious to escape British control.

At the Sands river Convention Britain recognized the independence of the Transvaal settlers, who were led by Andries Pretorius (1799–1853). The new state was called the South African Republic (1856).

However, all was not well in the Transvaal. The British suspected the Boers ('farmers') of enslaving Africans and coveting Bechuanaland (Botswana). The Boers quarrelled among themselves, especially over efforts to unite with the Orange Free State. The discovery of gold led to new territorial claims, more trouble with Africans, and the breakdown of government.

In 1877 Britain annexed the Transvaal, thereby becoming involved in war with the Zulu and, three years later, with the Boers themselves. By the Pretoria Convention (1881), Britain allowed self-government to the Transvaal but kept overall sovereignty.

1853
Verdi's *La Traviata*

It is primarily his gift for melody that makes Giuseppe Verdi (1813–1901) so continually popular as a composer of opera. *Rigoletto* (1851) was his first great international success. *Il Trovatore* ('The Troubadour', 1853) and *La Traviata* ('The Strayed One', 1853) confirmed his reputation. But Verdi's greatest work was done late in life: *Otello* first performed when he was seventy-four, *Falstaff* when he was eighty.

Giuseppe Verdi

1854
Outbreak of the Crimean War

The war in the Crimea – the peninsula of Russia that projects into the Black Sea – arose out of the weakness of the Turkish empire and the fear of Russian expansion at Turkish expense. It began with a dispute over the rights of Christians, whom Russia claimed to protect, in the Turkish empire. Russian troops moved into outlying provinces and the Turkish sultan declared war (October 1853). Britain and France came to Turkey's aid six months later, and their forces reached the Crimea in September 1854.

The allies defeated the Russians on the river Alma and advanced towards Sebastopol. Their campaign was badly organ-

ized and badly led: the most famous disaster, the result of an order misunderstood, was the suicidal charge of the Light Brigade (cavalry) straight at the Russian artillery during the battle of Balaclava (October). The Battle of Inkerman (November) was an allied victory, but Sebastopol still held out. During the winter siege, thousands died of cold and disease, and the city's defences did not fall until September 1855.

There were no more major battles, and peace was arranged in 1856 (Treaty of Paris). With minor changes, it left the situation much the same as it was when war began.

1854
Florence Nightingale goes to the Crimea

In the nineteenth century hospitals were filthy and fever-ridden, and nurses were often ignorant, brutal and drunk. When Florence Nightingale (1820–1910), a beautiful, wealthy girl decided to become a nurse, her parents were horrified.

Florence Nightingale's opportunity to help the nursing profession came with the outbreak of the Crimean War. She took a party of thirty-eight nurses to the hospital at Scutari, near Constantinople, where conditions were foul and miser-

The long and painful Siege of Sebastopol, at the end of the Crimean War.

able for the thousands of sick and wounded. She soon devoted herself to reorganizing the hospital, and provided blankets, medicines, soap and scrubbing brushes, nursing all the worst cases herself.

When she finally returned to England in 1856, Florence Nightingale had gained such a reputation for herself that a sum of £50,000 was collected to found the Nightingale Training School for Nurses attached to St Thomas's Hospital, London. This training by Florence Nightingale was to set new standards of skill, good behaviour and discipline in nursing.

1854
Emily Dickinson starts to write poetry

The American poet, Emily Dickinson (1830–86), was the daughter of a lawyer. In 1854 she withdrew completely from society and began to write poetry: at her death she had written over a thousand poems, most of which were published posthumously. Her intensely personal and often spiritual lyrics were almost immediately recognized as the work of a great poet.

1855
Hiawatha is published

Henry Wadsworth Longfellow (1807–82) was an American poet. He was professor of modern languages at Harvard University for twenty years but finally gave up his academic career to devote his life to poetry. *Hiawatha*, his long poem about Red Indians, is perhaps his most famous. Longfellow has always been extremely popular as a simple, romantic, story-teller.

1855
Whitman's *Leaves of Grass*

Walt Whitman (1819–92) is regarded as one of the greatest American poets and it was the publication of *Leaves of Grass* that made him famous. Although he was a lover of the classics, it was his own originality that gave his poetry its great vitality and compassion. He wrote in free unrhyming lines, largely about the lives of poor working men.

1855
Trollope's *The Warden*

Anthony Trollope (1815–82) was an English novelist who spent many years working in the Post Office. He nevertheless managed to write sixty novels, the best known being the Barsetshire novels which began with *The Warden*, published in 1855. Trollope was very successful in depicting provincial folk and more specifically provincial clergy, in a humorous and lively way.

1856
Invention of the Bessemer converter

In the mid-nineteenth century very little steel was being produced in Britain. In 1855 only about fifty thousand tonnes were being home-produced and that at the exorbitant average cost of £75 a tonne. Wrought iron was at that time still the main product of the British iron industry.

During the Crimean War (*see 1854 Outbreak of the Crimean War*) an English inventor called Henry Bessemer (1813–98) designed a new rotating artillery shell. Bessemer found his invention unsatisfactory because the traditional cast-iron cannon was too weak. As a result he developed his famous steel making process.

To produce steel, impurities such as silicon, manganese and phosphorus have to be removed from the pig-iron. Bessemer's idea was to blow a blast of air through the converter containing the iron, so oxidizing the silicon and manganese. This revolutionary process meant that steel could now be produced cheaply and swiftly.

1856
Keller's *Die Leute von Seldwyla*

Gottfried Keller (1819–90) was a Swiss-German poet and novelist. *Die Leute von Seldwyla* ('The People of Seldwyla'), was a collection of studies of Swiss provincial life. It included his *Romeo und Julia auf dem Dorfe* ('A Village Romeo and Juliet'), one of the most powerful *Novellen* (short stories) in the German language. A contemporary of Keller's, Theodor Storm (1817–88) was an equally important storyteller, who wrote several vivid, often eerie tales such as *Der Schimmelreiter* ('The White Horse').

1857
Madame Bovary is published

Gustave Flaubert (1821–80) is regarded by many as being France's greatest nineteenth century novelist. Born in Rouen, the son of a doctor, his literary aim was to produce a work of perfectly balanced prose. This he achieved in many ways with *Madame Bovary*, published in 1857, the tragic story of a young, unhappily married woman.

1857
Publication of *Les Fleurs du Mal*

Charles Baudelaire (1821–67) was not greatly appreciated during his lifetime, but is regarded now as one of France's finest poets and an important influence on modern European poetry. In 1857 Baudelaire's volume, *Les Fleurs du Mal* ('Flowers of Evil') was condemned and he was prosecuted for obscenity. The poems were written at various dates and express superbly the eternal conflict between good and evil in man.

1857
British enter Canton

There was already tension regarding trade between China and Great Britain when the British entered Canton in 1857.

Dissatisfied with the terms of the Treaty of Nanking (*see 1840 First China War*) the British wanted free travel in China, the residence in Peking of diplomatic representatives and the right of way in the Yangtze river for their merchant vessels. China, on the other hand, felt that it had ceded quite enough to the British and other European traders.

In the midst of civil war, China was not able to cope with these British demands, and war finally broke out over a comparatively minor incident. In 1856 the Chinese boarded a Chinese-owned but British-registered craft, the *Arrow*, which they suspected of piracy. The British retaliated the next year by taking Canton, and pressing on to Tientsin, they threatened Peking. In order to save their capital, the Chinese finally gave into the demands of the British.

1857
The Indian Mutiny

During the one hundred years that elapsed after the Battle of Plassey (*see 1756 The Black Hole of Calcutta*) great tension developed between Britain and India. British annexations of new areas caused alarm amongst the Indians and differences in belief, both cultural and religious, between Europeans and Indians added to the friction.

In 1857 the *sepoys*, Indian troops serving under British officers, revolted in Bengal. They had refused to handle cartridges that British officers had coated in cow and pig grease: the cow is a holy animal for the Hindus and the pig is considered too unclean to be touched by the Moslems. This, combined with other grievances, was a major cause of the Indian Mutiny which involved about eighty thousand native soldiers.

Ghastly atrocities were committed by both sides. The British troops were slow to grasp the gravity of the situation, while the mutineers took Delhi and Lucknow, a city where the British were besieged for months. The massacre of European women and children at Cawnpore caused more outrage than any other event.

When the mutiny was quelled under John Lawrence, chief commissioner of the Punjab, the British took away the political power of the East India Company. The Crown took over direct control under the Better Government of India Act (1858).

1858
Burton discovers Lake Tanganyika

Sir Richard Francis Burton (1821–90) was an exceptional British explorer. After a stormy education, he served in Sindh, India, where he mastered several languages including Hindustani, Persian and Arabic, and wrote vivid and faithful accounts of his life there. In 1853 he made a pilgrimage to Mecca disguised as an Indian Pathan.

Burton's most hazardous and dramatic expedition was his exploration of the Somali region of East Africa in 1854. Although accompanied by John Hanning Speke (1827–64), he accomplished the most dangerous part of his journey alone. No white man had entered Harrar, the Somali capital, but Burton stayed with the king for ten days, riding back over the desert, almost without food and water.

It was in 1857 that he and Speke set off to find the equatorial lakes of Africa. Quite independently Burton found Lake Tanganyika in 1858 and Speke found Victoria Nijanza. This infuriated Burton and the two went their separate ways.

1858
Brunel launches *Great Eastern*

Isambard Kingdom Brunel (1806–59) was a British engineer. Throughout his life he took an interest in the development of ocean steam navigation and in 1823 began work on the first Thames tunnel project.

Brunel was responsible for building three of the century's greatest ships. The first, the *Great Western*, built in 1838, was the first steamship to make regular trips across the Atlantic and it was followed in 1845 by the *Great Britain*. This was a huge, iron steamship the largest of its time.

It was in 1858 that his greatest ship was completed. Brunel's *Great Eastern* was a massive ocean liner, the only ship in history to be propelled both by a propeller and paddle-wheels. It was five times bigger than anything already built and was intended to be the finest passenger-carrying ship in the world. Unfortunately, it was a commercial failure and in 1888 it was sold as old iron and broken up.

The *Great Eastern* was the finest achievement of Isambard Kingdom Brunel, the great mechanical and civil engineer.

1859
On Liberty is published

John Stuart Mill (1806–73) was one of the principal British intellectual thinkers behind modern Liberalism. He was a humanitarian who felt that the greatest good was to serve society, and he is best remembered for his brilliant essay, *On Liberty*. His belief in votes for women and the freedom of thought and speech influenced both his own and future generations.

1859
Tennyson's *Idylls of the King*

Born in Lincolnshire, Lord Tennyson (1809–92) was one of England's most respected Victorian poets. Following the publication of his poem *In Memoriam* (1850) he became poet laureate in succession to Wordsworth. The first *Idylls of the King*, long poems based upon the legend of King Arthur, appeared in 1859, establishing him as a great poet of his age.

1859
Publication of Darwin's *Origin of Species*

Charles Darwin (1809–82) was always an enthusiastic naturalist and in 1831 he set off on a voyage as official naturalist on board the naval survey ship *Beagle*. It was as he sailed past the Galapagos Islands and across the Pacific to Australia that Darwin made detailed observations of different animals and fossils.

Years after his trip Darwin published his findings in his *Origin of Species*. He had noticed the constant struggle for survival in nature; how the fittest of a species would survive and reproduce its own kind, while the naturally weak would die out. He concluded that over millions of years species had adapted to survive their ever-changing environment.

A storm of controversy broke out; it was felt Darwin was denying the biblical account of the origins of man as found in *Genesis*. However, Darwin's theory of natural selection finally won the day and when he died he was buried in Westminster Abbey.

1860
Garibaldi invades Sicily and Naples

Giuseppe Garibaldi (1807–82) was an important Italian patriot and liberator. In 1834 he joined the 'Young Italy' nationalist movement, and condemned to death for his revolutionary activities, he escaped to South America where he fought in two civil wars.

Garibaldi's most spectacular achievement was in 1860, when the nationalists were busy unifying the small states of northern Italy. Leading red-shirted volunteers known as 'the thousand heroes', Garibaldi, aided by Count Cavour (1820–78), set out to capture the south which was held by the King of

Naples. Within three months he had conquered Sicily; he soon entered Naples in triumph, and Victor Emmanuel was proclaimed King of Italy.

Twice in later years Garibaldi tried to take the city of Rome from the Pope, believing that then only Italy would be truly independent. Both attempts failed and Garibaldi devoted his last years to writing on behalf of oppressed nations.

1860
Introduction of the antiseptic system

In 1846 Joseph Lister (1827–1912) attended the first operation ever performed with the aid of anaesthetics (see 1842 Ether is used as an anaesthetic). Although this was to make surgery easier, it did not do much to make it safer; more patients still died from infections caused by inflamed wounds than from the actual operations. No-one had yet discovered why these post-operative infections occurred, or how they could be treated.

Lister worked for twelve years to solve the problem. In 1860 he became Professor of Surgery at Glasgow, Scotland, and at the Royal Infirmary he showed how carbolic acid mixed with water or oil could be used to kill germs before they multiplied; hands, dressings and instruments were to be disinfected in the mixture.

The results of Lister's work were shattering. Patients began to recover without the earlier post-operative complications and the number of deaths fell rapidly. The introduction of this antiseptic system is often known as the 'Listerian revolution'.

1860
Golf: The first British Open

It has never been clearly established when golf started, but it seems that it was almost certainly Scottish in origin; there is a recorded sale of a golf ball for ten Scottish shillings in 1452. The British Open Championship is the oldest championship in golf, dating from 1860; the National Open Championship in the USA started in 1895.

1860
First internal combustion engine

Attempts to develop efficient types of engines continued during the eighteenth and nineteenth centuries (see 1765 Watt improves the steam engine). The internal combustion followed on as an improvement to the steam engine.

Like so many other mid-nineteenth century inventions, no single person can be said to have invented the internal combustion engine. It was more the result of one hundred years' research. The varieties of steam engines soon proved unsatisfactory for road transport because huge amounts of coal or wood had to be carried about to keep the fire in the engine alight.

In 1860 Etienne Lenoir (1822–1900) a Frenchman, built an internal combustion engine that gave a reasonably satisfactory service operating on illuminating gas. It worked on a two-stroke cycle and several hundred were sold over the next few years.

The modern engine used in cars, however, is based on a four-stroke petrol engine built by Nikolaus Otto in 1876. The century of the automobile had begun.

1861
Krupp's first gun

Krupp was the name of a German industrial family which owned one of the largest steel and armaments works in Europe, producing its first gun in 1861. The firm was well-known for its social welfare; good schools, houses and co-operative stores were available for the workers. During World War I the firm became internationally famous when it produced heavy guns like *Big Bertha*, a 42-cm. howitzer.

Their food supplies had run out, yet starving and weak from exposure they set off towards Adelaide. They struggled on, but Burke and Wills died. Only King survived, cared for by natives.

1861
George Eliot's *Silas Marner*

Mary Ann Evans was born in Warwickshire, England, and had a severely religious upbringing. Adopting the pen-name of George Eliot, she wrote stories which revealed both a sense of humour and compassion for the terrible tragedies that strike at ordinary, simple people. *Silas Marner*, published in 1861, is the story of a weaver who brings up a child which he finds on his doorstep.

1861
Expedition to Flinders river

One of the most tragic events in the story of Australian exploration was the expedition led by Robert O'Hara Burke (1820–61), an Irish-born police officer. The party was given a grand farewell as it set off for the Australian interior. When the second-in-command resigned, he was replaced by William Wills, the party's astronomical observer.

While waiting for members of his party at Cooper's Creek, Burke grew impatient and set off with only Wills, King and Gray as companions. It was a foolhardy and ill-fated decision, but the men finally reached Flinders river in 1861, hungry and exhausted.

The return journey was a nightmare; Gray died and the remaining three found their camp at Cooper's Creek deserted.

1861
Outbreak of the American Civil War

The American Civil War took place between the eleven states in the south and the rest of the Union, when tension over the question of slavery rose to a head. For two centuries African slaves had been shipped to America. The northern

A Union soldier (left) and Confederate soldiers (right) from the American Civil War.

states now joined Europe in their belief that slavery should be abolished; the southern states disagreed, and wanted to leave the Federal Union, calling themselves the Confederate States of America.

The army of the north was wealthier, better equipped and bigger than that of the south, but it took bitter fighting and the loss of nearly seven hundred thousand lives before the quarrel was resolved.

The southerners fought with grim determination led by several exceptional men such as 'Stonewall' Jackson and Robert E Lee. Abraham Lincoln (1809–65) President of the United States, led the north. In 1863, after the north's victory at the battle of Gettysburg, Lincoln delivered his famous speech on democracy: '. . . that government of the people, for the people, by the people, shall not perish from the earth . . .'

In 1864 the north took the offensive and the south surrendered to General Grant in 1865. After the war slavery was abolished.

1862
Turgenev's *Fathers and Sons*

When *Fathers and Sons* was published in 1862, Ivan Sergeievitch Turgenev (1818–83) was already a well-known novelist and short story writer. Disliked in Russia by both revolutionaries and reactionaries, his book was immediately recognized as a great work abroad, especially in England. His attack on Russian serfdom, *Sportsman's Sketches* (1852), brought him into disrepute with the Russian government.

1862
Bismarck becomes prime minister

Many factors inspired the unification of the German states (*see 1819 The start of the Zollverein*), but the man who finally created a powerful German nation was Otto von Bismarck (1815–98).

Bismarck became prime minister of Prussia in 1862. His methods of government were harsh and often unscrupulous and he believed in rule by 'blood and iron' rather than rule by Parliament. Bismarck's determination to do everything possible to unite Germany under Prussia and to drive Austria out of the German states was in later years to earn him the name 'Iron Chancellor'.

In 1864 Bismarck successfully fought a war with Denmark to decide who should own Schleswig-Holstein, and the Danish defeat gave Prussia an important naval base at Kiel. After his victorious 'Seven Weeks' War' with Austria, Bismarck had a freer hand in Germany: he annexed some of the smaller states and united the remaining ones with Prussia under the North German Confederation.

1863
First underground railway

The world's first underground railway was opened in London in 1863 by the Metropolitan railway. This early underground line ran from Bishops Road to Farringdon Street (about six kilometres); the lines were in cuttings beneath the street, roofed over to take the road surface. The first European underground railway (in Budapest) was opened in 1896.

1863
Maximilian becomes Emperor of Mexico

In 1860 Benito Juárez, a Zapotec Indian, led a revolt against the dictatorship of Miramón in Mexico and with the support of the USA succeeded in overthrowing the dictator. When Juárez declared that he could not pay the national debts of Miramón's regime to France,

Britain and Spain, all three countries sent troops to occupy Mexico.

Britain and Spain soon came to an agreement with Juárez and as a result withdrew their troops. France, however, remained, largely because Emperor Napoleon III felt he could establish a colony there and on June 7, 1863 French troops entered Mexico City and over-threw Juárez. Napoleon persuaded Arch-duke Maximilian, brother of the Em-peror of Austria, to become Emperor of Mexico in 1863.

The USA was outraged by Napoleon's actions (*see 1823 Monroe Doctrine*) and sent troops to support Juárez. When the French were forced to withdraw, Juárez and his men captured Maximilian and executed him in 1867.

1863
Football Association founded

In the mid-nineteenth century football clubs started spreading through Britain and it was soon felt that a definitive set of rules for the game should be prepared. In October 1863, representatives of the clubs met to form the Football Associa-tion. The Association grew slowly; in 1871 it introduced the FA Cup compe-tition, and today it is respected through-out the world.

1864
The First Socialist International

Marx was largely responsible for found-ing the First Socialist International in London in 1864, a union of communist or socialist movements. His ideas on sub-jects such as education, trade unions and co-operatives were to prove invaluable.

The International soon split up, leav-ing Marx time to write *Das Kapital* ('Capital'). The International failed part-ly because Marx quarrelled with the rival leaders, but also because Marx's theories (*see 1848 The Communist Manifesto*)

Karl Marx lived for a period in London, preparing his theories on international communism in the British Museum reading room.

clashed with the anarchists' theories. Mikhail Bakunin (1814–76), the leading anarchist, was Marx's most vigorous opponent. He believed that instead of a government, a self-controlling system of little societies, undisturbed by outside forces, would form the ideal basis for society.

Marx believed in the 'dictatorship of the proletariat', a belief which forms the basis of modern communism. This theory advocated a situation where the proletariat (the industrial working class) makes and controls a new state of its own. Bakunin, however, rejected the idea of the state altogether.

1864
Dunant founds Red Cross

In 1862 a Swiss called Jean Henri Dunant (1828–1910) published a booklet urging people to set up voluntary socie-ties that would help the sick and wounded in time of war. Dunant had been horrified to learn that soldiers were left to die in open battlefields, with no medical attention.

Dunant's appeal had immediate results. An international conference took place in Geneva, Switzerland, in 1864 and twenty-six governments were represented. The conference led to the 'Geneva Convention'; the emblem of a red cross on a white background (the Swiss flag reversed) was adopted, as well as the motto 'Charity in War'.

The Convention agreed that the wounded should be respected; that military hospitals should be regarded as neutral and that buildings or vehicles marked by the Red Cross should be safe from attack.

In the Middle East today, a Red Crescent replaces the Red Cross, while in Persia a Lion or Sun is used.

1865
Booth founds Salvation Army

William Booth (1829–1912) was a strongly religious Englishman. In 1852 he became a regular preacher of the Methodist Church but he broke away nine years later to become an independent preacher.

In 1864 Booth went to London where he conducted services in tents and in the open air. In Whitechapel he then founded the Christian Mission (1865) which later became known as the Salvation Army, modelling the organization along the lines of the army, with himself as 'General'.

Booth was a man who believed that unconverted people would be eternally damned. However, he had great compassion for those who were less fortunate than himself and who lived in filth, misery and squalor. Above all, his Army was devoted to bringing people to salvation.

Music, especially brass bands, has always been an attractive and important feature of the Salvation Army, as has its

charitable work. Today there are branches throughout the world.

1865
Mendel announces heredity laws

Gregor Johann Mendel (1822–84) was an Austrian monk who lived in what is now Czechoslovakia. In the monastery garden he performed experiments leading to the basic principles of heredity.

Mendel's work involved the crossing and subsequent observation of various kinds of garden pea. He showed that inheritance involved pairs of contrasting characteristics such as tallness and shortness. These characteristics were described as either dominant (strong) or recessive (weak) and Mendel showed how a tall pea crossed with a short one resulted in a tall offspring. This was unexpected; it had been believed that a medium-sized plant would be the result of such a union.

Mendel achieved fame only after his death, when in 1900 three other botanists obtained results similar to his. Mendel has since taken his place in history as one of the great influences in the story of genetics (the science of heredity).

1865
Alice in Wonderland

Alice in Wonderland is a strange and fantastic tale written for children by a shy and retiring man, known as Lewis Carroll (1832–98), whose real name was Charles Lutwidge Dodgson. The story was published in 1865 with wonderful illustrations by Sir John Tenniel (1820–1914) and was followed in 1872 by *Through the Looking Glass and What Alice Found There*.

1866
Queensberry rules set up

By the 1860s people in Britain were rather disgusted by the brutality of the professional 'bruisers', as boxers were called, and were in favour of laws being enforced. In 1866 the Amateur Athletic Club was founded and in the same year Lord Queensberry drew up a code of laws which came to govern all contests in Britain.

1866
War and Peace completed

Leo Tolstoy (1828–1910), Russian novelist and moral philosopher, wrote two masterpieces; War and Peace (about Napoleon's invasion of Russia) and Anna Karenina. When he grew uneasy about his prosperous life, he renounced his wealth, and evolving his own pure form of Christianity, took up the life of an ordinary peasant.

1866
US Civil Rights Act

Tension soon grew concerning the political and civil rights of Negroes (see 1861 Outbreak of the American Civil War). In 1865 slavery was abolished in the USA but the southern states immediately tried to restrict the freedom of the Negroes. In 1866 Congress adopted the Civil Rights Act.

The act gave the Negro the right to vote, to sign contracts, to sue and to give evidence. It gave him rights in the face of the law and protection from violence. An attempt was made to rehabilitate the whites and Negroes in the devastated south, but it failed. The southern states were determined to keep the Negroes in an inferior position and on principle always opposed the politics of the north.

1866
Crime and Punishment

Fyodor Mikhailovich Dostoevsky (1821–81) was born in Moscow. Arrested in 1849 for belonging to a socialist society, he was sent to Siberia for four years. The theme of his novels centres round his sympathy for ordinary people humiliated at the hands of society. His greatest works include Crime and Punishment (1866), The Idiot, The Brothers Karamazov and The Possessed.

1867
Fenian Rising

The Fenians were an Irish-American secret society formed to remove British control from Ireland. It was founded in 1858 in the United States and its name was derived from the legendary band of warriors in Ireland led by Finn Mac Cumhaill.

When Irish-Americans flocked to Ireland after the American Civil War there was an increase in Fenian activities and plans for a rising. The government heard of the plans, however, and took immediate action: the Fenian paper was suppressed and several members of the society imprisoned.

In 1867 several minor risings broke out in Ireland and there was an attempt to take Chester Castle. A policeman was killed in Manchester and the three Fenians hanged for this became known as the 'Manchester martyrs'. Clerkenwell Prison, London, was then blown up in an attempt to free Fenian prisoners, and twelve people were killed.

1868
Disraeli and Gladstone come to power

From about 1865 British politics were dominated by the great political duel between two famous men, Gladstone and Disraeli. William Gladstone (1809–98)

Gladstone addressing the House.

was a Liberal, serious, earnest and very conscientious. His rival, Benjamin Disraeli of the Conservative party, was clever, witty, colourful and very romantic.

In 1868 Disraeli became prime minister for the first time (his second period was 1874–1880), but there was a strong demand for reform throughout Britain and in the same year he lost the General Election to the Liberals led by Gladstone. Gladstone was prime minister four times, and was to carry through a programme of overdue reforms before a real age of Conservatism could set in.

Gladstone and Disraeli disliked one another intensely. Disraeli accused Gladstone of not being a 'gentleman' and Gladstone thought Disraeli was immoral. Gladstone's main interest lay in the rights of the individual and the right to vote, while Disraeli's thoughts moved on a larger scale, concerned with general social conditions. In foreign affairs Gladstone disapproved of British expansion, but Disraeli was a true Victorian Imperialist.

Despite these personal differences both men can be regarded as great British statesmen, who in their own ways were responsible for some very important social changes.

1868
Japanese Shoguns overthrown

In the seventeenth century the Shogun (the hereditary general in control) had expelled foreigners from Japan, once more cutting the country off from the western world. In 1853, however, Commodore Perry sailed to Japan with a fleet of US warships. The Japanese were terrified, but finally agreed to grant fishing rights to the Americans. This was the start of a new age of westernization for Japan.

After a great deal of turmoil and internal tension the repressive Shogun was overthrown and Emperor Komei, under

the title of Meiji (which means En-
lightened Government) was restored to
the throne. The Japanese called this
period *Isshin* (Restoration), for they felt
that rightful power had been restored to
the emperor.

It was not long before feudalism was
abolished, for it was clear that this was
necessary to achieve the unification of the
nation. As a further sign of change the
emperor moved his court, with great
pomp and ceremony, to Tokyo, the
largest city.

1869

Mendeleyev's *Periodic Table of Elements*

Scientists have always tried to organize
their facts and to point out any inter-
relationships that may exist between
them. As far as the elements are concerned the obvious classification was into
metals and non-metals.

In 1864 John Newlands (1837–98) an
English chemist, arranged the elements
according to atomic weights. Yet his *Law
of Octaves* in which he discussed his
theory was not taken seriously until
similar theories were exposed.

In 1869 the Russian chemist Dmitri
Mendeleyev (1834–1907) published his
Periodic Table of Elements which, in many
ways, was an extension of Newlands's
work. Mendeleyev recognized, however,
that some elements had not yet been discovered and left gaps for them in his
table. His prediction that the gaps would
be filled by elements yet to be discovered
was remarkably accurate. One of the elements, 'mendelevium' was named in his
honour.

1869

Suez Canal opened

Plans to connect lower Egypt to the Red
Sea go back to ancient times. France

The Suez Canal, the work of French engineer
Ferdinand de Lesseps, was the key to trade with the
East, by-passing the lengthy route round the Cape.

looks out onto the Atlantic and the Mediterranean, and this, combined with her
economic and political rivalry with England in the nineteenth century, encouraged her plans to pierce the isthmus of
Suez with a waterway.

In 1854 a French engineer, Ferdinand
de Lesseps (1805–94), conceived his
scheme for the Suez Canal and in 1860
work began on it. The British government refused to help the scheme, as it
feared France's expansion in Egypt. The
French continued, nonetheless, using
Egyptian labour, and by 1869
432,807,882 French francs had been
spent on the project. In August the Canal
was completed.

On November 17, 1869 there was a
grand ceremony to open the Canal,
headed by the French imperial yacht,
Aigle. The British, by now grateful to de
Lesseps for his good work, gave him a
British knighthood.

1869
Publication of Verlaine's *Fêtes Galantes*

Paul Verlaine (1844–96), who wrote some of the finest poems in the French language, mixed with the Paris writers who lived in and around the Paris cafés. His collection of poems, *Fêtes Galantes*, is considered by many to be his finest work. The poems evoke a past age, the eighteenth century, of painters such as Watteau and Fragonard.

1869
Brahms's *Requiem* performed

Johannes Brahms (1833–97) the German composer, always maintained a hatred for opera, but his *German Requiem*, first performed in 1869, is a very great choral work. Brahms's music was solidly based on classical foundations; he acts as a link between Beethoven, the classical composer, and Schumann the romantic. Brahms is responsible for some of the greatest violin concertos ever written.

1870
Smetana's *Bartered Bride*

1870, the date of the premiere of Smetana's *Bartered Bride*, marks the birth of a truly Czech national school of music. Bedřich Smetana (1824–84) was one of Czechoslovakia's greatest composers and in 1866 he became conductor of the new National Theatre for which he wrote most of his operas. He became deaf in 1874, but continued composing until 1883.

1870
Franco-Prussian War

Bismarck needed one more war to unite Prussia (*see 1862 Bismarck becomes prime minister*). He chose France as his enemy, making the dispute over who should inherit the Spanish throne the immediate cause.

A Hohenzollern Prussian prince was a candidate, but France created such a storm of protest, that the Prussian prince withdrew. Prussia refused to guarantee that it would oppose any similar event in the future and so France declared war in 1870.

The war was disastrous for France: Napoleon III surrendered and the main army, besieged at Metz, capitulated in October. Meanwhile the Second Empire was overthrown and the Prussians bebesieged Paris.

In September 1870 Léon Gambetta (1832–82) had with others declared France a Republic. He had escaped from Paris to Tours in a balloon, where he set up the headquarters for France's defence and he became dictator for five months.

Bismarck reviewing Prussian troops before the Franco-Prussian War.

Gambetta's determination was remarkable; even when Paris capitulated through famine and internal discontent, he wanted, in vain, to continue the war.

The German Empire, proclaimed in 1871, imposed heavy peace terms on the French in the Treaty of Frankfurt. France lost Alsace-Lorraine and had to pay a war indemnity.

1870
Education Act

The nineteenth century was a period of change as far as British education was concerned; change from minor concern about children's education to wide control. There had been an act in 1833 which made part-time education compulsory for children working in factories, but it did nothing for children working elsewhere.

The first real Education Act was in 1870. School boards were set up and each board had to arrange for children under ten years of age to attend school. The board also had to arrange to pay school fees for the poorest parents. By 1876 school attendance was compulsory all over Britain and by 1891 all elementary schools were made free.

Between this act of 1870 and the one of 1944, the State became more and more aware of the necessity for full-time education for children between the ages of five and fifteen.

1871
William becomes Emperor of Germany

During the Franco–Prussian War negotiations were pushed on for the uniting of all Germany outside Austria. When France had declared war, the German states had rallied round William, the King of Prussia (1797–1888), so that he knew he had the support of a united nation. On January 18, 1871, during the siege of Paris, William was finally proclaimed Emperor of Germany at his headquarters in Versailles.

The question of what the new state should be called was a problem. Bismarck wanted to revive the title of German Emperor, although William disliked the idea and Bavaria was unhappy too. Yet as always, Bismarck had the last word.

A new *Reichstag* (parliament) was elected from all Germany, but its powers were not clearly defined in the beginning. Nor was it clear to whom Bismarck, now Chancellor, was responsible; Bismarck felt he was responsible to the emperor, while the politicians felt he was answerable to the *Reichstag*. The parliament was opened by William on March 21 and on June 16 he entered Berlin at the head of his troops. After this William tended to leave the destiny of Germany in Bismarck's capable hands.

1871
Paris Commune

At the close of the Franco–Prussian War, the agreement that German troops should march in triumph through Paris humiliated the French, and prompted the outbreak of the Paris Commune on March 18, 1871.

Throughout the war the French had been split in two: the more reactionary loyalists in the provinces wanted peace with Prussia, while the revolutionaries in Paris had wanted war and to set up a more extremist Republic. The Commune was like a second siege of Paris, with the revolutionaries barricading themselves inside the capital.

It was Adolphe Thiers (1797–1877) who had persuaded the National Assembly to agree to peace, and now it was he who crushed the 'communards'. His troops stormed Paris on May 21. The violent fighting and massacre that followed (known as 'bloody week') resulted in the death of over twenty-six thousand Parisians. It was the end of what the French Socialists called the first 'workers' republic'.

1871
Rugby Football Union founded

Football was played in English public schools, yet no two schools had the same rules. All agreed, however, that the ball must never be carried or passed by hand. This rule was violated in 1823 in Rugby School, leading to the modern Rugby football. Its rules were codified in 1871 when a group calling itself the Rugby Football Union met in London.

1871
Livingstone meets Stanley

David Livingstone (1813–73) was a Scottish medical missionary and explorer. In 1858 he was commissioned by the British Government to explore eastern and central Africa, and it was on this trip that he discovered Lake Nyasa. For the first time he entered an area devastated by the slave trade and determined then to rid Africa of this human sacrifice.

In 1866 he set out on a private trip to continue his fight against the slave trade and to find the source of the Nile. In constant danger from Arab slave traders, he suffered terrible hardships, especially when his medical chest was stolen. In Europe he was given up for lost, but in November 1871 HM Stanley (1841–1904), who had been sent to Africa by an American newspaper, found Livingstone on the east coast of Lake Tanganyika and greeted him with the now famous words: 'Dr Livingstone, I presume'.

1871
Zola starts *Les Rougon-Macquart*

Emile Zola (1840–1902), the French novelist, evolved his pseudo-scientific theory of the 'naturalistic' novel around 1868. He believed that birth, background and circumstances formed a character and felt that the novel should be a form of human case history. The *Rougon-Macquart* series was a cycle of twenty novels, some quite brutal, based around the members of one family.

1871
Trade Unions legalized in Britain

British trade unionism grew very fast after 1825 when the Combination Acts were repealed, which meant that they were no longer regarded as criminal associations. They still had no legal status, yet in spite of this, and in spite of the harsh treatment of six labourers (see *1834 Tolpuddle Martyrs*) unionism spread.

In 1851 the Amalgamated Society of Engineers was formed, one of the most famous of the early trade unions. This union was to act as a model for others for it included several separate unions such as machinists, blacksmiths and fitters. The fight was now really on, and several other similar unions were formed; they were powerful and determined to make unions recognized, legal bodies and to strengthen themselves they elected a special committee to represent them.

Their determination was soon rewarded when in 1871 the Trade Union Act recognized them as legal associations. The Act also granted workers the right to strike and the right to picket.

1872
The Ballot Act

South Australia was the first state to introduce the secret ballot act (1856), since when it is usual to refer to it as the Australian ballot. The system then spread to Europe and America, reaching Great Britain in 1872. It was introduced through the Ballot Act to meet the growing public and parliamentary demand for the protection of voters.

1873
Ashanti War

In the nineteenth century the people of Ashanti (today a region in Ghana) conquered many of their coastal neighbours, hoping to increase their slave trade with Europeans. Britain abolished the slave trade and made peace with the coastal peoples, so the humiliated Ashantis attacked their neighbours. British troops soon moved in and destroyed the Ashanti capital, Kumasi, in 1874.

The Trade Unions, legalized in Britain in 1871, had grown to a powerful movement by the 1920s. The sense of pride in belonging to a Union was typified by the banners of each branch.

1873
Rimbaud's *Une Saison en Enfer*

Arthur Rimbaud (1854–91) was a young French poet, who wrote mainly between the age of fifteen and twenty. Greatly inspired by Baudelaire and his friend, Verlaine, Rimbaud was to become a master for the Symbolists. His collection *Une Saison en Enfer* illustrates his view that a poet must deliberately suffer mental anguish in search of experience.

243

1873
Verne's 'Around the World in Eighty Days'

Jules Verne (1828–1905) was the French author of innumerable adventure stories, combining a vivid imagination with a gift for popularizing science. *Le Tour du Monde en quatre-vingt Jours* ('Around the World in Eighty Days') was the story of Phileas Fogg who, accompanied by his valet Passepartout, wins a bet to travel round the world in eighty days.

1874
The first Impressionist Exhibition

In 1863 a painting called *Déjeuner sur l'herbe* was shown at the Salon des Refusés in Paris – established by Napoleon III for artists turned down by traditional exhibitions. It was by Edouard Manet (1832–83); the nude woman in the painting shocked the public, but the technique amazed the experts. With Manet, a number of artists who sympathized with his ideas, formed a new school, and in 1874 they held an exhibition at the studio of the photographer, Nadar.

A weekly paper ridiculed the artists for deserting the traditional school and called them 'Impressionists'. The name stuck – and Impressionism turned out to be one of the most revolutionary and lively experiences of nineteenth century art.

The Impressionists advocated painting in the open air, emphasizing the effects of light, and the use of a light palette. Claude Monet (1840–1926) who first painted in sunlight in 1866, painted the effects of sun and the smoke of the engines of the Gare St Lazare. Renoir (1841–1919) painter of the *Swing* had similar ideas to Monet, as did Pissarro and Sisley.

Other famous Impressionists include Edgar Degas, who painted several lovely ballerinas and a masterpiece, *l'Absinthe*, and Paul Cézanne, painter of the beautiful landscape *Montagne de Ste Victoire*.

1874
Mussorgsky's *Boris Godunov*

Modest Petrovich Mussorgsky (1835–81) resigned his commission in the army to devote his life to music. He was a member of a Russian nationalist group of musicians known as 'The Five' which included Rimsky-Korsakov, and first made his name with his songs. The opera *Boris Godunov*, his masterpiece, was based on a play by Pushkin and appeared in St Petersburg in 1874.

Richard Wagner and a scene from his opera *The Flying Dutchman*.

1876
Wagner's *Ring* at Bayreuth

Richard Wagner (1813–83) was a poet and one of Germany's greatest dramatic composers. He reformed the whole structure of opera, abandoning the traditional use of aria and recitative in favour of a perfect fusion of drama and music.

Wagner was the first to use the *leitmotif* successfully: musical themes introduce and identify different characters in his operas and this both aids dramatic development and psychological exposition.

In 1870 a theatre was built at Bayreuth and Wagner gave a full performance there of his work *The Ring of the Nibelungs* in 1876. This vast work is a cycle of four full-scale operas in which Wagner draws upon Teutonic mythology, using gods, dwarfs and giants to illustrate the corrupting effect of the lust for power in hearts which have renounced love.

Other operas by Wagner include *The Flying Dutchman, Parsifal, The Mastersingers* and *Tristan and Isolde*.

1876
The Battle of Little Big Horn

The massacre of the North American Indians by white men remains to this day a controversial issue, although it is generally believed that the Indians were justified in protecting their rights to live as they pleased. The Battle of Washita (1868) was the beginning of the end for the southern Plains Indians. George Armstrong Custer (1839–76) led his cavalry in this slaughter of the Cheyenne and it has since been called 'Custer's Massacre.'

Hostilities between Red Man and White Man continued. When Custer and

245

the seventh army were ordered against the Sioux, Custer was taken by surprise when he reached the valley of Little Big Horn. Instead of a few Indians, he was confronted by a well-prepared force and was soon hemmed in. It was to be 'Custer's last stand', for as he and his two hundred and twenty-six men rode into the midst of the enemy, they were slaughtered.

Tchaikovsky

1876
Tchaikovsky's *Swan Lake*

Piotr Ilyich Tchaikovsky (1840–93), the Russian composer, is best known for his ballet music, *The Sleeping Beauty*, *Nutcracker* and *Swan Lake* (1876). They are composed of short themes, but they are dramatic and contain some of his loveliest music. Tchaikovsky died of cholera soon after the first performance of the *Pathétique* symphony, a work reflecting his melancholy nature.

1876
Bell invents the telephone

Alexander Graham Bell (1847–1922) was a Scottish-American physicist and inventor. In 1876 he exhibited an apparatus embodying the results of his studies in the transmission of sound by electricity – the basis of the modern telephone. The first telephone message transmitted was from Bell to his assistant: 'Mr Watson, please come here: I want you.'

The world of Mark Twain: Huckleberry Finn and a Mississippi riverboat.

1876
Tom Sawyer is published

Mark Twain's real name was Samuel Langhorne Clemens (1835–1910). He was an American writer, who took his pen-name from the cry Mississippi pilots used when they were taking soundings ('mark twain', meaning 'by the mark two fathoms'). His famous novels *Tom Sawyer* and *The Adventures of Huckleberry Finn* (1884) have become world classics and give a wonderful picture of life on and around the Mississippi.

1876
Mallarmé's *L'Après-midi d'un faune*

Stéphane Mallarmé (1842–98), a French poet, has been described as 'the crown and conclusion of the Symbolist Movement'. He believed that poems should suggest rather than describe and that words had meanings beyond their everyday significance. His masterpiece, the pastoral short poem *L'Après-midi d'un faune* ('The Afternoon of a Faun'), which inspired the musician Debussy, was published in 1876.

1877
Whistler v. Ruskin

In 1877 James Whistler (1834–1903), an American artist, sued John Ruskin, English author and art critic, for libel. Ruskin (1819–1900) had accused Whistler of flinging a pot of paint in the public's face, and the lawsuit that followed was subsequently famous for representing two opposing nineteenth century attitudes to art. Whistler won the lawsuit and was awarded a farthing damages.

Whistler believed that a painting must, above all, be a work of art; that it should be a 'harmony' of perfect shapes and colours which would give pleasure independently of the subject matter. This kind of thinking led to the battlecry 'art for art's sake.'

Ruskin on the other hand, opposed this philosophy fiercely. A Victorian moralist, he was interested in social problems, education, morals and religion. He never sought to produce anything that he would call a 'work of art', but largely drew buildings or natural objects as they appeared to his eye.

1878
Edison patents the phonograph

Thomas Alva Edison (1847–1931), American inventor, was by the age of thirty, already highly successful. After producing many new devices to increase the efficiency of the Western Union Company's telegraph and telephone services, he went on to invent and patent an automatic repeater which sent messages from one wire to the next. His phonograph, or talking machine, was an early type of record player.

The phonograph used a revolving cylinder covered with tin foil which Edison had to turn by hand, as electric motors were not then in common use. Mechanical vibrations were created when the operator spoke into the recording tube and a needle transferred these on to the tin foil. The impressions on the tin foil represented the loudness and pitch of the recorded voice. Another needle was then moved along the impressions and the vibrations reproduced the voice in the hearing tube.

Edison and his phonograph.

1878
Edison and Swan produce light bulb

In 1860 Sir Joseph Wilson Swan invented an electric lamp, so it can be said that he was the real pioneer of electric lighting as we know it. Swan (1828–1914) was an English physicist and chemist, who also patented the carbon process for photographic printing.

Swan's lamp had contained a carbon filament which glowed, though not brightly. Nearly twenty years later both Edison (*see 1878 Edison's phonograph*) working on Swan's idea, and Swan himself, produced a greatly improved lamp.

The aim had been to produce a bulb which could be manufactured cheaply and easily: the secret lay in the filament. The 'Edison and Swan bulb' used a filament made from a length of carbonized sewing thread, mounted in an evacuated glass tube. This bulb produced a glow for forty hours. In 1882 the people of New York watched as Edison switched on the world's first electric light system.

1879
Zulu War

European powers did not hesitate to grab African territory to further their own trade. The British and Dutch fought over the south and in so doing the British confronted the Zulu people of the Bantu tribes. The Zulus were finally crushed by the British, and the government annexed Zululand (now a part of South Africa) to the crown in 1887.

1879
Panama Canal started

When explorers after Columbus found that the two American continents were a barrier to the far east, interest in the possibility of an interoceanic waterway was aroused. In 1879 the Panama Canal company was founded with de Lesseps as president (*see 1869 Suez Canal opened*). By 1889 work stopped because the firm went bankrupt, but the Canal was finally opened in 1915.

The Zulus strongly resisted the encroachment of European settlers.

1880
Death of Ned Kelly

After 1776 the British began to use Australia as a penal colony, even though a number of the criminals sent to Australia were guilty of only petty offences such as poaching. Much of Australia was therefore colonized by freed prisoners and gold diggers. These were lawless times and many lawbreaking colonialists were ruthlessly hunted down by the police and their Aborigine scouts. Life generally became very difficult for them in this repressive situation.

As a reaction to their hardships many of these men became outlawed bushrangers. Their spectacular raids on banks and towns, their horse-thieving and attacks on policemen made them notorious – and over the years many became national heroes.

The most famous and often-told story is that of the bushranger Ned Kelly (1855–80) who after a shoot-out at Glenrowan was hanged. His name lives on and in Australia it is said that a brave man is 'as game as Ned Kelly'.

1881
The First South African War

In 1881 the descendants of Dutch settlers in South Africa, known as Boers, rose against the British in an attempt to regain the independence that they had previously given up in return for protection against the warlike Zulus. The

British were defeated at Majuba, and at the Convention of Pretoria, the Transvaal received a degree of self-government, pioneer Paulus Kruger (1825–1904) becoming president in 1883.

The quarrel was not over. Non-Boer European settlers (or *Uitlanders*, mainly British) swarmed into the Transvaal, soon threatening to out-number the Boers. Kruger denied them an effective vote. In 1895 L S Jameson (1853–1917) of the British South Africa Company led an unofficial raid into the Transvaal with the connivance of Cecil Rhodes (1853–1902) premier of Cape Colony. The raid did not succeed, and the hoped-for *Uitlander* uprising did not occur. (*See 1899 The Second South Africa War.*)

1881
Ibsen's 'Ghosts' published

Henrik Ibsen (1828–1906) was a Norwegian poet and an outstanding pioneer of social drama. His *Dukkehjem* ('A Doll's House') and *Genganere* ('Ghosts') were disliked at the time as they dealt with controversial questions such as marriage, venereal disease and corruption. A stroke in 1900 ended his literary career, but he had already caused a revolution in the world of drama.

1881
Parnell imprisoned

As an MP Charles Stewart Parnell (1846–91) was a leading figure in the struggle to win independence for Ireland. He used two methods to focus attention on Irish grievances: he deliberately obstructed debates at the House of Commons; and he organized the Irish peasants into boycotting unpopular, absent landlords.

In October 1881 Parnell was imprisoned for a short time for inciting the Irish, but while he was in prison disorders in Ireland grew worse and so Gladstone released him. In 1882 Irish terrorists murdered the Chief Secretary and Under-Secretary for Ireland as they were walking through Phoenix Park in Dublin. Parnell denounced the murders and later won a libel action against *The Times*, which had maintained that he had been involved.

Parnell remained a powerful political figure until he became involved in a sensational divorce case. Gladstone and public opinion swung against him immediately and he lost his hold on the Irish party.

1881
James's *Portrait of a Lady*

The American novelist, Henry James (1843–1916) is regarded as the master of the psychological novel, and one of the greatest influences on twentieth century literature. *Portrait of a Lady* is largely concerned with the impact of American life on the older European civilization.

1882
Koch isolates TB bacillus

Tuberculosis is a serious disease that occurs throughout the world. The most common form is tuberculosis of the lungs, popularly called 'consumption'.

For years it was believed that the disease might be contagious, but the infecting agent was not discovered until 1882, when the German bacteriologist Robert Koch (1843–1910) isolated the tubercle bacillus.

He discovered that the lungs are invaded by the bacilli bacteria and that the infected person expels them into the atmosphere when he coughs or talks. The bacilli are tough and resist disinfectants, but can be killed quickly by sunlight or ultra-violet light.

Tuberculosis used to be called the 'white plague' and was incurable, but thanks to Koch's work and modern treatment, patients can now be completely restored to normal health.

1882
Australia wins the Ashes

When an Australian cricket team visited England in 1882 the Australians won the match by seven runs; a stump was 'cremated' in celebration and the ashes placed in an urn. The shattering English defeat was given an obituary notice in the *Sporting Times* and since then test matches between England and Australia have been called the 'Ashes'.

1883
Treasure Island is published

Robert Louis Stevenson (1850–94) was born in Scotland. *Treasure Island* was his first popular romantic thriller and is read by both adults and children all over the world. Other well-known works by this traveller constantly in search of health, include *Kidnapped* (an adventure story of the Scottish highlands) and *The Strange Case of Dr Jekyll and Mr Hyde*.

A scene from Stevenson's *Treasure Island*.

1883
Founding of Fabian Society

In the winter of 1883 a Socialist group calling itself the Fabian Society was formed by a small gathering in London. Its aim was to spread socialism by peaceful means and so gradually to reconstruct society in accordance with the highest moral possibilities.

The Fabians, who were joined and later led by George Bernard Shaw and Sidney Webb, were influenced by Marxism, but they based their economic philosophy not on Marx but on John Stuart Mill (*see 1859 On Liberty is published*). Unlike the Marxists, who believed that the state should be overthrown, the Fabians regarded the state as a social machine which should be used to develop social welfare.

Beatrice Webb, Sydney's wife, later joined the society and together in 1894

they published their classic *History of Trade Unionism* and started the journal *The New Statesman* in 1913.

The society was and is largely a body of intellectuals and many leading trade unionists have been members.

1883
Krakatoa erupts

The volcano of Krakatoa (between Java and Sumatra) had been dormant for two hundred years when in 1883 it burst into violent eruptions that could be heard from west Australia. Dense, volcanic clouds and ash were hurled into the air as huge waves, over thirty-six metres high, swamped the coasts of Java and Sumatra, drowning thirty-six thousand people.

1883
'Thus spake Zarathustra' is published

Friedrich Wilhelm Nietzsche (1844–1900) was a German philosopher and critic who was strongly anti-Christian. He believed that mankind was divided into two: a large herd, which he despised and a small, aristocratic master-class. His idea of a 'superman', developed in *Also sprach Zarathustra* ('Thus spake Zarathustra'), appealed particularly to the Nazis, although they often misinterpreted his philosophy.

1884
First steam turbo-generator

Sir Charles Algernon Parsons (1854–1931) was an English engineer, famous for his work on the steam turbine engine which he first constructed as a turbo-generator in 1884. In 1894 Parsons took out a patent to use the generator in ship propulsion; the first ship to be driven in this way was the *Turbinia* (1897).

1884
First gramophone record is made

The oldest existing record is a cylinder record made in 1884. It was made by a man called Emile Berliner and was a recording of him reciting the Lord's Prayer. The first practical foil cylinder phonograph was manufactured in the USA in 1886 (*see 1878 Edison patents the phonograph*). In 1888 Berliner invented the flat disc to replace the cylinder.

1884
Toulouse-Lautrec settles in Montmartre

Henri de Toulouse-Lautrec (1864–1901) was a French painter permanently crippled after an accident. In 1884 he settled in Montmartre which his paintings and posters were to make famous. Lautrec's studies of prostitutes, barmaids, clowns, actors and cabaret stars leave us with a vivid picture of the café and gay night-club life of Paris in *la belle époque*.

1884
William Morris forms Socialist League

William Morris (1834–96) was an English poet, artist and socialist and possibly one of the most talented of Britain's Victorians. He and a group of friends known as the 'brotherhood', used to meet and together read theology, ecclesiastical history, and medieval poetry. Morris adored the middle ages for their beauty and good craftsmanship and devoted his life to work which would rid society of the uglier aspects of a modernized, industrial civilization.

Morris set up a business which included the artists D G Rossetti (1828–82) and Burne-Jones (1833–98) to undertake church decor, carving, stained glass, chintzes and paper-hangings – always using pure colour and handwork.

In 1884 he helped set up the Socialist League and was arrested several times for his public speaking. However, he became less prominent when the Anarchist section took over. It was said by friends that his socialism was tinged with an inaccessible idealism, but his influence both on art and politics still lives on.

1885
Benz's first motor car

Karl Benz (1844–1929) was a German engineer. In 1879 he founded an engine factory of his own, having constructed a two-stroke engine model, but he left the firm when his backers refused to finance a mobile engine.

Benz then set up another firm, Benz and Co., *Rheinische Gasmotorenfabrik*, where he developed a light high-speed four-stroke engine, finally completing his first car in 1885. This was one of the earliest petrol-driven vehicles. He sold this car, which could do between 10 and 16 kph, and then joined the firm of Panhard and Lavasseur.

Meanwhile Gottlieb Daimler (1834–1900) was involved in similar work, making his first motor bicycle in 1885 and his first four-wheeled vehicle in 1886. In 1890 he founded the Daimler *Motoren-Gesellschaft*. In 1926 Benz's firm merged with Daimler's.

1885
Death of Gordon

Charles George Gordon (1833–85) was a British soldier and a colonial administrator. He had served in the Crimean War, and had taken part in the capture of Peking when in 1863 the Chinese asked for his help in suppressing a number of rebellions. His success in crushing the rebels earned him the name of 'Chinese Gordon'.

General Gordon, killed in Khartoum by rebels of the Mahdi.

In 1877 Gordon was appointed governor of the Sudan where his feats of government astounded the world. He returned a few years later having brought peace and order to the land.

Early in 1884 he was sent back to the Sudan to deal with an armed revolt led by the Mahdi. Instead of evacuating Khartoum as ordered, Gordon was determined to quash the Mahdi, whose troops surrounded Khartoum. The siege lasted for five months, but a relief expedition sent by Britain arrived too late. Khartoum had fallen and Gordon had been killed on the palace steps.

1886
Lawn Tennis Association founded

In about 1874 the All England Croquet Club, at Wimbledon, a suburb of London, discovered that it was short of money. In an attempt to boost the funds it added 'Lawn Tennis' to its title and several grass courts to its facilities. The first championships were held there in June 1877. In 1886 the English Lawn Tennis Association was founded.

1886
Canadian Pacific Railway completed

In 1886 the Canadian Pacific Railway was completed, linking the Pacific to the Atlantic. Until then Canada had been no more than a loose association of colonies which were beginning to feel acutely their isolation from one another. On May 23, 1887 the first train ran from the east to Vancouver, a distance of about 5,380 kilometres.

1887
Sherlock Holmes's first case

Sherlock Holmes, the super-observant amateur detective, was the creation of English novelist Sir Arthur Conan Doyle (1859–1930). *A Study in Scarlet*, which appeared in 1887, introduced Holmes and Dr Watson, his good-natured, questioning friend and partner in crime detection. Over the years, Holmes and his frequent interjection 'Elementary, my dear Watson!' have become household words.

1887
Strindberg's 'The Father' is published

Johan August Strindberg (1849–1912) was a Swedish dramatist, novelist and poet, born in Stockholm. His plays *Fadren* ('The Father') and *Fröken Julie* ('Miss Julie', 1888), form a landmark of importance in the history of naturalism in the European theatre. Other similar plays followed, most of which were concerned with Strindberg's attack on marriage, a result of his own marital tragedy.

1888
Van Gogh paints *Sunflowers*

Vincent van Gogh (1853–90) was a Dutch post-Impressionist painter whose strong brush strokes and vigorous use of colour make his paintings unmistakable. In 1888 he moved alone and in poverty to Arles, France, where the sunbaked, violent landscape was to influence him in paintings such as *Sunflowers*. In 1889 he entered an asylum after cutting off his ear, and in 1890 he shot himself.

1888
Pasteur Institute founded

Louis Pasteur (1822–95), a French chemist, was responsible for revolutionizing medical science. His researches led him to discover that fermentation and mould in food was not caused by a chemical reaction, but by microscopic living organisms. These findings led to the modern study of bacteriology. They also led Pasteur to find that germs could be killed by moderate heat. This process ('pasteurization') could be used to prevent beer, wine and milk from going bad.

Pasteur is perhaps best remembered for his vaccination of sheep and cows against anthrax, when he discovered that to inject an animal with a weakened culture of a disease would prevent the animal from developing the disease itself.

His last triumph was the development of a rabies vaccination and in 1888 the Pasteur Institute was founded in Paris to produce this vaccine. There are now over sixty Pasteur Research Institutes in the world.

1888
Rimsky-Korsakov's *Scheherazade*

Nikolai Andreievich Rimsky-Korsakov (1844–1908), the Russian composer was a member of 'The Five' (*see 1874 Mussorgsky's Boris Godunov*). In 1877 he published a collection of Russian folk songs and from 1887–8 he produced his three great orchestral masterpieces, *Capriccio Espagnol, Easter Festival* and *Scheherazade*. His operatic masterpiece was the pastoral *Snow Maiden* (1882).

1889
Mayerling tragedy

Rudolph of Hapsburg (1858–89), Crown Prince of Austria, was the only son of the emperor Francis Joseph I of Austria and his wife, Elizabeth.

Rudolph was an extremely talented boy, and his father had great hopes for his future, but while the emperor was chiefly intent on his son's military education, Rudolph was keenly interested in natural history and the arts. He had a wide knowledge of modern literature and philosophy and as his revolutionary views became more apparent, he drifted away from his father.

Rudolph was married but soon became involved in a passionate love affair with the young and beautiful Baroness Marie Vetsera. The emperor ordered him to break off this liaison and in January 1889 came the tragic news: in a fit of despair Rudolph had shot the Baroness and then committed suicide. The bodies of the two lovers had been found in Rudolph's hunting lodge in Mayerling.

1889
Eiffel Tower is built

The Eiffel Tower was erected between 1887–89 at the time of the great Paris Exhibition. The engineer responsible for it, Gustave Eiffel (1832–1923), had already designed several notable bridges and viaducts. The Tower was built on the Champ-de-Mars in Paris at a cost of £260,000 and was three hundred metres high on completion.

1889
Second Socialist International

The Second Socialist International set up in Paris in 1889 was a second attempt at the organization of International Socialism (*see 1864 First Socialist International*).

It was not a highly centralized association as its predecessor had been and did not establish a formal secretariat until 1900.

The movement was seriously weakened by internal conflict and in 1905 the International in Amsterdam condemned the participation of socialist parties in 'bourgeois coalitions'. The outbreak of World War I in 1914 totally shattered the association, for the International had approved resolutions demanding joint action by the workers to prevent war, but the various national parties failed to respond. (*See 1919 Comintern formed.*)

1890
Fall of Bismarck

After the peace of Frankfurt (*see 1870 Franco–Prussian War*) Bismarck's policy, both domestic and foreign, concentrated on consolidating and securing the young German empire.

His domestic policy was marked by universal suffrage, nationalization of the Prussian railways, codification of the law and many attempts to combat socialism. However, he distrusted movements with international affiliations and quarrelled bitterly with the Roman Catholics in the 1870s (Bismarck feared the political power of the Vatican) and with the Socialists in the 1880s.

Two years after the accession of the young William II (1859–1941), the emperor dismissed Bismarck. The Chancellor now found himself out of step with the younger generation in Germany and quarrelled with William over home and foreign policy.

William sought a new course for Germany, asserting the country's claim to world leadership. A long spell of personal rule now followed for the emperor, helped out by political favourites such as Holstein and Van Bülow.

Oscar Wilde, (second from left) surrounded by figures of London Society.

1891

Oscar Wilde writes *Dorian Gray*

Oscar Fingall O'Flahertie Wills Wilde (1854–1900) was an Irish writer and poet who achieved immortality with plays such as *Lady Windermere's Fan* (1893) and *The Importance of Being Ernest* (1899), which are masterpieces of humour. Wilde became a notorious figure in London society, for his witty epigrams and unconventional behaviour.

His concept of 'art for art's sake', the idea that aesthetic pleasure was an end in itself, found an echo with many European intellectuals at a time when the mainstream of European literature was concerned with naturalism and social issues. The aesthetic approach of Wilde's novel *Dorian Gray* (1891) is also to be found in an extreme expression in the French novel *A Rebours* ('Against Nature', 1884) by J K Huysmans (1848–1907), and the illustrations of Aubrey Beardsley (1872–98). The figure of the aesthetic poet, striking a pose, became a favourite target of cartoonists in *Punch* and other humorous magazines.

1891
Gaugin starts Tahiti paintings

Paul Gauguin (1848–1903) was a French post-Impressionist painter. He had a deep-rooted hatred of civilization which led him to abandon his wife and family in favour of a primitive life. He spent some time in Martinique and then in Tahiti, which inspired his tapestry-like paintings in distinctive purples, greens, reds and browns.

fuel; the air is heated before the fuel is let in and then the oil is sprayed into the cylinder so that tiny drops are ignited in the hot air. Today diesel engines are commonly used for buses, taxis and lorries.

1893
Lilienthal successfully flies a glider

Otto Lilienthal (1849–96) was a German aeronautical inventor. He studied birds in flight with the idea of building a heavier-than-air flying machine like the birdman designs of Leonardo da Vinci.

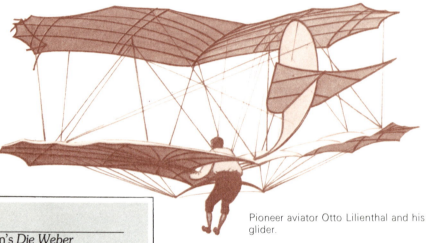

Pioneer aviator Otto Lilienthal and his glider.

1892
Hauptmann's *Die Weber*

Gerhart Hauptmann (1862–1946) was a German dramatist and novelist, born in Silesia. His first play, *Vor Sonnenaufgang* ('Before Sunrise'), introduced the social drama of Ibsen, Zola and Strindberg to Germany, but his plays contained a new sense of compassion which other plays often lacked. *Die Weber* ('The Weavers') is the tale of Silesian weavers in revolt in 1844.

Lilienthal made over two thousand short glides, but in 1896 he was caught in a gust of wind and he crashed to his death.

1893
Dvořák's *From the New World*

Antonin Dvořák (1841–1904) was a Czech composer born near Prague; his close friend was Brahms. His most famous work is his ninth symphony which he wrote in 1893 in New York, calling it a symphony *From the New World*. It contains some American folk themes, but the beautiful solo of the cor anglais is particularly noteworthy.

1892
Diesel invents engine

The first diesel engine was made in 1897 by the German inventor Rudolf Diesel (1858–1913). The engine uses oil as a

1893
Nansen sets sail in the *Fram*

Fridtjof Nansen (1861–1930) was a Norwegian explorer, whose most spectacular achievement began in 1893, when he set out on his voyage to the North Pole. Nansen decided to let his ship get frozen into the ice north of Siberia and drift with the current towards Greenland; the *Fram* had been specially built to survive the ordeal.

By September 1893 the *Fram* had reached the most northerly point of Siberia, where the ice was ten metres thick. The ship made fast to an ice-floe and began to drift northward, and in 1895 Nansen and a companion set off on foot across the ice. They came to within three hundred and twenty kilometres of the North Pole, farther north than any previous explorers, but turned back, exhausted by the extreme cold.

The *Fram* turned up a week after they had returned to Norway. As Nansen had hoped, it had drifted round the North Pole.

1894
The Dreyfus scandal

In October 1894 Alfred Dreyfus (1859–1935), an Alsatian Jewish officer on the French General Staff, was court-martialled for treason and sentenced to life imprisonment. The evidence consisted of military letters, apparently in Dreyfus's handwriting, that were betraying France.

Dreyfus's family never ceased to believe in his innocence. When in 1896 the new Chief of Intelligence tried to re-open the case, he was silenced and transferred to Tunisia. He had named the real traitor as Major Esterhazy, who was tried but acquitted by a court-martial.

The French Radicals were soon aroused, believing that the anti-Semitic General Staff were guilty of prejudice. The author, Zola, and Clemenceau took up the case and eventually it was dis-

covered that false evidence had been used against Dreyfus. The Dreyfusards pressed for acquittal and in July 1906 the court-martial verdict was quashed. Dreyfus was finally re-admitted to the army and given the Legion of Honour.

1894
Kipling's *Jungle Books* published

Rudyard Kipling (1865–1936) was an English writer born in India. His best-loved books are his two *Jungle Books* (1894–95) and *The Just-So Stories* which display his great genius for story-telling. The story of Mowgli, the man-child brought up in the jungle by the wolf family is read by children all over the world.

India is the setting of Kipling's famous story *Kim*, about a child spy.

1895
Marconi's first wireless message

Guglielmo Marconi (1874–1937) was an Italian physicist and the inventor of the first practical system of wireless telegraphy. In 1895 he succeeded in transmitting wireless signals between sending and receiving points without the use of connecting wires, to a distance just over two kilometres.

In 1896 Marconi went to London where he met William Preece, engineer-in-chief of the post office. Preece offered him help and encouragement and Marconi took out his first patent in England in June. During that year he gave a series of demonstrations using balloons and kites to obtain greater height for his aerials. In 1898 Marconi managed to arrange wireless communication between ships and the shore and in 1899 he set up the first wireless communication between Britain and Europe.

Marconi's greatest triumph was to come in 1901, when he successfully transmitted wireless signals across the Atlantic ocean between England and America.

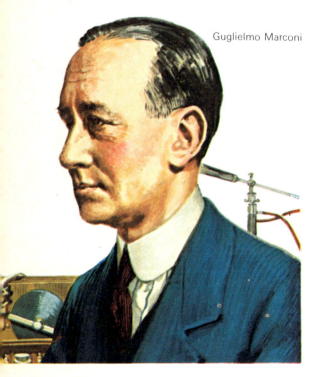

Guglielmo Marconi

1895
The Lumière cinematograph

August Lumière (1862–1954) and his brother Louis (1864–1948) were French pioneer film-makers. In 1889 Thomas Edison patented a form of peep-show machine for showing photographic mov-

ing pictures to one viewer at a time (*see 1878 Edison's phonograph*). The Lumière brothers then began to manufacture films for the Edison peepshow and by 1895 they had patented a device which would both photograph and project films.

Throughout the year the Lumière brothers gave demonstrations of their cinematograph to photographic societies, and in the winter they rented a room in a café for their first public shows. It was the first time that films had been shown to a paying audience.

Parallel projects were, of course, pursued in other countries, particularly in the USA. In 1896 the first 'screen kiss' was made, between May Irwin and John C Rice from their stage success *The Widow Jones*.

1895
Röntgen discovers X-rays

It was in 1895 that the German physicist Wilhelm Konrad von Röntgen (1845–1923) made his most important discovery. He noticed that when electrons travelling at high speed hit an aluminium anode at one end of a cathode ray tube

Röntgen's invention was to have many uses. X-rays can be used by engineers to show up metal defects.

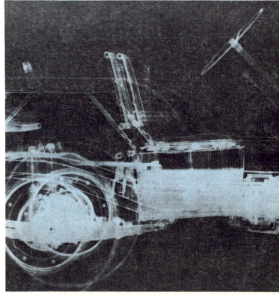

curious rays escaped from the tube. This new radiation was called X-rays.

The discovery of X-rays started a new era in physics and medicine. In physics they can be used to find out how atoms and molecules are grouped in crystals and how they are arranged together in some of the major chemicals found in the body. In medicine X-rays can be used to check broken or badly-formed bones (the first X-ray picture taken by Röntgen in 1898 showed the bone structure of his wife's hand) and higher energy rays can be used to treat cancer.

For his work on X-rays Röntgen was awarded the Rumford medal in 1896 and in 1901 the Nobel prize for physics.

1895
Freud starts psycho-analysis

The real founder of modern psychology was the Austrian, Sigmund Freud (1856–1939). Born at Freiburg, Moravia, of a Jewish family, he carried out a great deal of research as a young man into the physiology of the nervous system and then set up as a specialist in nervous diseases.

Freud soon found that he was able to cure one patient of hysteria by allowing her to talk freely while under hypnosis. Finding hypnosis inadequate Freud then encouraged patients to ramble on with their thoughts while in a state of relaxed consciousness. This method of drawing memories from the unconscious to the conscious mind became known as 'psycho-analysis'.

Freud had many great followers including Carl Jung (1875–1961) and Alfred Adler (1870–1937). Their pioneer work into the subconscious processes of the mind has had a far-reaching effect on people's attitude to the mentally ill.

1895
Maison de l'Art Nouveau opens

The *Maison de l'Art Nouveau* was a shop specializing in modern design which opened in Paris. The Art Nouveau movement was a series of decorative styles linked by a desire to be new and to keep up with the demands of the new age of technology. The style was used particularly in illustration and achieved its most dramatic effects in the work of Aubrey Beardsley (1872–98). Other artists involved in the movement include Mucha, Klimt and Schiele.

1895
Michelin's first car tyre

The first pneumatic tyres (patented by civil engineer R W Thompson in 1845) were demonstrated publicly for the first time in 1846. In 1895 the Paris cycle-tyre manufacturer, Edouard Michelin, fitted the first pneumatic motor-car tyres to a four hp Daimler, which he drove in the Paris–Bordeaux Race on June 11. Michelin had to change the tyres twenty-two times over the 1,200 kilometre long route.

1895
H. G. Wells: *The Time Machine*

Herbert George Wells (1866–1946) the English novelist, was writing at a time when science and engineering were changing the face of the world. His scientific stories are highly imaginative; *The Time Machine* (which tells of a machine which could travel into the future) and other stories including one about a drug which could make a man invisible, are fantastic adventures.

1895
Kiel Canal opened

The Kiel canal connects the North Sea and the Baltic and is the safest, most convenient, shortest and cheapest route for ships going from the one to the other. It is over one hundred kilometres long and fourteen metres deep and runs from the mouth of the Elbe to Hortenau, near Kiel.

Construction of the canal was started in 1887 and took eight years, and at one point over eighty thousand men were working on the canal. One of the main reasons for building it was to provide the German navy with means of communication between the naval stations at Wilhelmshaven and Kiel; since then it has been used for merchant vessels.

Occasionally ice-breakers have to be used in winter, but the canal is never closed and ships may pass through under their own power or may be towed, providing they keep to a speed limit between 5·4 and 8·1 knots.

1896
Nobel establishes prizes

Alfred Bernhard Nobel (1833–96), the Swedish inventor, was the son of an explosives manufacturer. In 1867 Nobel was assisting his father when he discovered how to make a safe and manageable explosive – dynamite. At his death he left a fortune of over £2,000,000, most of which he left for annual prizes in the fields of physics, chemistry, medicine, physiology, literature and peace.

Alfred Nobel

1896
Tchekov: *The Seagull*

The work of Anton Pavlovitch Tchekov (1860–1904) possesses a timeless quality, although it also reflects perfectly the life of middle-class Russian families. Tchekov was a great humanist who above all wanted to point out to his fellow countrymen the futility and falsity of their lives. *The Seagull, The Three Sisters* and *The Cherry Orchard* contain a delicate irony and humour that have made Tchekov one of the best-loved Russian authors.

1896
Olympic Games re-introduced

The Olympic Games (*see c. 776 BC The first Olympics*) had not been held since AD 394. It was through the efforts of Baron Pierre de Courbetin (1863–1937), a brilliant French scholar that the Olympic games were revived. Courbetin felt that nothing but good could result if amateur athletes from throughout the world were to meet once every four years. A new marble stadium was constructed in Athens for the first cycle of the games.

1896
Puccini's *La Bohème*

Giacomo Puccini (1858–1924) was the son of an Italian family of musicians. *Manon Lescaut* (1893) was his first great success and three years later followed his masterpiece, *La Bohème*, the story of which is the touching, but over-romanticized picture of student life. These, as well as *Madame Butterfly* and *Tosca*, have remained popular favourites.

A scene from *La Bohème*, Act III.

1897
Discovery of the electron

Sir Joseph John Thomson (1856–1940) the British mathematical physicist, was one of the outstanding pioneers of nuclear physics. His early work involved the application of dynamics to physics and chemistry.

In 1897 Thomson discovered that cathode rays consisted of negatively charged particles (electrons). Thomson measured their speed and charge and came to the conclusion that these electrons must be nearly two thousand times smaller in mass than the lightest known atomic particle, the hydrogen ion.

It was Thomson's work that led to a much greater understanding of electric currents, for current is made up of a flow of electrons; when electrons in a metal wire move at random there is no current; when a current flows the electrons all move in the same direction.

1898
The Spanish-American War

Tension between the USA and her Latin-American neighbours flared into war in 1898. Annoyed by Spain's harsh treatment of her colony of Cuba, disturbed by the effect of Cuban unrest on American investment, and provoked by the blowing-up of USS *Maine* in Havana harbour, the USA declared war on Spain. Spain was forced to give up the Philippines, Guam, and Puerto Rico. Cuba became independent, but was held closely under US political and economic influence.

1898
Tsiolkovsky: principles of rocket propulsion

With man's dream of flying soon to become a reality, one man was already looking ahead to the days of space flight. Russian school teacher Konstantin Tsiolkovsky (1857–1935) was one of the first to take the idea of space travel seriously.

As early as 1898 Tsiolkovsky stated the principles of rocket reaction propulsion, and in 1903 he published a paper in which he pointed out that the rocket engine alone would work in the vacuum of space.

Further development of rocket theory came in the 1920's from German Hermann Oberth, and also from American Robert Hutchings Goddard, who fired the first liquid-fuelled rocket (primitive solid-fuelled rockets having been used by the Chinese as early as 1232). In the Second World War the Germans developed the V-2 rocket, used to bomb London, and after the war both the USA and the USSR used German scientists and technology to found their space programmes of the 1950s.

1898
The discovery of radium

A major discovery was made in 1898, which was to change the course of science and transform medicine. French physicist Pierre Curie (1859–1906) and his Polish wife Marie (1867–1934) discovered, in the course of their experiments, the radioactive elements radium and polonium.

Their discovery of these elements was the birth of modern nuclear physics and led to the whole science of radiotherapy. The couple were awarded the Nobel Prize in 1903, which they shared with French physicist Antoine Henri Becquerel (1852–1908) who had first discovered the rays emitted by uranium salts.

Pierre Curie was killed in an accident, but Marie became Professor of Physics at the Sorbonne in his place, and went on to isolate the new elements in 1910. Her achievements were recognized by a further Nobel Prize and an honorary professorship in radiology at Warsaw.

1899
The Second South African War

The struggle between British and Dutch settlers (or Boers) in South Africa continued. The Jameson Raid of 1895 (*see 1881 The First South African War*) had cleared the way for a major war, and in 1899 it broke out in earnest.

In the first months the Boers had the upper hand, besieging the British garrisons at Ladysmith, Mafeking and Kimberley.

Lord Roberts (1832–1914) and Lord Kitchener (1850–1916) launched the counter-attack; the garrisons were relieved, amidst general rejoicing in England. Kruger fled, and in June 1900 the British took Pretoria. With their capital taken, the Boers took to a guerilla campaign, harassing British units. Kitchener set up blockhouses and moved civilians who supported the Boers into concentration camps.

Peace finally came with the Treaty of Vereeniging in 1902; Transvaal and the Orange Free State became part of the British Empire, and by 1909 the two sides had sufficiently settled their differences to form the Union of South Africa.

1899
Sibelius composes *Finlandia*

In 1899 Finnish composer Jean Sibelius (1865–1957) wrote a symphonic poem, *Finlandia*, that reflected his passionate love of his native country. His symphonic poems, symphonies and violin concerto all showed an originality that won him international renown. His last published work, *Tapiola* appeared in 1926.

1899
Sarah Bernhardt founds theatre

In 1899 a theatre was founded in Paris by the most remarkable actress of the day. French *tragédienne* Sarah Bernhardt (1844–1923) had made her début with the Théâtre Français in 1862, and within a few years was appearing throughout Europe and America. In 1915 she had a leg amputated, but continued her acting career, a legend in her own time.

1900
The Boxer Rebellion

At the turn of the century the traditional Chinese way of life was threatened by contact with the west. In 1894 China had lost Korea to Japan, and the Germans, Russians and British had all taken over Chinese territory. In 1900 a young nationalist movement known as the 'Boxers' or the 'Society of Harmonious Fists' rose against the foreigners.

Christians and missionaries were killed, and foreign-owned railways attacked. A riot occurred in Peking, supported by the Dowager Empress Tzu Hsi (1834–1908). The German minister was killed, and foreign embassies besieged.

A six-nation force (from Japan, Britain, Russia, France, Germany and the USA) relieved the embassies, and then looted the city. The indemnities demanded from China for the revolt fostered further bitterness. Anti-foreign feeling grew, culminating in the nationalist movement of San Yat-Sen (*see 1911 China declared a republic*).

The Boxer Rebellion in Peking.

1900
Elgar's *The Dream of Gerontius*

In 1900 the English composer Edward Elgar (1857–1934) wrote his oratorio *The Dream of Gerontius*. Although it was not successful at its first performance, together with the *Enigma Variations* (1899) it established his position as a great figure in English music. Other works by Elgar include two symphonies, concertos for violin and cello, and the popular *Pomp and Circumstance* marches.

1900
Max Planck's Quantum Theory

In 1900 a German scientist, Max Planck (1858–1947), who was professor of physics at Berlin University, published his Quantum Theory. Put simply, this stated that energy is emitted in small units called quanta. It successfully explained certain scientific phenomena which Sir Isaac Newton's laws on physics had been unable to account for.

Planck's new theory was to influence almost every development in modern physics. Albert Einstein successfully applied the Quantum Theory to light and was thus able to formulate his theory of relativity. The Danish scientist Niels Bohr (1885–1962) made use of Planck's ideas in his research into atomic structure, which eventually led to the development of nuclear energy. In 1918 Max Planck was awarded the Nobel prize for physics for his work and in 1926 he was elected a member ot the Royal Society.

1900
Conrad's *Lord Jim*

In 1900 the Polish-born British novelist Joseph Conrad (1857–1924) published *Lord Jim*, the story of a man who tries to redeem himself after an act of cowardice. Like many of Conrad's other novels, including *An Outcast of the Islands* (1896) and *The Nigger of the Narcissus* (1897), it is concerned with life at sea in faraway places.

1901
The accession of Edward VII

In 1901 Queen Victoria died at the age of eighty-two; she had reigned over Britain for sixty-three years. The Victorian era had seen the peak of British imperialism and industrial advance; a quarter of the globe had come under the British flag. The queen had set strict standards of morality, and expected others to conform to them.

The Prince of Wales (1841–1910) who acceded to the throne as Edward VII on his mother's death, was a very different character: known throughout Europe for his life of idle pleasure and love of pageantry, he was nevertheless a popular figure and proved an able king in his short rule of nine years. He established the *Entente Cordiale* with France, and improved relations with Japan and Russia. He did not live to see the First World War, being succeeded by his second son, George V (1865–1936).

1901
Opening of the Trans-Siberian Railway

In 1891 work began on the Trans-Siberian Railway which was to link European Russia with the Pacific Coast. The railway was officially opened in 1901 although the final section was not completed until 1917. The longest continuous stretch of railway in the world (9,300 kilometres), it made possible the large-scale industrial development of Siberia.

1901
Thomas Mann's *Buddenbrooks*

In 1901 the German writer Thomas Mann (1875–1955) published his first novel, *Buddenbrooks*. Recognized as a masterpiece, it traces the story of a German family through several generations. Other works by Mann include *Der Tod in Venedig* ('Death in Venice', 1913), *Doktor Faustus* (1947) and *Der Zauberberg* ('The Magic Mountain', 1924), for which he was awarded the Nobel Prize. In 1933 Mann left Germany because of his opposition to the Nazi regime.

1901
Roosevelt becomes president

In September 1901 William McKinley, the twenty-fifth president of the United States, was assassinated by an anarchist. He was succeeded in office by the vice-president, Theodore Roosevelt (1858–1919), who became the youngest president in the history of the country. McKinley had supported expansionist policies, and during his term of office the United States acquired the Philippines and Puerto Rico.

Roosevelt was an energetic and ambitious man, who had become famous during the Spanish–American War of 1898, when he commanded a volunteer force of 'rough riders' in Cuba. His aggressive foreign policy was designed to secure US dominance over South America and in 1903 he obtained control of the Panama Canal Zone.

At home Roosevelt expanded the powers of the presidency and took action to restrict the growth of big business organizations. Re-elected president in 1904, he retired in 1909, and was defeated when he stood again for office in 1912.

1902
André Gide's *L'Immoraliste*

André Gide (1869–1951) published his novel *L'Immoraliste* ('The Immoralist'), about a man who follows his own desires without regard to the feelings of others. Gide enhanced his reputation with novels like *La Symphonie pastorale* ('The Pastoral Symphony', 1919) and *Les Faux-Monnayeurs* ('The Coiners', 1925). He was also a playwright, poet and critic.

1902
W. B. Yeat's *Kathleen ni Houlihan*

In 1902 the play *Kathleen ni Houlihan* by the Irish poet and dramatist William Butler Yeats (1865–1939) was first performed. Yeats, who was a leading figure in the Irish literary revival, had already achieved success with *The Land of Heart's Desire* (1894). He is chiefly remembered for his fine volumes of lyric poetry, including *The Wild Swans at Coole* (1917) and *The Winding Stair* (1939).

1903
The Wright brothers' first flight

In the United States two brothers Orville (1871–1948) and Wilbur Wright (1867–1912) became interested in aviation when they read about the gliding experiments of Otto Lilienthal in Germany. While running a cycle manufacture and repair business they began building and flying gliders.

In 1903 they constructed an aeroplane fitted with a 12-horsepower petrol engine, which was successfully flown by Orville later that year near Kitty Hawk, North Carolina – the first controlled flight made by man in a heavier-than-air machine. They went on to build other aeroplanes and in 1905 had a machine which could stay airborne for more than

The Wright brothers' *Flyer*.

thirty minutes at a time.

Wilbur Wright toured Europe where he made pioneering flights with their aeroplanes in Britain, France and Italy, and in 1909 the brothers formed their own aircraft production company. After Wilbur's death, Orville devoted most of his life to research.

1903
First Tour de France

By the 1890s cycling racing had become a popular sport in many countries. In 1903 a French cyclist Henri Degrange (1865–1940) established the Tour de France which has remained the most famous international cycling race. The contestants cover some 4,000 kilometres in about twenty-one daily stages in flat and hilly country, mainly in France and Belgium.

1903
Women's Political and Social Union formed

As early as 1792 English writer Mary Wollstonecraft had been campaigning for women's rights, and parliamentary lobbying had gone on throughout the nineteenth century with little progress except entitlement vote in local elections (1894).

Foremost amongst the 'suffragettes' as the campaigners for women's suffrage were called, were Emmeline Pankhurst (1857–1928) and her daughters Christabel (1880–1958) and Sylvia (1882–1960). As all women's suffrage bills were rejected, the Women's Social and Political Union (founded in 1903) resorted to increasing militancy, cutting telephone lines, damaging property, chaining themselves to railings; in 1913 Emily Davidson even gave her life by throwing herself under the horses at the Derby.

All protests were met with brutal suppression; militants were sent to prison, where their hunger-strikes were dealt with by crude forced feeding that nearly killed some.

The First World War involved women for the first time in industry, and traditionally male areas of work. Public attitudes soon changed and the end of the war saw votes for certain categories of women (*see 1928 Votes for all women in UK*).

A demonstration in the campaign to gain the vote for women.

1904
J. M. Barrie's *Peter Pan*

In 1904 *Peter Pan*, a play by the Scottish novelist and dramatist James Barrie (1860–1937) was first performed. The story of a little boy who does not want to grow up, it has remained a great favourite with children. Other popular plays by Barrie include *The Admirable Crichton* (1902) and *Dear Brutus* (1917), and his best-known novel is *The Little Minister* (1891).

1904
Rodin's *The Thinker*

In 1904 the French sculptor Auguste Rodin (1840–1917) completed his statue *The Thinker*. Rodin had already established his reputation with such works as *The Burghers of Calais* (1886–95), *Balzac* (1891), and *The Kiss* (1898). He was influenced by the great sculptors of the Italian Renaissance and by sculpture of the Gothic period.

1904
Le Douanier Rousseau's *Jungle with a Lion*

During 1904–06 the French painter Henri Rousseau (1844–1910), known as 'Le Douanier', produced his *Jungle with a Lion*. Rousseau was a so-called 'primitive' painter who ignored the conventions of perspective and colour, and this is one of the best examples of his work. Other paintings by him include *Sleeping Gipsy* (1897) and *The Cart of Père Juniet* (1908).

1904
Russo-Japanese War

During the nineteenth century Russia was continually trying to expand its eastern frontiers at the expense of a weakened Chinese Empire. However, Japan, which was rapidly transforming itself from a backward feudal state into a modern industrial power, also began to make demands on China. A clash between Russia and Japan became inevitable when both countries attempted to extend their influence in Manchuria and Korea.

In February 1904 without warning the Japanese navy attacked the Russian fleet at Port Arthur, a Chinese seaport which had been leased to Russia as a naval base. The Japanese army subsequently defeated the Russians at the Yalu river between Korea and Manchuria – the first time the Japanese had won a victory over a Western nation.

In May 1905 a Russian fleet which had sailed all the way from the Baltic was almost completely destroyed by Japanese warships off the island of Tsushima. A humiliated Russia made peace with Japan in September 1906.

1905
Unrest in Russia

At the beginning of the twentieth century there was considerable unrest among the Russian people, because Tsar Nicholas II (1868–1918) refused to establish a constitutional government. Opposition to his autocratic rule came to a head when Russia suffered humiliating defeats at the hands of the Japanese in the war of 1904–05.

On January 20, 1905, troops opened fire on demonstrators in St Petersburg (now Leningrad) and hundreds of people were killed or injured. This incident, known as 'Bloody Sunday', led to strikes and other disturbances in many parts of the country, and mutinies in the army and navy. In October 1905 Russia was paralyzed by a general strike and it seemed possible that revolutionaries might seize power.

With great reluctance Nicholas II issued the so-called 'October Manifesto' which promised to set up an elected parliament and to grant the Russian people full civil liberties.

1905
Einstein's Special Theory of Relativity

In 1905 the German physicist Albert Einstein (1879–1955) published his Special Theory of Relativity. This was one of the most important developments in the history of science, because it completely changed man's ideas about the nature of the universe.

It is impossible to understand Einstein's theory without a thorough knowledge of mathematics and physics, but we can state some of its basic principles, which upset traditional notions about the measurement of time and space.

Einstein showed that there is no such thing as absolute motion, but that all motion is relative. Time, like motion, is not absolute, so that it is impossible to speak of two events occurring in different places as happening at the same time. Einstein also showed that there is no real difference between matter and energy, and that the mass of an object increases with the speed at which it travels.

In 1915 Einstein put forward his General Theory of Relativity which made fundamental changes to ideas about gravitation which had been held since the time of Sir Isaac Newton. Einstein was awarded the Nobel Prize in 1921.

1905
Norway achieves independence

Norway, which had long been a dependency of Denmark, was united to Sweden in 1814. The Swedish king also became King of Norway, although the Norwegians kept their own parliament – the *Storting*. The Norwegians grew increasingly discontented with their subordinate position and in 1905 the union with Sweden was ended. A Danish prince became king of an independent Norway as Haakon VII.

1905
Debussy's *La Mer*

In 1905 the French composer Claude Debussy (1862–1918) wrote his orchestral piece *La Mer*, a striking impression of the sea. It showed the same originality of musical expression which had already made his piano music famous. Other works by Debussy include *L'Après-Midi d'un Faune* (1894), *Pelléas et Mélisande* (1902), numerous pieces for piano, and chamber music.

1906
First Grand Prix

Motor racing had begun in 1894 between Paris and Rouen. In 1906 the French car manufacturing industry established at Le Mans a new kind of event, the Grand Prix, with no limitations on the number of cars entered by any country. In Britain the first track especially built for motor racing was opened at Brooklands, Surrey, in 1907.

1906
The Fauve movement

Fauvism was a style of painting which flourished in France in the early 1900s. When an exhibition by painters of this group was shown in Paris in 1905, one art critic, shocked by the violence of their work, referred to them as *fauves* ('wild beasts'), and this name remained attached.

By 1906 Fauvism had become established as an important art movement, with Henri Matisse (1869–1954) as its leader and most talented exponent. Paintings by the Fauves were characterized by the use of brilliant, intense colours, applied straight to the canvas in an apparently indiscriminate manner, with forceful brushstrokes, in order to create an explosive effect. Other notable Fauvist painters were André Dérain (1880–1954), Georges Rouault (1871–1958) and Maurice de Vlaminck (1876–1958).

By 1908 the Fauvist movement had come to an end but it had been a significant development in modern painting, which prepared the way for even more fundamental changes.

1906
The first Cubist painting

The most outstanding painter of his time was Spanish-born Pablo Picasso (1881–1973). Having quickly mastered both traditional and impressionist forms of painting, he sought an entirely new artistic expression. In 1906–7 he painted *Les Demoiselles d'Avignon*, which initiated the Cubist movement. The influence of Cubism spread among a number of young French painters, notably Georges Braque (1882–1963) and Fernand Léger (1881–1955), and the first Cubist paintings caused a storm. These artists explored geometrical forms, distorting and abstracting the conventional representation of the subject.

Picasso produced a vast amount of work during his life, constantly developing and modifying his style. His greatest masterpiece is *Guernica* (1937) a large canvas expressing his horror at the bombing of this town in the Spanish Civil war.

1906
The San Francisco earthquake

San Francisco had already experienced earth tremors on three occasions in the past fifty years when on April 18, 1906, it suffered a severe earthquake. This caused widespread devastation and was followed by a fire in the centre of the town. Much of San Francisco was destroyed, hundreds of people died, and more than 200,000 were made homeless.

1906
First radio broadcast

In December 1906 an American physicist, R A Fessenden, broadcast the first-known radio programme from his experimental station at Brant Rock, Massachusetts, USA. The programme, which included some items of music and a talk, was heard by listeners with receiving equipment up to twenty-four kilometres away. However, proper sound broadcasting to large audiences did not begin until the 1920s.

1907
Rilke's *Poems*

In 1907–08 the Austrian poet Rainer Maria Rilke (1875–1926) published his *Poems*. He had already established his reputation with *Life and Songs* (1894) and *Poems from the Book of Hours* (1905). Rilke is one of the greatest lyric poets in the German language and his finest work is generally considered to be the *Duino Elegies* and *Sonnets to Orpheus*, both of which appeared in 1923.

1908
Revolt of the Young Turks

In the early 1900s there was much resentment in Turkey over the repressive regime of Sultan Abdul Hamid II (1876–1909). Many Turks who had fled abroad in order to escape his harsh rule became influenced by Western political ideas. They wanted liberal reforms, including the restoration of the more democratic Constitution of 1876.

The exiles made contact with discontented Turkish army officers who rose in revolt in Macedonia in July 1908. The rebels were led by an organization known as the Committee of Union and Progress. Realizing he could not rely on other army units to put down the revolt, Abdul Hamid agreed to restore the Constitution and to summon a Parliament.

When in 1909 he attempted to stage a counter-revolution he was deposed and exiled. Turkey was now under the effective control of the 'Young Turk' army officers, who adopted a strongly nationalistic policy.

1908
Ravel's *Ma Mère l'Oye*

In 1908 the French composer Maurice Ravel (1875–1937) wrote his piano duet *Ma Mère l'Oye*. He had already achieved success with other piano pieces like *Pavane pour une Infante défunte* (1899), and *Sonatina* and *Miroirs* (both 1905). He went on to even greater fame with his music for the ballet *Daphnis et Chloé* (1912) and his opera *L'Enfant et les Sortilèges* (1925).

1908
Belgium annexes the Congo Free State

The opening up of vast tracts of Africa in the late nineteenth century led to a race to found colonies there by the powerful nations of Europe. From 1885 the Congo Free State, the country now known as Zaïre, was ruled by an international association under King Leopold II of Belgium. He opened up trade and communication, subdued the Arab slave traders, and settled territorial claims by France and Portugal. Charges of corrupt administration and atrocities led the Belgian government to take over the state in 1908. Their rule was to last fifty-two years. (*See 1960 The Belgian Congo Crisis.*)

1908
Boy Scout movement founded

In 1908 Robert Baden-Powell (1857–1941), a British army officer, founded the Boy Scout movement, an organization which taught boys to be good citizens and to become skilful in various outdoor activities. So great was its popularity that Boy Scout movements quickly grew up in other countries. In 1910 a similar organization for girls – the Girl Guides – was also established.

Baden-Powell and the first boy scouts.

1909
Ford produces the Model T

In its early days motoring was the preserve of the rich man or the specialist.

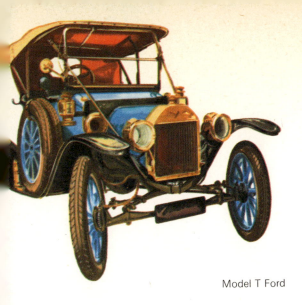

Model T Ford

and bitter cold. In 1908 he set out on the expedition which was to bring success, in the polar exploration ship *Roosevelt*.

Wintering in Grant Land, he set out across the ice from Cape Columbia in March 1909. As supplies ran low Peary sent his men back, until only Matt Henson and four Eskimos remained with him. They pressed forward, and on reaching the Pole spent thirty hours taking observations and soundings. Peary made the return journey in safety, but lost one member of his team; in 1911 he was made a Rear-admiral.

1909
Blériot flies the English Channel

In the early days of aviation bi-planes and tri-planes were much in favour. Louis Blériot (1872–1936) was a French engineer and aviator who was an early advocate of the monoplane. Having founded the first aircraft factory in France in 1906, Blériot made several pioneering flights within France. On July 25, 1909 he left Calais in a small 24 hp monoplane, and landed successfully at Dover. He was awarded a prize of £1,000 by the *London Daily Mail*.

1909
Diaghilev brings Nijinsky to Paris

Sergei Diaghilev (1872–1929) was a Russian impresario who brought Russian opera and ballet to Europe. The

Nijinsky dances with Tamara Karsavina.

When Henry Ford (1863–1947) set up the Ford Motor Company in Detroit (USA) in 1903, he planned to bring motoring within the reach of all. By introducing mass production techniques, such as the continuously moving assembly line, he hoped to produce a cheap standardized car that required little maintenance.

Ford's solution was the Model T, a small family car that was to make his fortune. 'Any customer can have a car painted any colour that he wants, so long as it is black', announced Ford.

For eighteen years Ford produced nothing but the Model T, selling in this period nearly sixteen million cars. The 1909 price for a Model T was $950; by 1922 it was $295, and a new car was leaving the production line every fifteen seconds. The age of popular motoring had arrived, revolutionizing social habits and changing the face of the world.

1909
Peary reaches the North Pole

On April 6, 1909 Robert Peary, a commander in the US Navy, became the first man to stand at the North Pole. Peary (1856–1920) was the veteran of several Arctic expeditions in which he and his men had experienced extreme hardship originality of his productions such as Mussorgsky's *Boris Godunov* inspired a vitality long absent from the Western European stage. In 1909 he brought Vaslav Nijinsky to Paris as his leading dancer. Nijinsky (1890–1950) became an extremely popular dancer, though his choreography was less successful; he became insane in 1917.

1910
The arrest of Crippen

In 1910 the British public was scandalized by news of a brutal murder. Dr Crippen was an American who settled in London, and murdered his second wife for love of his secretary. Fleeing to Antwerp, he boarded an Atlantic liner with his secretary disguised as a boy. The captain was suspicious and telegraphed Scotland Yard – the first time radio had been used for police work. The arrest was dramatic: a detective disguised as a pilot boarded the liner and took them into custody. Crippen was tried and executed.

1911
Richard Strauss: *Der Rosenkavalier*

Richard Strauss (1864–1949) was a German composer who in works such as *Also Sprach Zarathustra* ('Thus spake Zarathustra', 1896) proved himself to be master of symphonic form. Turning to opera, he again achieved success: *Der Rosenkavalier*, a musical comedy with a libretto by the Austrian writer Hugo von Hofmannsthal (1874–1929), is a sensitive work, set in eighteenth-century Vienna.

1911
Jung's *The Psychology of the Unconscious*

Until the publication of this work in 1911 the Swiss psychiatrist Carl Jung (1875–1961) was the leading collaborator of Sigmund Freud. His research into psychoanalysis led him to disagree with Freud's interpretations, and his life's work transformed the study of psychology. Much of this work was concerned with the symbolism of dreams, myths and religions. (*See 1895 Freud's first work on psychoanalysis.*)

1911
Alexander's Ragtime Band

The most popular song of 1911 was an early jazz tune by the American composer Irving Berlin: *Alexander's Ragtime Band*. The invention of the gramophone and the mass production of records led to a revolution in popular musical taste. In Britain the music halls provided a wealth of popular songs, but for some years the influence of American folk music and minstrel shows had been growing.

Negro work songs and spirituals led to the musical style known as 'blues', songs reflecting the hard life of the American negro. In New Orleans military band instruments accompanied parades, and negro pianists developed a style of playing known as 'ragtime' using syncopation, i.e. the stressing of normally unaccented beats.

From all these sources there evolved 'jazz', a highly rhythmic music relying on improvization. This unconventional music, much imitated by whites, soon became 'respectable' and very popular in both Europe and the USA.

1911
China declared a republic

In the unstable years after the 1900 Boxer rebellion, China was oppressed by foreign powers and seething with internal discontent. In 1911 a revolution under Sun Yat-Sen (1866–1925) finally swept away the Manchu dynasty, and a republic was declared. Yuan Shih-k'ai (1859–1916) became president, but soon China reverted to political chaos and civil war.

1911

The Expressionist Exhibition

In December 1911 a first exhibition of paintings was held in Munich, Germany, by artists calling themselves the *Blauer Reiter* ('Blue Rider') Group. This group, including Wasilly Kandinsky (1866–1944) and Franz Marc (1880–1916) were part of a literary and artistic movement known as Expressionism, whose influence was to spread to drama, film, music and architecture.

Expressionism was a youthful reaction against the conventions of its day. Inspired by Marx and Nietzsche, the Expressionists wanted to involve the artist in the creation of a new age. They rejected the Impressionists' idea of recording light and atmosphere in order to reproduce the appearance of nature, preferring instead the powerful, tragic paintings of the Norwegian Edvard Munch (1863–1944). Other painters influenced by Expressionism were Paul Klee (1879–1940) and Oscar Kokoschka (*b.* 1886).

The Expressionist viewpoint appeared in the extremely emotional, fragmented literature of Germany at this time, and was later reflected in films such as Lang's *Dr Caligari*. The musician Arnold Schönberg was a member of the *Blauer Reiter* group (*see 1921 Schönberg: Twelve-note System of Composition*).

1911

Amundsen and Scott reach the South Pole

In 1911 two expeditions were battling through the hostile and unknown landscape of Antarctica. Roald Amundsen (1872–1928) was a Norwegian experienced in polar exploration, whose expedition had set out the previous year. In December Amundsen became the first person to reach the South Pole.

The second expedition was headed by Robert Falcon Scott (1868–1912) a captain in the Royal Navy. His sledge team, including Wilson, Oates, Bowers and

Amundsen's expedition reaches the South Pole.

Evans, finally reached the pole on January 17, 1912, only to find that Amundsen had beaten them by a month.

Disaster struck the return journey. Ferocious blizzards hindered their progress, and Evans died. A month later Captain Oates became too ill to continue. Rather than endanger his friends further, he walked out of his tent into a blizzard. The weather became worse and the situation hopeless; the remaining three perished at the end of March 1912. Their bodies, together with their diaries and records, were found by a search party eight months later.

1912

Shaw writes *Pygmalion*

Pygmalion is the story of a professor of phonetics who transforms a cockney flower girl into a lady of high society. Shaw named his play after a legendary king of Cyprus who fell in love with a statue and caused it to come to life. This play proved very popular, being filmed in 1938, and adapted into the musical *My Fair Lady* in 1956.

George Bernard Shaw (1856–1950) was born in Ireland; settling in London he soon became renowned as a fiery critic and pamphleteer. An energetic socialist involved in the Fabian Society, Shaw wrote plays with a message for his age, including *Arms and the Man, The Devil's Disciple, Candida, Caesar and Cleopatra, The Apple Cart, St Joan*.

1912
Sinking of the *Titanic*

The British ocean liner *Titanic* was intended to be the pride of the Atlantic crossing. At 46,300 tonnes she was the largest ship afloat and was widely regarded as unsinkable, so there was no shortage of passengers for her prestigious maiden voyage. The captain was eager to reach New York in daylight, but he underestimated the danger of icebergs. At 2.20 a.m. on April 15, 1912, the disaster struck: the *Titanic* ran into an iceberg at full speed and quickly sank. Of 2,224 passengers there were only 711 survivors. The disaster shocked the world, and led to a greater concern for maritime safety procedures.

1913
Alain-Fournier: *Le Grand Meaulnes*

Henri-Alban Fournier (1866–1914), better known by his pen name of Alain-Fournier, was killed in the First World War, having produced one of the outstanding French novels of this century. *Le Grand Meaulnes* ('The Wanderer', 1913) deals with a young man's awakening to love, and his yearning for the lost world of childhood.

1913
Robert Frost: *A Boy's Will*

Robert Frost (1874–1963) is recognized as one of the foremost American poets of the century. Born in San Francisco, he studied at Harvard; his poetry portrays the countryside and everyday life of New England. Frost spent three years in Britain, 1912–15, where he was encouraged to publish *A Boy's Will* which gained him an international reputation.

1913
Stravinsky: *The Rite of Spring*

Igor Stravinsky (1882–1971), the outstanding musical genius of the century, found fame with the Diaghilev ballet's production of *The Firebird* and *Petrushka* (*see 1909 Diaghilev brings Nijinsky to Paris*). Primitive rituals of his native Russia form the basis of *The Rite of Spring*; its harsh dissonance and strange rhythms caused an outrage at its première. Stravinsky's interest extended to opera, choral and instrumental work, and eventually to twelve-note composition.

1913
Invention of the geiger counter

When a material is suspected of being radioactive, or a radiation leak is thought to be occurring, a geiger counter is used to detect the radiation. The device was invented by the German physicist Hans Geiger (1882–1945) as part of his investigations with Rutherford into beta-ray radioactivity in 1913.

Further developed with the help of Müller the counter, across which a high voltage is applied, contains a gas held at low pressure, which surrounds a metal cathode cylinder. This has a thin wire anode running down the centre. If any particles of ionizing radiation enter, the gas is ionized, and a momentary current runs through the tube. The charge in voltage is amplified electronically to give a reading.

Radioisotopes are widely used in medicine, and radiation can also be a

A modern geiger counter.

dangerous hazard in much scientific and industrial work. Instruments measuring radioactivity are vital to health and safety.

1913
Albert Schweitzer founds his hospital

In 1913 a remarkable man appeared at the Lambaréné mission station on the Ogowe river in French Equatorial Africa (Gabon). Alsatian-born Albert Schweitzer (1875–1965) had already become internationally famous as a musician and theologian when he decided to devote the rest of his life to humanitarian work. He studied medicine, and with the help of his new wife set up a hospital at Lambaréné to fight sleeping sickness and leprosy.

For the rest of his life he worked at his hospital village, for which he raised funds by giving organ recitals in Europe.

Although paternalistic towards the local people, Schweitzer devoted himself to their welfare with vigour and application, developing an ethical code based on the principle of 'reverence for life'. His achievements were recognized by the award of a Nobel Peace Prize in 1952. Despite his tireless activities he found time to write a number of works on ethics and accounts of his experiences in Africa.

1913
Proust writes Du Côté de Chez Swann

Du Côté de Chez Swann ('Swann's Way') was the first of the thirteen volumes that make up the great work of French novelist Marcel Proust (1871–1922): *A la Recherche du Temps Perdu* ('Remembrance of Time Past').

Proust delves into the inner emotions of his characters; he is concerned with the role of memory in the subconscious, and with the passing of time.

1913
Apollinaire writes Les Alcools

Just as the Cubists rejected the artistic traditions of their day, many poets tried to achieve exciting new approach to their work. The French poet Guillaume Apollinaire (1880–1918) used no punctuation and experimented with typography; in a poem about rain the letters fall down the page like raindrops. His main poetic works were *Les Alcools* ('Alcohol'), (1913) and *Calligrammes* (1918).

1914
Charlie Chaplin enters Hollywood

In the years before the First World War the film business was in its infancy. The best known star of the early silent films

Images of Hollywood: Charlie Chaplin; *The Great Train Robbery* (the first western); Greta Garbo, star of the 1930s.

was Charlie Chaplin, whose trademark of bowler hat and cane won international renown. Charlie Chaplin was born in poverty in London, in 1889, and his early stage experience was in vaudeville. He came to Hollywood in 1914, and in his portrayal of the down-and-out splay-footed tramp in films such as *The Gold Rush* is still popular today. He later turned to directing films.

The film industry grew in the USA as nowhere else. Giants such as directors Sam Goldwyn (*b.* 1882) and Cecil B de Mille (1881–1959) laid the foundations, and in the post-war years stars such as Mary Pickford, Rudolph Valentino, Laurel and Hardy and Buster Keaton became household names.

1914
Holst composes *The Planets*

The Planets, composed by English composer Gustav Holst between 1914 and 1917, is a seven-movement suite inspired by the astrological significance of each planet. This popular work showed Holst (1874–1934) as a major composer for the first time. Other works include the *Hymn of Jesus* (1917) and the *Concerto for Two Violins* (1929).

1914
Outbreak of First World War

The great European powers had long been suspicious of each other's motives, eager for power, and intent on arming themselves against the possibility of war. Tension between France and Germany had not relaxed since the Franco–Prussian war of 1871; Germany had the best army in Europe and was now rivalling Britain in naval power. Austria, Hungary and Russia were vying for power in the Balkans. In this mood of fear and aggression, both great and small powers were divided into two hostile camps: Europe was sitting on a keg of gunpowder.

The fatal spark that set it alight occurred on June 28, 1914. Archduke Franz Ferdinand, heir to the Austro-Hungarian throne, was driving through Sarajevo, a Bosnian town under Austrian rule. Gavrilo Princip, a young Bosnian in the crowd, shot him dead.

Austro-Hungary held Serbia responsible for the assassination. Russia mobilized to support Serbia, backed by her ally France. Germany mobilized, declaring war on Russia and France. Britain had a friendly agreement with France, known as the *entente cordiale*, and also stood to guarantee Belgian neutrality. So when Germany attacked France and invaded Belgium, the result was inevitable. At midnight on August 3, 1914 Britain entered the war.

1914
The early battles

At the beginning of the war Britain and Germany were seized by patriotic fervour; enthusiastic crowds flocked to the recruiting stations. It was not thought that the war would last for long.

Trench warfare: British troops advance to the German lines, under heavy artillery fire.

The Germans had planned a rapid sweep to Paris through Belgium, but were hindered by determined resistance. The British Expeditionary Force made a stand at Mons, but the Anglo-French forces under the French General Joffre (1852–1931) were pushed back to the Marne. Here the German advance was halted, and the armies dug in. By the end of the year the Western Front was a vast line of trenches, stretching from the North Sea to Switzerland.

In the East the Russians seized Galicia, but were defeated at Tannenberg in East Prussia by the German General von Hindenburg (1847–1934). The Russians received another setback when Turkey entered the war on the side of Germany.

It was clear that this war would be a long and bitter struggle.

1915
Gorky commences trilogy

In 1914 a writer returned to the political turmoil of Russia to engage in revolutionary propaganda. Alexei Peshkov (1868–1936), whose pen-name was Maxim Gorky, had had a hard and eventful life. Rejecting his earlier romanticism for realism, in 1915 he began his autobiographical trilogy: *Childhood, In the World* and *Reminiscences, of My Youth.* Gorky was an advocate of 'social realism' in Soviet art and literature.

1915
The sinking of the *Lusitania*

For the first time in history, civilians became totally involved in war, as air raids and submarine warfare took their toll. At times German submarines attacked merchant shipping and passenger liners indiscriminately. When the British liner *Lusitania* was torpedoed in 1915, American citizens were killed. This hardened anti-German feeling in the USA, which was still neutral.

1915
Execution of Edith Cavell

On October 12, 1915 British nurse Edith Cavell faced a German firing squad. She was matron of a hospital in Brussels which had become a Red Cross hospital when Belgium was invaded. Although she had tended German and Allied patients impartially, she was found to be assisting in the escape of Allied prisoners. Her execution shocked the British public.

1915
The Dardanelles expedition

With the Western front in a stalemate, and Russia under pressure from the Turks, the Allies decided to attack the Dardanelles. These straits, a vital supply route to the Russians, had been closed when Turkey entered the war. The naval campaign (planned by Winston Churchill) and the army attempts to take the Gallipoli peninsula were costly failures.

1915
Somerset Maugham: *Of Human Bondage*

William Somerset Maugham (1874–1965) was a British writer who mastered the art of the short story and was a successful novelist. *Of Human Bondage,* published in 1915, is a great autobiographical novel. His early experience in medical practice and his later travels gave him an acute insight into human behaviour.

1916
The Easter Rising

On the outbreak of the First World War the British government had pledged limited Home Rule for Ireland, on the condition that it did not take effect until the war was over. Whilst many Irishmen volunteered to fight in the war, many could see the opportunity to revolt that they had been waiting for. With German and Irish-American money, the Sinn Fein party built up their rebel army.

Sir Roger Casement (1864–1916), a convinced Irish nationalist, visited the USA and Berlin to gain support for the Irish cause. On April 2, 1916 he returned to Ireland in a German submarine, accompanied by a boat full of arms, which was intercepted and sunk by a patrol. Three days later Casement was captured by the British, who later hanged him as a traitor.

Despite this setback an armed rising did take place. On Easter Monday 1916 the rebels captured the general post office in Dublin and key points in the city. Padraig Pearse (1879–1916) commanded the rising, and he and his colleagues held out for a week under bombardment. On April 30 he surrendered.

The execution of the fifteen rebel leaders further embittered the Irish people, and whilst negotiations continued, the resistance movement was rebuilt (*see 1921 Formation of the Irish Free State*).

1916
Kafka writes 'Metamorphosis'

'Metamorphosis' (*Die Verwandlung*) is the story of a man who wakes up to find himself transformed into an insect. Franz Kafka (1883–1924) was born in Prague of a Jewish family. His introspective, morbid personality resulted in a number of remarkable works, notably 'The Trial' (*Ein Prozess*) and 'The Castle' (*Das Schloss*), in which the individual is lost in a bewildering, seemingly pointless society.

The Battle of Jutland: the British fleet encounters heavy fire in a night action.

1916
Assassination of Rasputin

In the last years of Czar Nicholas II an extraordinary figure became a favourite at the Russian court. Grigoriy Rasputin (c.1871–1916) was a debauched monk who exerted a magnetic influence over his followers, including the czarina. His political influence became intolerable to many, and a group of noblemen shot him dead, having failed in an attempt to poison him.

1916
The third year of war

The war had spread: Italy had joined the Allies, Bulgaria the Central Powers. Britain had occupied Palestine. In France the war dragged on in miserable conditions, the soldiers living and dying in a devastated area of mud and barbed wire. Horrific new weapons appeared: the Germans introduced poison-gas shells, the British introduced tanks.

In the winter of 1916 the Germans launched a massive attack on the French at Verdun, but were held by the French under Pétain. In July 1916 the British counter-attacked fiercely along the Somme. Casualties were heavy: in one day 60,000 British soldiers were killed.

At sea Britain maintained a blockade of Germany, despite submarine losses and a running battle off Jutland in May 1916, where neither fleet gained advantage. In June 1916 Lord Kitchener, who had organized the British army for war, was lost when HMS *Hampshire* struck a mine off Orkney.

1916
The Dada movement is formed

Many artists and writers, having no sympathy with the climate of war, fled to neutral Switzerland. A Zurich group which included the Romanian poet Tristan Tzara and the Alsatian painter and sculptor Hans Arp (1888–1966) started producing satirical revues and engaging in artistic discussion. Sticking a pin into a French-German dictionary at random, they found the word *Dada*, and called their movement after it. They set out to attack all traditional aesthetic ideals, valuing the impact of shock, protest and change above all: 'art is nonsense' declared their manifesto of 1918.

French painters Francis Picabia (1879–1953) and Marcel Duchamp (1887–1968) exhibited every day objects as works of art; the latter scandalized artistic circles with his reproduction of the *Mona Lisa* with a moustache. The movement spread to France, Germany, Italy and the USA, greatly influencing twentieth century attitudes to art.

1917
USA enters the war

At the beginning of 1917 the outlook was bleak, and the weary armies seemed to be locked in a fight to the death. Few people at home in Britain and Germany grasped the realities of modern warfare. Battle followed battle and the carnage continued: Messines, Passchendaele, Vimy Ridge, Cambrai. There was mutiny in the French army, and the Russian troops were deserting in droves.

Two political events dominated 1917, which had a crucial effect on the war. Firstly, in March 1917 the czar abdicated; in December the Bolsheviks signed an armistice with Germany.

This setback for the Allies was balanced by the second important political development of the year: on April 6, the USA decided to enter the war. President Woodrow Wilson (1856–1924) was finally forced to enter for a number of reasons: submarine warfare had killed innocent American civilians; Germany had been wooing Mexico with the promise of returning US territory to them, public opinion had rallied behind the Allied cause. A US expeditionary force was followed up by large numbers of troops, and fresh soldiers arrived to take on an exhausted enemy.

1917
Van Doesburg publishes *De Stijl*

De Stijl is Dutch for 'The Style' and was the name of an arts periodical published in 1917 by Theo van Doesburg (whose real name was CEM Küpper, 1883–1931). A movement of painters, sculptors, architects and designers grew up around van Doesburg, notably the painter Piet Mondrian (1872–1944). Their work sought to express in abstract terms the underlying order of nature.

1917
Outbreak of the Russian Revolution

For some years Russia had been in a state of political unrest (*see 1905 Unrest in Russia* and *1916 Assassination of Rasputin*). The terrible conditions of the war had demoralized the armed forces, and the masses were starving: strikes and hunger marches met with repression.

Czar Nicholas II (1868–1918) was an unimaginative ruler, lacking self-assurance and dangerously out of touch with modern times. Convinced of the absolute authority of his office his gestures towards democracy were too few and too late. When the Duma (parliament) pressed him for reforms in March 1917, he refused outright. The Duma formed a provisional government, and forced the abdication of the czar, who could no longer find any military support. The Romanov dynasty had finally collapsed.

The government that came to power in the spring of 1917 was made up of liberals and social democrats, known as Mensheviks, under the inept leadership of Alexander Kerensky (1881–1970). He could not maintain order, and his decision to continue in the war was unpopular. In Petrograd (formerly St Petersburg) a Soviet of Workers' and Soldiers' Deputies was formed to oppose the government, made up of radical revolutionaries known as Bolsheviks.

Bolshevik leaders returned from long years of foreign exile to participate in the forthcoming revolution. Vladimir Ilyich Lenin (formerly Ulyanov, 1870–1924) returned from Germany, to address workers and organize the Bolsheviks. He was joined by Leon Trotsky (formerly Bronstein, 1879–1940) and Joseph Stalin (formerly Dzhugashvili, 1879–1953). On November 7, 1917 (October 25 according to the Russian calendar then in use), the Bolsheviks rose against Kerensky's government, and the revolution quickly spread from Petrograd. Kerensky fled and Soviet power was established. Land

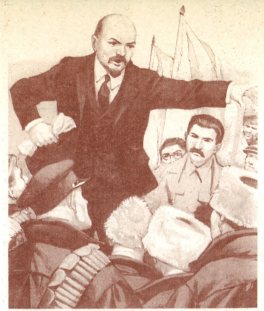
Lenin (left) with Stalin.

was given over to the peasants, local councils ('Soviets') were set up, companies were nationalized, and the Orthodox Church penalized. The following years were a bitter struggle, but the communists maintained their power (*see 1918 Murder of Czar Nicholas II and Civil War*).

1917
The Balfour declaration

The origins of the modern Arab–Israeli conflict can be traced back to the year 1917, when a declaration was made by the British foreign secretary Lord Balfour (1848–1930) promising the Jews a national home in Palestine.

The Zionists, a Jewish nationalist group, were to be offered settlement in the hope that this would secure British interests in the Middle East and gain support for the allied war effort from world Jewry. The declaration, supported by France, Italy and the USA, was open to a number of interpretations, and conflicted with promises made to the Arabs, whom the British had encouraged to revolt against the Turks.

In December 1917 Jerusalem was taken by the British General Allenby (1861–1936) and the fall of Damascus in 1918 secured the British position in the

Middle East. Between the wars Jewish immigration grew amidst growing Arab discontent (*see 1948 State of Israel founded*).

1918
Death of Wilfred Owen

In 1918 a young English poet was killed in action on the Western Front. Wilfred Owen (1893–1918) had produced some remarkable verse expressing his horror at the bloodshed he had witnessed.

Many young writers had gone into the war optimistically. Rupert Brooke (1887–1915) produced some fresh lyrical verse before dying on Skyros on his way to the Dardanelles.

Siegfried Sassoon (1886–1967) survived the war. Initially sharing Brooke's optimism, his experience soon made him hate war with a ferocious bitterness, expressed in his *Counterattack* (1918). Sassoon edited Owen's work after his death.

The casualties of the First World War have been called the 'lost generation'. The work of these war poets stands as a monument to the memory of those who were killed, or who spent the rest of their lives crippled or suffering from the effects of gas poisoning.

1918
The end of the First World War

By 1918 the Allied blockade was causing Germany extreme hardship, and many hoped for peace. The German General von Ludendorff decided to risk all in one final push, and smashed through British lines. The swift advance was finally halted at the Marne, and the tide turned as the Allies broke through the German defences of the Hindenburg line.

One by one the Central Powers surrendered. Kaiser Wilhelm II fled to neutral Holland, and an armistice was signed with Germany on November 11, 1918. The First World War was not known as the Great War for nothing.

Peace – but for how long? The Treaty of Versailles was signed in 1919 by Lloyd George, Woodrow Wilson and Clemenceau.

Sixteen nations had mobilized sixty-five million men; well over eight million young men were killed, and countless more were maimed and injured for life. The war left a scar across the face of Europe that did not heal quickly. The map of the world was altered, and the structure of society changed.

The terms of peace were decided the next year. British Prime Minister Lloyd George, US President Woodrow Wilson and French Premier Clemenceau dominated the conference. The Treaty of Versailles was severe. Germany lost her colonies and Alsace-Lorraine, her military development was to be closely controlled, and she was to pay large sums of money to the victors (*see 1920 League of Nations founded*).

1918
Czechoslovakia and Poland become independent

The Treaty of Versailles changed the map of Europe. In the East, the Central Powers were forced to recognize the independence of Poland and Czechoslovakia. The Polish nationalist movement

under Josef Pilsudski (1867–1935) and the Czechoslovak under Thomas Masaryk (1850–1937) finally achieved their aim, although their political stability was at first uncertain.

1918
G. M. Hopkins first published

In 1918 the poet Robert Bridges (1844–1930) published posthumously the work of a friend, English poet Gerard Manley Hopkins (1844–89). This unconventional work had a mixed reception, but later Hopkins was recognized as a master, considered by some as the father of modern English verse. A Jesuit, Hopkins experimented with what he called 'sprung rhythm', producing poems of great beauty and sensitivity.

1918
The *Bauhaus* founded

In 1918 a German architect, Walter Gropius (1883–1969) was made director of art schools in Weimar. He reorganized the schools into a centre of architecture, craft and design, known as the *Bauhaus*.

Transferred to Dessau in 1925, the school was closed down with the rise of the Nazis.

At a time when industry and mass-production were spreading rapidly, and scientific progress was creating new technologies, the *Bauhaus* proved that function and beauty were compatible. Art and craft were to unite, and pupils were trained to think in terms of mass-production. The school had an enormous influence on international architecture, as well as industrial and graphic design, and art.

The *Bauhaus* attracted many of the great artists of the day as teachers. The Swiss artist Paul Klee taught there for twelve years, producing his *Pädagogisches Skizzenbuch* ('Educational Sketchbook'), and Wasilly Kandinsky, the Russian painter, was for a time director (*see 1911 the Expressionist Exhibition*).

1918
Murder of Czar Nicholas II

The Bolsheviks who had swept to power under Lenin in 1917 had more than their share of problems. Having moved the capital of Russia from Petrograd to Moscow, they now faced the task of organizing the economy of a vast and chaotic country.

In 1918 civil war broke out between the Reds (the Bolsheviks) and the Whites (their opponents). Although the Whites received military assistance from Allied units, the Red Army under Trotsky virtually crushed all opposition within two years.

The czar was a liability to the Bolsheviks. Since his abdication, he and his family had become used to a life very different from the one they had known. In the turbulence of the civil war, they were exiled to Eastern Russia, where they were apparently all shot by Red Guards in 1918, it is thought at the order of a local commander (*see 1919 Comintern formed*).

1919
Birth of the Weimar Republic

The new peace found Germany bitter, starving, and torn with political dissent. November 1918 saw a naval mutiny at Kiel, the signing of the armistice, and the formation of soviets on Russian lines in Berlin. With the Kaiser in Holland, the way was open for the formation of a republic, but its nature was only to be decided by fighting.

The communists, known as Spartacists, held the balance of power for a time, but in January 1919 were defeated by the counter-revolutionaries on the streets of Berlin. Spartacist leaders Karl Liebknecht and Rosa Luxemburg were murdered.

The new republic formed under the Weimar Constitution of 1919 allowed for a considerable degree of democracy, but in the long run was unable to stand up to economic disaster and manipulation by undemocratic elements. First president of the Weimar Republic was Friedrich Ebert (1871–1925) (*see 1925 Hindenburg becomes German President*).

1919
Comintern formed

As the Civil War raged in Russia, the involvement of units from the Allied powers on the side of the Whites spurred on the communist party to call the Third Communist International, or *Comintern*. Foreign groups discussed how to spread the revolution abroad.

However, attempts to establish soviet systems elsewhere in Europe at this stage failed. The social democrats won the day in Germany, and in Hungary a communist government under revolutionary Béla Kun (1886–1937) collapsed after five months.

The Soviet Republic in Russia, from 1922 known as the Union of Soviet Socialist Republics, was bankrupt, and in 1921 Lenin was forced to moderate his economic policy. His New Economic

Plan allowed a certain amount of private enterprise and the country became economically viable. The USSR gradually received official recognition by the West (*see 1924 Death of Lenin*).

1919
Formation of fascist parties

The Europe of 1919 had all the seeds of new conflict. Disillusionment and fear of communism led some towards an extreme nationalism in which the authority of the state was thought to be supreme, and to justify any inhumanity. Fascism derived its name from the *fasces* of ancient Rome, a bundle of rods with an axe carried as a symbol of state authority.

Boastful and obsessed with power for its own sake, Benito Mussolini (1883–1945) formed his fascist group in Italy in 1919. Dropping his professed socialist ideals, he allied himself with industrialists and landowners while his thugs broke up opposition groups. In 1922 the black-shirted fascists marched on Rome, establishing Mussolini as dictator, although outnumbered ten to one in parliament.

The violent methods of Mussolini were duplicated by the German fascists, or Nazis, whose minute National Socialist German Workers' party had a new recruit in 1919 – a former corporal turned army informer, called Adolf Hitler (1889–1945).

1919
Alcock and Brown fly Atlantic

On June 14, 1919, aviation history was made when a Vickers Vimy aircraft successfully crossed the Atlantic Ocean without stopping. The arduous crossing was carried out by Captain John Alcock (1892–1919), a famous air ace of World War I, and Lt. Arthur Whitten Brown (1886–1948). The aircraft took sixteen hours twelve minutes to cover the three thousand kilometres between St John's,

Newfoundland, Canada and Clifden, Ireland. Their remarkable achievement was recognized when both men were knighted. However tragedy struck Alcock later in the year, when his amphibian plane crashed in Normandy, on the way to Paris, and he was killed.

Alcock and Brown's achievement followed closely on that of Lt. Albert C Read of the US Navy, who with five crew in May 1919 had flown the Atlantic from Newfoundland to Lisbon in a Curtiss NC-4 flying boat – but not without stopping.

1919
Rutherford's atomic experiments

A brilliant scientist became Cavendish Professor of Physics at Cambridge in 1919. New Zealand-born Ernest Rutherford (1871–1937) was a pioneer in his field, and radically altered our understanding of atomic physics.

Rutherford had previously studied at Cambridge under Sir J J Thomson (1856–1940), the discoverer of the electron, and had researched into uranium radiation. Whilst Professor at McGill University, Canada, in 1898, Rutherford upset the laws of conservation of matter with his theory of atomic disintegration. Moving to Manchester in 1907 he worked with the Danish physicist Niels Bohr (1885–1962), and gave us a new insight into the structure of the atom. The atom was revealed as a nucleus surrounded by electrons.

Ernest Rutherford

Rutherford's experiments of 1919 were remarkable, proving that atomic transformation took place in atmospheric nitrogen bombarded with alpha-rays, liberating hydrogen nuclei. In 1920 Rutherford foresaw the existence of the neutron, which was confirmed by Chadwick in 1932.

1920
Pirandello writes 'Six Characters in Search of an Author'

Italian writer Luigi Pirandello (1867–1936) had made his name as a novelist and short story writer when he turned to drama, producing his best known work in 1920. *Sei personaggi in cerca d'autore* ('Six Characters in Search of an Author') was performed throughout Europe.

Pirandello's constant theme is illusion and appearance. He received the Nobel Prize for Literature in 1934.

1920
The League of Nations established

An important part of the Treaty of Versailles in 1919 was the establishment of a League of Nations, an earlier version of the modern United Nations Organization. It was the first real attempt at international co-operation and peace-making.

The Geneva-based league was made up of an Assembly of all member nations, a Council, consisting of the major powers and four other members, and a Secretariat. A world court would be set up to settle international disputes. On January 10, 1920 twenty-four members assembled for the first time.

The USA did not join the League. Opposing the personal wish of President Woodrow Wilson, Congress decided to avoid all foreign involvements. The USSR joined in 1934.

Although there were eventually sixty members, the League never had the military support to be effective, and was so constituted that most important international action could be blocked by use of the veto.

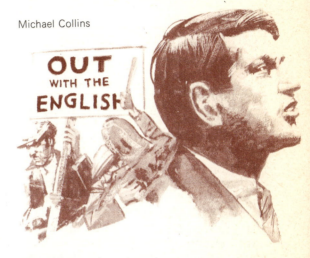

Michael Collins

1921
Formation of the Irish Free State

In Ireland the anti-British campaign had been continued since 1916. Whilst Sinn Fein leader Eamon de Valera (1882–1975) wanted a full republic, another leader, Michael Collins (1890–1922) was prepared to settle for the same status as Canada and Australia within the British empire.

Collins, a popular hero of the Easter Rising, managed to come to agreement with the British, and headed a provisional government, but was shot dead in a Republican ambush. A bitter feud between the rival parties lasted for years, but the Irish Free State was agreed by both the British parliament and the *dáil éireann* (Irish assembly) in December 1921.

The new state did not include Northern Ireland, where the largely protestant population insisted on remaining part of the UK. This problem was to cause lasting bitterness and suffering, and when a complete republic was finally declared in 1949, Northern Ireland was still excluded.

1921
Schönberg: *Twelve-note System of Composition*

Arnold Schönberg (1874–1951) was a self-taught Austrian composer, whose originality soon became apparent: the performance of his first *Chamber Symphony* in 1907 caused a riot. Involved in the Expressionist movement, he became a friend of the composer Mahler, and taught Berg and Webern. In these years he came to abandon the classical concept of tonality, and write in an 'atonal' style.

His theoretical work led him to publish in 1921 his *Twelve-note System of Composition*, in which he organized his atonal system into a structure based on a 'note row'. The composer arranges the twelve notes of the semitone scale in a sequence, each note appearing once but at any pitch. This sequence determines the relationship of the notes for the rest of the work.

Forced into exile by the Nazis, Schönberg settled in the USA; his system, also known as 'serial music', became a major influence on musicians such as Stravinsky.

1921
The first birth control clinic

In this century the rapid increase in world population has made measures to control the birth rate vital. One of the pioneers of birth control was a remarkable woman called Marie Stopes (1880–1958), a university science lecturer and suffragette. Her views caused a storm of controversy, but in 1921 she founded the first clinic for marital advice and birth control, in North London.

1922
Egypt becomes independent

In the First World War Britain had succeeded in bringing to an end the power of the Turks in the Middle East. In 1914 Egypt had been declared a British Protectorate. In 1922 the British granted Egypt independence, but were keen to protect their interests in the Suez Canal zone. They therefore retained some military bases and a degree of control.

1922
T S Eliot publishes *The Waste Land*

Perhaps the most influential English-language poet of this century has been American-born T S Eliot (1888–1965), who took British nationality in 1927. *The Waste Land* (1922) was widely recognized for its quality and was followed by outstanding poetry including *The Four Quartets* (1944). Eliot also wrote a number of successful plays, including *Murder in the Cathedral* (1935) and *The Cocktail Party* (1950).

1922
BBC begins regular broadcasts

After the war the growth of interest in radio (or 'wireless telephony') was rapid. Many amateurs became interested in experimenting with crystal sets. From 1922 the privately run British Broadcasting Company started making regular broadcasts for entertainment and the primitive radio sets became more and more sophisticated.

A station was erected at Daventry in 1925 which made for easy reception all over Britain, and the broadcasts could now be picked up on the continent as well. The broadcasting revolution meant that for the first time music of quality could be heard by all: the potential of this new medium was enormous – for education as well as for entertainment and information.

In 1927 the government established the British Broadcasting Corporation in place of the Company, an independent body responsible to the state. The age of the radio was here to stay.

1922
Tutankhamun's tomb is discovered

On November 4, 1922 a British archaeologist on Lord Carnarvon's expedition to Egypt, Howard Carter (1873–1939) uncovered steps leading to a royal tomb of ancient Egypt. When the tomb was

This magnificent throne, over three thousand years old, was discovered in 1922 in the tomb of Tutankhamun.

opened it was revealed as a unique treasure house, which had not been disturbed for over three thousand years (*see 1362–1356 BC The reign of Tutankhamun*).

1922
Valéry writes *Charmes*

The French writer and poet Paul Valéry (1871–1945) was notable for his complex symbolism. In 1922 his greatest work appeared, *Charmes* (Charms), in which he compresses his ideas into an exact poetic language. His interest in mathematics and philosophy is reflected in his verse. Poems in *Charmes* include *Le Cimetière Marin* and *L'Ébauche d'un serpent*.

1922
James Joyce publishes *Ulysses*

1922 saw the publication in Paris of a novel that was quite unlike any that had gone before it. In *Ulysses* Irish writer James Joyce (1882–1941) dispenses with the normal time sequence, to plunge the reader into the world of the subconscious. Joyce's minute observation of everyday life and interweaving of themes provides a brilliant if complex masterpiece. Joyce's other great work is *Finnegan's Wake* (1939).

1923
Atatürk founds modern Turkey

When the Ottoman empire broke up at the end of the First World War, nationalist groups pressed for an independent Turkish state free of all external commitments. This was set up in 1921, and in 1923 Turkey became a republic. The first president was national hero Mustafa Kemal Pasha (1881–1938), who later took the name of Atatürk.

Over the next fifteen years Atatürk introduced reforms to change centuries of tradition. For the first time the Islamic faith became separate from the state. Women were able to vote and participate in political life, and the offices of the

Kemal Atatürk

Ottoman empire were abolished. Traditional dress was forbidden, and Western laws, coinage and alphabet introduced.

Turkey had become a modern republic with a democratic basis, although Atatürk wielded the power of a dictator. Achieving friendship with Britain and the West, as well as with the USSR, Turkey remained free to develop its new identity in the years between the wars.

1923
Hitler imprisoned

Continuing political unrest in Germany led the government to fear a Communist revolution might take place. The greatest threat to them however proved to be from extreme right-wing groups such as the Nazis. Political murder was the order of the day, and the leniency of the courts did little to deter right-wing terrorists.

In November 1923 an alliance of extreme right-wing groups attempted to seize power in Bavaria. The Nazis marched through Munich, much as the Italian fascists had marched on Rome the previous year. The police, however, gunned down the column, killing sixteen and wounding Göring.

Hitler narrowly escaped and was imprisoned for nine months. In jail he wrote his autobiography *Mein Kampf* ('My Struggle'), a work that reveals Hitler's peculiar psychological make-up and his ruthless brand of politics. Released from prison, Hitler continued to push for power, attempting to gain support from the big industrialists.

1924
Macdonald becomes first Labour prime minister

In 1874 the first trade union-sponsored MPs had entered parliament, and 1900 saw the formation of the Labour Party as we know it, by pioneers such as Keir Hardie (1856–1915). The longstanding domination of Parliament by the Conservatives and the Liberals finally ended in January 1924, when a minority Labour government came to power under Ramsay Macdonald (1866–1937).

Dependent upon the Liberals for a majority in the House of Commons, Macdonald introduced no radical changes, and his government fell to Conservative Stanley Baldwin (1867–1947) after only eleven months.

Despite this first showing by a Labour government, the future balance of power in British politics lay between the Conservative and Labour parties. Labour was returned again in 1929, but when in the economic depression of 1931 Macdonald formed an all-party National Coalition, he was bitterly opposed by many of his party.

1924
The Surrealist Manifesto

Of all the artistic and literary movements which sprang up in Europe at this time, one of the most influential was Surrealism, a more positive development of the Dadaist movement, that was received with abuse by a mystified public.

The term 'Surrealist' was first used by Apollinaire to describe a play, and was

Surrealist images feature in this copy of a Salvador Dali.

when in 1924 he died (*see 1919 Comintern formed*). There followed a battle for power in the Communist party, and the victor was Joseph Stalin, an astute but totally ruthless politician. Within three years his main rival, Leon Trotsky, was expelled from the party and exiled; Stalin's position as leader was secured.

Stalin introduced a series of five-year economic plans to increase the number of collective farms, expand nationalized industry, and increase production.

His economic successes, despite considerable setbacks and widespread famine, were only achieved by the brutal suppression of all opposition. Peasants, intellectuals and original revolutionaries who had devoted their lives to the cause of communism were exterminated or imprisoned: the country of revolution had become a brutal police state. Trotsky, exiled in Mexico, was murdered by Soviet agents in 1940.

explained by French writer André Breton (1896–1966) in his *First Surrealist Manifesto* of 1924: surrealistic art was inspired by the subconscious, by the associations that spring into one's head, by the world of dream. The pictures of surrealist artists show a world of fantasy, of 'super reality': clocks melt, bodies are distorted, a train roars out of a fireplace.

Perhaps the best known surrealist painter is Spanish-born Salvador Dali (*b.* 1904), who also collaborated with Spanish film director Luis Buñuel (*b.* 1900) to produce surrealist films. The German, Max Ernst (*b.* 1891), the Belgian René Magritte (1898–1967) and the Italian Giorgio de Chirico (*b.* 1888) all contributed to this new artistic approach.

1924
The death of Lenin

Lenin was just succeeding in getting his economic plans for the USSR under way,

1924
E. M. Forster writes *A Passage to India*

English novelist EM Forster (1879–1970) wrote a number of fine works (*A Room With a View*, 1908; *Howards End*, 1910) before he produced his masterpiece in 1924. *A Passage to India* is a gentle, ironical look at the uneasy co-existence of two civilizations in British India. This sensitive portrait was widely acclaimed at the time.

1925
The Great Gatsby and the Jazz Age

The USA and Europe were on the road to economic disaster. But on the surface things were booming, and those who had the money spent it lavishly. Freed from wartime austerity, the younger generation shocked their elders with fast cars, cocktail parties and dance crazes such as the Charleston. Women wore their hair short, smoked cigarettes and wore short dresses.

This was the golden age of traditional jazz (see 1911 Alexander's Ragtime Band); the greatest artist of the day was a young trumpeter called Louis Armstrong (1900–71). The spirit of the twenties was captured by US writer F Scott Fitzgerald (1896–1940) in works such as *The Great Gatsby* (1925).

The glitter of the Jazz Age concealed violence and corruption. Unpopular laws prohibiting alcohol in the USA led to 'bootlegging' (illicit trafficking in liquor), opening a market for gangsters such as Al Capone (1899–1947). Gang warfare erupted in the streets, but only the economic depression brought an end to the gay life of the twenties.

1925
Hindenburg becomes President of Germany

The death in 1925 of Friedrich Ebert, the first president of the Weimar Republic, gave cause for concern in Germany and abroad: his successor, ageing war hero Paul von Hindenburg (1847–1934) was a monarchist of the right wing. However, Hindenburg proved to be a supporter of the republican constitution, and Germany became more stable.

Monetary reform was introduced, and the Treaty of Locarno signed, with the result that Germany confirmed their respect for the Belgian and French frontiers, and their renunciation of Alsace-Lorraine. Allied troops began to leave the occupied Rhineland.

Party politics, however, became increasingly bitter, and the strident chorus of the (still small) Nazi party made itself heard. Germany's economic recovery had depended largely on foreign credit,

and when the worldwide depression set in, Germany was affected worse than most. In the 1932 election Hindenburg received 54 per cent of the vote to Hitler's 36 per cent, but Hitler was not easily deterred (see 1933 Hitler comes to power).

1925
Eisenstein makes *Battleship Potemkin*

Hollywood was the centre of the world cinema industry (see 1914 Charlie Chaplin enters Hollywood). In Europe, notably in Germany and the USSR, the artistic possibilities of the new medium were also being explored. Soviet film director Sergei Eisenstein (1898–1948) was to be perhaps the major influence on the development of cinematic art. Powerful films such as *Battleship Potemkin* (1925) and *Alexander Nevski* (1938) show Eisenstein as a master of film technique.

Noël Coward

1925
Noël Coward produces *Hay Fever*

English dramatist and actor Noël Coward (1899–1973) was renowned for his witty dialogue and elegant satire. His plays, revues and musicals were extremely popular. *Hay Fever* was the success of 1925, and was followed by many others, including *Private Lives* (1930) and *Blithe Spirit* (1941). Noël Coward received a knighthood in recognition of his work.

Strikers clash with police in the general strike.

1926
The general strike

In 1926 there were about five million trade-union members in Britain, out of a wage-earning population of fifteen million. For the first time a direct confrontation arose between the Trades Union Congress and the Conservative government under Stanley Baldwin.

The general strike started off with a miners' strike against less pay for longer hours. The mine owners would not climb down, and the TUC sanctioned a general strike that spread throughout the country.

Rail, transport, building, printing, iron and steel production all ground to a halt. The press closed down, and both government and TUC published their own newspapers. The government was determined not to give in. Baldwin called in troops and armed special constables. Hundreds of strikers were arrested.

After nine days a peace was negotiated, but it was bitterly resisted by the miners, who remained on strike for the whole summer, until economic conditions forced them to submit.

1926
The death of Rudolph Valentino

The film industry in the USA created an entirely new approach to entertainment (*see 1914 Charlie Chaplin enters Hollywood*). The big film companies publicized 'stars', who were adulated internationally. Rudolph Valentino (1895–1926) was the first great screen lover in films such as *The Sheikh* (1921). He died at the height of his popularity, and his New York funeral was attended by hysterical thousands.

1926
T E Lawrence: *The Seven Pillars of Wisdom*

British soldier T E Lawrence (1888–1935) led the Arab revolt against Turkish rule in the First World War. A brilliant, unconventional man, he was unable to achieve all he had hoped for the Arab cause after the war, and retired from public life to join the RAF under an assumed name. Killed in a motorcycle accident, his marvellous account of his desert life appears in *The Seven Pillars of Wisdom* (1926).

1926
Virginia Woolf writes *To The Lighthouse*

One of the most original modern English novelists and essayists was Virginia Woolf (1882–1941), whose poetic, impressionistic style is combined with acute psychological perception. She committed suicide in 1941. Her novel *To the Lighthouse* (1926) was followed by *The Waves* (1931) and some excellent essays.

1926
Invention of television

Scottish inventor John Logie Baird (1888–1946) was forced to give up his business career by illness. Settling in Hastings, England, he set up a small attic workshop in which he experimented with light projection. In 1925 he managed to transmit the image of a face from one room to another, and in 1926 he gave the first demonstration of a television image, to the Royal Institution of Great Britain, in London.

Baird at last received support for his research, and in 1929 his 240-line mechanically-scanned system was taken by the BBC. Other researchers were close behind him, in particular Russian-born American Vladimir Zworykin (*b.* 1889) whose 405-line electronically scanned system was adopted in 1937.

Baird also produced images in 3D, colour, and with stereophonic sound before his death in 1946. Television was to become the most important communications medium in the world after the Second World War.

1927
The first 'talkie'

Until 1927 films were silent, normally accompanied in the cinema by a piano or organ. Warner Brothers' *The Jazz Singer* was the first talking picture. Film-star Al Jolson's voice was converted into an optical soundtrack of varying intensity. In projection this was scanned by a photoelectric cell. The variations in current were amplified and fed into a loudspeaker to reproduce the voice.

1927
Hesse writes *Steppenwolf*

After Thomas Mann, Hermann Hesse (1877–1962) was perhaps the greatest German novelist of his day. His constant theme is the conflict between the spiritual and the wordly, and the path towards a harmonious inner self. *Steppenwolf* (1927) is a remarkable vision of the dilemma of modern man. In 1947 Hesse was awarded the Nobel Prize for his novel *Das Glasperlenspiel* ('The Glass Bead Game').

1927
Lindbergh flies Atlantic solo

In 1925 US aviator Charles Lindbergh (1902–74) decided to compete for a $25,000 prize offered for a New York to

Paris flight. Having found the financial backing to build a special plane, which he called the 'Spirit of St Louis', by 1927 he was ready for the solo attempt.

Having made a record overland flight from San Diego to New York City, he left Long Island at 7.52 a.m. on May 20 and arrived at le Bourget airfield at 10 p.m. Paris time. His achievement received international acclaim: the French cross of the Legion d'honneur, the British RAF Cross, the US distinguished flying cross and Congressional medal.

An air tour of the States, Mexico, Central and South America and the West Indies was followed by a flight from the USA to Denmark. Lindbergh settled in England in 1935, and returned to the USA in 1939.

The 'Spirit of St Louis' – the famous plane in which Lindbergh crossed the Atlantic.

the House of Commons: Nancy Astor (1879–1964) became the first female MP. Women were still not equal, and it was not until 1928 that the age of female voters was lowered to twenty-one, the age at which men could vote.

Women's position elsewhere in the world varied greatly. Victory for the US women's suffrage movement came in 1920. New Zealand enfranchised women as early as 1893, Australia in 1901, Denmark in 1915. The USSR offered political equality at its start. French women did not receive the vote until 1944, and Swiss women only received the vote in 1971.

1928
Votes for all women in UK

The struggle of the women's movement in England had not been in vain. The cruel opposition to them (*see 1903 Women's Political and Social Union founded*) could not survive a war in which women had taken over many jobs traditionally done by men.

In 1918 the Representation of the People Act allowed married women, women householders, and women graduates over thirty to vote. A subsequent act was passed allowing women to sit in

1928
Lorca writes *Romancero Gitano*

Spanish poet and dramatist Federigo Garcia Lorca (1899–1936) was best known for his gypsy songs – *Canciones* ('Songs', 1927) and *Romancero Gitano* ('Gypsy Romance', 1928), masterpieces of poetic form, subtle imagery and rhythmic control. Lorca achieved success as a playwright too before being killed at Granada in the Spanish Civil War.

1928
Chiang Kai-Shek takes Peking

China was in a state of turmoil; as the traditional way of life crumbled in the face of twentieth-century values, political factions fought for influence. Sun Yat-Sen (*see 1911 China declared a republic*) accepted Communist support into his Kuomintang party. When he died in 1925 his successor Chiang Kai-Shek (1887–75) led Kuomintang armies northward from Canton.

In 1927 however the Communists and their opponents within the Kuomintang party fell out. Chiang Kai–Shek opposed the Communists, and they withdrew from the party to form their own headquarters at Hankow. The Kuomintang's base was at Nanking.

Chiang Kai-Shek's armies swept north, and in 1928 took Peking. They soon controlled much of China, though the Communists held some areas, and warlords were still powerful. Fighting between Nationalists, under Chiang, and Communists under Mao-Tse Tung (1893–1976) lasted up to 1949, although both factions united to fight against Japanese aggression in the 1930's (*see 1949 Mao Tse-Tung proclaims Chinese People's Republic*).

1928
Brecht produces 'The Threepenny Opera'

Few have had such an influence on modern drama as German playwright and poet Bertolt Brecht (1898–1956). In the *Dreigroschenoper* ('The Threepenny Opera'), a 1928 play based on Gay's *Beggars' Opera*, with music by Kurt Weill, Brecht satirizes bourgeois society. A Marxist, Brecht put his theories of drama into practice with his *Berliner Ensemble* company, when he returned to East Germany from wartime exile in the USA.

1928
Evelyn Waugh writes *Decline and Fall*

Decline and Fall was the first of a number of novels by English writer Evelyn Waugh (1903–66) which form a witty commentary on the society of his day. Waugh's later work includes a number of masterpieces of sardonic humour, such as his popular trilogy, *Men at Arms* (1952), *Officers and Gentlemen* (1955) and *Unconditional Surrender* (1961).

1928
Fleming discovers penicillin

Twentieth-century medicine was revolutionized by the discovery of a powerful antibiotic. Scottish bacteriologist Sir Alexander Fleming (1881–1955) had already been a pioneer in the use of anti-

Sir Alexander Fleming

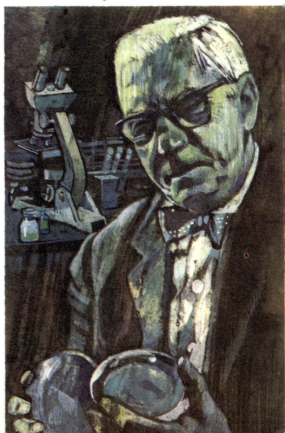

Penicillium notatum

typhoid vaccines, when in 1928 he discovered penicillin by accident.

In one of his tests he noticed a strange mould had formed. When he examined this *penicillium notatum*, one of the same family of moulds that grow on blue cheese and jam, he found it to have extra-ordinary antibiotic qualities.

It was another eleven years before a satisfactory method of producing penicillin as a practical medicine was found by two biochemists, Howard Florey and Ernest Chain. A formidable weapon had been added to man's warfare on harmful bacteria, and during the Second World War antibiotics became widely used. In 1945 all three men were awarded the Nobel prize.

1929
Wall Street Crash

On October 24, 1929, disaster hit the US stock exchange on Wall Street. The worst stock crash in history marked the start of a worldwide depression that was to bring misery and ruin to millions over the next decade.

World finance had never really recovered from the massive cost of the First World War and the industrial chaos it caused. Trading was made no easier by the high tariff barriers which individual countries had set up to protect their national interests.

The financial crash caused panic everywhere. Both the USA and the European countries underwent great hardship. By 1932 thirteen million were unemployed in the USA, farmers were starving, and people were living in the streets. In England, France and Germany the story was similar (*see 1936 The Jarrow Hunger March*).

Political upheaval followed in the wake of the depression. In 1933 US President Herbert Hoover (1874–1964) lost to Franklin Delano Roosevelt (1882–1945), whose 'New Deal' programme offered some hope.

1929
Cocteau publishes *Les Enfants Terribles*

Jean Cocteau (1891–1963) was a French writer of great versatility and originality and *Les Enfants Terribles*, a study of adolescence, is his best-known novel. His numerous publications included poetry, plays, works of criticism, and scenarios for ballets and musical compositions. He was associated with modern artistic movements and also became famous as a film director.

1929
J. B. Priestley publishes *The Good Companions*

The English essayist and critic John Boynton Priestley (*b.* 1894), achieved immense popularity with his novel *The Good Companions*, a story about a company of touring actors. He added to his reputation as a novelist with *Angel Pavement* (1930). His plays such as *Dangerous Corner* (1932) and *Time and the Conways* (1937) show that he was also a gifted dramatist.

1929
Graf Zeppelin flies around world

The early belief in the airship as a practical means of transport resulted in many models being manufactured during the First World War and post-war years. In 1929 the German *Graf Zeppelin* flew from New York to Friedrichshaven, Germany in $55\frac{1}{2}$ hours, and flew around the world in 21 days 7 hours.

Subsequent airship disasters – such as the British *R101* in 1930, the German *Hindenburg* in 1937 – discouraged further development.

1929
William Faulkner publishes *The Sound and the Fury*

The Sound and the Fury is considered by many to be the finest work of the American novelist, William Faulkner (1897–1962). Like many of his other novels including *Intruder in the Dust* (1948) and *Requiem for a Nun* (1951), it is set in the southern United States. In 1949 he was awarded the Nobel Prize for literature.

1930
W. H. Auden publishes *Poems*

Poems was the first collection of verse to be published by the English poet, Wystan Hugh Auden (1907–73). He was a very gifted writer who was deeply worried about contemporary events such as mass unemployment and the rise of fascism. During the 1930s Auden became the leader of a group of English writers who felt strongly about social conditions.

1930
Amy Johnson flies to Australia

On May 5, 1930 a young Englishwoman, Amy Johnson (1904–41), set off alone from London in a tiny plane to fly to Australia, completing the journey in nineteen days. She did not break the record, but her achievement as an inexperienced pilot made her famous. She later broke records in flights to Tokyo in 1931 and to Cape Town in 1932.

1930
Ortega y Gasset: *La Rebelión de las Masas*

José Ortega y Gasset (1883–1955) was a Spanish philosopher and writer who encouraged the literary revival in twentieth century Spain. He was also greatly concerned with contemporary problems and *La Rebelión de las Masas* ('The Rebellion of the Masses') describes the conflicts in Spanish society which eventually led to civil war in 1936.

1931
Gandhi attends London conference

Mohandas Karamchand Gandhi (1869–1948) was a Hindu lawyer who gave up his career in order to devote himself to the achievement of Indian independence from British rule by peaceful means. In 1920 he led a campaign of civil disobedience and non-cooperation with the British government in India and was imprisoned during 1922–4.

In 1930 a conference was held in London to discuss the future constitution of India, but the Congress Movement, the main Indian nationalist party, which was led by Gandhi, refused to take part.

In 1931 he attended a London conference, but was unable to solve the important problem of the conflicts be-

Mohandas Gandhi

tween the various communities in India.

Gandhi undertook long fasts in the continuing struggle, and was imprisoned for civil disobedience several times. His campaign of non-violence and his insistence on revitalizing the traditional culture of the Indian village were instrumental in achieving independence (*see 1947 India, Pakistan and Ceylon achieve independence*).

1932
Sir Malcolm Campbell breaks the land speed record

In 1932 the British racing motorist Sir Malcolm Campbell (1885–1948) reached a speed of nearly 409 kilometres per hour in his car *Bluebird*, beating his own previous record. In 1935 he became the first motorist to exceed 483 kph. He also held the world water-speed record at the time of his death.

Campbell's *Bluebird*

1932
De Valera wins general election in Ireland

Although he had been one of the leading figures in his country's fight for independence from Britain, Eamon de Valera (1882–1975) did not become head of the Irish government until 1932 when his party, Fianna Fail, came to power. He held office for more than twenty years and during this time he made Ireland a completely sovereign state.

1932
Francois Mauriac: *Le Nœud de Vipères*

François Mauriac (1885–1970) was already a major French novelist when in 1932 he published *Le Nœud de Vipères* ('The Vipers' Tangle'). It tells the story of an old man's conflict with his family and is considered by many to be Mauriac's best work. Like his other novels it shows the influence of the author's strong Catholic faith.

1932
The splitting of the atom

Sir John Cockcroft (1897–1967) and Ernest Walton (*b.* 1903) were two British scientists engaged in research work at the Cavendish Laboratory in Cambridge under the supervision of Lord Rutherford (*see 1919 Rutherford's atomic experiments*). In April 1932 it was announced that they had succeeded in splitting the nucleus of a light metal called lithium by a process known as 'bombardment' by accelerated protons.

This was an important step forward in the search to extract and control the tremendous energy contained in the nucleus of atoms. It led eventually to the construction of the atomic bomb and the use of atomic power for industrial purposes. In 1951 Cockcroft and Walton were awarded the Nobel Prize for physics.

Adolf Hitler

1932
Aldous Huxley's *Brave New World*

In 1932 Aldous Huxley (1894–1963), the English writer, published his most famous novel *Brave New World*, a gloomy picture of a future in which human beings are mass produced in a laboratory. Among Huxley's other novels are *Antic Hay* (1923) and *Point Counter Point* (1928). He also wrote *The Doors of Perception* (1954), which studied the effects of drugs.

1933
Hitler comes to power

In January 1933 Adolf Hitler, the leader of the Nazis (*see 1919 Formation of fascist parties*), became chancellor or head of government in Germany. He at once called for a general election, since his party did not have a majority in parliament.

In February the *Reichstag*, the parliament building, was burnt down, probably by a Nazi gang. Blame was laid on the communists, and Hitler used the apparent Communist threat against the state to suspend the ordinary liberties of the people and to conduct a violent election campaign. The Nazi Party won only a small majority but Hitler now took steps to make himself absolute ruler of

Germany by suppressing all other political parties.

However, there were some Nazis, led by Ernst Röhm, who demanded sweeping changes in German society, including the abolition of capitalism. But Hitler did not wish to annoy the German industrialists and financiers, and in June 1934 Röhm and many of his supporters were executed without trial. In July 1934 a group of Nazis tried unsuccessfully to seize power in Austria and murdered the Austrian chancellor, Engelbert Dollfuss.

1933
Jacob Epstein's *Ecce Homo*

Sir Jacob Epstein (1880–1959) was a sculptor born in New York of Russian-Polish parents, who spent most of his life in England. *Ecce Homo* was a symbolic religious work which expressed the artist's emotions and was very different from traditional sculpture. Epstein's other works included *Madonna and Child* (1927), *Genesis* (1931), and *Christ in Majesty* (1957).

1934
Benny Goodman forms his own band

Benny Goodman, who was born in Chicago in 1909, joined his first jazz band when he was only sixteen. In 1934 he formed his own band and made swing music, which was a form of jazz played by big bands, popular all over the United States. The 1930s was the swing era and the big bands usually featured solo performers. Benny Goodman, who was an outstanding clarinet player, became known as the 'king of swing'.

There were many other well-known bands including those led by Count Basie, Jimmy Dorsey, Duke Ellington and Glenn Miller, who was killed in an aircraft crash during the Second World War.

In the late 1930s a lively dance called the jitterbug, which was performed to swing music, and boogie-woogie, another variety of jazz, became very popular.

1935
Italy invades Abyssinia

In December 1934 there was fighting between Italian and Abyssinian soldiers on the frontier of the Italian Somaliland in an area which both Abyssinia and Italy claimed as their own. Mussolini, the fascist dictator of Italy, was determined to expand his country's empire in East Africa, and used this incident as an excuse to attack Abyssinia.

In October 1935 Italian forces, armed with modern military equipment, which

Benito Mussolini

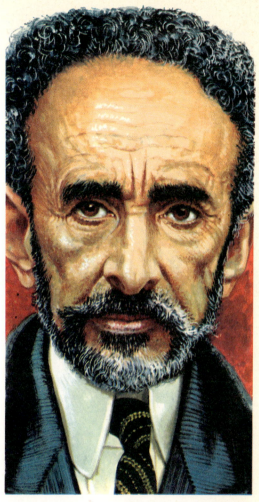

Haile Selassie, Emperor of Abyssinia (now Ethiopa) was ousted by the Italians in 1936, and restored by the British in 1941.

included tanks, artillery, aircraft and poison gas, invaded Abyssinia. The poorly armed Abyssinian soldiers were no match for the Italians and by May 1936 they had been almost completely defeated.

The emperor of Abyssinia, Haile Selassie (1891–1975), was forced to leave his country, which became part of Italian East Africa. However, in 1941 British forces drove the Italians out of Abyssinia and Haile Selassie was restored to his throne. An unsuccessful attempt was made by his own people to overthrow him in 1960, and he was finally deposed in 1974.

299

1935
Giraudoux: *La Guerre de Troie n'aura pas lieu*

French writer Jean Giraudoux (1882–1944) was a symbolist poet and novelist, but is best known for his plays. These are often based on Greek mythology or biblical subjects, but are nevertheless relevant to modern times. *La Guerre de Troie n' aura pas lieu* ('There shall be no Trojan War') was written in 1935.

1935
Sholokhov's *And Quiet Flows the Don*

In 1935 there appeared *And Quiet Flows the Don*, an English translation of part of a long novel by the Russian writer Mikhail Sholokhov (*b.* 1905). This was a vivid description of life in Russia during and after the Revolution of 1917. Sholokhov was also the author of *Virgin Soil Upturned* (1935) and in 1965 he was awarded the Nobel Prize for literature.

1935
Watson-Watt develops radar

In 1935 a Scottish physicist, Robert Watson-Watt (*b.* 1892), working at the National Physical Laboratory at Teddington, not far from London, perfected a method for locating distant objects in space by the use of radio waves. This device, which was later to become known as radar (from *ra*dio *d*etecting *a*nd *r*anging), provided early warning of an air attack, since enemy aircraft could be detected while they were still many miles away.

In 1936 a number of radar stations were set up in England. In 1938 the battleship HMS *Rodney* became the first ship successfully to detect approach-ing aircraft by using radar. By 1939 a chain of twenty radar stations had been installed along the east coast of England and they were to prove very important in the air defence of Britain during the Second World War.

Radar is now used for many purposes and is especially important in helping ships and aircraft to navigate in darkness and fog.

1936
Civil War breaks out in Spain

In February 1936 the Popular Front, an alliance of left-wing parties, formed a government in Spain. It introduced a sweeping programme of social reform, including the redistribution of land. This aroused the opposition of the land-owners, the Roman Catholic Church and the army.

In July 1936, led by General Francisco Franco (1892–1975) and other officers, many army units rose in revolt against the government. They quickly occupied large areas of the country, but failed to capture Madrid and Barcelona. Since most of the army was controlled by the rebels, or Nationalists as they were called, the government was forced into arming the workers in order to defend itself.

It was also helped by volunteers from many countries who formed groups known as the International Brigades. The Nationalists received considerable support in the form of soldiers, aircraft and other military equipment from Fascist Italy and Nazi Germany.

Gradually the Nationalists captured more territory. In 1937 they took control of the Basque region in northern Spain after heavy bombing attacks, during which the town of Guernica was almost completely destroyed. In 1938 they began to occupy the eastern part of the country. The war ended with the surrender of Madrid in April 1939, and General Franco became head of state until his death in 1975.

CRUSADE

OVER 3 MILLION JOBLESS

The Jarrow 'Crusade' or hunger march: unemployed men from North-East England march to London to demand work.

1936
Abdication of Edward VIII

In January 1936 Edward VIII (1894–1972) became King of Great Britain and Northern Ireland on the death of his father King George V. As Prince of Wales he had travelled widely while performing many official duties on behalf of his father and had achieved great popularity with the ordinary people.

Later in 1936 there was a constitutional crisis when King Edward announced his intention of marrying an American lady, Mrs Wallis Warfield Simpson. Since she had just divorced her husband there was a general feeling that she would not be acceptable as queen of England. However, the king was determined to marry Mrs Simpson, and he had no choice but to give up the throne.

In December 1936 he announced his abdication, and was succeeded by his younger brother, the Duke of York, who became King George VI. Edward, who married Mrs Simpson in June 1937, received the title of Duke of Windsor.

1936
The Jarrow Hunger March

In 1929 the US Stock Market collapsed and caused a severe slump in the country's economy. This in turn had a serious effect upon international trade. There began a period called the Great Depression in which there was a general decline in prosperity in most European countries and a sharp rise in unemployment. By the early 1930s more than two million men were out of work in Britain, and the industrial north of England was badly affected.

In 1933 the shipbuilding yard at Jarrow in County Durham was forced to shut down. More than two-thirds of the town's entire labour force was thrown out of work. In 1936 Ellen Wilkinson (1891–1947), the MP for Jarrow, led a march of workers to London to seek help from the government. Attempts were made to bring new industries to Jarrow, but the town did not really recover until after the Second World War.

Hitler held massive Nazi rallies at Nuremberg.

1936
Germany builds the Siegfried line

In 1936, shortly after the German re-occupation of the Rhineland, work began on the Siegfried line, a series of fortifications to protect Germany's western frontier in time of war. By 1939 it consisted of more than twelve thousand steel and concrete forts armed with heavy guns, stretching from the Dutch frontier in the north to Switzerland in the south.

1936
The Olympic Games in Berlin

Adolf Hitler wanted the Olympic Games to be a triumph for Nazi racialist theory and was outraged when the outstanding

athlete proved to be an American Negro, Jesse Owens (*b.* 1913). Nevertheless the Olympics were made into a magnificent film by Leni Riefenstahl (*b.* 1902) who also directed a documentary film of one of the Nazi Party's Nuremberg rallies.

1936
Prokofiev composes *Peter and the Wolf*

Peter and the Wolf was a piece of music written especially for children by the Russian composer Sergei Prokofiev (1891–1953). Prokofiev was a gifted composer and his best-known works include the opera *The Love of Three Oranges*, the ballet *Romeo and Juliet*, the *Classical Symphony*, piano and violin concertos, and film music.

1938
Germany annexes Austria

Adolf Hitler's plans for the expansion of Germany included the *Anschluss*, or annexation of Austria by Germany. There was considerable support for this in Austria especially among Nazi sympathizers in that country, and in 1934 they had made an unsuccessful attempt to seize power in Vienna.

In February 1938 Hitler made his position in Germany even stronger by becoming supreme commander of the armed forces. Later the same month he summoned the Austrian chancellor, Kurt von Schuschnigg (*b.* 1897) to Germany and demanded that the Austrian Nazis be given important posts in Schuschnigg's government.

Schuschnigg wanted the Austrian people to decide by voting whether to accept union with Germany. However, threatened with a German invasion, he resigned. On March 12 German troops entered Austria peacefully and on the following day the union between the two countries was proclaimed. A government headed by the Austrian Nazi Arthur Seyss-Inquart (1892–1946) was established in Vienna.

1938
The Munich Agreement

After his annexation of Austria earlier in 1938 Adolf Hitler was now determined to destroy Czechoslovakia. This country contained more than three million German-speaking people living in the Sudetenland region and many of them strongly supported the idea of union with Germany. In April 1938 their leader Konrad Henlein (1898–1945) demanded full self-government for the Sudetenland. This brought about a threat of war between Germany and Czechoslovakia, which might involve other countries.

The British prime minister, Neville Chamberlain (1869–1940), who was anxious to preserve peace at all costs, flew to Munich in September 1938 to attend a conference with the French prime minister, Hitler and Mussolini. A settlement of the crisis was reached and the Sudetenland region and its population were transferred to Germany. On his return to England Chamberlain said to cheering crowds, 'I believe it is peace in out time.' However, in March 1939 Germany annexed the rest of Czechoslovakia.

1939
Steinbeck publishes *The Grapes of Wrath*

In 1939 the American novelist John Steinbeck (1902–68) published *The Grapes of Wrath*, the story of a farming family from Oklahoma who emigrate to California in search of a better life. Like his other well-known novels *Tortilla Flat* (1935), *Of Mice and Men* (1937) and *Cannery Row* (1952) it shows his concern for the sufferings of ordinary people.

1939
Outbreak of the Second World War

After Germany had annexed Austria and Czechoslovakia Hitler now began to threaten Poland. Britain and France realized that there was no limit to Hitler's ambitions and in March 1939 promised to help Poland if it should be attacked by Germany. In August 1939 Germany and the USSR signed a treaty in which they guaranteed not to attack each other and to remain neutral if either country was involved in a war.

On September 1 Germany invaded Poland and on September 3 Britain and France declared war on Germany. Despite heroic Polish resistance, German mechanized divisions supported by overwhelming air power overran the country in four weeks. Russian troops invaded Poland from the east and occupied a large area of Polish territory, leaving the rest in German hands.

In Britain there was a mass evacuation of children from London and other large towns, because of the fear of German air-raids, although very few air attacks on Britain took place early in the war.

At sea there was a spectacular battle off the coast of South America between three British cruisers and a German battleship, the *Graf Spee*, which was badly damaged and later sunk by its crew.

1939
Henry Moore's *Reclining Figure*

In 1939 *Reclining Figure* established the reputation of Henry Moore (*b.* 1898) as one of the most original of modern English sculptors. Among his other works is the *Madonna and Child* (1943) and he created some notable sculptures for the UNESCO headquarters in Paris. During World War Two he also produced a series of famous drawings of people in air-raid shelters.

1940
Germany invades Denmark, Norway and the Low Countries

On April 9, 1940 German troops invaded Denmark which surrendered without fighting. On the same day German sea-borne forces landed in various parts of Norway. British and French forces were sent to help the Norwegian army, but had to be withdrawn later because they were needed in France. Norwegian resistance to the Germans did not finally cease until June 10.

On May 10 German armies invaded the Netherlands, Belgium, and Luxembourg. The Dutch port of Rotterdam was severely damaged by German air attacks before the Dutch army surren-

In occupied Poland, Nazi troops transported thousands of Polish Jews to brutal concentration camps.

dered on May 15. The British Expeditionary Force, which had been in France since September 1939, was sent into Belgium to help the Belgian army, together with some French troops.

Strong German armoured forces broke through the French defences at Sedan, near the French border with Belgium, and moved swiftly towards the English Channel. In this way they cut off from the main French army those British and French soldiers who were fighting in Belgium. They were gradually being forced back by the Germans and their position became extremely dangerous when the Belgian army surrendered on May 26.

1940
Ernest Hemingway: *For Whom the Bell Tolls*

Ernest Hemingway (1898–1961) was already a well-known American novelist when he published *For Whom the Bell Tolls*. It describes the heroism of an American fighting in the Spanish Civil War. Physical courage is a dominant theme in Hemingway's other novels which include *The Sun also Rises* (1926) and *A Farewell to Arms* (1929).

1940
Churchill becomes prime minister

In May 1940 Neville Chamberlain resigned as prime minister of Britain because many Members of Parliament were not satisfied with his leadership. He was succeeded by Winston Churchill (1874–1965) who had for a long time been a strong opponent of Chamberlain's policy of appeasement of Nazi Germany.

Churchill formed a coalition government of Conservative, Labour and Liberal members, and the leader of the Parliamentary Labour Party, Clement

Attlee (1883–1967), became his deputy prime minister. In his first speech to Parliament as prime minister on May 13, at a time of grave national crisis, Churchill declared, 'I have nothing to offer but blood, toil, tears and sweat.'

The same month, the Home Guard, a force of part-time volunteer soldiers, was formed to help defend the country against the expected German invasion. By midsummer more than one million men had enrolled.

1940
Graham Greene: *The Power and the Glory*

The Power and the Glory by the English novelist Graham Greene (*b*. 1904) tells the story of a fugitive priest in a country where Christianity has been outlawed. It shows the author's concern as a Roman Catholic with the problem of good and evil. Other novels by Graham Greene include *Brighton Rock* (1938) and *The Heart of the Matter* (1948).

1940
Evacuation from Dunkirk

The surrender of the Belgian army and the arrival of German armoured forces at the Channel ports in France meant that by the end of May 1940 the British and French troops in Belgium were encircled on all sides. The British government decided to evacuate these troops by sea from Dunkirk, a port in northern France, just south of the Belgian border.

In order to carry such a large body of men nearly a thousand ships of all sizes were hastily sent across the Channel from England. Fortunately for the soldiers retreating towards Dunkirk, the German forces halted their offensive for a time.

Between May 26 and June 4 about 200,000 British and over 120,000 French soldiers were taken away from Dunkirk under very difficult conditions. They were under constant attack from German aeroplanes and, without the protection provided by British fighter aircraft and the courage and discipline of the men involved, the evacuation would never have been possible.

1940
The fall of France

On June 5, 1940 the German armies in France launched a big attack. After some resistance the French defence collapsed completely and the German forces moved rapidly southwards. On June 10 Italy declared war against France and Britain. Four days later the Germans entered Paris. The French military position was now hopeless and a new French government, led by Marshal Philippe Pétain (1856–1951) asked for an armistice.

Under the terms of the armistice (June 22, 1940) France was divided into two zones. One was to be under German military occupation and the other, with the town of Vichy as its capital, was to remain under French sovereignty. Pétain became head of state of Vichy France, as it was called, and Pierre Laval (1883–1945) was chief minister. Although Vichy France was occupied by the Germans in 1942 its government remained in existence until 1944. Many Frenchmen refused to accept the armistice and, under the leadership of Charles de Gaulle (1890–1970), formed the Free French movement in London which was determined to continue the fight against the Nazis. Inside France itself a strong resistance movement grew up and many acts of sabotage were committed against the Germans.

The Battle of Britain

1940
The Battle of Britain

In July 1940 Adolf Hitler began to make plans for the invasion of Britain. Before this could take place it was necessary for the *Luftwaffe*, the German air force, to destroy British air power. The *Luftwaffe* launched a series of attacks, first against shipping and targets on the English coast, then against airfields, and finally against London and other towns.

The German planes greatly outnumbered the defending British aircraft. However, the use of radar (*see 1935 Watson-Watt develops radar*) gave the Royal Air Force advance warning of the direction in which the attacks would come, and so its aircraft could be ready in position. Moreover, the German bombers were easy targets for the British fighter planes.

By the end of October 1940 the *Luftwaffe* had lost more than 1,700 aircraft in a vain attempt to destroy the Royal Air Force and Hitler was forced to give up the idea of invading Britain.

1941
Shostakovich's *Leningrad Symphony*

In 1941 the Russian composer Dmitri Shostakovich (1906–75) wrote his seventh symphony, the *Leningrad Symphony*, while Leningrad was besieged by the Germans. It enjoyed great popularity in the USSR and other countries. Although Shostakovich is best-known for his symphonies, he also wrote a violin concerto, piano concertos, ballets and operas.

1941
Whittle's jet engine

Frank Whittle (*b.* 1907), an officer in the Royal Air Force, invented a jet aeroplane engine in which the means of propulsion was provided by a stream of gas being forced out backwards at great speed. In May 1941 his new engine was fitted into a specially built aircraft which made a successful flight. By the end of the

Frank Whittle

The Japanese attack Pearl Harbor.

Second World War, the Gloster Meteor, the first British jet fighter aircraft, was being produced.

In Germany a jet engine similar to Whittle's was used in an aircraft which first flew in August 1939, and in 1944 a jet-powered German military aircraft was in service.

After the war there was a rapid development in the use of jet engines for combat aircraft. In 1952 the De Havilland Comet, the first commercial airliner to be fitted with jet engines, went into regular service. By 1970 the majority of the world's aircraft were jet-powered.

1941
Germany invades the USSR

On June 22, 1941, Germany, in alliance with Romania, Hungary and Finland, invaded the USSR. The first German attacks met with great success. The Russians were taken by surprise and their army suffered heavy losses. By December

1941 German forces were only a few kilometres from Moscow. Leningrad was cut off by the Germans and during a heroic siege which lasted nearly eighteen months large numbers of its inhabitants died of starvation.

However, the Germans had under-estimated both the severity of the Russian winter and the almost limitless supplies of Russian manpower. A Russian attack in December forced the Germans to re-treat almost everywhere.

In June 1942 the Germans were able to launch a new offensive with the aim of gaining possession of the Caucasus region in the southern USSR. In August 1942 German armies began to attack the town of Stalingrad, an important communica-tions centre on the Volga river. But the Russian defenders resisted strongly for four months and the attacking German forces were themselves surrounded and captured.

This was the turning-point in the war. However, huge battles between the Russians and Germans involving hun-dreds of thousands of men and thousands of tanks were to be fought before the Germans were finally driven out of the USSR.

1941
The Japanese attack Pearl Harbor

On December 7, 1941 Japanese aircraft launched a surprise attack upon Pearl Harbor, the main US naval base in Hawaii, sinking and damaging many warships. On December 10, two days after the United States and Britain had declared war on Japan, two British battle-ships were destroyed by Japanese air-craft.

Japan now had naval and air supremacy in the Pacific and during the next five months Japanese forces won control of nearly the whole of South-East Asia. They occupied Malaya, Singapore, the Dutch East Indies (now Indonesia) and the Philippines, and invaded Burma.

The first American successes were in naval battles in May and June 1942 when US aircraft inflicted heavy damage on the Japanese fleet. The Japanese were gradually driven out of the many Pacific Island territories they had occupied. In October 1944 the reconquest of the Philippines began and by May 1945 the Japanese had been defeated in Burma.

The Japanese fought with fanatical courage and in the later stages of the war 'Kamikaze' airmen deliberately flew their aircraft, loaded with explosives, straight at enemy ships: the Japanese thought it shameful for soldiers to surrender. Be-cause of this they treated their British, Australian and American prisoners of war with great brutality and many died in captivity.

1942
Camus publishes L'Etranger

In 1942 the French writer Albert Camus (1913–60) published his novel L'Étranger ('The Out-sider'). It tells the story of a man who pointlessly kills somebody and illustrates the absurdity of human existence. His other well-known books include the novel La Peste ('The Plague') and L'Homme révolté ('The Rebel'), which shows how pure ideals be-come corrupted.

1942
The Desert War

The war in the Middle East began in September 1940 when an Italian army from Libya invaded Egypt in order to attack the British forces stationed there. The British counter-attacked and drove them back into Libya. In March 1941 the Italians were reinforced by a mecha-nized German force, the Afrika Korps, commanded by General Erwin Rommel (1891–1944), who quickly compelled the British to retreat into Egypt. However, a British garrison in the Libyan port of Tobruk withstood a siege by the Ger-mans and Italians for nine months.

Desert warfare: Montgomery's final offensive.

In November 1941 the British army began another offensive. In May 1942 Rommel counter-attacked and pushed his forces deep into Egyptian territory until they were halted at El Alamein. It was from here in October 1942 that General Bernard Montgomery (1887–1976), commanding a force of British, Australian, New Zealand and Indian soldiers, launched a final offensive which was to lead to the expulsion of German and Italian troops from North Africa.

1943
The surrender of Italy

In November 1942 Allied (US and British) forces landed in Morocco, Algeria and Tunisia. In May 1943, together with the British army advancing from Egypt, they compelled the German and Italian armies in North Africa to surrender. Two months later Allied forces occupied Sicily and in September they invaded the mainland of Italy.

In July Benito Mussolini's Fascist regime had been overthrown. A new Italian government under Marshal Pietro Badoglio (1871–1956) surrendered to the Allies and later declared war on Germany. Mussolini was arrested and imprisoned, but rescued by German soldiers. He was, however, captured and executed by Italian partisans in 1945.

The Germans sent large forces into Italy and these put up a stubborn resistance. In an effort to speed up their advance, in January 1944 the Allies landed troops at the seaport of Anzio near Rome. But it was not until spring 1945, after much fierce fighting, that the Germans were finally driven out of Italy.

1943
Perón comes to power in Argentina

In June 1943 the government of President Ramón Castillo (1873–1944) of Argentina was overthrown by a group of army officers led by Juan Perón (1895–1974). Three years later Perón was elected president of Argentina and his supporters won a majority in parliament.

Perón at once began a five-year plan of economic reform and rapid industrialization. His programme of social welfare brought many benefits to the working classes and gained him great popularity with the mass of the people although he was in fact a dictator. Perón's wife Eva (1919–52) played an important part in her husband's career.

He was deposed and exiled in 1955 after he had aroused the hostility of many powerful people. However, he still had numerous supporters and, following years of political unrest in Argentina, he returned there in 1973 to form a new government. He died the following year.

1944
The Allied invasion of France

On June 6, 1944 ('D-Day', as it was called) a huge force of American, British and Canadian soldiers landed on the Normandy coast of France. They were commanded by the American General Dwight D Eisenhower (1890–1969). Before the invasion took place railways and bridges in northern France had been heavily bombed, making it very difficult for the Germans to move their armies quickly.

After fierce fighting the Germans were forced to retreat. On August 15 Allied troops landed in the south of France and by the end of September most of the country had been freed from German occupation.

On September 3 British troops entered Belgium. Later the same month a large force of paratroops was dropped at Arnhem in the Netherlands in an unsuccessful attempt to obtain a bridgehead over the Rhine.

The Allied forces were halted at the German frontier by the Siegfried line. In December the commander of the German army, Field Marshal Gerd von Runstedt (1875–1953), launched a surprise counter-attack in the Ardennes region of Belgium which had some success. In February 1945 the Allies broke through the Siegfried line. In March they crossed the Rhine and began the invasion of Germany.

1944
The Liberation of Paris

By the end of July 1944 the Allied forces which had invaded Normandy in June were advancing rapidly through France. On August 17 American troops entered the town of Orléans only 113 kilometres from Paris. Two days later the French resistance forces in Paris rose in revolt against the Germans. On August 25 a French armoured division under General Leclerc (1902–47) entered the city and received the surrender of the German garrison. Paris was finally liberated after four years of occupation.

On August 26 General Charles de Gaulle, who had led the Free French movement in London, took part in a triumphant procession along the Champs Elysées in Paris. Afterwards he attended a service of thanksgiving in Notre Dame Cathedral, bravely defying the bullets of hidden German snipers.

De Gaulle became head of a provisional government which maintained authority in France until a new constitution could be drawn up.

1944
Jean Anouilh's *Antigone*

In 1944 *Antigone*, a play by the French dramatist Jean Anouilh (b. 1910), was first performed. Like some of his other plays it is based on a story in Greek mythology, but the characters wear modern dress and are concerned with contemporary problems. Many of Anouilh's plays were successfully presented in England including *Ring round the Moon* (1947), *The Waltz of the Toreadors* (1952), and *Becket* (1959).

1945
The Yalta Conference

In February 1945 an important conference was held at Yalta in the Crimea. It was attended by President Franklin D

Roosevelt of the United States, the British prime minister, Winston Churchill, and the prime minister of the USSR, Joseph Stalin. They were accompanied by their foreign ministers and the chiefs of staff of their armed forces. The aim of the conference was to discuss a number of military and political problems.

The three leaders agreed upon plans for the final defeat of Germany. They also made arrangements for Germany to be divided into four zones after the end of the war, to be occupied by Britain, The United States, the USSR, and France respectively.

The future frontiers of Poland were settled and the USSR agreed to enter the war against Japan after Germany had surrendered. Finally, the conference discussed plans for the setting up of the United Nations organization.

1945
Surrender of Germany

In January 1945 Russian forces had reached the eastern frontier of Germany. In the west the British and American armies were preparing for the final offensive. Meanwhile the Allied air forces continued their bombing campaign and in February caused widespread destruction and many thousands of deaths when they raided the town of Dresden, Germany.

In March the American army crossed the Rhine and by the end of April had joined up with the Russians on the river Elbe. Russian troops entered Berlin on April 24 and captured the city after fierce street fighting. Adolf Hitler committed suicide in his underground fortress in Berlin on April 30. In May the German armies began surrendering and the war in Europe finally came to an end on May 8. The leaders of the victorious powers held their last wartime conference in Potsdam, on the outskirts of Berlin, during July–August 1945.

Churchill, Roosevelt and Stalin meet at Yalta.

1945
The concentration camps are discovered

As they began to overrun countries previously occupied by Germany and then Germany itself, the Allied forces were horrified to discover the concentration camps. These had originally been established in 1933 as places of detention for opponents of the Nazi regime. Later they were used to house Jews and other minority groups. By 1939 six camps had been established in Germany, containing more than 20,000 prisoners.

After the outbreak of the Second World War further concentration camps were built in Germany itself and Poland to take people from all over Nazi-occupied Europe. They were kept short of food in dreadful living conditions, and were also forced to undergo cruel medical experiments.

Later the concentration camps were used for the systematic killing of Jews in poison gas chambers, since Adolf Hitler's plan to create a 'master race' required the extermination of so-called inferior peoples. More than five million people were murdered or died of starvation and disease in the camps.

1945
The surrender of Japan

Between 1942 and 1945 the Japanese armies were slowly driven from the territories they had overrun during the first six months of the war in the Pacific. In April 1945 the Americans invaded the island of Okinawa which they captured after much fierce fighting. They now had a base only 515 kilometres from the mainland of Japan.

In the following months American aircraft launched a series of heavy air raids on Japanese cities and industrial centres. After the collapse of Germany in May 1945 Japan had been left without allies. However, although her military position was now desperate, she still had a large army to defend her.

The US president Harry S Truman (1884–1972) realized that the conquest of Japan would cost many American lives. He therefore decided to try and bring the war to a quick end by the use of the atomic bomb. This terrible new weapon, which had an explosive power far greater than any ordinary bomb, had been developed by scientists in the United States. On August 6 a bomb was dropped on Hiroshima and on August 9 a second on Nagasaki, killing more than 120,000 people and causing widespread devastation. On August 14 Japan surrendered.

1945
The Nuremberg Trials

During 1945–6 many Nazis, accused of war crimes, were put on trial by the Allies at Nuremberg. Some were sentenced to death and others given long terms of imprisonment.

In Britain William Joyce ('Lord Haw-Haw'), who had broadcast Nazi propaganda from Germany during the war, was executed for treason, as was Pierre Laval, the former prime minister of Vichy, in France.

1945
The United Nations formed

In April 1945 delegates from fifty countries met at San Francisco in the United States to draw up a charter for the United Nations Organization which was to be the successor to the League of Nations. The charter, which was signed on June 26, 1945 declared that the organization was an association of states whose aim was to maintain international peace and encourage co-operation between nations.

The United Nations consists of six main bodies: the General Assembly, the Economic and Social Council, the Trusteeship Council, the International Court of Justice, the Security Council, and the Secretariat. It also contains a number of special agencies, such as the Food and Agriculture Organization and the UN Educational Cultural and Scientific Organization.

The Secretariat, which is the administrative body of the United Nations, is headed by a secretary-general chosen by the General Assembly on the advice of the Security Council. The first secretary-general was a Norwegian, Trygve Lie (b. 1896), who held office from 1946 to 1953.

Hiroshima, Japan, was devastated by the first atomic bomb.

Although the United Nations was unable to ensure that its member countries would remain permanently at peace with one another, its special agencies carried out much useful work.

1945
Landslide Labour victory

The British general election of July 5, 1945, was won by the Labour Party with a huge majority over all other parties. The new government, led by Clement Attlee, immediately began a sweeping programme of economic and social reforms, which were to transform Britain into the 'Welfare State'.

Among the most important measures were the nationalization of various industries including coal mining, the electricity supply industry, and the Bank of England. Another significant event was the establishment of the National Health Service which provided free medical care for everybody.

However, the war had left Britain's economy in a very serious condition and the country recovered its prosperity only very slowly, with the help of generous loans from the United States. It was a time of great hardship, and rationing of food, which had been introduced during the war, did not end until the early 1950s.

1945
France: the end of the Third Republic

In October 1945 elections were held in France for an Assembly which was to draw up the country's new constitution. The Assembly later proclaimed General Charles de Gaulle head of a provisional government, but de Gaulle resigned in January 1946.

The new constitution was finally adopted by a referendum in October 1946 and the Fourth French Republic came into existence. After elections in

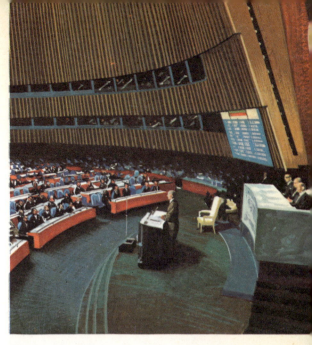

The General Assembly of the UN, founded in 1945 meets in New York.

November the Communists became the largest party in the National Assembly. However, the Communists in the government quarrelled with their colleagues and were removed from office in May 1947. They now opposed the government as did the new right-wing party formed by de Gaulle later the same year.

France's difficulties were increased by economic problems, strikes and a war in the French colony of Indo-China (now Vietnam). The next ten years were a period of political instability, during which there were frequent changes of government.

1945
Birth of modern jazz

In the 1940s some American jazz musicians tried new harmonic ideas and produced a kind of jazz known as bebop. Inspired by Charlie Parker, Dizzy Gillespie, Thelonius Monk and others, modern jazz later developed in the 1950s and 60s a number of different styles, including the so-called 'cool' or relaxed jazz. The Modern Jazz Quartet found inspiration in the forms of classical music.

1945
George Orwell's *Animal Farm*

In 1945 the English writer George Orwell (1903–50) published his novel *Animal Farm*, the story of a group of animals who overthrow their human masters. A satire on communism, it created a great impression, as did his last novel, *Nineteen Eighty-Four* (1949). This is set in a nightmare world of the future, in which the state has complete control over people's lives.

1945
Benjamin Britten's *Peter Grimes*

In 1945 *Peter Grimes*, an opera by the English composer Benjamin Britten (*b.* 1913), had its first performance. It was a great success and he went on to write other operas including *Billy Budd* (1951) and *The Turn of the Screw* (1954). Britten is also well known as a composer of songs and choral works.

Benjamin Britten

1945
Sartre's *Chemins de la Liberté*

In 1945 Jean-Paul Sartre (*b.* 1905), the French writer and philosopher, published the first two parts of his four-volume novel *Les Chemins de la Liberté* ('The Roads to Freedom'). Like his earlier novel *La Nausée* ('Nausea', 1939) and his plays *Les Mouches* ('The Flies', 1943) and *Huis-clos* ('In Camera', 1944), it expresses his philosophical views.

Sartre's philosophy of existentialism denies the existence of God, but says that man is free to give a meaning to his life by his actions. He must constantly be making a choice of what he will do, for he will be judged by his acts and not by his intentions.

Existentialism had a considerable influence on French life and literature after the Second World War, and Sartre himself played an active part in politics. He was a successful dramatist and his other plays include *Les Mains Sales* ('Crime Passionnel', 1948) and *Nekrassov* (1956).

1945
Le Corbusier's *Unité d'habitation*

In 1945 work began at Marseilles, France, on the *Unité d'habitation*, one of a number of tall buildings designed by the Swiss architect Le Corbusier (1887–1965) according to a mathematical system of proportions. Le Corbusier had a great influence on town planning and modern architecture, and among his other achievements was the designing of the town of Chandigarh in India.

1946
Jackson Pollock: action painting

In the early 1940s the American artist Jackson Pollock (1912–56) began to develop a strange new style of abstract painting known as action painting. The artist creates an unusual pictorial effect by applying paint to the canvas in a random manner – smearing, dripping or splashing it on to the surface. This can be seen in his *Untitled*, an action painting of 1946.

1947
India and Pakistan achieve independence

Before the Second World War the Indian Empire consisted of British India, directly administered by Britain but ruled by native Indian princes. Although both Hindus and Muslims in India wanted complete independence for their country, the Muslims were afraid that their rights would be ignored by the large Hindu majority.

After the British government tried unsuccessfully to meet the wishes of both religious groups, the Muslim leaders demanded the creation of a separate state and the Hindus reluctantly agreed to the partition of the country.

On August 15, 1947 India and Pakistan came into existence. The division of the Punjab and Bengal between them meant that millions of Hindus and Muslims had to be transferred from one country to another. During these mass migrations there was much fighting and many people were killed. Moreover, there was a dispute over Kashmir. It was claimed by India, but Pakistan objected on the grounds that the majority of the population was Muslim.

Gandhi travelled all over India trying to keep the peace between the Hindus and Muslims, but he was eventually assassinated by a Hindu fanatic on January 30, 1948.

Ceylon (now Sri Lanka), which had been a British colony, became independent in February 1948.

1947
Thor Heyerdahl's Kon-Tiki expedition

In 1947 a Norwegian scientist Thor Heyerdahl (b. 1914), with five companions, set off from Callao in Peru on the west coast of South America in a raft made of locally grown balsa wood. His object was to sail across the Pacific Ocean to Polynesia.

Heyerdahl had already noticed that certain aspects of Polynesian culture resembled that of the ancient inhabitants of Peru. He believed that the Polynesians were not Asiatic in origin and wanted to show the possibility that in ancient times people from South America could have crossed the ocean on primitive rafts and settled in Polynesia.

After an epic voyage of three and a half months over 8,000 kilometres of ocean, Heyerdahl landed in Tuamotu Island in the South Pacific. His exploit made him world famous and he wrote about the voyage in *The Kon-Tiki Expedition* (1948).

1947
The Dead Sea Scrolls

In 1947 some ancient manuscripts were discovered in a cave near the Dead Sea, about 12 kilometres south of Jericho. When the manuscripts were examined by experts it was found that they belonged to a community of Jews who lived around the time of Christ. They have provided much important information about Jewish history and the origins of Christianity.

1947
Tennessee William's *A Streetcar Named Desire*

A Streetcar named Desire by the American playwright Tennessee Williams (b. 1914) is about the disastrous consequences of a visit by a neurotic frustrated woman to her married sister. Like many of Williams's best-known plays including *The Glass Menagerie* (1945) and *Cat on a Hot Tin Roof* (1955) the scene is set in the 'Deep South' of the United States.

1947
The Marshall Plan

In 1947 the countries of Western Europe, which had suffered severely during the Second World War, were in some danger of economic collapse. In June of that year the US secretary of state, George C Marshall (1880–1959), announced in a speech that the United States would be willing to help Europe in its efforts towards recovery.

In July 1947 seventeen Western European countries met in Paris to try and co-ordinate their plans for economic stability and to decide what assistance would be necessary from the United States. This was the European Recovery Programme, or Marshall Plan as it was popularly called.

The countries supporting the Programme subsequently set up a permanent body, known as the Organization for European Economic Co-operation, which was to administer aid given under the Marshall Plan. In 1948 the United States began to supply material and financial aid to Europe, which continued until 1952.

1948
Communist government in Czechoslovakia

Czechoslovakia, which had been occupied by the Germans since March 1939, was finally liberated by the Russian army in May 1945. A provisional government was appointed and began a programme of nationalization and agricultural reform.

Elections held in May 1946 gave the Communist party the largest number of seats in parliament. A new government took office with the Communist Klement Gottwald (1896–1953) as prime minister and other Communists holding important positions. In February 1948 the Communists seized control of the country by force and Jan Masaryk, the foreign minister was found dead.

Between 1945 and 1948 all the countries of eastern and south-eastern Europe, with the exception of Greece and Turkey, came under Communist domination. Non-Communists were expelled from positions of power and governments subservient to the USSR were formed. Only Yugoslavia, although a Communist country, under the leadership of Marshal Tito (b. 1892) remained independent of the USSR.

1948
The Berlin Airlift

After the surrender of Germany to the Allies in 1945 Berlin was divided into four sectors, each under the control of one of the Allies. In 1948 the Western Allies (Britain, the United States and France) formed their zones of Germany into a single economic unit.

This was done in the face of opposition from the Russians, who began to blockade the city of Berlin, which lay right in the centre of their zone of occupation in Germany. All communications by rail and road with the west were cut off. The Russians moreover declared that the four-power administration of the city was no longer functioning and that the Western Allies had no right to be there. They went on to set up their own municipal government in the Russian sector of Berlin.

West Berlin was saved by a massive airlift of vital supplies by the British and Americans, which continued until the blockade was lifted in May 1949.

1948
Mount Palomar's reflecting telescope

In 1928 the California Institute of Technology received a grant from the Rockefeller Foundation for the construction of a reflecting telescope with a diameter of

200 inches (508 centimetres). It was to be housed in an observatory built at the height of nearly 1,800 metres on Mount Palomar in California.

The dome containing the gigantic telescope and the building supporting the dome were erected in 1938. The dome is nearly 43 metres high and about the same width. The telescope itself was to be fitted into a heavy steel framework which could be easily moved despite the enormous weight it carried.

The preparation of the disc for the telescope's mirror took nearly ten years and the finished mirror weighed about 15 tonnes.

In 1948 the telescope was finally completed and installed. Mount Palomar Observatory now had the largest telescope in the world.

The Mount Palomar telescope.

1948
State of Israel proclaimed

Many Jews settled in Palestine after the First World War (*see 1917 The Balfour Declaration*) developing industry and agriculture. The Arabs living in Pales-tine strongly opposed the arrival of large numbers of Jews and there was frequent fighting between the two communities. The persecution of the Jews during the Second World War led to even greater immigration into Palestine. The British authorities tried to limit their numbers, but many entered illegally and Jewish terrorist organizations conducted a campaign of violence against the British.

In 1947 the United Nations voted in favour of partitioning Palestine into a Jewish state and an Arab state. The British withdrew from the country and in May 1948 the state of Israel came into existence. The territory allotted to the Arab state became part of Jordan, and the holy city of Jerusalem was divided between Israel and Jordan.

1949
Founding of NATO

After the Second World War in face of the growing hostility of the USSR the countries of western Europe decided to form a protective alliance with the United States. In April 1949 the North Atlantic Treaty Organization (NATO) was formed. The treaty was signed by delegates from twelve countries and provided for mutual assistance against aggression.

1949
The establishment of the German Federal Republic

After the surrender of Germany in 1945 the country was divided into four occupation zones. Growing hostility between the USSR and the Western Allies made it impossible for Germany to be treated as a single political and economic unit as had been intended.

In order to deal with the desperate postwar plight of the Germans, which included near starvation and an enormous influx of refugees from the east, the

British and Americans decided in 1946 to merge the economies of their two zones. They also began to hand over much responsibility for local administration to the Germans. In 1948 the three Western Allies went ahead with their plans for the creation of a centralized German government.

In April 1949 the German Federal Republic came into being as an independent sovereign state. Elections were held in August of that year and the Christian Democratic Party, led by Konrad Adenauer (1876–1967), took office in the parliament at Bonn. Theodor Heuss (1884–1963) became federal president.

1949
Mao Tse-Tung proclaims Chinese People's Republic

Mao Tse-Tung as a young man.

The struggle between the Chinese Nationalists and the Chinese Communists for the control of their country had begun in the 1920s (*see 1928 Chiang-Kai-Shek takes Peking*). Civil War between the opposing sides continued until the Japanese invasion of China in 1937. After the defeat of Japan the civil war was resumed.

The Chinese Communists, under the leadership of Mao-Tse Tung (1893–1976) equipped themselves with enormous quantities of arms left behind by the Japanese. Their Nationalist opponents proved both incompetent and corrupt and gradually lost popular support. Although they received military assistance from the Americans, they were unable to win any significant victories over the Communists.

In 1948 the Nationalist armies suffered a series of defeats and began to disintegrate. In 1949 the remaining Nationalist forces, led by Chiang Kai-Shek (1887–1975), were driven off mainland China and took refuge in the island of Formosa. On October 1 of that year Mao Tse-Tung proclaimed the establishment of the Chinese People's Republic.

1949
Arthur Miller's *Death of a Salesman*

In 1949 *Death of a Salesman* by the American playwright Arthur Miller (*b.* 1915) had its first performance. It is the story of a man who believes that happiness in life depends on success in business. It made its author world famous and like his other well-known plays *All My Sons* (1947) and *The Crucible* (1953) it attacked the values of American society.

1950
Bertrand Russell receives Nobel Prize

In 1950 the English philosopher and writer Bertrand Russell (1872–1970) was awarded the Nobel Prize for literature. Russell began his long and distinguished career as a lecturer in mathematics at Cambridge University. He went on to make his reputation as an outstanding philosopher with such books as *Principles of Mathematics* (1903) and *Principia Mathematica* (1910–13).

During the First World War he was sent to prison for writing an article in a pacifist journal. After the war he became a lecturer and journalist, and wrote popular books on a variety of subjects, including philosophy, marriage, education, and sociology.

Throughout his life his outspoken views on morals and politics brought him into conflict with authority. In the 1950s he became associated first with the Campaign for Nuclear Disarmament and subsequently with its more militant branch, the Committee of 100, which advocated civil disobedience in support of its beliefs.

Bertrand Russell

1950
The Korean War

After the surrender of Japan in 1945, Korea, which had been under Japanese rule since 1910, was occupied by US and Russian troops. The Americans took the southern half of the country and the Russians the part north of the 38th parallel of latitude.

Although it had been agreed that a democratic government should be set up for the whole of Korea, in 1948 the Americans recognized South Korea as an independent state. The same year a Communist government was established in North Korea, which claimed authority over the entire country.

In June 1950 North Korean forces invaded South Korea. The United Nations asked member countries to stop the North Korean advance. By the end of 1950 a UN force, mainly composed of Americans, had pushed the North Koreans right back to the Chinese border. China now intervened on the side of North Korea, and after much fierce fighting an armistice was eventually signed in 1953.

1950
McCarthy investigates 'Un-American' activities

In the early 1950s Americans became worried about Communist influence in the United States when several people were convicted of spying for the USSR. An American senator, Joseph McCarthy (1908–57), exploited their fears with wild accusations that Communists held important positions in government departments. He set up an investigation committee and many innocent people lost their jobs before McCarthy was finally discredited.

1951
Defection of Burgess and Maclean

In 1951 two British diplomats, Guy Burgess and Donald Maclean, who had been passing secret information to the Russians, suddenly fled to the USSR. They had been warned that they were under suspicion by Kim Philby, a trusted member of the British Intelligence Service, who had in fact been a Soviet spy for many years. In 1963 Philby was himself unmasked and defected to the USSR.

1951
Sugar Ray Robinson becomes boxing champion

In 1951 the American Negro, Sugar Ray Robinson (b. 1920), won the world middleweight boxing championship, keeping his title until 1955. During his career Robinson had fought successfully as a featherweight and a lightweight, and was also world welterweight champion. His style and personality made him popular with boxing fans everywhere.

1951
Barbara Hepworth's *Contrapuntal Forms*

In 1951 the English sculptor Barbara Hepworth (1903–75) exhibited her striking abstract carving *Contrapuntal Forms* at the Festival of Britain exhibition. She was one of the leading sculptors of her time and examples of her work, including *Empyrean* (1953–54), *Winged Figure* (1962), and *Single Form* (1963), are to be found in public buildings throughout the world.

1953
Eisenhower becomes president

In 1952 Dwight D Eisenhower (1890–1969), who had led the Allied armies in the invasion of Europe in 1944, was nominated as the Republican Party's candidate for the presidency of the United States. When the elections were held in November of that year Eisenhower won an impressive victory over the Democratic Party's candidate, Adlai E Stevenson (1900–65), and took office as president in January 1953.

Eisenhower's first term as president was characterized by the growing prosperity of the United States. In his domestic politics he pursued a moderate policy. In foreign affairs he made great efforts to improve international relations, in the hope of lessening the tensions caused by the Cold War.

He was re-elected president in 1956 and during his second term of office he travelled widely, visiting other heads of state and received the Soviet prime minister, Nikita Khrushchev, on a visit to the United States.

1953
Conquest of Everest

Mount Everest, which lies in the Himalayan Range on the border between Nepal and Tibet, is the highest mountain in the world, rising to a height of more than 8,800 metres. Many attempts had been made to climb it, and although some mountaineers had come very close to the summit, none had actually reached it.

In 1953 the Royal Geographical Society of London and the Alpine Club sponsored a new expedition led by Colonel John Hunt. Elaborate preparations were made before the climb began, and the expedition followed a route which had not been tried before. By May 28 the mountaineers had reached a height

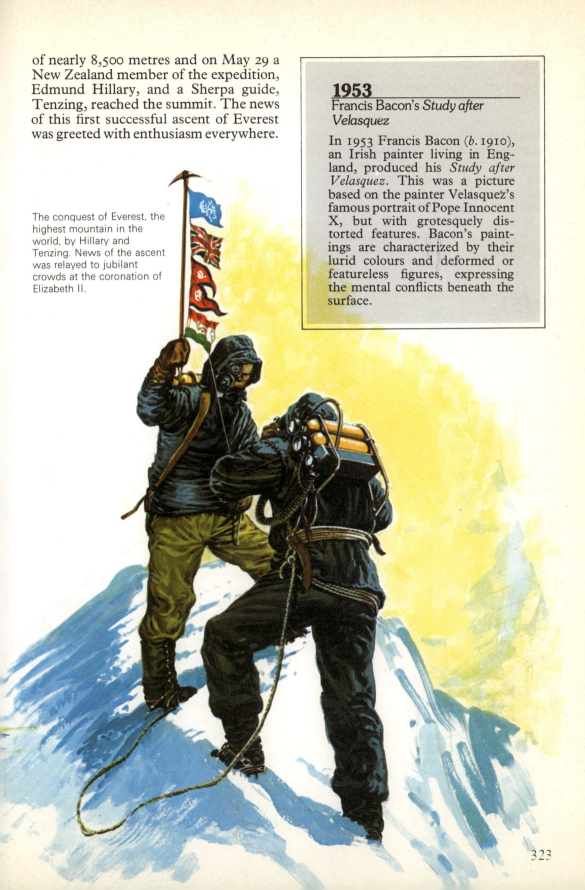

of nearly 8,500 metres and on May 29 a New Zealand member of the expedition, Edmund Hillary, and a Sherpa guide, Tenzing, reached the summit. The news of this first successful ascent of Everest was greeted with enthusiasm everywhere.

The conquest of Everest, the highest mountain in the world, by Hillary and Tenzing. News of the ascent was relayed to jubilant crowds at the coronation of Elizabeth II.

1953
Francis Bacon's *Study after Velasquez*

In 1953 Francis Bacon (*b.* 1910), an Irish painter living in England, produced his *Study after Velasquez*. This was a picture based on the painter Velasquez's famous portrait of Pope Innocent X, but with grotesquely distorted features. Bacon's paintings are characterized by their lurid colours and deformed or featureless figures, expressing the mental conflicts beneath the surface.

1953
Bathyscaphe descends to the ocean depths

In the late 1940s the Swiss scientist, August Piccard (1884–1962), already famous as a high-altitude balloonist, began designing a bathyscaphe, a diving apparatus for exploring the ocean bottom. In 1953 he reached a record depth of more than 3,500 metres. In 1960 his son Jacques, in a new version, descended to a level of nearly 10,900 metres.

1953
Discovery of DNA structure

One of the most important developments in biology has been the cracking of the 'genetic code'. The work started by Mendel (*see 1865 Mendel announces heredity laws*) and others had become a complex and advanced branch of science when Francis Crick and James Dewey Watson discovered the structure of the DNA (deoxyribose nucleic acid) molecule, so opening for good or bad the possibilities for genetic 'engineering'.

1954
The fall of Dien Bien Phu

During the Second World War the French south-east Asian colonies of Tonkin, Annam and Cochin-China were occupied by the Japanese. After the defeat of the Japanese (*see 1945 The surrender of Japan*) Ho Chi-Minh (1892–1969) leader of a Communist-dominated nationalist party, the Viet Minh, proclaimed the independence of the three colonies as the Democratic Republic of Vietnam.

The French attempted to re-establish their control in the country and in 1946 fighting broke out between their forces and the Viet Minh. Unable to secure a decisive victory, the French attempted to set up a rival non-Communist national-ist government.

However, by 1953 French forces were rapidly losing ground in the northern part of the country and in May 1954 the Viet Minh overran an important French military position at Dien Bien Phu. Following a conference held at Geneva the same year Vietnam was divided into Communist North Vietnam and French controlled South Vietnam.

1954
Hydrogen bomb exploded

In the early 1950s American scientists were working on the construction of the hydrogen bomb, whose destructive power was many times greater than the atomic bomb. One hydrogen bomb was tested in the Pacific in 1952. Another test took place on Bikini Atoll in the Pacific in March 1954, causing such a devastating explosion that there was worldwide protest against the continuation of such tests.

A nuclear test in the Pacific.

1954
Bannister's four-minute mile

On May 6, 1954 a young English athlete and medical student, Roger Bannister (*b*. 1929), competing in a race at Oxford, became the first man to run the mile (1·6 kilometres) in less than four minutes. His actual time was 3 minutes 59·4 seconds. Bannister also captured the European 500 metres record the same year.

1954
Dylan Thomas's *Under Milk Wood*

1954 saw the publication of the drama *Under Milk Wood* by Welsh poet Dylan Thomas (1914–53). This poetic evocation of a day in the life of a small Welsh town enjoyed an instant popular success. Thomas established his reputation as a poet with *Eighteen Poems* (1934); he was also well-known for his volume of short stories *Portrait of the Artist as a Young Dog* (1940).

1954
C. Day Lewis's *Collected Poems*

In 1954 the English poet, C Day Lewis (1904–72), published his *Collected Poems*. He first established his reputation in the 1930s with collections of verse like *From Feathers to Iron* (1931) and *Overtures to Death* (1938), which brought fresh imagery and new ideas to English poetry. He was also well known as a writer of detective novels.

1955
Scientists appeal against nuclear weapons

After the United States had exploded a hydrogen bomb in the Pacific Ocean (*see 1954 Hydrogen bomb exploded*) there was growing alarm at the possible harmful effects of radioactivity if the tests continued. In July 1955 a group of world-famous scientists, including Albert Einstein and Bertrand Russell, appealed for the renunciation of warfare, and warned against the dangers resulting from thermonuclear explosions.

In 1958 the Campaign for Nuclear Disarmament (CND) was formed in England to press for the unilateral abolition of nuclear weapons by the British government. In 1960 Bertrand Russell, who had helped to found CND, broke away from the main body to found 'The Committee of 100', which proposed to use civil disobedience as a method of protest. Both groups were active in the early 1960s and a regular event was the Easter march by CND supporters from the Atomic Weapons Research Establishment at Aldermaston in Berkshire to Trafalgar Square in London.

The CND peace symbol.

1956
John Osborne's *Look Back in Anger*

In 1956 *Look Back in Anger* by the English playwright, John Osborne (*b*. 1929), had its first performance. It is the story of a young working-class man who protests against a society dominated by middle-class attitudes. Osborne and other young writers, including John Wain, Colin Wilson and Kingsley Amis, who were critical of contemporary social values, became known as the 'angry young men.'

1956
The rock'n roll era

In the 1950s rock 'n roll quickly established itself as the dominant popular music in the United States. Made famous by such performers as Bill Haley and Elvis Presley, it was characterized by a heavily stressed, repetitive dance rhythm. It rapidly became popular with Britain's teenagers who were enjoying a new prosperity and dressing in the 'teddy boy' fashion, which resembled men's clothes of Edwardian times.

1956
Khrushchev denounces Stalin

Joseph Stalin died in 1953, after nearly thirty years of dictatorship. Power in the USSR passed to three men; Georgi Malenkov, Vyacheslav Molotov and Lavrenti Beria. But the man who was to dominate Soviet politics for the next decade was First Secretary of the Communist Party, Nikita Khrushchev (1894–1971), who by 1958 was also head of the government.

A down-to-earth, obstinate figure, with a marked sense of humour, Khrushchev was to be a thorn in the flesh of Western politicians until 1964 (*see 1961 Kennedy becomes US President*).

The most remarkable feature of Khrushchev's internal politics was 'de-Stalinization'. In 1956 Khrushchev denounced Stalin, his brutal methods, and the cult of personality in politics.

Liberal reforms were introduced: thousands of prisoners were released from labour camps, and curbs on writers and artists were partially eased. The full extent of the misery created by Stalin became known to the world.

Nikita Khrushchev

1956
The Cyprus crisis

The British took over Cyprus from Turkey in 1878, and by 1930 many of the predominant Greek Cypriot population were pressing for *enosis*, or union with Greece, against the will of the Turkish Cypriot community.

After the Second World War, the *enosis* movement was led by Archbishop Makarios III (*b.* 1913). It flared into violence with a campaign by Georgias Grivas (1898–1974) and his EOKA guerilla organization. In 1956 the British deported Makarios, and fighting broke out against the British and between the two communities. In trying to establish a constitution for an independent Cyprus, the British were unable to satisfy all parties, as the Turkish Cypriots demanded partition.

Independence in 1960 brought no long-term solution, although both sides were guaranteed representation under Makarios's presidency. UN forces were sent in, in the 1960's; in 1974 a National Guard coup temporarily ousted Makarios and Turkey invaded part of the island amidst bitter fighting.

1956
Beckett writes 'Waiting for Godot'

En Attendant Godot ('Waiting for Godot') was originally written in French by Irish author Samuel Beckett (*b.*1906); it was the theatrical success of 1956. Beckett, formerly secretary to James Joyce, portrays a stark, seemingly pointless world, in which characters are unable to communicate; the play is both amusing and tragic. It was followed by *Fin de Partie* ('Endgame') in 1957.

1956
Rothko paints *Orange, Red and Yellow*

In the 1950s New York took over from Paris as the art capital of the world, aided by collectors such as Peggy Guggenheim and artists such as Jackson Pollock and Willem de Kooning. Abstract painting was at its peak, and at its best in the canvases of Mark Tobey, Franz Kline and Mark Rothko.

1956
The Suez Crisis

In 1952 an army revolt in Egypt forced the corrupt King Farouk (1920–65) to abdicate; Gamal Abdel Nasser (1918–70) became president of the new republic in 1954. Nasser secured an arms deal with Czechoslovakia in 1955, and an Anglo-US offer of financial assistance for the building of the Aswan Dam. British troops withdrew from the Suez Canal Zone.

In July 1956 Britain and the USA became worried by Egypt's apparently pro-Communist sympathies and withdrew their Aswan Dam offer. Nasser replied by nationalizing the private Suez Canal Company, whose stockholders were mainly British and French.

In October Israeli troops invaded the Sinai. Britain and France demanded an end to Egypt–Israeli hostilities, but Egypt ignored them. Britain and France, anxious about the future of the Suez Canal, attacked Egypt. The UN ordered Britain, France and Israel to withdraw, and they were replaced by UN forces on the Egypt–Israeli border. Nasser turned to the USSR to finance the Aswan Dam.

1956
The Hungarian Revolution

The new Communist countries of Eastern Europe soon began to resent the extent of USSR control. June 1953 saw rioting in East Berlin, and in 1956 there were bad riots in Poznan, Poland after which Polish Communist leader Wladyslaw Gomulka (*b.*1905) managed to secure an increased measure of independence.

In October 1956 revolution broke out in Hungary. Students demonstrating against the degree of Soviet control were joined by workers and fought with Hungarian police. When the Hungarian Communist Party requested Soviet assistance, bitter fighting broke out with the troops sent in by the USSR.

Imre Nagy (1896–1958), a national Communist, became Prime Minister and introduced sweeping reforms. Soviet troops were withdrawn from Budapest, political prisoners released, the one-party system abolished. Hungary withdrew from the Warsaw Pact and appealed to the UN.

This was too much for the USSR. On November 4, 1956 they sent troops and tanks into Budapest and suppressed the revolution. A pro-USSR government was installed; Nagy was later captured and executed.

1957
The EEC is formed

The 1950s saw the first attempt at economic co-operation in Western Europe.

In 1952 France, West Germany, Italy, Belgium, the Netherlands and Luxembourg successfully formed the European Coal and Steel Community.

In 1957 the experiment was extended and the same countries established the European Economic Community (EEC). Customs duties between member states were lowered, and a common market set up with a single tariff on imports. In 1958 a European parliament was formed.

In 1959 the rest of Europe formed a rival, less rigid economic union, which had none of the EEC's aspirations towards 'a greater Europe'. The European Free Trade Association (EFTA) included Great Britain, Austria, Denmark, Norway, Sweden, Switzerland and Portugal.

Britain applied for EEC membership in 1963, but its application was vetoed by France. Only in 1973 did Britain finally enter the EEC, together with Ireland and Denmark. Britain's entry was confirmed by referendum in 1975. Greece joined the EEC in 1981.

1957
Sputnik I is launched

The exploration of space, mankind's greatest adventure, began on October 4, 1957, with the launching of the first man-made earth satellite by the USSR. Sputnik I, as it was called, was a sphere of about fifty-eight centimetres in diameter and weighed eighty-three kilograms. Orbiting the earth every 96·2 minutes and reaching a maximum altitude of 896 kilometres, Sputnik I sent out a steady stream of signals.

The USSR followed this success a month later with the launching of Sputnik II, a five-hundred kilogram satellite containing the first space traveller – a dog called 'Laika'. The USA launched Explorer I, on January 31, 1958, a small satellite of fourteen kilograms.

It was fitting that these achievements took place in International Geophysical Year (July 1957 – December 1958) a successful attempt at worldwide co-operation in the scientific study of our planet (*see 1961 First man in space*).

1957
Pinter writes *The Birthday Party*

British dramatist Harold Pinter (*b*. 1930) caused a stir with his first plays: *The Birthday Party* (1957) and *The Caretaker* (1958) are full of the seemingly illogical, tortuous conversations that make up everyday talk, and this unusual dramatic language baffled critics of the day. Pinter has also written *The Homecoming* (1965) and a number of successful film-scripts.

1957
A Long Day's Journey into Night produced

In 1957 *A Long Day's Journey into Night* by American Eugene O'Neill (1888–1953) was produced in New York. This masterpiece about the tragic Tyrone family is based on O'Neill's early life. O'Neill had a long career as a dramatist, writing *Mourning Becomes Electra* in 1931 and *The Iceman Cometh* in 1946. In 1936 he became the first US dramatist to receive the Nobel Prize.

1958
De Gaulle becomes President of France

In the post-war years France suffered from political chaos (*see 1945 France: the end of the Third Republic*). No party had a majority in the National Assembly, and shaky coalitions were unable to pass any effective legislation. French military action in Indo-China (Vietnam) had been disastrous, and in 1958 a report that

France was to grant independence to the Algerians led to riots by French colonials in Algiers.

The government collapsed, and wartime leader of the Free French General Charles de Gaulle (1890–1970) was called out of retirement. An election in November 1958 gave his party office, and in December de Gaulle became First President of the Fifth Republic, with sweeping personal powers.

An ardent nationalist, de Gaulle's aggressive foreign policy and controversial home measures kept him in power until 1969. (*See 1962 Algeria achieves independence*, and *1968 Student revolts*). He died in 1970.

De Gaulle in 1944, leading the triumphal procession after the liberation of Paris. He became President of France in 1958.

1958
Dr Zhivago published

Boris Pasternak (1890–1960) had a longstanding reputation in the USSR as a poet and translator, but it was his first novel that caused a sensation. Pasternak misjudged the extent of post-Stalin liberalization, and this fine novel about the revolution caused his expulsion from the Writers' Union. Despite his disenchantment he was a Marxist and a patriot, and was compelled to refuse the Nobel Prize.

1959
Grass writes *The Tin Drum*

Perhaps the best-known West German writer of post-war years is Günter Grass (*b.* 1927), whose work provides a penetrating analysis of the Germany of his day. *Der Blechtrommel* ('The Tin Drum', 1958) and *Hundejahre* ('Dog Years', 1962) are marked by black humour and strange fantasy. Grass is also a campaigner for the Social Democratic Party in West Germany.

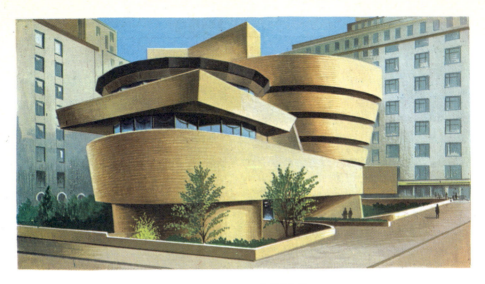

1958
Frank Lloyd Wright: The Guggenheim Museum

One of the greatest architects of the twentieth century was American Frank Lloyd Wright (1869–1959). He is particularly famous for his unconventional designs for private homes and his introduction of 'open plan' rooms. His best large work is the Guggenheim Museum of Art in New York, which was built between 1943 and 1958.

1958
Nautilus crosses the North Pole

In 1958 the first US nuclear submarine *Nautilus*, under Commander William Anderson, performed an epic voyage by travelling 2,928 kilometres under the polar ice cap from Point Barrow, Alaska, to the Greenland Sea, crossing the North Pole on August 3. In 1960 the USS *Trident* completed the first submerged circumnavigation of the world. The age of the nuclear submarine was here.

(Above) The Guggenheim Museum of Art, New York, completed in 1958.

(Right) The age of nuclear power: *Nautilus*, and details of her reactor.

1959
First hovercraft flight

The first hovercraft flight took place at Cowes, Isle of Wight, in 1959. The four-tonne Saunders-Roe SR-N1 was soon able to reach sixty-eight knots. Invented by Briton Christopher Cockerell (*b.* 1910), the hovercraft soon proved its worth as a means of crossing water, marsh, or flat land, easily manoeuvrable on its cushion of air.

1959
Castro overthrows Batista

Cuba under the dictatorship of President Batista (*b.* 1901) was corrupt and oppressive. A rising under revolutionary Fidel Castro (*b.* 1927) had failed in 1953, but returning to Cuba in 1956 Castro recovered from an initial setback to mount a guerrilla campaign from the Sierra Maestra mountains.

In January 1959 Castro finally overthrew Batista, who fled to the Dominican Republic. On becoming prime minister Castro reformed Cuba on communist tations.

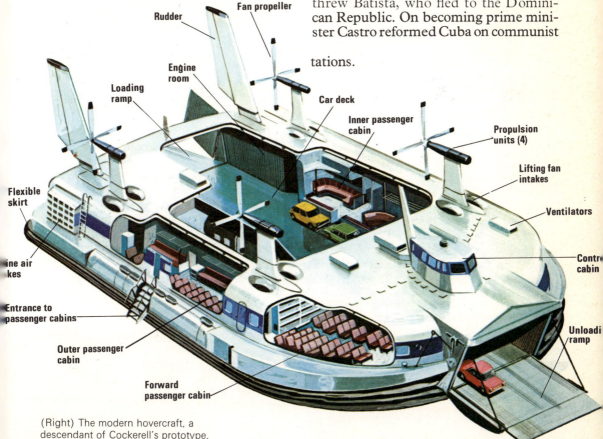

Rudder

Fan propeller

Engine room

Loading ramp

Car deck

Inner passenger cabin

Propulsion units (4)

Lifting fan intakes

Flexible skirt

Ventilators

ine air kes

Contr cabin

Entrance to passenger cabins

Outer passenger cabin

Forward passenger cabin

Unloadi ramp

(Right) The modern hovercraft, a descendant of Cockerell's prototype, can travel at speeds up to 90 kph and ferry cars across the English Channel.

Cuba soon developed a close relationship with the USSR, and the USA became increasingly worried at the thought of having a pro-Soviet country only 150 kilometres off the coast of Florida.

In 1961 an unsuccessful attack on Cuba was made by US-trained Cuban exiles in the Bay of Pigs, and the next

Fidel Castro, leader of the Cuban revolution.

This term was coined by Françoise Giroud to cover the exploratory film work of François Truffaut, Jean-Luc Godard, Louis Malle, and other young French directors.

Hiroshima Mon Amour, a film of the New Wave.

year saw the USA and the USSR on the brink of war, when US intelligence revealed Soviet missile sites in Cuba (*see 1961 Kennedy becomes US President*).

1959
Launching of NS *Savannah*

In 1959 the world's first nuclear-powered merchant ship was launched in the USA. The NS *Savannah*, capable of carrying sixty passengers and 10,000 tonnes of cargo introduced a new era in shipping. Her nuclear reactor weighs 2,500 tonnes, but the amount of uranium oxide used is so small that she could travel fourteen times round the world without refuelling.

1959
Films of the New Wave

Alain Resnais' film *Hiroshima Mon Amour* (1959) which examined the effects of war upon human relationships, was one of the *Nouvelle Vague* (New Wave) films produced in the 1950s and 1960s.

1959
Wesker writes his trilogy

British writers of the 1950s were very concerned with social conditions (*see 1956 John Osborne's Look Back in Anger*), and Arnold Wesker (*b.* 1932) was no exception. His trilogy *Chicken Soup with Barley, Roots,* and *I'm talking about Jerusalem* (1959–60), and later plays such as *Chips with Everything* (1962), are good theatre and convincing social comment.

1960
Macmillan's 'Wind of Change' speech

In a speech on January 10, 1960 during a visit to Ghana, the British prime minister, Harold Macmillan (*b.* 1894) said that '. . . the wind of change is blowing through Africa'. He referred to the rapid emergence of African countries towards independence as representing a major new development in the world.

During the 1950s no less than twenty-five African countries achieved independence, and the map of the continent was changed beyond recognition. New names appeared: Ghana, Tanzania, Malawi, Mali and many others. By 1961 eighty percent of Africa was free from foreign control.

Conservative Prime Minister Harold Macmillan.

The new nations of Africa faced many crises during the 1960s; tribal loyalties often conflicted with the new national interests, and different political factions fought for power. Whilst foreign control had largely gone, foreign powers such as China, the USSR, and the USA sought influence by providing aid and technology.

1960
Fighting in Belgian Congo

At a meeting of Belgian and Congolese representatives in Brussels from January 20 to February 20, 1960, it was agreed that the Belgian Congo should be granted full independence on July 30 of that year.

Peace did not come easily: the rest of the year was marked by a series of tribal disputes in various parts of the country. In July many tribes were fighting, the *Offices des Transports du Congo* (Otraco) went on strike, and the army mutinied. Belgian forces in the country were put on immediate alert.

Katanga Province and Kasai Province broke away from the rest of the country and there were several serious disturbances in Leopoldville, the capital. An emergency United Nations force was sent to the Congo but it was not until early 1963 that the rebellion was suppressed.

Congolese affairs remained unstable for many years, but in 1970 Joseph Mobutu (b. 1930) was proclaimed President and the country was renamed Zaïre in 1971.

1960
First working laser

The principle of the laser (Light Amplification by the Stimulation of Radiation) was first propounded in 1958 by A L Schawlow and C H Townes. Two years later T H Maiman announced the building of the first working laser in the USA and since then it has been utilized in many different spheres. These applications include welding, surgery, and holography (a type of three-dimensional photography).

A laser beam cuts through metal.

John F Kennedy

Kennedy's home policy was marked by civil rights legislation; he was a keen supporter of a federal policy for the desegregation of schools and universities, supported by his brother Robert Kennedy (1925–69), the Attorney-General. Kennedy's promising career was, however, doomed to tragedy (*see 1963 Assassination of President Kennedy*).

1961
First man in space

The world's first spaceman was the Russian Yuri Alekseyevich Gagarin (1934–68). On April 12, 1961, in the spacecraft *Vostok I*, he orbited the earth once, remaining in space for one hour 48 minutes, the actual orbit lasting 89·34 minutes.

Vostok I was launched from Tyuratam space base, Kazakhstan, at 9·07 a.m. Moscow Time (6·07 GMT). The capsule orbited the earth at a maximum speed of 28,090 kph at altitudes between 258 and 340 kilometres.

1961
Kennedy becomes US President

After the most closely contested election in American history, Democrat John Fitzgerald Kennedy (1917–63) was inaugurated as President of the United States on January 20, 1961. He was the first Roman Catholic president and the youngest man to hold this office.

Kennedy's first year in office was marked by an attempted invasion of Cuba by forces trained in America (*see 1959 Castro overthrows Battista*). On April 17, 1961 anti-Castro Cuban exiles mounted an abortive invasion in the Bay of Pigs.

The failure of this bid led the Soviet Premier, Nikita Khrushchev, to assume that Soviet ballistic missiles could be based in Cuba, but in October 1962 Kennedy imposed a naval 'quarantine' around the island to prevent Soviet ships delivering weapons. For a week it looked as if the USA and the USSR were on the brink of nuclear war; this eventuality was averted when Khrushchev halted work on the missile sites. In 1963 Kennedy secured a treaty with Russia partially banning nuclear tests.

Yuri Gagarin

The return to earth was accomplished by the firing of retro-rockets after the craft had been turned round automatically. *Vostok I* seared into the earth's atmosphere and Gargarin was ejected from the craft and carried earthwards by parachutes. He landed in a ploughed field near the village of Smelovaka, much to the amazement of two local farmworkers.

With his epic flight (as Gagarin himself said) 'the road to the stars had opened'.

1961
Dag Hammarskjöld receives Nobel Prize

Dag Hammarskjöld (1905–61), Swedish economist and statesman, was second secretary-general of the United Nations from 1953 to 1961. His leadership improved the effectiveness and reputation of the UN.

Hammarskjöld died in an air crash whilst on a peace mission in Katanga (*see 1960 Fighting in Belgian Congo*) and was posthumously awarded the Nobel Peace Prize later that year.

1961
Building of the Berlin Wall

Following a decree passed on August 12, 1961 by the East German *Volkskammer* (People's Chamber) a fence of barbed wire was erected around West Berlin to cut off communication with East Berlin and East Germany. At a later date the barbed wire was replaced by a concrete wall manned by armed guards.

Berlin had been divided into four sectors, British, American, French, and Russian, at the end of the Second World War. During the 'Cold War', a war of words and economic weapons with little military involvement, the Russian sector (East Berlin) was separated from the other three.

From 1948 some 1,500,000 people had used Berlin to escape from communist domination to a freer life in the West. The East Germans built the wall to stem this flow but many people still attempted crossings in spite of the fact that the communist troops had no hesitation in shooting the escapees.

1962
Fonteyn and Nureyev debut at Covent Garden

Dame Margot Fonteyn (*b.* 1919) and the finest ballet have been synonymous ever since her debut with the Vic-Wells Ballet in 1934. But in 1962 she reached a new

The Berlin Wall, symbol of the Cold War.

peak in her brilliant dancing career when she began her celebrated partnership with the Russian ballet star Rudolf Nureyev (b. 1938).

1962
First Beatles record

The British pop group 'The Beatles' (Paul McCartney, b. 1942, John Lennon, b. 1940, George Harrison, b. 1943, and Ringo Starr, b. 1940) revolutionized the world of popular music.

They started making records in 1962 and within a short time had taken the world by storm. Their music inspired many other performers and marked the beginning of an era of youthful revolution in the arts.

1962
Algeria achieves independence

In 1947 Algeria became unified politically with France, but the eighty-six percent Moslem (Arab and Berber) population resented continuing domination by the French colonialists, and in 1954 started the fight for independence.

Guy Mollet (b. 1905) was elected to the French premiership, but neither he nor

his successor Félix Gaillard could find a peaceful solution to the Algerian problem. During the Algerian crisis the French were to employ half a million troops against the rebels.

In 1958 rumours that the French government was giving in to the rebels led to a riot of French colonialists in Algiers. Instead of suppressing the riot, the French military joined it. It looked as if France itself could be torn by Civil War, and de Gaulle was called upon to take over (*see 1958 de Gaulle becomes President of France*).

Despite terrorist acts by the OAS (the Secret Army Organization, dedicated to keeping Algeria French) de Gaulle pursued his plans for Algerian independence, which was finally achieved in July 1962.

Charles de Gaulle

1962
Launch of *Telstar*

Telstar I, launched on July 10, 1962 was the first communications satellite to receive and transmit live television pictures across the Atlantic.

The first trans-Atlantic transmission via *Telstar*, from Andover, Maine, USA to Pleumeur Bodou, France, was made on July 11.

Telstar opened up a new era in world communications and paved the way for modern satellites that carry several programmes simultaneously.

1963
Death of Pope John XXIII

His Holiness Pope John XXIII (*b.* 1881) Angelo Giuseppe Roncalli, died on June 3, 1963.

Although Pope John's reign of four and a half years was one of the shortest on record, it proved extremely significant. His convening of the œcumenical council, on October 11, 1962, to promote unity in the Christian Church was particularly important.

Kennedy's presidency saw the start of the space age: US rocket base Cape Canaveral was renamed Cape Kennedy in his memory.

1963
Assassination of President Kennedy

John F. Kennedy, President of America, was assassinated in Dallas, Texas on November 22, 1963 whilst driving through the city.

As the motorcade proceeded through the city three shots were fired from the sixth story of a warehouse. Kennedy immediately slumped forward in the car, shot in the head and the neck.

Kennedy and Governor Connally, who had been injured in the shooting, were rushed to Parkland Hospital but the president died half an hour after admission.

A twenty-four year old ex-marine, Lee Harvey Oswald, was arrested and charged with the murder but he was never tried. On November 24 Oswald was shot and killed by Jack Leon Ruby, a night-club proprietor.

Upon the death of John Kennedy vice-president Lyndon Baines Johnson (1908–1973) was sworn in as President.

Whaam! by Roy Lichtenstein.

1963
Lichtenstein paints *Whaam!*

The 'pop art' movement grew up in the late 1950s and 1960s. It was concerned with the trivia of modern materialistic society, such as comic strips and advertisements, and revelled in the 'bad taste' of its subjects. Principal pop artists in America include Roy Lichtenstein (*b.* 1923), Andy Warhol (*b.* 1927) and Claes Oldenburg (*b.* 1929); in Britain, Richard Hamilton (*b.* 1922) and Peter Blake (*b.* 1932).

1964
Muhammed Ali becomes world heavyweight champion

On February 25, 1964 American boxer Muhammad Ali (Cassius Marcellus Clay, *b.* 1942) knocked out Charles (Sonny) Liston in a match at Miami Beach, Florida, USA, to become world heavyweight champion. Ali's title was not recognized universally, however, until he outpointed Ernie Terrell, the World Boxing Association Champion, at Houston, Texas on February 6, 1967.

1964
Escalation of the Vietnam War

The Geneva Agreement of 1954 (*see 1954 The fall of Dien Bien Phu*) confined the Communist Viet Minh, under Ho Chi-Minh, to North Vietnam, with their capital at Hanoi; South Vietnam and its capital Saigon was held by anti-communists supported by France and the USA, who feared the spread of Communism in Asia. The Agreement intended that elections for a unified government should be held, but the South refused to co-operate.

US military advisors were sent to South Vietnam, and in 1963 Kennedy increased their number to sixteen thousand. In 1964 incidents involving American and North Vietnamese ships in the Tonkin Gulf led to total US involvement and the most horrific war of recent years.

From 1965 President Johnson ordered the sustained bombing of North Vietnam. The number of US military personnel was raised to over half a million. Australia and South Korea sent units to support the US, and money and weapons from the Communist world poured into Hanoi. First Laos and then Cambodia were drawn into the battle arena.

The growing outcry in America and abroad and the US failure to achieve a military success led to President Johnson's retirement from politics. Peace talks held in Paris achieved little but by 1973 the USA was ready to wind down its war effort, and withdraw. In 1975 Southern Vietnamese communists (Viet Cong) took Saigon, renaming it Ho Chi-Minh City.

Martin Luther King

1964
Stockhausen composes *Moments*

Perhaps the most influential composer of the last twenty years has been the German Karlheinz Stockhausen (*b.* 1928), who has gone beyond the 12-note system to experiment with electronic sounds and strange effects. *Moments* (1964) is scored for a soprano solo, a chorus, and thirteen instrumentalists, yet it includes a remarkably diverse range of sounds.

1964
Martin Luther King receives Nobel Prize

The Rev Dr Martin Luther King (1929–68), an American Negro clergyman, was awarded the Nobel Peace Prize on November 14, 1964 for his work in promoting peaceful solutions to American racial problems.

King first came to prominence in the American civil rights' movement in 1954 when he led a boycott of transport in Montgomery, Alabama to force desegregation on the city's buses. Six years later he resigned his Baptist Ministry to devote his full attention to the cause of his people.

Although King was acknowledged to be a great leader of men, his non-violent policies to promote the cause of civil rights were not always popular. Militant members of the 'Black Power' movement attacked his ideas, white segregationists

abhorred his aims. On April 4, 1968 he was assassinated by a sniper in Memphis, Tennessee.

1965
Death of Winston Churchill

The whole of Britain mourned when statesman Sir Winston Churchill (1874–1965) died on January 24, 1965.

A great war leader, member of the House of Commons for over sixty years, eminent historian, brilliant orator, and gifted artist, he will be remembered by many as 'the greatest Englishman of his time'.

Winston Churchill, wartime leader.

1965
First space walk

On March 18, 1965 the Russian cosmo-
naut Aleksei Arkhipovich Leonov (*b.*
1934) became the first man to leave a
space vehicle and to 'walk' in space.

Leonov was connected to the space vehicle *Voskshod II* by a cable in this
experiment essential to the furtherance
of space exploration. He floated in space,
freed from the effects of gravity, for
twenty minutes.

1965
Indo-Pakistan War

In April 1965 forces of India and Pakistan fought in a recurrence of the border
troubles that had led to the Sino–Indian
War of 1962 when China sided with
Pakistan on the Kashmir problem. Further clashes occurred in May and September 1965 until a UN resolution
brought agreement from both sides.

1965
Rhodesia declares UDI

In November 1965 the Rhodesian
government, under the leadership of Ian
Smith (*b.* 1919) made a unilateral declaration of independence.

The Rhodesians took this action as
Britain would not consider granting independence to the country because it
considered that the administration, controlled by a white minority, to be
insufficiently representative of the
people.

In March 1970 the Rhodesian government renounced its allegiance to the
British throne and declared Rhodesia to
be a republic, in the face of continuing
economic sanctions by the UK and
many other countries.

In the 1970s opposition to Smith's
government from African nationalists
took the form of guerrilla warfare.

Leonov floats in space, connected to his spacecraft
by a cable.

1966
Chichester's round-the-world voyage

Between 1966 and 1967 a remarkable
man, Francis Chichester (1901–72), well-
known aviator and yachtsman, achieved
the first solo circumnavigation of the
world by yacht.

On July 7, 1967 Chichester was
knighted by Queen Elizabeth II with the
very sword used by Elizabeth I to knight
Sir Francis Drake following his circumnavigation (*see 1577 Drake sets out in
the Pelican*).

1966
Cultural Revolution in China

The Great Proletarian Cultural Revolution in China from 1966 to 1969 was organized by the Communist Party Chairman Mao-Tse Tung (1893–1976).

Mao's objective was to bring into line those elements of political and cultural life that appeared to be moving away from the strict ideological lines that he advocated. It was felt that if these 'backsliders' were allowed to continue they would ultimately damage Mao's system of Marxist–Leninist ideology that forms the basis of the Chinese communist state.

The people, and in particular the specially formed youth movement 'The Red Guard', were invited to question the ideological correctness of those in authority. They were encouraged to criticize any administrator who did not conform to Maoist thought.

Although the political scene was purged during the cultural revolution it caused enormous disruption in industry and agriculture and almost brought civil war to many areas of China.

Francis Chichester, solo yachtsman.

1966
Assassination of Dr Verwoerd

Dr Hendrik F Verwoerd (1901–66), South African Prime Minister, was stabbed to death by a parliamentary messenger, Dimitri Tsafendas on September 6, 1963.

At his trial in October Tsafendas was deemed to be mentally disorientated and unfit to plead. He was committed to prison.

1967
Military coup in Greece

After a long period of political instability the Greek army overthrew the constitutional government of Greece on April 21, 1967 to form a 'National Government'.

On May 9 the new government passed two new Acts: one to provide for the creation of a new constitution and the second to empower the government to rule by decree until the first had been ratified. The rule of the military junta was rigid and all opposition was ruthlessly suppressed.

Six years later, on June 1, 1973 Greece was proclaimed a republic under the presidency of George Papadopoulos and the monarchy was abolished two months after.

By the end of the year Papadopoulos

himself had been overthrown, by a fast and bloodless *coup d'état* on November 25. Lieut-General Phaedon Ghizikis was made President on the same day and a new cabinet was formed.

The military dictatorship ended in July 1974 when the armed forces called upon nine former leading politicians to form a new government.

1967
The Six-Day War

One of the shortest wars in history started on June 5, 1967. Six days later the battle, between Israel and Egypt, was over.

Tension had started mounting on May 18 when Egypt demanded the withdrawal of the UN peace-keeping force stationed along the Israeli–Egyptian border since 1956.

During the ensuing weeks the tension built up and eventually erupted into full-scale war. Israel gained the upper hand on the first day of fighting when its air force delivered devastating attacks on air bases in Egypt, Jordan, Syria, and Iraq. The United Nations called for a cease-fire but this was not accepted by all the countries concerned until June 10. By this time Israel had achieved substantial territorial gains.

The peace was, however, an uneasy one during the following years and on October 5, 1973 war broke out again as Egypt laid claim to territories lost during the Six Day War. Fighting continued until October 22, 1973, but the situation remained tense.

1967
First heart transplant

On December 3, 1967, at the Groote Schuur Hospital in Cape Town, South Africa, Professor Christian Barnard (*b.* 1922) performed the world's first successful human heart transplant. The recipient was a fifty-six year old man Louis Washkansky and the donor a twenty-five year old woman, Denise

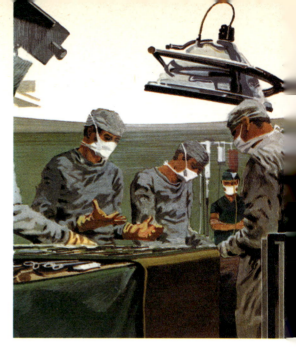

The rapid advance in modern surgery made a heart transplant operation possible.

Darval, who had been killed in a car crash.

Unfortunately Washkansky died on December 21, 1967. His death was caused, not by heart failure, but by the failure of his lungs following double pneumonia.

1968
Invasion of Czechoslovakia

Communist Party leader Alexander Dubček (*b.* 1921) was the principal instigator of liberalism in Czechoslovakia in 1968. His influence led to the relaxation of press censorship and the importation of foreign literature. But as the spirit of freedom increased within Czechoslovakia the deep anxiety felt by other Warsaw-pact countries increased also.

A letter of protest to the Czech leaders, an anti-Dubček campaign in the Soviet press, an ominous build-up of Soviet troops along the border, and talks between Czech and Soviet leaders did little to deter Dubček and his followers from their chosen course.

During the night of August 20–21 sixty thousand troops of the USSR, East

Germany, Poland, Hungary, and Bulgaria invaded Czechoslovakia. The Czechs showed open defiance towards the invaders but gradually censorship was reintroduced, the liberalization programmes were phased out, and all leaders associated with such policies were removed from office to be replaced by pro-Soviet leaders.

1968
Start of troubles in Ulster

Religious differences, long a feature of life in Ireland, flared into battle in Ulster on October 5, 1968 when civil rights demonstrators clashed in Londonderry.

Catholics fought Protestants and the British army tried to keep them apart. The Catholic movement was supported by the IRA (Irish Republican Army) and in 1972 the UDA (Ulster Defence Association) was formed to promote the Protestant cause. The struggle continues amidst increasing violence and bloodshed.

1969
First moon landing

With the words 'That's one small step for a man; one giant leap for mankind', the American astronaut Neil Armstrong (*b.* 1930) stepped down from the lunar module of *Apollo II* on July 21, 1969 to become the first man to step foot on the moon.

With Armstrong on that epic flight were Colonel Edwin Aldrin and Colonel Michael Collins.

Apollo II was launched by a *Saturn 5* rocket from Cape Kennedy (Cape Canaveral) on July 16. Twelve minutes after take-off the third stage of the rocket (the first two stages having been fired and jettisoned) put the ship into earth orbit before the start of its 328,000 kilometres journey to the moon.

The astronauts remained on the moon's surface for twenty-two hours, exploring, collecting soil samples, and setting up experiments. Then the lunar module *Eagle* took off, taking the astronauts back to the command ship *Columbia*. Armstrong and Aldrin clambered back into the command module to join Collins who had remained at the controls in lunar orbit.

After splashdown in the Pacific on July 24 the astronauts were received on the aircraft carrier *Hornet* by President Nixon who greeted them with the words: 'This has been the greatest week since the Creation.'

Man walks on the moon: Armstrong's historic moment.

1970
War in Biafra

On May 30, 1968 the Eastern region of Nigeria broke away from the federation and declared independence as the Republic of Biafra. Colonel Yakubu Gowon (b.1934), head of the Nigerian government, imposed economic sanctions against Biafra and mobilized his forces to effect a blockade of the breakaway state.

Fierce fighting throughout the rest of the year culminated in the fall of Enugu, the rebel capital, in October. Starvation was widespread and thousands perished. By December it looked as if Biafra's fight for independence was at an end. In June 1969 the two sides met for peace talks at Kampala and later at Addis Ababa, but they failed to reach agreement and the fighting continued.

The Biafrans held out until January 1970 when General Odumegwu Ojukwu (b. 1933), the Biafran leader, fled the country. Fighting ceased on January 12 and the country was once again united.

1971
Bangladesh declares independence

The first one-man-one-vote election in Pakistan in December 1970 resulted in a wide split between the racial and linguistic groups that formed the populace – the Punjabis of West Pakistan and the Bengalis of East Pakistan.

By March 1971 the split had widened so much that the first meeting of the Pakistan Constituent Assembly was postponed indefinitely. Sheikh Mujibur Rahman (1920–75) of East Pakistan and his separatist party the Awami League called for a campaign of civil disobedience amidst increasing demands for independence.

On March 23, Pakistan's Republic Day, people in the eastern state hauled down the national flag and replaced it with the flag of Bangladesh. Fighting broke out and Rahman was arrested and charged with treason, but the state formally declared its independence on April 17, although bitter fighting continued until the end of the year, with the secessionists supported by the Indian army.

Sheikh Rahman, who was elected President during his imprisonment, received a tumultuous welcome when he returned to Bangladesh in January 1972, but his problems were not over. Natural disasters and famine compounded the political problems of corruption and fighting between factions. Sheikh Rahman was killed in 1975.

1973
The Watergate affair

The subject uppermost in the minds of Americans and much of the rest of the world in 1973 was the 'Watergate' scandal. During the year the increasing disclosures revealed a tangled web of political intrigue that eventually enveloped even the office of the president.

Richard Nixon

On January 10, 1973 the trial of five men involved in the break-in and bugging of the Democrat headquarters in the Watergate apartments, Washington on July 17, 1972 was opened. The men, members of the Republican organization CREEP (Committee for the Re-Election of the President), pleaded guilty to the burglary.

It appeared to be a straightforward

affair until two reporters on the *Washington Post* followed up some of the loose ends to discover that the corruption was not minor. It involved White House officials, and even President Nixon (*b.* 1913) appeared to be implicated. Many called for his impeachment.

On August 8, 1974 Nixon became the first American president in history to resign from office and his vice-president, Gerald Ford, was sworn in on the next day.

1973
Skylab launched

Skylab I was launched on May 14, 1973 and remained in orbit for twenty-eight days. During this time the astronauts, Charles Conrad, Dr Joseph Kerwin, and Paul Weitz, carried out important experiments. These researches were largely concerned with human adaptation to long periods of weightlessness.

Initially it appeared that the mission would have to be abandoned as a set of solar energy panels failed to open and the craft's meteor shield had broken off soon after launch. The launch of the astronauts was postponed until May 25 and the following day they affixed an umbrella-like 'sunshade' over *Skylab* to provide shelter from the intense sunlight. This enabled them to continue with their scheduled mission after which *Skylab* was left in orbit ready to be used by the second (July 28 to September 25) and third (November 16, 1973 to February 8, 1974) missions.

1974
Overthrow of Caetano

On April 25, 1974 army insurgents in Portugal overthrew the extreme rightwing government of President Américo Tomás and Prime Minister Dr Marcello Caetano. For years Portugal had been struggling to maintain African colonies such as Angola and Mozambique, but the new head of state, General António de Spínola (*b.* 1910) saw that there was no military solution in Africa, only a political one.

Wide-ranging reforms were promised. These included the formation of a provisional civil government, free elections within a year, and the disbandment of the secret police. The African colonies were to receive independence.

The overthrow of Caetano was generally welcomed and socialists, communists, and other leftist leaders returned from exile. On May 15, 1974 a largely civilian government was sworn in. Spínola was replaced by the more radical General Francisco da Costa Gomes in September 1974. Constituent Assembly elections were held in April 1975, but much of the year was marked by disruption as the various parties of the left struggled for power.

1975
American-Russian space link

Years of combined effort and co-operation between the world's leading space powers culminated in July, 1975 with the first international manned space mission.

On July 15 *Soyuz 19* was launched from the Baikonur Cosmodrome, Kazakhstan, USSR. On the other side of the world, seven and a half hours later, an *Apollo* craft was launched from Cape Kennedy, Florida, USA.

On the following day both craft adopted a circular orbit 225 kilometres above the earth and the two were linked together at 16.12 GMT on July 17. They remained docked together for two days.

1975
Death of Franco

Francisco Franco, who had been head of state of Spain since the end of the Civil War in 1939 (*see page 300*), died in November 1975. His death was followed by the restoration of the monarchy under

Juan Carlos and a gradual return to democratic government. Political parties were legalized and in June 1977 the first general election was held since 1936.

1978
First test-tube baby

On July 25, 1978, the first so-called test-tube baby, Louise Joy Brown, was born at Oldham General Hospital, Lancashire. She was conceived by implanting in her mother's womb an embryo which had been developed from an egg fertilized outside her mother's body.

1979
Margaret Thatcher becomes prime minister

Margaret Thatcher, who had been leader of the Conservative Party since 1975, became Britain's first woman prime minister following her party's victory in the general election of May 1979.

1979
Islamic Revolution in Iran

During 1978 there was increasing opposition to the Iranian government, centred on religious leaders calling for a return to Islamic principles. As rioting and bloodshed grew worse the army could no longer maintain order. In January 1979 the Shah left the country (he died in exile in Egypt in July 1980) and in February a revolutionary government took office. Later that year, under the leadership of the Ayatollah Khomeini, the country was proclaimed an Islamic Republic.

1979
Soviet invasion of Afghanistan

In December 1979 Soviet forces invaded Afghanistan, overthrew the government and installed a regime which was under the effective control of the USSR. During the following year they occupied much of the country in the face of fierce opposition from Muslim guerrillas.

1980
Zimbabwe achieves independence

In April 1980 Zimbabwe (formerly Rhodesia) became an independent republic under the premiership of Robert Mugabwe. His party, the Zimbabwe African National Union, had been victorious in the elections held in February 1980 under a transitional British government, after a ceasefire had ended some years of guerrilla warfare.

1981
Reagan becomes US President

The American presidential election, held in November 1980, resulted in a victory for the Republican candidate, the former film actor, Ronald Reagan, who took office as the 40th US president on January 20, 1981.

1981
Flight of Space Shuttle

On 12 April, 1981, the US Space Shuttle *Columbia*, crewed by two men, made a successful trip. It took off vertically like a conventional rocket and, after two days in orbit around the Earth, glided down to land at an airforce base in California like an ordinary aircraft, thus becoming the first re-usable spaceship.

Index

347

351